DARING INSIGHTS
INTO SCHOOL LEADERSHIP AND BOARD GOVERNANCE

Published in association with

OPTIMAL SCHOOL GOVERNANCE

DARING INSIGHTS

INTO SCHOOL LEADERSHIP AND BOARD GOVERNANCE

Stephen Codrington

Solid Star Press
Sydney

© 2025 Stephen Codrington

All rights reserved. No part of this publication may be reproduced, copied, or transmitted in any form or by any means, electronic or mechanical, including photocopying, scanning, recording or any information storage and retrieval system without prior written permission from the author (stephen@optimalschool.com).

optimalschool.com

DARING INSIGHTS
into school leadership and board governance

Stephen Codrington

ISBN 978 0 9756426 6 5

An earlier edition of this book was published in 2024 featuring 72 insights without colour images under the title *Insights into school leadership and board governance*, ISBN 978 0 6489937 5 9.

The author and publisher are grateful for permission to reproduce copyright material. Where copyright material has been reproduced, this is acknowledged in the text or at the end of the chapter. Every effort has been made to trace all holders of copyrights, but where this has not been possible the publisher will be pleased to make any necessary arrangements at the first opportunity.

DEDICATION

To the educators, leaders, and boards in schools around the world who devote themselves selflessly every day to the most important of all vocations – shaping the future of our world .

Preface

After forming my specialist consultancy service Optimal School Governance over a decade ago, I have been working with school leaders and school boards to improve the quality and effectiveness of school governance. My work has involved spending time with hundreds of board members and school leaders around the world, helping them through workshops and discussions as well as providing support with strategic planning, performance reviews, policy development and analysis, advice in crises, recruitment of principals – indeed anything that can support their quest to improve leadership and governance.

As part of my ongoing support to school leaders and boards, I have been publishing free articles on my website at optimalschool.com. This book is an updated and enhanced collection of 115 of these articles, assembled into book form at the request of many of my regular users.

– Dr Stephen Codrington
Sydney, Australia

Contents

Insight 1 – Advice for new Principals	13
Insight 2 – Advice to school leaders and boards from 1932	18
Insight 3 – AI, ChatGPT, and the future of education	24
Insight 4 – Allowing school boards to be responsible	29
Insight 5 – An expectations reality check	31
Insight 6 – Antidote to a disengaged school board	35
Insight 7 – Antifragility	38
Insight 8 – Authentic leadership is more than management	42
Insight 9 – Autonomy boosts morale and productivity	45
Insight 10 – Black Swan crises and adaptive governance	50
Insight 11 – Board Manuals in our digital age	53
Insight 12 – Board-Staff Interaction	59
Insight 13 – Boeing's lessons for school boards and leaders	65
Insight 14 – Branding	72
Insight 15 – Can a school be a real community?	75
Insight 16 – Chinese mice do not eat cheese	79
Insight 17 – Civility and respect on school boards	83
Insight 18 – Codes of Practice for School Boards	86
Insight 19 – Committees	89
Insight 20 – Common pressures on school boards	94
Insight 21 – Communicate to persuade	101
Insight 22 – Conflict resolution and mediation	115
Insight 23 – Conflicts of interest	121
Insight 24 – Consensus building – six approaches	126
Insight 25 – Converting congeniality into collegiality	135
Insight 26 – Courage	138
Insight 27 – Dealing with poorly performing employees	143
Insight 28 – Debating skills: secret weapon for board chairs	146

Insight 29 – Deconstructing school governance	152
Insight 30 – Developing antifragility in every school	156
Insight 31 – Disagreeing agreeably on school boards	160
Insight 32 – Diversity enhances effective board leadership	164
Insight 33 – Dysfunctional boards – exit, voice and loyalty	166
Insight 34 – Effective boards	171
Insight 35 – Effort grades boost student outcomes	173
Insight 36 – Empathy enhances leadership	177
Insight 37 – Empathy shapes school culture	181
Insight 38 – Ethics for school boards and leaders	186
Insight 39 – Euphemisms and jargon	189
Insight 40 – F-shaped reading can help digest reports efficiently	194
Insight 41 – Face-to-face or remote?	198
Insight 42 – Finance officers should be on tap, not on top	203
Insight 43 – Firing an employee humanely	206
Insight 44 – Free riding	210
Insight 45 – Generational differences affect educational leadership	215
Insight 46 – Getting governance right – advice for new schools	223
Insight 47 – Good. Cheap. Fast. Can schools have all three?	229
Insight 48 – Governing is not the same as governance	231
Insight 49 – Handling disrespectful remarks	233
Insight 50 – Hat, haircut or tattoo	237
Insight 51 – How frequently should your school board meet?	240
Insight 52 – I can't believe we used to …	244
Insight 53 – Idealism and pragmatism in school leadership	248
Insight 54 – Improving the sustainability of small schools	253
Insight 55 – Intentional Cultural Change	257
Insight 56 – Interim headships	263
Insight 57 – International experience benefits everyone	265
Insight 58 – Interviews	270
Insight 59 – Is there an ideal board size?	276
Insight 60 – It's not fair	279

Insight 61 – Knowing when it's time to go	284
Insight 62 – Language and communication in board meetings	297
Insight 63 – Language matters	300
Insight 64 – Looking in the mirror before joining a School Board	303
Insight 65 – Lying applicants	307
Insight 66 – Making decisions using data	311
Insight 67 – Making schools green	313
Insight 68 – Managing a crisis	319
Insight 69 – Measure what you treasure	322
Insight 70 – Measuring things	335
Insight 71 – Melting the cultural iceberg	339
Insight 72 – Mission drift	344
Insight 73 – Muddy puddle or leaking ceiling	348
Insight 74 – Nailing the Principal's annual performance review	352
Insight 75 – Normalisation of deviance	357
Insight 76 – Operationalising a strategic vision	360
Insight 77 – Overcoming negativity – perhaps your own	363
Insight 78 – Parents who are board members	366
Insight 79 – Perfection can be a prison	371
Insight 80 – Principled Leadership	377
Insight 81 – Priorities when finances are beyond tight	384
Insight 82 – Purpose trumps convenience	387
Insight 83 – Recruiting a new head of school	392
Insight 84 – Related parties transactions	396
Insight 85 – Resuscitating a bored board	400
Insight 86 – Retaining excellent staff	404
Insight 87 – Riding a dead horse	407
Insight 88 – Risk management	412
Insight 89 – Roots and wings	415
Insight 90 – School Board Chairs are superheroes	420
Insight 91 – Servant leadership and falling into a river	424
Insight 92 – Setting tuition fees – the annual agony	430

Insight 93 – Should board members be required to donate?	435
Insight 94 – Should school boards be innovative?	438
Insight 95 – Successful successions	440
Insight 96 – Succession planning	443
Insight 97 – Term limits	446
Insight 98 – The best, most complex job in the world	450
Insight 99 – The board's most important duty	456
Insight 100 – The board's relationship with the school community	459
Insight 101 – The board's role in thinking strategically	462
Insight 102 – The first hundred days	465
Insight 103 – The great resignation	469
Insight 104 – The red line between governance and management	474
Insight 105 – The Village Venus Effect	477
Insight 106 – Thinking strategically	481
Insight 107 – Time management	484
Insight 108 – Trust and truth	488
Insight 109 – Truths about truth	493
Insight 110 – Turns are permitted	496
Insight 101 – Values define our identity	498
Insight 112 – What is truth?	504
Insight 113 – What new board members should know	509
Insight 114 – When should board members step down?	512
Insight 115 – You have been asked to join a school board	516
About the Author	520

Insight 1

Advice for new Principals

It is said that all new school principals enjoy a honeymoon period. If that is so, then mine may have set a record for its brevity.

I will never forget the first day of first term of my first headship. Less than an hour after I arrived at school, just as the first students began returning after the summer break, I received a phone call from the headmaster at my former school to tell me that a student I had known very well, a member of my tutor group for several years, had taken his own life a couple of days previously. He had received a severe spinal injury in a Rugby match some time before and been rendered quadriplegic, but he had not been able to come to grips with his situation and had driven his wheelchair into a swimming pool.

Within half an hour of receiving that news, one of my Heads of Department (who was also the Board Chair's brother-in-law) handed me his written letter of resignation over a long-standing issue to do with how his subject was to be taught in the integrated Year 7 Core. I accepted his resignation reluctantly on the principle that written letters reflect a well-considered action. As a result, he became wildly angry, even phoning the Board Chair (who he knew very well, of course!), claiming that he wanted his position returned to him because never expected me to accept his resignation – his (unstated) intention had been for me to refuse to accept his resignation and then back down over the Year 7 Core program.

My initial idealism to transform the world through education was starting to dissipate well before lunch time on that first day. By the time I drove home that afternoon, I was close to being shell-shocked!

In hindsight, I can see that my experiences on that first day were crucially important in my formation as a Principal. That day helped me understand why I was occupying the Principal's Office – I was there to be the solution to the students' and the school's Big Problems. My dependence on God rather than my own resources was thrown sharply into focus that day, and it shaped all my subsequent work as a School Principal.

I spent 25 years as a School Principal. During that period, I came to lead five schools in four different countries. I agree with many of my fellow Principals that leading a school is the best job in the world. It can also be one of the loneliest and most challenging jobs in the world.

Given that background, what general advice might I offer now to a new Principal who is about to commence? Hundreds of thoughts spring to mind, but I think a few stand out as being applicable to almost any school – large or small, primary or secondary, single-sex or co-educational, international or national, faith-based or secular, day or boarding, and so on.

- **Carry around a notepad**, at least for the first couple of months. You will see things that irritate you in your new school, and these are probably things that irritate students, staff, and visitors as well. After a couple of months, you may no longer notice these irritations because you become so used to them. That is why it is a good idea to make notes when you first arrive and get the irritations fixed while you remain sensitive to them.

- **Never hesitate to phone your predecessor** to get background information regarding situations arising in the school. Institutional memory does not have to evaporate when a new Principal arrives to lead a school, and the insights gleaned from background information is invariably helpful. I have never known a former Principal to be reluctant to share whatever insights might be helpful to a successor.

- Make it a priority to **meet each staff member for a one-on-one conversation**. Staff are the means through which almost all the school's work is performed, and a strong, positive working relationship with every teacher, administrator and member of the grounds staff is essential to your effectiveness as a Principal.

- It follows from this that **you should not make any changes until you learn at least one strength of every staff member**. New principals are often under pressure from their board to make significant changes that "everyone thinks are overdue" or which "are essential to the school's survival". It is more important to make changes effective and sustainable than be reactive or hasty.

- **Make people the priority.** As a young Principal I was often frustrated that I struggled to get my paperwork completed because of all the interruptions with people coming to my office door – which I admit I always left open when not in a meeting so I would be as open and accessible as possible. With help from an elderly colleague, I came to realise that people – not paperwork - were my real work, and paperwork was how I filled in my time when no people were demanding my attention.

- **Schedule a regular 'open door' time each day.** Gaining easy access to the Principal is often a challenge for staff. However, this can be partially addressed by scheduling a regular daily 'open door' time when any staff can come to discuss a matter that takes five minutes or less without making an appointment. For more substantial matters that take more than five minutes, it is reasonable to schedule an appointment with the Principal's PA.

- **Meet key personnel on a weekly basis.** It is important to address situations before they escalate, so having regularly scheduled meeting times for key personnel such as the Deputy, Head of the Primary Section, Boarding Supervisor, Chaplain, and of course the Board Chair, are essential for maintaining communication. Needless to say, urgent matters affecting these people (and indeed, anyone) will be handled with more immediate conversations.

- **Spend as little time in the office as possible.** It is important for you as Principal to see the school in everyday action and "sniff the mood". Moreover, staff and students appreciate your presence and the easy accessibility it offers to them. I always made a point of taking one or two walks through every part of my schools while I was Principal, and I invariably gained insights in doing so. It also helped me to overcome the lack of fitness that can come to afflict office-bound Principals.

- **Make an effort to get to know the students.** Schools exist for their students. Building relations with students can be a challenge, especially in larger schools where putting a name to every face can present a major headache to a busy Principal. In several of my headships, I addressed this challenge by inviting students to my office on their birthdays for a one-on-one chat, during which I gave them a hand-written card and (before sugar became known as 'white death') a chocolate frog. I loved the way this simple gesture removed any stigma about going to the Principal's office, and it was often the highlight of my (and their) day.

- **Share the school's mission** (core values and enduring purpose) **as often as possible**. Every school assembly, staff meeting, parents' gathering and newsletter (and, these days, every blog or social media post) should reflect – and preferably emphasise – the reasons why the school exists, what it is seeking to achieve, and what are its uniquely positive attributes.

- **Make "How may I help you?" your mantra.** A Principal is there to serve the school community, not to be served. This mantra should be repeated almost to the point of irritation – whenever a child is upset or injured, whenever guests gather for a school function, whenever a teacher feels overwhelmed, whenever a parent is angry about something – and whenever the Principal's spouse inevitably complains that work is dominating life at home with the family.

- **Avoid competition with the former Principal.** Although Boards often appoint new Principals to implement a new direction, or a 'pendulum swing', away from the former Principal's direction, it doesn't follow that an incoming Principal should try to tarnish their predecessor's reputation. Indeed, my observations have shown that incoming Principals who try to discredit their predecessor seldom last long in the job. A new Principal should always focus on the future rather than the immediate past. In general, new

Principals are perceived as statesmanlike when they extend courtesy and respect to predecessors, as opposed to being seen as petty and insecure when they criticise former Principals.

While I hope these few tips may be helpful, it is also important to remember that Murphy's Law operates strongly in schools – "What can go wrong will go wrong". (I have often suspected that Murphy was a School Principal).

When things go wrong – and they will – my final piece of advice is to realise that you can't make everyone happy, not should you try to do so. It's time to make a rational decision about which people it is better to upset and which people it is most important to satisfy.

The answer to this last dilemma will almost always be "it is most important to keep the Board happy". This makes sense because the Board has ultimate responsibility for achieving the school's mission and direction (its ultimate purpose). This is achieved by the Board through its delegated powers – powers which are delegated to you alone as Principal. As Principal, you are the one and only person who is directly accountable to the board.

It could be argued that everything you do as a new Principal will either become a mere footnote, or else the essential means, to achieving this central purpose of enhancing the school's mission and vision.

Insight 2

Advice to school leaders and boards from 1932

One of the five schools where I served as Principal was an all-boys' school in Australia with a history (now) of over 150 years. The first time I walked into my office after taking up the headship, I was greeted by a large and very impressive collection of old books on somewhat dusty bookshelves.

There were certainly some unusual titles among the books I inherited. There was volume 2 of "Demosthenes' Orations", but not volume 1. There was the three-volume set of "The Life of Gladstone" and the four-volume set of the "Works of Edgar Alan Poe". There was a book called "Two-minute Bible readings for Use in Opening School and in Hospital Wards". Another book was titled "The Schoolboy – his nutrition and development", and it talked about hunger (and I quote) "as a manifestation of the carnal sin of greed, to be suitably repressed".

Perhaps the most surprising title I found was "The Life of the Bee", published in 1901. I was probably the only Headmaster in the world at the time to have "The Life of the Bee" on his office shelves, and it was a 351-page manual on apiculture, or beekeeping. Perhaps one of my predecessors had seen a parallel in raising bees and raising boys, because there was a bookmark at page 47 in the chapter headed "the swarm".

One very interesting 216-page book dating from 1932 was called "The Romance of School" by Rev Dr Charles John (CJ) Prescott, Headmaster of Newington College in Sydney, Australia from 1900 to 1931. The book contained 37 chapters with diverse headings such as 'Boys', 'Girls', 'The Dining Room', 'Pocket Money', 'Epidemics', 'Latin', 'The Joy of Learning', 'Schoolboy Friendships', 'Public Spirit' and 'The Product'.

Given Prescott's career, chapter 1 naturally focussed on the topic of 'Headmasters', and the book opened with these words at the top of page 1:

"Headmasters are naturally in a class of their own. They have many qualities in common imposed upon them by the conditions of their work, but outside of these they are as varied as the flowers. One excels in scholarship, another is a proved athlete, another is great in administration, another a masterly disciplinarian, but one and all they are autocrats and rule in their spheres as kings. Yet in some relations the autocracy is tempered. They do not rule their governing bodies as they rule their boys. In a certain sense they are subject to them: from them they receive their appointment, and by them they may be dismissed. Their relations may be genial and friendly, sometimes they are unpleasant, in some cases they are stormy. Instances have been known in which voting bodies or individual members have tried to treat headmasters merely as paid servants, but these are exceptional. As a rule, a working understanding is reached, and as both have the same object in view, the welfare of the school, this makes for mutual tolerance and sympathy."

In chapter 9, titled 'Governing Bodies', Prescott explores the relationship between Heads of School and their Boards in more detail. I'll reproduce a substantial excerpt from this chapter, partly for its entertainment (and sometimes horror) value to modern educators, but mostly as a basis of comparison for today's school leaders and boards to reflect on their own practices.

"Many schools are incorporated, subject to the law of incorporation. In such cases the body is the legal owner of the premises, the trustee for endowments and property of all kinds, and the party responsible for debts, if these exist.

"It therefore holds the purse-strings. It makes its own financial arrangements with the staff. In certain cases in the past, it has let the establishment to the headmaster who has paid a rent nominal or real, and then has paid his assistants what he thought just and made what he could out of it. House masters in like manner have conducted their houses on the same principle.

"The system still obtains; but in Australian schools the tendency is to give fixed salaries to all the staff, and to keep the financial management in the governors' hands. Their function therefore is an important one and offers opportunities to men of business ability. People of academic training are not usually financiers (though there have been notable exceptions) and a few men with good business training can render high service.

"While the reputation of a school will depend upon the work of its staff, the ruling body can do much to support that reputation. The (board) members can use their personal influence to secure an ample inflow of new boys; sometimes their very names are a guarantee for the soundness of the institution they control. Many such bodies are very wide awake to the interest of the school, and its prosperity has been aided by their active co-operation.

"An obvious danger is that the numerical and financial aspect should become the prominent one. If the numbers increase or are maintained and there is a gratifying balance on the right side at the end of the year, there is satisfaction: but if numbers decline, or if the profit is a small one, or is replaced by a loss, the tendency is for every member to become discouraged and sometimes disagreeable; this, too, even when in other respects the school has been doing its best work.

"Of course, the financial test is one of the legitimate tests, as is the numerical. Yet one of the most brilliant and scholarly headmasters in England in the nineteenth century, when his boys were shining conspicuously at the universities, was never rewarded by large numbers, and the financial test may be equally misleading. In a bank or a commercial enterprise, or a trading concern, or a mine, or a shipping firm, it is accepted as the just test; though even here a truer one might be whether or not these enterprises are discharging a useful public service.

"But a school is not a bank, nor a business, nor a speculation. The question is: Is it doing the work for which it was founded? Is its teaching sound, its training effective? Is its general tone good? Is it turning out worthy and capable men? These are the supreme questions to be asked, the others though legitimate and necessary are of minor importance.

"Apart from this, a governing body is exposed to two opposite dangers, the one of ill-directed and excessive zeal, the other of laxity. If it is a large body, it probably will contain some, placed upon it for the sake of the supposed value of their names, whose interest is skin-deep, who rarely attend its meetings and

"A Meeting of the School Trustees", a painting by Robert Harris (1885) National Gallery of Canada, Public Domain, https://commons.wikimedia.org/w/index.php?curid=4376166

do not concern themselves with what is going on. Such a body may say: 'We take some trouble to give the place the best head we can find, and it is his business to do the rest.' This means, of course, that it makes no attempt to help the man of their choice, even though it is in their power to do so, if they would take the trouble.

"On the other hand, members of the ruling body may magnify their office, and think that their position entitles them to visit, to enquire, and to criticise at their sweet will; sometimes a headmaster has been treated as though he was simply and solely a paid servant. Dr Arnold (Headmaster of Rugby School in the UK from 1828 to 1841) was emphatic on this point. The remedy of a governing body, he said, was not interference, but dismissal; and by that assertion he added one more valuable element to the store of benefits he gave to English education.

"To the boys of a school there is no greater man, on his own ground, than the headmaster. The old story that Dr Busby (Headmaster of Westminster School in the UK for almost 57 years, from 1638 to 1695) kept his hat on in the presence of Charles II, lest his boys should think that there was any greater man in the Kingdom than himself, is suggestive of a time when boys did not know so much of the big world outside as the daily reading of the newspapers teaches them to-day. It was an extravagant assertion of authority, and perhaps only the Merry Monarch would have tolerated it, but there may be places even to-day where some assertion would not be out of place.

"As a rule, the governing body selects the headmaster. This places immense power in their hands and calls for very judicious exercise. Sometimes personal acquaintance, or relationship, comes in to interfere with a purely impartial choice; in some cases, political views or ecclesiastical prejudices distort a just judgment. Many a time a first-rate man has been refused a headship for such reasons, and an inferior appointment has been made with ill results. But so much depends upon a prudent choice that it forces one to raise the question whether proper prudence is displayed in selecting the ruling body itself.

"When once a choice has been made, the supreme need is that there should be mutual trust. Of course, cases may arise in which for good or bad reasons that trust breaks down. Then the only course open is for the headmaster to resign or for the ruling body to dismiss him. Instances of both have occurred in the great English schools. But until such breaking point is reached, each side should trust the other.

"The management of finances belongs to the governing body. But the management of the school, the settlement of its curriculum, the principles of its internal government, the direction of the masters, should be left to the man who, if he is worth his salt, has made a study of these things and ought to know more about it than any of his councillors, and who, if he is doing his duty, has his finger upon the pulse of the school, and understands it better than any outsider, even though that outsider was at one time a boy in the school himself.

"The heroic enterprise of Dr Thring (Headmaster of Uppingham School in the UK from 1853 to 1887) in raising Uppingham from a tiny, endowed grammar school to one of the great schools of England, is one of the romances of the nineteenth century. It attracted universal attention, it set scores of other people thinking, and it marked him as one of the most stimulating forces in the educational life of the land. Yet his biographer has to relate that there was, to the end of his life, almost constant friction between him and his trustees. Thring was undoubtedly a man of exceptionally strong character and had a profound conviction as to the soundness of his methods and his plans, which indeed were justified by the results. Any co-operation with him was easily carried on when he was recognised as the dominant partner; but perhaps not otherwise.

"Yet it remains a pathetic story that such a man should have been thwarted, opposed, and hampered by a body of men who with one shining exception, had not eyes to see the quality and power of the one whom they themselves appointed to be the ruler of their, originally, tiny school.

"And what an honourable function it is to be a ruler of a great school! In the motherland, the proudest of the aristocracy, even royalty itself, counts it an added honour if their names are associated with some great school. They have nothing personal to gain, but it is a fine form of public service. To help to maintain its reputation, to make its future eclipse its splendid past, to be a nursing father to its annual cohorts of glorious boys setting out for the battle of life – this is a task that any good citizen might well envy. And out of a sympathetic heart, he will be moved from time to time to make some fitting gift, and when he makes his will, while he makes generous provision for his widow and his children, he will joyfully insert a little clause that will cause his school to remember him when he has passed away."

Clearly, 1932 was a vastly different world educationally than today. CJ Prescott concludes his book on page 216 with a conversation he is having with his own adult son soon after his retirement.

"Are you asleep, dad? Your pipe has gone out. I crept into the room five minutes ago, and you were so still that I was afraid I should wake you."

"I must have been dreaming, my dear. I was back at school again and living over my schooldays."

"And didn't you wish to be a boy again, dad?"

"Yes, for a time. They were happy days, and I like to recall them. But there are other things. I wasn't married to your mother then, and what should I do without my girls? It was good to be a boy; but better still to be the father of a family like mine."

"And were all your memories pleasant, dad?"

"Nearly all, but not quite. The last thing I dreamed of was that old N. had reported me to the Head for gross disobedience and I was in his study. It was a clear case, I must admit. Just as he said, 'Bend over,' you spoke to me, and I woke up, and you saved me from a hiding."

Reference:

Prescott CJ (1932) *The Romance of School: A Headmaster's Retrospect.* Sydney: Angus & Robertson.

Insight 3

AI, ChatGPT, and education's future

In early December 2022 a research group in San Francisco named OpenAI released a free preview of a new artificial intelligence platform, ChatGPT (Generative Pre-trained Transformer). Anyone who registered could enter a request for information about almost anything and receive an eloquently written response in just a few seconds.

A flurry of articles soon followed, both on social media and in the established media, expressing concern that artificial intelligence (AI) was becoming so powerful that it was taking human thought and creativity on a swift path towards obsolescence.

As Stephen Brook wrote in an article in Melbourne's Sunday Age on 18th December:

> When asked, it wrote instructions on how to remove peanut butter from a VCR in biblical verse: "And it came to pass that a man was troubled by a peanut butter sandwich, for it had been placed within his VCR, and he knew not how to remove it." It created a dairy-free recipe for macaroni cheese and an essay comparing and contrasting the nationalism of political scientist Benedict Anderson and philosopher Ernest Gellner. It refused to write about the benefits of eating glass, declaring "there are none".

For a few decades, educators have been increasingly wary of assignments submitted by students that were not their own work. Indeed, ghost-writing students' assignments has been a growth industry in the last decade, especially for students who are required to submit assignments that are not in their first language. To get a free, persuasively written assignment in less than five seconds must seem like a dream come true for a student who is facing a looming deadline – a dream for the student, but a potential nightmare for the teacher who must assess the student's performance fairly and justly.

So, how good is ChatGPT? I decided to give it a test run in January 2023, soon after its public release.

The first request I entered reflected my interest in the challenges facing school boards – I typed "Why is it important to declare conflicts of interest on school boards?" Five seconds later I had the following response on my screen, ready for copying and pasting:

Declaring conflicts of interest on school boards is important because it helps to ensure that decisions made by the board are objective and unbiased. Conflicts of interest can arise when a member of the board has a personal or financial interest in a matter being considered by the board. For example, a board member who owns a company that provides goods or services to the school district may have a conflict of interest when the board is considering a contract with that company.

If conflicts of interest are not declared and managed properly, they can lead to perceptions of corruption or favouritism and undermine public trust in the school board. By disclosing conflicts of interest, board members can avoid the appearance of impropriety and help to maintain the integrity and transparency of the decision-making process. In some cases, board members may be required to recuse themselves from discussions or votes on certain matters if they have a conflict of interest. This helps to ensure that decisions are made in the best interests of the school district and its students, rather than being influenced by personal or financial considerations.

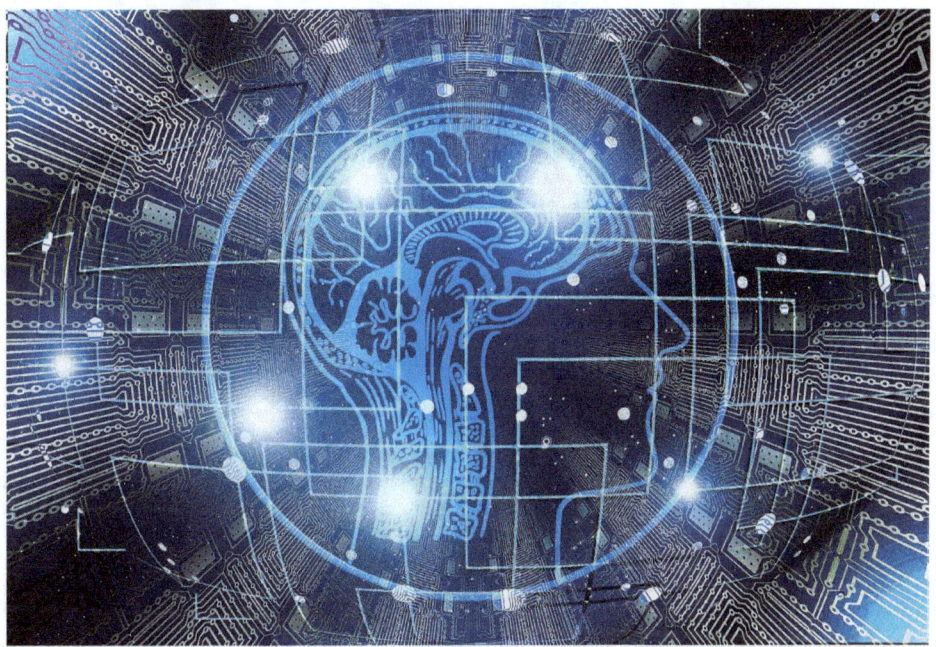

I was quite impressed, so I decided to try and enter something less generic that could not possibly already be in ChatGPT's memory: "In what ways are school boards different in Australia and Uganda?" Five seconds later…

School boards, also known as school governing bodies or school councils, play a similar role in both Australia and Uganda, but there may be some differences in the specific responsibilities and powers of school boards in these two countries.

In Australia, school boards are responsible for setting the strategic direction of a school and working with the school's principal to ensure that the school is meeting the needs of its students and community. School boards in Australia are typically made up of elected parents, teachers, and community members, and they may have the power to make decisions on issues such as the school's budget, curriculum, and policies.

In Uganda, school boards are also responsible for setting the direction of a school and working with the school's headteacher to ensure that the school is meeting the needs of its students and community. School boards in Uganda may be composed of a variety of stakeholders, including parents, teachers, community members, and government representatives. In addition to setting the strategic direction of a school, school boards in Uganda may also have the power to make decisions on issues such as the school's budget and resource allocation, as well as the hiring and evaluation of teachers.

Overall, while school boards in both Australia and Uganda play a similar role in the governance of schools, there may be some differences in the specific responsibilities and powers of school boards in these two countries, as well as in the composition of school boards and the processes for selecting their members.

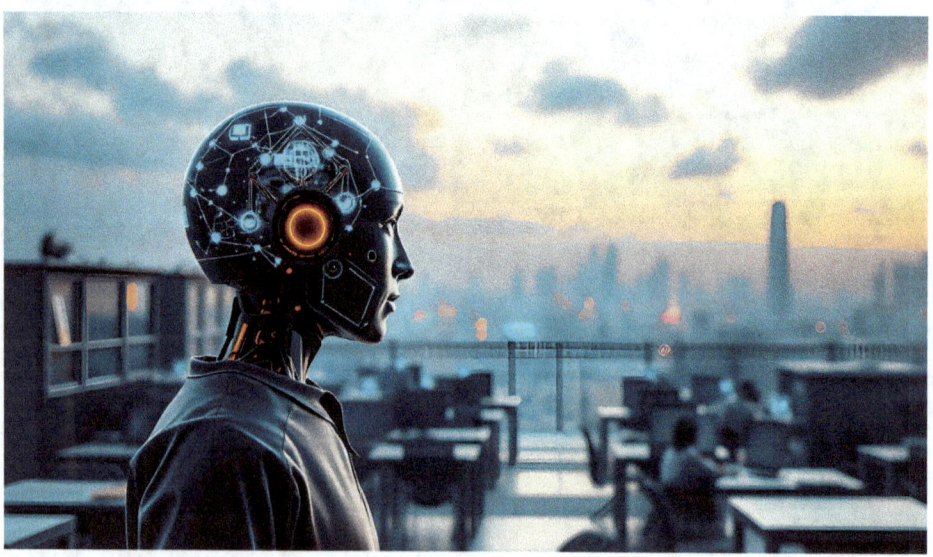

Once again, factually correct (if not especially insightful), grammatically immaculate and confidently – almost compellingly - articulated. So, I tried one final question on a topic that Chat GPT should understand: "How can a teacher tell the difference between an assignment that is written by a student without cheating and an assignment written by ChatGPT?". This time the answer took about seven seconds to be typed on my screen:

There are a few ways that a teacher can tell the difference between an assignment written by a student and one written by a tool like ChatGPT:

- *Style: ChatGPT and other language models are able to generate text that is structurally and grammatically correct, but it may lack the unique style and voice that a student's writing would have.*
- *Originality: ChatGPT and other language models are trained on a vast amount of text, so they may generate responses that include information that is widely available online or in books. A student's assignment should show their own original thoughts and ideas, rather than simply repeating information that can be found elsewhere.*
- *Understanding: A student's assignment should demonstrate their understanding of the subject matter, while an assignment generated by a tool like ChatGPT may not show the same level of understanding. A teacher can ask questions or give a quiz on the material to assess a student's understanding.*
- *Plagiarism: It is important for a teacher to check for plagiarism in any student's assignment. Plagiarism is the act of copying someone else's work and presenting it as your own. If a student has cheated by using ChatGPT or a similar tool, it is likely that the assignment will include content that is copied from other sources. Plagiarism detection software can be used to check for this.*

It is important for teachers to be aware of the potential for students to use tools like ChatGPT and to take steps to prevent and detect cheating.

That sounds like good advice from ChatGPT – I have always thought the presence of a few minor errors, the insertion of some personal anecdotes, and evidence of discernment and reflections, together with good footnotes and bibliography, were signs of originality in assignments.

I suspect that Chat GPT could well challenge and even replace Google and other search engines before long. I know that is a bold claim, but it is surely far quicker and more efficient for a student (or a teacher) to receive a single coherent response to a question than to receive millions of links that must be individually read, sorted, considered, filtered, and then amalgamated. On the other hand, ChatGPT is somewhat like "Wikipedia for Dummies" in that everything it says is essentially derivative rather than original, and unlike Wikipedia, it doesn't routinely quote sources.

I can understand the threat to original thinking, and to fair assessment, that AI may present to the world of education. Although the challenges need to be addressed and not ignored, I am much more optimistic about the future than the writers of many recent articles and social media posts (see the reading list below).

Rather than fearing the impact of AI on education, I think we need to tame it and embrace it as a tool to improve teaching and learning. The reality is that ChatGPT is a disrupter, just like ball-point pens, calculators and photocopiers were disrupters to earlier generations of educators. AI tools such as Chat GPT won't disappear any time soon. The genie is out of the bottle, and its algorithms will almost certainly improve in quality.

I really believe schools need to adopt the same discerning but optimistic spirit that earlier generations used to embrace innovative disrupters, if for no other reasons that genuine disruptors never go away, they fundamentally change ways of working, and indeed they become integral components of the future society that today's students will enter and eventually lead.

One example of teachers embracing Chat GPT could be to use AI as an aid to develop challenging Units of Enquiry or arguments for students to critique. Students could use AI to correct grammatical and spelling errors more quickly and thoroughly than at present, just as they will probably be doing in decades to come as AI becomes a near-universal, indispensable tool in everyday work.

To give you an idea of its editing potential, I typed this question into ChatGPT: "this sentents hav lots & lots and lots of gramarticle and spel mistracks, so can U fiks it 4 me?" In less than two seconds, this response appeared on my screen:

Sure, here is a revised version of the sentence with the grammar and spelling errors corrected: "This sentence has lots and lots and lots of grammar and spelling mistakes, so can you fix it for me?"

It seems that the possibilities are enormous if educators and school leaders can adopt a "solutions-based approach" and embrace this huge advance in AI capability.

Postscript: Perhaps ChatGPT can't replace humans just yet. I asked it to write a funny joke for me describing a school board's interview of a prospective school principal. The response from ChatGPT was: *"Why did the prospective school principal bring a ladder to the interview? Because he heard it was a high position!"*.

Nice try, but I don't think "Dad jokes" should be a threatened species just yet.

Insight 4

Allowing school boards to be responsible

Soon after I completed my fifth and final Headship, I returned to Australia and was asked by a former colleague, "What is your number one take-away after a quarter of a century as a school Principal?" I had to consider not only the schools where I had served as Principal, but also the many others I had visited or evaluated as a member of various accreditation teams. I am by nature a positive person, and yet I eventually replied using an uncharacteristic double negative: "I cannot think of a single school that could not be improved with better Board governance".

That does not mean that most Boards are disastrous any more than it implies that most schools are disastrous. However, it does suggest that most Boards are operating sub-optimally, probably unknowingly, and most likely because of inertia.

My answer surprised my colleague. School Boards and Administrators devote considerable energy and resources to improving student outcomes, raising teacher morale, developing facilities, and ensuring sound management practices. However, unless they are deep in crisis, very few school Boards give sufficient time or attention to their own welfare, efficacy, operations, or procedures. Even fewer Boards consciously consider the impact of their own 'Board health' on the operations and reputation of the school.

Are Board Members prepared to accept a sub-optimal level in their own operations that they would not tolerate in the school's day-to-day operations?

Having worked directly with hundreds of Board Members, and having been a Board Member myself, I can count on the fingers of just one hand the few Board Members I have met who might place their own interests above those of the school. School Board Members rank among the most sacrificial, public-spirited, and generous people I have ever worked with or known. And yet, even with that immense generosity of spirit, Boards can fall into the trap of blaming others when the reality is that their own policies, procedures, and processes might be inhibiting the school's effectiveness.

Boards know that they must accept responsibility for the school's finances, legal obligations, risk management, mission, policies, safety, and the appointment and oversight of the Principal, as well as ultimately the school's reputation and its viability. Yet too few Boards seem to appreciate how important their responsibilities to self-evaluate and to be evaluated are for the school.

Why is Board evaluation so important? Quite simply, effective Boards that operate according to best practices add value to their school. And Boards can only ensure that they are operating optimally if they can measure performance against clear, impartial criteria. Warm fuzzy impressions simply don't make the grade in today's competitive environment.

In the United States, school Boards routinely monitor their own performance, both through regular formal self-evaluations and independent external consultants. To date, such practices have been less common in Australia. However, as Boards appreciate the significant impact they have either to enhance or diminish their school's effectiveness, it is imperative that regular Board training also becomes the expected norm here.

Insight 5

An expectations reality check

Let's be honest - the culture of schools is quite different to the culture of most of the institutions in our society today:

- The **mission** (enduring purpose) of schools contrasts with missions in the corporate sector, as schools primarily exist to transmit knowledge and values.
- Unlike most businesses, schools do not focus on profit maximisation (or some similar metric) but on **viability** – making ends meet in a way that is more akin to the philosophy of a family budget.
- Schools are often more **resistant to change and innovation** than many other institutions (except perhaps families and churches), with teachers (rightly) demanding to know the details of "why?", "what?" and "how?" for any proposed change. When change does occur, it often comes to mean "addition" rather than "replacement", leading to overload.
- Schools are subject to very high **compliance** demands, especially by governments.
- The largest component of a school's **personnel** – the teachers – usually have a strong service ethic and a desire for job security, and seldom a thirst for risk and competition. More than the employees in most organisations, teachers tend to **work co-operatively** while also loving autonomy, and this requires patience and improvisation on the part of managers seeking change. Most teachers would like higher salaries, but they react badly to the concept of merit pay as they operate with a strong collegial/communal ethic and are motivated by qualitative rather than quantitative outcomes.

Of course, these are all generalisations, but they are generalisations that I have found to be widely applicable from my own observations over several decades.

If the culture of schools in general is different from mainstream society, it should also be recognised that the culture of most independent schools (also known as private schools in some countries) demonstrates some additional contrasts when compared with the general culture of government (or state schools). For clarity, please note here that I am emphatically NOT generalising that one type of school culture or the other is inherently better, simply that they are different.

It is probably inevitable that parents who are paying money for something they could otherwise get for free will expect something 'extra' in return for their sacrifice – some kind of 'value-added' factor. On occasions, these parental expectations may even extend into the territory of expecting something 'exceptional'. In that context, a child who is under-performing compared with their parents' expectations presents a situation (sometimes called a 'problem') that requires an explanation.

Time and cultural factors play a significant role here. Several decades ago, when I started my teaching career, a student's under-performance invariably demanded a robust explanation from the student to the parents. These days, a robust explanation is still required, but it is more likely to be demanded from the teacher. At least, this is often the case in Western societies – in Hong Kong and other parts of China where I have worked, it is still student who must do the explaining, sometimes in response to a question like "You got 98% - what happened to the two marks you dropped?".

Expectations vary from family to family, and from school to school. One of the great benefits of independent schools is that they have the freedom to emphasise the values, aims, culture and mission that define the school's identity and purpose. Sometimes the emphasis is academics, sometimes sports, sometimes culture, sometimes faith, and so on. Most commonly, a school's culture is a curated balance of these and other factors that form a coherent, holistic philosophy.

When I was working in the US about a decade ago, I often interacted with **interim principals**. The role of interim principal is used much more frequently during headship transitions in the US than elsewhere, and there is a large army of highly experienced, often retired former principals who take on these roles, almost invariably for a maximum of one year while the appointment of a new principal is underway.

The role of interim principal tends to be used differently in the US than elsewhere. In most countries, interim principals operate in a maintenance capacity, just 'holding the fort', explicitly avoiding significant decision-making that might be seen as potentially binding the incoming permanent principal in some way.

By contrast in the US, interim principals are usually asked by the board to fix up as many major and long-standing problems as possible before the incoming principal arrives. This is to minimise the number of unpopular decisions an incoming principal must face in the early days a new headship, thus preserving political capital and prolonging as far as possible the 'honeymoon' period during which the new principal is getting to know the school and its people.

One experience I had with an interim principal while in the US provides a good example of managing expectations and tailoring them to the school's mission, vision and values.

I remember her telling me that shortly after she arrived at a school to take up the interim principalship, the board asked for her initial impressions. Her first response was that the school needed to change the way it promoted itself through its messaging and marketing because it was not accurately reflecting the school's identity and purpose.

She felt that the photos portrayed on the school's website and social media posts made the school appear more like a holiday camp where students spend most of their time out of the classroom on co-curricular activities, outdoor programs, sports, theatre arts or amusements rather than engaging in academically rigorous lessons. It was an interesting observation because the board saw all these activities as worthwhile value-adding programs that distinguished it from narrowly academic schools. Nonetheless, the interim principal argued that these were all activities that the children had access to away from the school. She argued further that when parents were paying for their children's education, they really wanted to know that they were getting something that neither they nor local public schools could provide, which was the chance to succeed in today's highly competitive society.

Of course, that begs the question – **what does success really mean?** And what is the ultimate purpose of achieving this so-called success? This is where a school board has a responsibility to define, articulate, guide, and monitor the mission, vision and values of the school (and keep interim principals in check!). As a statement of the school's enduring purpose, the mission is the "true north" point towards which the school must head with deviation if it is to be true to its identity. Expectations only make sense when they can be measured against a clear statement of intent on the part of the school's leadership.

The school board in question did have a clear mission and vision, which was far more **holistic and faith-based** than the academic rigour being demanded by the interim principal. However, many parents had chosen the school for its high behavioural standards, its compassionate approach to pastoral care, its strong university acceptances, and its strong uniforms policy rather than its faith position, although they were more than happy to tolerate the faith position provided the other standards were not neglected.

In this context, the interim principal's argument to change the school's marketing image was largely pragmatic rather than visionary. She understood the expectations of the school's parents in the context of its marketplace. She understood that a school which functions like a holiday camp is unlikely to make a compelling case for fee-paying parents. At her initiative, the marketing was changed, and enrolment applications increased. **However**, the increased focus on academic achievement and financial results diluted clarity of the school's (and the board's) mission, and this needed to be re-addressed when the new permanent principal took up duties the following year.

Defining and maintaining a school's mission is hard work, but it is centrally important if a school is to be successful in achieving its outcomes – and meeting the legitimate expectations of its community.

Insight 6

Antidote to a disengaged school board

Do you feel your board merely rubber stamps the motions that are put before it? Do board meetings feel more like a "show-and-tell" session than a genuine, robust exploration of ideas, initiatives and alternatives? Do you hear nothing but silence from board members between meetings?

If any of these scenarios rings true for you, it may be that you are working with a disengaged board, or at least a board whose members don't appreciate how important their input is for the health of the school.

The answer is not to sack the board (or those disengaged members), or to give up on them or ignore them. Board chairs and Heads of Schools should begin with the assumption that board members love the school, they believe in its mission (its enduring purpose), and they want it to flourish. You should almost certainly also assume that they want to make a meaningful contribution.

A change of mindset may be an important foundation for re-engaging board members who appear to be disengaged.

Proceeding from this assumption that board members love the school and believe in its mission, a four-step approach can often be an effective way to re-engage them in the board's work.

STEP 1: Reiterate the school's mission and identify the priority strategic consequences. The school's mission is its foundational philosophy – why the school was established and why its continued existence is worthwhile. The mission should provide a strong sense of purpose for everyone in the school community, especially the board. The board should be constantly aware of its current priorities in achieving the mission, although this will be most acute when starting its regular strategic planning process. These priorities should give an automatic sense of urgency and purpose to the board's work that will focus the attention and the imagination of every board member.

STEP 2: Target the input required. Once the strategic priorities have been identified and agreed by the Board, the Board Chair and the Head of School should work as a team to present the operational consequences to board members. This discussion should allocate board members to individual positions of responsibility to monitor or guide the implementation of these priorities, such as chairing a committee, monitoring specific areas of interest, and so on. The delegation of these tasks must not leave any room for inaction, precluding a mediocre outcome such as "That was a great conversation and your input was really valuable".

STEP 3: Complete the circle. This critically important step is often neglected, which weakens the effectiveness of the board's work. Every board member should be asked to provide regular reports on progress and identify any barriers to achieving the goals. Reporting back provides the idea (and important) opportunity to acknowledge the efforts of board members, to highlight the value they bring to the school, and to thank them meaningfully for their ongoing service. For most board members, this simple step will lead to deeper engagement with the significant challenges being addressed by the board.

STEP 4: Share stories. This should be an ongoing, perpetual process. The real value of a board's work isn't shown in statistics or financial metrics – these are just means to a greater end. The purpose of any school is to make a real and significant difference as it educates its students to the highest possible standard in accordance with the school's mission, or enduring purpose. It follows from this that one of the most encouraging things a board can do is allow time at every meeting for the Head and any board member to share real stories of recent examples where the school is making a transformative difference in the lives of its students.

Kurt Hahn in his office at Gordonstaun School, colourised from the original B/W, By Ryswyles - Own work, CC BY-SA 4.0, https://commons.wikimedia.org/w/index.php?curid=97490386

The famous educator Kurt Hahn once observed: "There are three ways of trying to win the young. You can preach at them — that is a hook without a worm. You can say, "You must volunteer" — that is of the devil. And you can tell them, "You are needed" — that appeal hardly ever fails."

I suggest that in this sense, board members are not unlike adolescents; they need to be reminded from time to time that the school needs them if they are to be expected to rise to the challenges of board engagement.

Insight 7

Antifragility

The term "antifragility" only became part of our language relatively recently. Introduced by Nassim Nicholas Taleb in his 2012 book "Antifragile: Things that Gain from Disorder", antifragility is much more than the opposite of fragility.

The thinking goes like this – if something is fragile, it will break when it is hit or dropped. If something is robust or resilient, it will not break if it is hit or dropped. Antifragility goes beyond being robust or resilient. If something is antifragile, it will actually thrive from the disruption of being hit or dropped.

If the "something" is actually a "someone", the same principles apply. A fragile person will 'break' or suffer irredeemably when hit with a physical, emotional, financial or other difficulty. A resilient person will recover and then continue as previously, whereas an antifragile person will flourish and advance as a result of adversity.

Nassim Nicholas Taleb defines antifragility in these words:

"Some things benefit from shocks; they thrive and grow when exposed to volatility, randomness, disorder, and stressors and love adventure, risk, and uncertainty. Yet, in spite of the ubiquity of the phenomenon, there is no word for

> *the exact opposite of fragile. Let us call it antifragile. Antifragility is beyond resilience or robustness. The resilient resists shocks and stays the same; the antifragile gets better. This property is behind everything that has changed with time: evolution, culture, ideas, revolutions, political systems, technological innovation, cultural and economic success, corporate survival, good recipes (say, chicken soup or steak tartare with a drop of cognac), the rise of cities, cultures, legal systems, equatorial forests, bacterial resistance ... even our own existence as a species on this planet."*

Many experienced educators sense that students in schools today are less emotionally resilient than they were a generation ago. Teachers anecdotally illustrate these views by referring to higher absenteeism, declining persistence in meeting challenges, increasing incidence of mental health issues, difficulties in forming relationships (away from screens), inattention in class, refusal to attend school, and decreasing capacity to accept personal responsibility. Similarly, many school principals feel that young teachers today are less emotionally resilient than their predecessors, anecdotally referring to increasing periods of stress leave, declining compliance with regulatory demands, difficulty in controlling even small classes, and entrenchment of a 'work-to-rules' mentality.

Realistically, these observations probably reflect changes in society as a whole rather than school environments specifically. Nonetheless it raises an interesting question – if the increase in personal emotional fragility is seen as a negative trend, should our target be to raise more resilient people, or should we be seeking to raise more antifragile people?

It's a fair question to ask in this era of incessant disruptive change. Is it sufficient to be able to recover from a financial, emotional or other blow, battered and bruised but surviving, or should we be seeking the skills to grow – to flourish – through adversity? Rather than just recovering from mistakes, can we actually become stronger?

Writing in 2013, the US author Buster Benson identified ten principles from Taleb's book that can help develop an antifragile life:

1. Stick to simple rules.
2. Build in redundancy and layers (no single point of failure).
3. Resist the urge to suppress randomness.
4. Make sure that you have your soul in the game.
5. Experiment and tinker — take lots of small risks.

6. Avoid risks that, if lost, would wipe you out completely.
7. Don't get consumed by data.
8. Keep your options open.
9. Focus more on avoiding things that don't work than trying to find out what does work.
10. Respect the old — look for habits and rules that have been around for a long time.

These principles can probably be summed up by the metaphor of seeking to run a marathon rather than a sprint, always keeping options open, and experimenting by trying lots of different things in life while maintaining an open mind towards new opportunities and circumstances. Schools ought to be better placed than most organisations to achieve antifragility because they are inherently based upon a culture of learning and adaptability – or if not, they should be. This may mean sacrificing efficiency in the short-term for long-term gain, or in other words, thinking ahead to second-order consequences of decisions.

In his 2013 book "The Most Important Thing", the investor Howard Marks explains the importance of second-order thinking (which he calls second-level thinking) in these words:

> "First-level thinking is simplistic and superficial, and just about everyone can do it (a bad sign for anything involving an attempt at superiority). All the first-level thinker needs is an opinion about the future, as in "The outlook for the company is favourable, meaning the stock will go up." Second-level thinking is deep, complex and convoluted".

Second-order thinking therefore deliberately goes beyond immediacy and seeks to understand consequences by asking questions such as "And then what?" or "And so what?". In order to engage in second-order thinking, it can help to create a flow diagram of scenarios like the one shown below. Identify your decision, think through the possible consequences, write them down and then evaluate the balance between the "positives" and the "negatives". If this process is undertaken regularly, it should prepare you or any individual to enhance the capacity for antifragility.

Many of the things that happen to people in everyday life are the result of events or actions that are first-order negative but second-order positive. Therefore, even situations which seem inherently negative may not be once the second-order consequences are explored. This is

where antifragile people can flourish compared with fragile and even resilient people – antifragile people are more likely to see the positive second and third-order consequences than others who struggle to see beyond the immediate first-order consequences.

Second-order thinking may take more effort than first-order thinking because it is not always easy to think in terms of systems, interactions, and time. However, it is the key to developing anti-fragility.

So, what does antifragility look like in practice? For a teacher or a school principal, it might take the form of being dismissed from a school and thus being forced to look for a new position, which results in professional growth, opportunities for travel and enhanced family life beyond anything that was previously possible. For a school student, it may mean failing a subject, being forced to take up an alternative area of study, and then thriving through the unforeseen opportunities that arise.

Of course, any disruptive scenario is also capable of spiralling downwards into disaster. The defence against a downward spiral is antifragility – maintaining alternative options, being prepared to take risks, and visioning consequences, perhaps helped by a healthy dose of optimism.

References:
Benson B (2013) *How to Be Antifragile: Live Like a Hydra*, Better Humans.
Marks H (2013) *The Most Important Thing Illuminated*, Columbia Business School.
Taleb NN (2012) *Antifragile: Things that Gain from Disorder*, Random House.

Insight 8

Authentic leadership is more than management

Separating the roles of governance and management is fundamentally important to the effective functioning of every school. It is also one of the most common areas of confusion. Indeed, I have written about this at length in Insight 104.

The nature of leadership defines the roles of both school boards and senior management.

At its best, leadership is a peculiar art. It is also an endangered art. Society cries out for authentic leadership on the one hand, but as we saw during the election campaign earlier this year, society can also be cynical about leadership in the name of egalitarianism. A similar dynamic can often be seen in schools.

In our rational moments, we seldom need to be convinced that to be led is preferable to anarchy, even if we are less clear about who should be giving the lead and in what direction.

I suggest that a leader is not always someone with an impressive title, significant responsibilities, and a reserved car parking spot. A leader need not even be someone with rank, power, or position.

Quite simply, a leader is someone who someone else is following.

This means that any of us can be a leader. If our words direct and our actions inspire, we are leading. If we cause another to follow our example, or to follow our direction, we are leading. And at times, if our words and actions cause a reaction from those who disagree, then it is more than likely that we are not only leading but probably effecting authentic change! Leaders are change-initiators who often find themselves surrounded by change-resistors, and the art of leadership is to effect authentic and worthwhile change within such a scenario.

The question remains of course – in what direction are leaders leading? A person may have charismatic qualities and the capacity to encourage blind devotion, but they may be leading their acolytes into adopting values and behaviours that are unworthy and perhaps even dangerous. Discernment of vision and a commitment to serving others are crucially important for any leader.

This highlights the huge difference between leadership and management. It was Ian Percy who commented "Managers count seeds in the apple, while leaders envision how many apples there are in one seed". Another writer, Abraham Zaleznik, wrote: "Leaders have

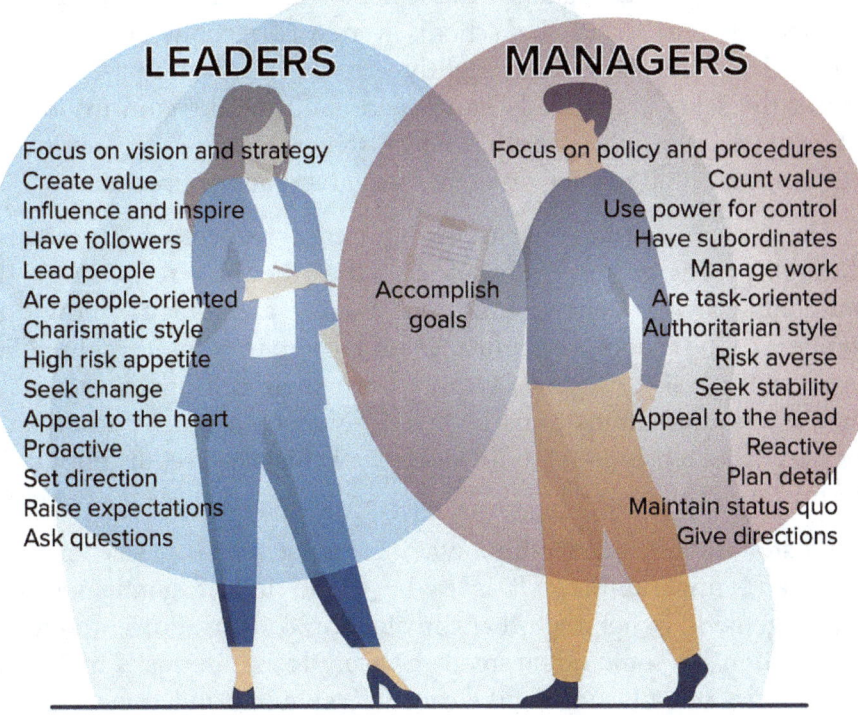

much more in common with artists, scientists, and other creative thinkers than they do with managers".

In short, the difference between leadership and management is the difference between shaping and controlling. Leaders yearn to create interdependencies; managers create dependencies. Leaders seek to recreate the ways people frame their thoughts; managers seek to re-structure organisations.

Leaders and managers are plentiful in the ranks of both boards and principals. It is probably fair to say that school principals have leadership positions which are among the most complex anywhere. It is said that to be a successful Head of a school, one must have the friendliness of a child, the enthusiasm of a courting teenager, the assurance of a soccer player, the diplomacy of a wayward husband, the curiosity of a cat, the memory of an elephant, and the good humour of an idiot.

School principals are expected, not unreasonably, to provide leadership by being committed contributors and exemplars. They are expected to have integrity, be willing to speak out as individuals on behalf of others, whilst being a team member par excellence, fully conversant with precedents in the school while simultaneously being expected also to drive the school in new directions for changing times. They are expected - rightly - to be interventionists, visible around the school, genuinely concerned about students in trouble, or lost, or weaker, or who simply need a listener, and yet they are loaded with mundane and routine tasks that take them out of circulation.

They are expected to be fearless in giving considered, balanced, and thoroughly researched advice to the board, respecting the confidentiality of deliberations on policy and about individual members of the school community, even though in being loyal to policy they run the risk of losing intimacy with their colleagues, especially when unpopular stands must be taken. Nonetheless, it is a necessary and inevitable tension - it would surely be a mistake to court popularity and mistake it for respect.

Most authentic leadership, whether in schools or elsewhere, is covert and unassuming. It is to be found in the gentle word of encouragement, in helping others, in steering conversations, in offering a suggestion, or some other small service. These are tasks that every person in a school community can and should fulfil, meaning that everyone should find themselves in positions as leaders from time to time.

During my career in various schools in several countries, I have usually found that the most effective leaders are those in ANY positions whatsoever who guide, steer and direct others without them necessarily being aware of it. As the Chinese sage, Lao Tzu, wrote in the 6th Century BC (when all leaders were male): "A leader is best when people barely know he exists. When his work is done, his aim is fulfilled, they will say 'we did this ourselves'".

Insight 9

Autonomy boosts morale and productivity

Let's begin not in the world of schools, but in the world of marketing and advertising – a world that interests many school board members who are keen to see enrolment numbers grow. In the late 1980s, one of the most prestigious advertising agencies in the world was Chiat/Day. Based in Los Angeles (USA), the company had an enviable reputation for innovation and creativity based on the spectacular success of Apple's famous "1984" launch of the Macintosh computer at the 1983 Super Bowl, an advertisement that was developed by Chiat/Day, followed by subsequent iconic ads starring the Energizer Bunny bursting through any and all competing products.

In 1993, the company's co-owner, Jay Chiat, announced a radical plan to boost creativity within his own company. The proposal was to eliminate separate offices, individual cubicles and even desks. These would all be replaced with open spaces that would be "zany, playful and stylish".

The famous Canadian-American architect Frank Gehry was commissioned to design the changes for Los Angeles headquarters. His design was certainly creative. It included a four-storey high sculpture of a pair of binoculars surrounded by randomly spaced, curved two-seater pods based on amusement park rides that were thought to encourage creative thoughts and discussions.

Design of the company's New York office was handled by the Italian designer, Gaetano Pesce. It included a wall-sized mural of a pair of red lips and a luminous multi-coloured floor covered with hieroglyphs. The floor in front of the men's toilet featured a large picture of a man urinating, while the round tables that were shared for work, rest and eating, would amusingly grab and hold important papers used for meetings. Some of the chairs had springs instead of legs, and they would tip backwards unexpectedly to the amusement of everyone present (who was not wearing a skirt!).

The new offices quickly became famous for their colour, fun and creativity, and design magazines featured enthusiastic coverage of their innovations. Chiat/Day even started charging for tours of their offices by tourists. The New York Times published an article claiming that the New York office was "the apotheosis of the dream factory" and that agency staff were "happily at home inside the dream".

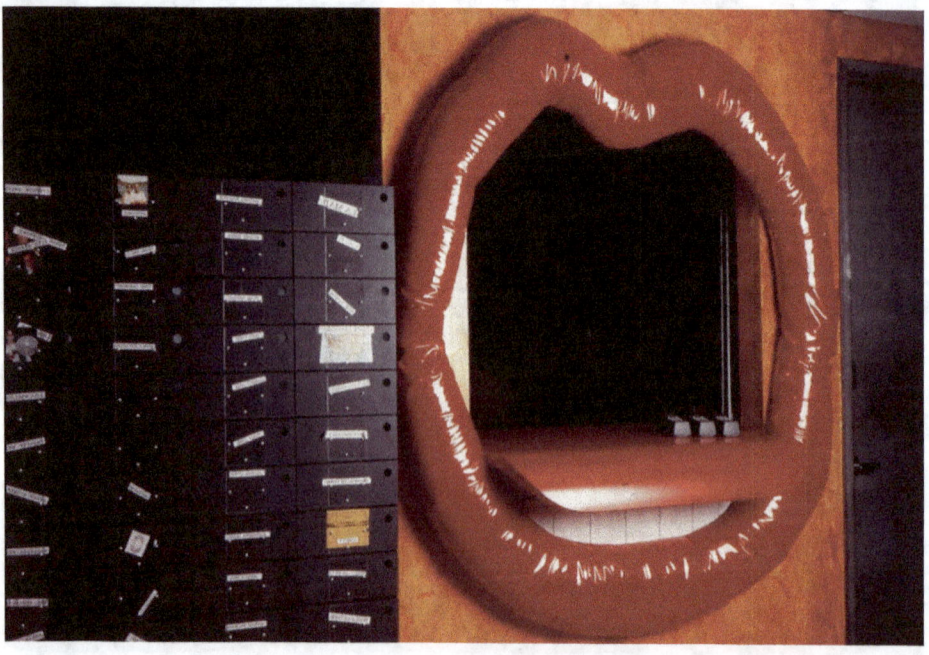

Chiat/Day's "free range" office concept was certainly ahead of its time. Many schools and companies now consciously use mobile technology, 'hot desking' and bright colours to encourage creativity and allow work to be done in whichever location within the "campus" works best for the task and the individuals concerned.

Unfortunately for the employees whose desks and spaces had suddenly disappeared, problems quickly began to emerge. Disgruntled employees found themselves carrying their temperamental, clunky laptops and heavy armfuls of paperwork all over the office in search of a temporarily vacant desk. Some employees chose to convert the boots (trunks) of their cars into filing cabinets, walking out to the car park when they needed to retrieve a document needed for their work.

Rather than being able to retain their shared clunky portable phones and computers from day to day, employees had to return them each evening and then sign in to retrieve a different one when they returned to the office the following day – if there was one available – and often there were not. Because of the shortage of shared equipment, employees would line up outside the office several hours before the doors opened each morning to get their precious phone and computer, then go home to sleep for a few hours, before later returning to do their day's work. Senior staff would arrange for their subordinates to arrive a few hours before them to secure their equipment on their behalf for the day's work. Rather than creating flexibility to work anywhere at any time, the new system had staff queuing before daybreak just to collect basic equipment. It wasn't long before disenchantment started building into resentment.

The "dream factory" was becoming a "nightmare" for those who had to work there.

In 2010, Alexander Haslam and Craig Knight conducted research into why some office spaces alienate workers, whereas others make them happier and more efficient. They examined four types of office space:

1. The "lean" office was a sanitised-looking space containing only the items necessary to perform the tasks required: a pencil, paper, a bare desk and a swivel chair.
2. The "enriched" office had these basic supplies but was decorated with plants and art, including several large, bright pictures.

3. The "empowered" office provided the same plants and art that were in the enriched office but participants were allowed to arrange them however they chose or not use them at all.

4. In the "disempowered" office, participants were given the opportunity to decorate, but when they had finished doing so, the experimenter rearranged the office so that it matched the enriched condition.

The results were very clear. People in the enriched office worked about 15% faster than those in the lean office, with no more errors, and they reported fewer health-related environmental complaints. Productivity and wellbeing increased even more – by about 30% – in the office that participants customised themselves. However, when employees' personal choices were overridden (in the fourth type of office), their performance and wellbeing dropped back to the same levels they showed in the lean office.

Haslam and Knight conclude their study with these words:

"Why are people who work in spaces to which they feel a personal connection happier and more productive – even healthier? We think that when people feel uncomfortable in their surroundings they are less engaged – not only with the space but with the work they perform in that space. Arranging offices in ways that ignore employees' preferences and individuality can undermine production and focus, even if well-meaning planners intend the opposite. When employees get to surround themselves with personally meaningful objects at work, the

efficiency gurus, enrichment experts and plastic palm-tree peddlers can all stay home."

The lesson here is that office design matters far less than letting people design their offices.

This helps explain why the "zany, playful and stylish" spaces that Chiat created, and which were so loved by magazine editors, architects, visitors and designers, were reviled by those who had to work there. The employees were not responding to the aesthetics but to the feeling of disempowerment they were experiencing as the aesthetics were imposed upon them by an over-confident employer. As one of Jay Chiat's deputies recalled, "Jay didn't listen to anybody. He just did it".

Jay Chiat summed up his office experiment by claiming that it was "the only thing I ever did in business that I was satisfied with". His employees disagreed, and the bold interior designs were torn down after just a few years.

So, here is the key lesson for school leaders and their boards. If the aim is to enhance teachers' productivity, effectiveness and morale, then give them the autonomy to make their own decisions about the workspaces where they spend their days.

The photos in this article show the Chiat/Day office in New York in 1995. Photos by Donatella Brun and originally published in Domus 769, March 1995.

References:

Berger, W (1999) Lost in Space, *Wired Magazine*.

Haslam, AS & Knight, C (2010) Cubicle, Sweet Cubicle: The Best Ways to Make Office Spaces Not So Bad, *Scientific American*.

Muschamp, H (1994) It's A Mad Mad Mad Ad World, *New York Times*.

Zanco, F (1995) *Hot desking in 1995: an office by Gaetano Pesce*, Domus Archive.

Insight 10

Black Swan crises and adaptive governance

The term "black swan event" springs from the idea that, for centuries, people in Europe assumed that all swans were white because no one had ever seen otherwise. This belief was shattered when Dutch explorers under the leadership of Willem de Vlamingh discovered black swans in Western Australia in 1697.

The phrase "black swan event" has evolved to symbolise an unexpected, seemingly unpredictable occurrence that completely upends existing assumptions. It is an exception to the prevailing wisdom that undermines accepted assumptions. The expression was popularised by Nassim Nicholas Taleb in his 2007 book "The Black Swan", where he defined a black swan event as rare (it lies outside regular expectations), high impact (its consequences are extreme) and retrospectively predictable (after it happens, people try to rationalise it as if it should have been foreseen).

Recent examples of "black swan events" include the 2001 attacks on the World Trade Centre in New York, the 2008 global financial crisis, the global COVID-19 pandemic, and some assert perhaps even the disruptive rise of Donald Trump in US politics.

There is no way that a school board can establish enough policies and procedures to eliminate every risk. Therefore, when school boards and leaders **fulfil their duty to manage risk** in the school, they typically focus on identifying risks according to two main criteria: their likelihood and their consequences. Risks that are highly likely to occur and have severe consequences understandably become the highest priority areas for school boards to address. Risks that have less likelihood and/or less significant impacts can be placed lower on the priority list.

Almost by definition, "black swan" risks lie outside this formulaic framework as they are unpredictable (except, perhaps, in hindsight, as Taleb points out). Furthermore, "black swan" risks typically come from sources that are external to the school, making them even more difficult to forecast. Every "black swan" event is different, but there are certain frameworks that a school board can set in place to minimise (or at least ameliorate) their impact.

For schools, one type of "black swan" event is more dangerous than any other, and that is a crisis which threatens the school's Mission. The Mission is the school's enduring purpose – why the school was established and why it is important for it to continue to operate. School boards can provide some defence against "black swan" events which pose an existential threat to the school by practising what has become known as 'adaptive governance'. This is a flexible, learning-based approach that is designed to manage complex and uncertain situations in ways that enhance the capacity of an organisation to deal with and adapt to changes while protecting the same organisation from becoming unstable.

Adaptive governance is widely applied in black-swan-like situations such as climate change adaptation, water resource management and biodiversity conservation – situations where uncertainty and complexity require continuous learning and co-operation. Strategies of adaptive governance include keeping up with and utilising new knowledge and changing conditions, dispersing decision-making power, engaging diverse groups to collaborate and work together to build resilience and adaptation, and using adaptive management strategies to test and refine policies over time.

Adapted from Krantzberg, G. and Song, Z. (2020) How Does Adaptive Governance Help Restore and Protect Shared Waters?. *Open Access Library Journal*, 7, 1-19.

In school situations, using the practice of adaptive governance to help prepare for and ameliorate unforeseeable black swan events involves three broad steps:

Step 1: Map out the school as a system, identifying inputs, outputs, functions, outcomes, and the interrelationships between the different parts.

Step 2: Identify potential disruptors to this system. Cast a wide net to identify those scenarios that could create great disruption for the school or offer new opportunities. Start at a large scale and then narrow down the identification so that the focus becomes concentrated on those events that will have the greatest impact on the school's mission.

Step 3: Ask "what if" questions. After identifying risks or opportunities, the board's inclination may be to go immediately to mitigation or creation strategies. However, it is more important first to ask "what if" questions. These questions will help uncover the school's greatest vulnerabilities and the most promising opportunities.

Risk identification should be done by as broad and diverse a range of people as possible, including board members, operations staff, teachers in charge of critical areas, part-time staff, contractors, volunteers, and perhaps even students. Identifying potential risks is one area where diverse perspectives are really needed.

Insight 11

Board Manuals in our digital age

In the long-distant past, by which I mean before computers became commonplace in the 1990s, school boards revered their policies and procedures so much that they kept them in beautifully preserved, classically bound books. Standards of board professionalism were so high that members very seldom had to refer to these books as their conduct was highly professional and respectful, and so conflicts almost never arose. In any case, board members fulfilled their duties more by habit and chivalrous behaviour than by policy, so the Board Manual (or Board Handbook) never really needed checking, updating or revision.

Everything in that previous paragraph is, of course, complete fictional fantasy. For many school boards in the pre-digital era, the reason that the Manual was almost never used was because it often didn't exist, at least in form of a single collection of documents. School boards would have had a brief document outlining the method of appointing new members and their term of office, they would have kept a file of the minutes of board meetings, and they would have had their constitution (or Memorandum and Articles of Association – or an equivalent under some other name), and often not much else. Even when these documents existed, they were seldom consulted.

During this pre-digital age, boards usually kept what documents they needed in ring binders which could be updated as required by inserting replacement pages. Some school boards used filing cabinets instead, especially where many years of minutes had accumulated, with files arranged alphabetically, numerically or by subject. Documents were typically handwritten or typed with typewriters, with copies being made using carbon paper, at least until photocopies became widely available.

These systems required meticulous organisation, frequent manual updates, significant physical storage space, and someone with a well-developed set of organisational skills. Not every school board rose to these requirements.

The digital age has completely transformed the traditional Board Manual as schools now try to make the storage of data more secure and the retrieval of information more efficient. These days, school boards use technologies such as digital document management systems (DMS) like Google Drive or Microsoft SharePoint, or online portals such as a secure section of the school's own website, where the Manual is split into themed files using standard formats such as Microsoft Word, Apple Pages or Google Docs, or preferably converted PDFs which ensure consistency in formatting and prevent unauthorised edits.

It is sound practice to keep at least two backups of the Board Manual and all-important documentation offsite, either at remote locations and/or on a reputable cloud storage platform such as Google Drive, Apple's iCloud, Microsoft OneDrive or Dropbox. All these platforms are secure and allow collaboration on editing drafts if desired, with tracked changes and ready availability of previous versions.

In the high-compliance environment in which today's schools operate, it has never been more important for school boards to maintain thorough, complete, up-to-date board manuals. This is important for new board members who need information about the school, the board's structure and operations as part of their orientation. It is also important for continuing board members and senior staff who need to refer to an expanding array of policies, precedents, minutes of meetings and financial records to perform their duties with proficiency.

The contents of a Board Manual will vary from school to school depending on its location, size, and legal requirements. When I conduct workshops on this topic with school boards, I provide a VERY comprehensive checklist of possible items to be included in the Board Manual, but such a long list is unlikely make captivating reading here, so I will simply list some of the most common key requirements:

The Board.
- Board member names and contact information.
- Board member biographical summaries, written in a standard format, with photos.
- Board member periods of service and expiry of current term.
- Statement of the board's powers, responsibilities and duties.
- Board member responsibilities (such as committees, positions of responsibility, etc).
- Committee descriptions and membership.
- Record of Board members' professional development.
- Related Parties transactions register.
- Latest Board Performance Review Report.

Historical and foundational documents for the organisation.
- Brief written history and/or fact sheet.
- Articles of Incorporation, including relationship with the School's owner.
- Constitution.
- Licence to operate, registration documents, accreditation documents (if applicable) not-for-profit status (if applicable), etc.

Bylaws.
- Procedures to appoint or elect members.
- Meeting procedures, including provisions for a quorum, etc.

Strategic framework or plan.
- Mission, vision, and values statements.
- Current strategic framework or plan.
- Progressive updates on progress in meeting strategic goals.

Board policies.
- Anti-discrimination.
- Child protection.
- Code of Practice.
- Complaints.
- Conflict of interest.
- Confidentiality.
- Document retention and destruction.
- Gift acceptance.
- Harassment.
- Insurance coverage.
- Legal liability.

- Record retention and destruction.
- Related Parties Transactions.
- Removal of Board members.
- •Social media.
- Technology appropriate use.
- Tendering for contracts and services.
- Travel and meeting expense reimbursements.
- Whistleblower
- Others that apply to your board.

Staff.
- The Head of School's job description.
- The Board-Head relationship.
- Staff list and positions.
- Organisation chart.

Finance.
- Financial reports for the previous 7 years.
- Auditor's reports for the previous 7 years.
- Current annual budget.
- 5-year financial projections.
- Finance policies (such as, investments, reserves and endowments).
- Risk management policies.
- Current risk management template.

Other information.
- Annual board calendar.
- Minutes from the last three years' board meetings.
- Current advertising and prospectus brochures.
- Website and social media information.

Schools across the world have never had to operate in such high-compliance environments as they confront today. A few decades ago, the documentary demands of a Board Manual were far more rudimentary, and it was usually possible to fit everything into a thin binder. If today's requirements for policies and legal documents had existed in the pre-digital age, they would have been unmanageable in the absence of a large support staff. School leaders may justifiably curse the documentary demands made upon them these days, but they can be grateful for digital innovations that help to generate, update and keep track of those documents.

Insight 12

Board-Staff Interaction

"We never see board members."
"We don't even know who they are."
"They make huge decisions that affect us all, but they never engage with us."
"They are invisible."

That is an amalgam of comments I have often heard from teachers and other staff in many schools I have worked with (indeed, far too many!).

I also often hear comments from teachers and staff along opposite lines:

"The board needs to keep its grubby hands out of our work."
"They interfere too much. Can't they just leave us alone and let us do our work?"

It is clear that staff in schools, and some board members, may not be clear on the appropriate boundaries between the board and the school's employees. Clearly, many school boards fail to get the balance right.

In order to understand the "right" balance, it is important to understand the board's role with respect to the Principal (Head of

School). The essence of that relationship is that the Board has only one employee, and that is the Principal. This doesn't mean the Principal is paid from the bank account of a separate legal entity than everyone else who works at the school. It does mean, however, that the Principal has a unique relationship with the Board that is not shared with anyone else working at the school.

The Principal serves as CEO (Chief Executive Officer) of the School and, as such, will have delegated authority from the Board to manage all day-to-day operations of the School. In return, the Principal is uniquely accountable to the board for the effectiveness of all the day-to-day operations in the school, including executing the general policies and directives of the Board, supervising and controlling all of the operational and educational affairs of the School, and so on. This is the "accountability-responsibility relationship" between governance (the board's work) and management (the Principal's work) shown in the diagram below. The Board delegates day-to-day operations and implementation of the school's Mission to the Principal, and in return, the Principal is accountable to the Board for the effective implementation of the Mission through the day-to-day operations.

The Principal's duties will include, but not be limited to, speaking on behalf of the School, recruiting and supervising teachers, planning

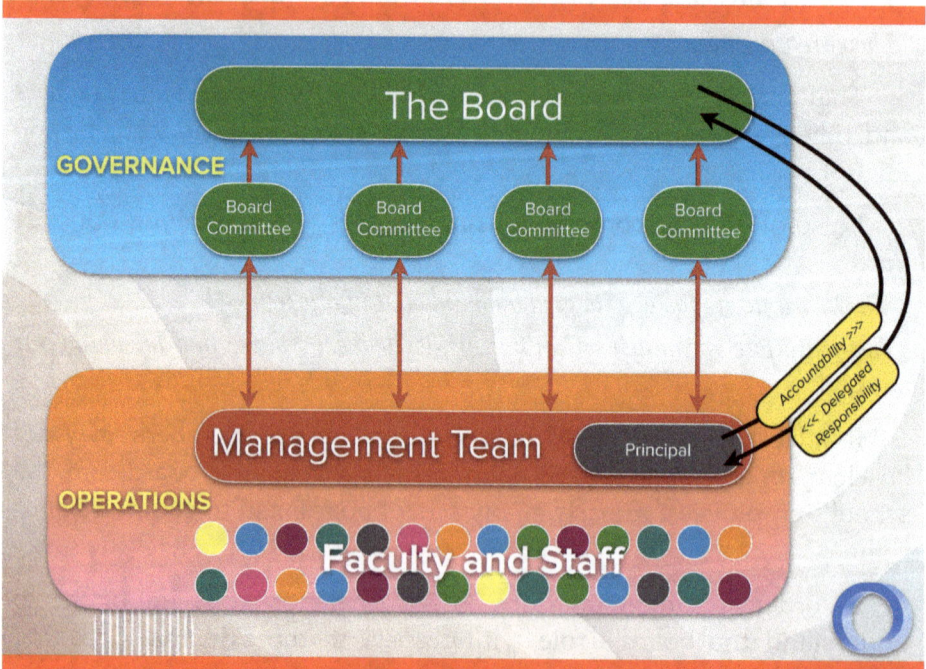

and implementation of school curriculum and student admission standards, overseeing general supervision of students, financial matters, building and grounds, fundraising, and acting as a liaison with the staff, administrative and parent bodies. Being accountable to the Board, the Principal will attend Board meetings, prepare and transmit timely reports to the Board, work with the Board to set the strategic plan and mission for the School, and will monitor the School's overall performance and development.

Every teacher and member of the non-teaching staff is employed by the Principal, and is thus accountable to the Principal. Only the Principal is employed by the Board, and only the Principal is directly accountable to the Board.

This accountability-responsibility relationship is essential to the effective working of any school that aims to implement the board's strategic vision in everyday practice. Unfortunately, it is also the rationale for board members in some schools to think they should never associate with the staff on the grounds that doing so might short-circuit or blur the clear line of accountability from the Board through the Principal to the staff.

In everyday practice, it is usually helpful for Board member to get to know members of the staffs – not to hear their complaints or to be lobbied behind the Principal's back, but to establish a two-way relationship of trust and respect. Establishing a clear, open, accessible line of communication is especially important so it is available in the rare but serious event that a formal complaint needs to be made about the Principal to the Board.

It follows from this that board members should be seen around the school and at school events such as sports matches or musical performances, but not too often, and never in a way that undermines the Principal's role as the primary line of two-way communication between the Board and the staff.

Apart from extremely rare events such as discovery of financial mismanagement, a crisis, or a lack of confidence in the Principal, the Board should never normally be involved in day-to-day management of school operations. Leaving aside these types of circumstances, is it possible for the board to swing the pendulum too far to the other end of the spectrum and become too removed? Undoubtedly this can happen. If all information is channelled solely through the Principal without any triangulation or checking on the Board's part, the Principal's authority may become dangerously unrestrained, and it can even disconnect the board from the culture of the school, its staff, students, parents and the wider community.

How can the Board ensure it is getting the balance right and receiving honest, fair and balanced reports from the Principal? Perhaps the most constructive way is to conduct an independent annual performance review of the Principal that seeks input from the Principal's direct reports, other teaching and non-teaching staff, students and parents, and includes questions pertaining to school culture, morale, academic performance, and so on.

One highly effective way for board members to engage with staff is through board committees. Board committees can be thought of as the Board's workforce. Committees report to the Board and make recommendations, but they generally do not have the power to make decisions – this authority should always rest with the Board. Although typically chaired by a board member, board committees may include members of the staff and even parents or members of the community with particular expertise or skills. For example, the Finance Committee would normally include the School's Bursar (Chief Finance Officer) and the Building and Grounds Committee would usually include the Chief

Operating Officer and/or the Property Manager. As the Principal is always an ex officio member of every board committee, the committee structure can offer a well-structured, appropriate formal channel for board-staff interactions.

Another effective way for the board to engage with staff is through regular written communications in the area of governance. For example, in my role as Chair of the Board of a school for Indigenous students in Queensland (Australia), I write a summary of the Board's relevant discussions and decisions after every board meeting for the Staff Bulletin. The Staff Bulletin is prepared and distributed by the Executive Principal (who also attends the board meetings), and so no short-circuiting of proper and appropriate occurs as staff are embraced as trusted, well-informed members of the decision-making process.

At a less formal level, when staff see board members walking around the school or at a school musical production or sports match, how should they interact? Quite often, both the board member and the staff member will be equally nervous and similarly aware of the need to behave within acceptable boundaries. But where do those boundaries lie?

Is it appropriate for a board member to give instructions directly to a member of the staff? No.

Is it necessary for a staff member to accept instructions from a board member? Also no.

Is it appropriate for a staff member to take aside a board member to complain about something they don't like or a decision the Principal has made? No, because operational issues are not within board members' responsibilities. The Principal is responsible for all management issues and supervising the staff, so when a staff member approaches a board member with a management complaint, it is important for the board member to react properly. In general, the board member should simply encourage the staff member to meet and discuss the concerns with his or her line supervisor or the Principal, reiterating that Principal is responsible for overall management and is therefore the person who can address the concern. No board member should ever act as a court of appeal against a decision the Principal has made that upsets a staff member.

The only exception to this general rule would be if a serious complaint about the Principal's conduct, ethics or honesty were to be made. In such cases, the verbal or conversational complaint should not be entertained by the board member, but the staff member bringing the complaint should be encouraged to document the concern and forward it to the Board Chair as a matter of urgency. It is important that every school has an established grievance policy and a complaints mechanism (such as a well-publicised e-mail address with direct access to the Board Chair) to handle such rare but serious situations.

In the dynamic world of education, the relationship between teachers and school board members is a two-way balancing act of professionalism, collaboration, and mutual respect. Contacts should not be artificially avoided, but approached with clear communication, ethical boundaries, and of course a shared commitment to building the best possible futures for the student. Board members and school staff are on the same team, but they serve in different roles. When everyone ensures that conversations are constructive, respectful, and student-centred, educators and board members can turn even the most awkward discussions into opportunities for growth. After all, good schools are never built on conflict – they are built on co-operation and teamwork.

Insight 13

Boeing's lessons for school boards and leaders

On the evening of 5th January 2024, a fairly new Alaska Airlines Boeing 737-9 MAX was flying from Portland (Oregon, USA) on a flight to Ontario (California, USA). It was still over suburban Portland, climbing just above 4,500 metres altitude, when one of the cabin windows/emergency exit plugs and its holding panel separated from the aircraft, together with parts of one un-occupied seat (26A), leaving a gaping hole in the side of the aircraft. As the plane rapidly depressurised, a boy sitting in row 26 had his t-shirt sucked off him while his mother held on to him to prevent him being sucked out of the airliner as well. Several phones and some unsecured hand luggage were sucked out of the plane before it returned to Portland and landed about 20 minutes after take-off. Miraculously, no injuries were reported – almost certainly because no passengers happened to be sitting in seats 26A and 26B at the time – even though an entire panel on the left-hand side of the aircraft was missing!

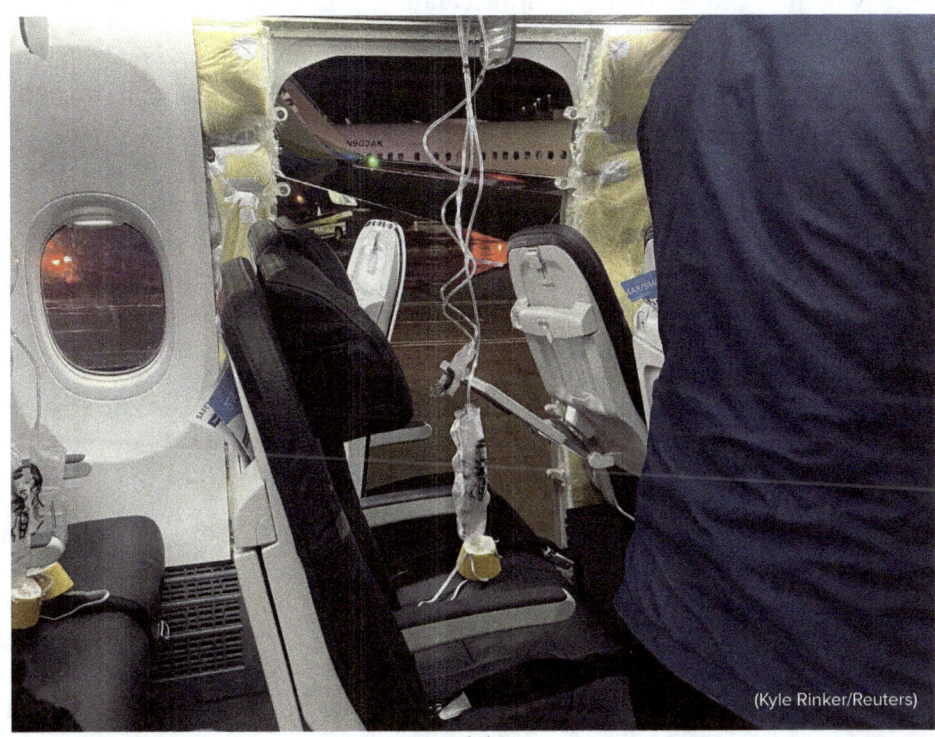

(Kyle Rinker/Reuters)

Subsequent investigations suggested that the fault occurred because several bolts that secure the exit panel plug to the plane had not been installed when Boeing had worked on the aircraft prior to its delivery to Alaska Airlines.

In a press conference on 10th January, the CEO of Boeing, David Calhoun, admitted that the blowout on the Alaska Airlines aircraft had been caused by a "quality escape". At the direction of the FAA, inspections were conducted on all Boeing 737-9 MAX aircraft in service with all airlines, and both United Airlines and Alaska Airlines found loose door bolts in a number of their aircraft.

"Quality escape" seems like a somewhat trivial euphemism for a manufacturing fault that almost killed 171 passengers and six crew on an airliner. Quite rightly, Calhoun has been criticised for drawing upon such a bland euphemism, with words like "bizarre" and "tone deaf" being used by journalists, commentators and airline passengers.

Perhaps surprisingly, school boards and leaders can learn several important points from Boeing's mishaps. In order to appreciate the full significance and relevance of these lessons, however, it is important to know a little more about the background to Boeing's problems with the 737 MAX. The Alaska Airlines incident was not an isolated occurrence – it was just one element of an escalating crisis Boeing has faced for more than a decade with their 737 MAX airliners.

Boeing's challenges with the 737 MAX arose from in part its rushed introduction. In 2011, American Airlines was on the verge of ordering a large fleet of airliners from Boeing's major competitor, Airbus. This competitive pressure led to Boeing's hurried decision to abandon plans for a new 'clean sheet' airliner it was developing and rush development of an updated version of its long-established 737 airliner, the first version of which had flown some 45 years earlier in 1967. The result was the 737 MAX.

The hectic timeframe which followed, together with insistence from another large customer (Southwest Airlines) that the new model include as few changes as possible from earlier 737 models to simplify pilot training and maintenance, seems to have led to poor build quality and major design flaws. One particular challenge was finding a way to fit new, larger diameter engines under the wings. Rather than lengthening the undercarriage, which would have then required other expensive re-design and regulatory changes, Boeing's "cheap and easy" solution was to mount the engines forward and in front of the wings. This changed the centre of gravity of the plane, so to restore stability and the handling characteristics to resemble earlier models (to reduce the cost of transitional pilot training to the new model), Boeing developed a software solution known as MCAS (the Manoeuvring Characteristics Augmentation System).

N704AL, the aircraft involved in the accident – Nick Dean - https://www.flickr.com/photos/44691276@N06/53293840699/

MCAS was intended to address the new aircraft's tendency to pitch upwards by forcing the nose downwards to prevent a stall when sensors indicated the need to do so. Unfortunately, Boeing didn't include any information about MCAS in its pilot manuals, nor did it fully disclose the way it worked to the regulators when they certified the new model. MCAS subsequently played a central role in causing two fatal crashes – Lion Air Flight JT610 in October 2018 and Ethiopian Airlines Flight ET302 in March 2019 – which together killed all 346 people on board. Although Boeing tried to blame the airlines' maintenance procedures and poor pilot training, investigations revealed that inaccurate sensor readings triggered the MCAS, causing the planes to nosedive uncontrollably (some commentators say the planes behaved like lawn darts). These tragic incidents resulted in the global grounding of all 737 MAXs, substantial financial setbacks for Boeing, increased regulatory scrutiny, and a comprehensive reassessment of the aircraft's design and safety protocols.

So what can school boards learn from Boeing's experience with the 737 MAX? I suggest there are at least ten "takeaways" for school leaders:

1. **Prioritise Quality Over Finances:**

Boeing has been widely criticised for prioritising profits and timelines over safety concerns. Rather than investing in new products over the past decade or more, Boeing used its surpluses to inflate its stock market value through share buybacks, a strategy that was directly fuelled by the finance-driven KPIs given to its managers by the board. School boards should ensure that the quality of education and the safety of the school community are the top priorities in educational environments, and focus on these as KPIs rather than financial returns, even if it means adjusting budgets or timelines.

2. **Transparent Communication:**

Boeing faced scrutiny for its lack of transparency and communication regarding the issues with the 737 MAX. It kept MCAS a secret from customers and regulators until it had to be revealed as the cause of a fatal crash. It has been secretive about its own internal investigations, presumably on the advice of its legal team, although this has paradoxically resulted in escalating legal challenges and litigation. Furthermore, most of Boeing's communications were handled by its PR team (rather than its CEO or Board Chair), and these communications came across as bland, formulaic and excessively constrained by lawyers' phrasing. School boards should prioritise personal, factual, transparent communication with all stakeholders, including students, parents, teachers, staff, alumni and the general community. This is especially so in times of crisis or when considering important changes.

3. **Regulatory Compliance:**

Boeing's main regulatory authority in the US is the FAA (Federal Aviation Administration). As funding to the FAA was reduced over the years, the FAA allowed manufacturers such as Boeing to self-regulate many aspects of their operations. This cosy relationship ended when the 737 MAX crashes revealed the inadequacy of self-regulation. The FAA's response was to impose a far more intense level of scrutiny that has subsequently revealed even more problems at Boeing, delaying certification of new airliners and slowing production rates. School boards and leaders should emphasise strict, full adherence to accountability requirements and regulations, working closely in partnership with relevant authorities to ensure compliance through harmonious, professional relationships.

4. Ethical Leadership:

Boeing's repeated public claims following every 737 MAX incident that "Safety remains our top priority" now seem somewhat hollow after a decade of mishaps, quality control shortcomings and accidents. Boeing 737 MAX crises highlight the importance of ethical leadership where leaders say what they mean and mean what they say. Similarly, school boards should insist that every level of educational and financial leadership in the school makes decisions based on ethical considerations that demonstrate a commitment to the well-being of students and the broader educational community. Needless to say, school boards should act in precisely the same manner to enhance the school's mission and vision.

5. Accountability and Oversight:

Following each 737 MAX incident, Boeing tried to divert blame to external sources – pilots, maintenance officers, their own suppliers, the regulators. Boeing's internal oversight and accountability mechanisms were questioned. School boards should establish robust oversight mechanisms to monitor the implementation of policies, ensure compliance, and hold individuals accountable for their actions.

6. Continuous Training and Professional Development:

Southwest Airlines, one of Boeing's major customers and a key operator of older 737 airliners, demanded that pilot training for transitioning to the 737 MAX be minimal. The airline insisted on maintaining a high level of commonality with earlier 737 models to minimise the need for additional training and certification. Boeing agreed to this demand, requiring just four hours training on an iPad for pilots to transition to the 737 MAX, additionally promising to pay Southwest Airlines $1 million per plane rebate if any simulator training was needed. A year before one of its 737 MAX airliners crashed, Lion Air tried to introduce simulator training for its pilots, and Boeing refused to allow it, claiming (in internal communications) that it would undermine a key selling point for the aircraft. Understandably, Boeing faced subsequent criticism for lapses in the pilot training protocols and undisclosed documentation of new features. In contrast to Boeing, school boards should invest in continuous training and professional development for teachers and staff – and themselves! – to ensure they stay updated on best practices and educational advancements.

7. **Crisis Preparedness:**

Clearly, Boeing struggled with its crisis management and continues to pay the price in terms of lost sales, delayed certification, production delays and severe reputational damage. School boards should develop comprehensive crisis management and risk reduction plans to address a full range of actual, potential and perceived issues promptly, thus minimising adverse impacts on the school, its students and staff, and its ongoing reputation.

8. **Cultural Shift Towards Safety:**

Boeing's culture has been heavily criticised, with claims that it prioritised production targets and share prices over safety. School boards have a duty to ensure that schools are safe, secure environments for everyone present, including visitors, contractors, and volunteers as well as its own students and staff. Fixing risks posed by maintenance oversights, deteriorating infrastructure, inadequate security, and so on, must always be a top priority on a school's expenditure and efforts – an integral component of a prevailing culture that values safety and welfare.

9. **Collaboration and Interdepartmental Communication:**

Boeing faced significant communication shortcomings between its different departments that exacerbated its safety and quality challenges. For example, there were many reported communication breakdowns between engineers and management. When engineers reported problems, they were often ignored because fixing the issue would slow production, miss deadlines or raise costs. In several cases, the engineers who reported the problems were sacked from their jobs, lowering overall morale, and leading to a culture of hiding mistakes. In contrast to Boeing's culture of blame, school leaders and their boards should encourage open, transparent collaboration and frank, respectful communication between various departments to ensure a cohesive and coherent approach to solving problems and advancing the school's mission and vision.

10. **Learning from Mistakes:**

Boeing's response to the 737 MAX (and other) incidents has highlighted the importance of learning from mistakes. School boards should do everything they can to create an authentic learning culture that encourages applying the lessons acquired from both successes and

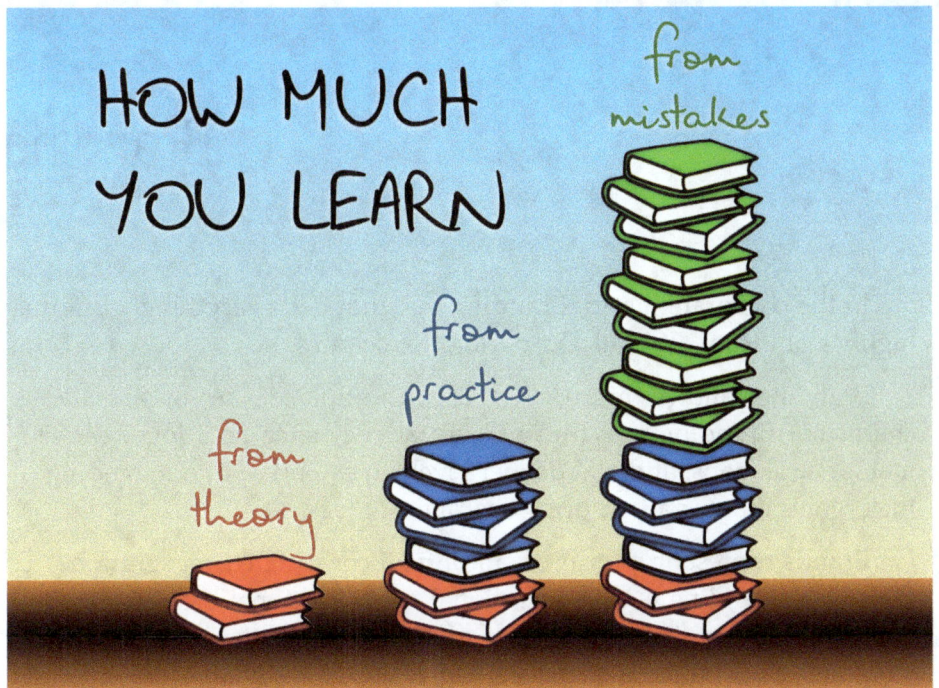

failures to continuous improvement in the educational system. Boeing seems to have been incapable of developing a true learning culture over the past decade or two; it would be a sad indictment indeed if schools – that is, educational organisations that specialise in teaching and learning – fell into the same vortex. No school would want to suffer the long-term reputational damage Boeing has experienced, with seemingly miniscule chances of a quick (or even medium-term) recovery.

Insight 14

Branding

In the corporate world, branding may not be "everything", but it is highly significant. It is also important for schools.

Branding allows high-speed identification of an organisation's character. Branding may include visual cues such as a logo, easy-to-memorise slogans, and at a deeper level, an extensive understanding of the organisation's values, priorities, and uniqueness.

Brands represent a form of simplified, constructed recognition. At their best, branding is also intentional. Unintentional branding occurs when a brand is "trashed", such as through negative media articles, well-known incompetence or negligence, internal divisions, or even co-ordinated social media attacks. As anyone who is involved with branding knows only too well, it takes much longer to build up positive branding than it takes to destroy a brand's reputation.

Despite the best efforts of advertising agencies, brands do not have their own innate personality or consciousness. They do not have a moral compass. They do not feel pressure or pain or indeed any emotion. People and organisations can own brands, they can create brands, and they can direct brands, but they should never aspire to be a brand. Brands reflect identity and character; brands do not determine identity or character.

Perhaps the ultimate example of the power of corporate branding is the Nike logo. When we look at Nike's global operations, the Nike logo is the most profitable part of the organisation because it is the only thing that is "authentically Nike". Everything in Nike's operations apart from the logo is outsourced. The manufacturing is outsourced to supplier organisations, the advertising and marketing are outsourced, and retailing is done through other companies. In effect, Nike IS the logo (and nothing else).

For schools, branding is expressed through visual symbols such as the crest / logo and the motto, and more deeply through mission and vision statements. At their best, logos and mottos, the mission and

vision, all work together harmoniously to communicate the character and reputation of the school.

An important question arises from this principle – if branding communicates identity, who are the targeted recipients for such communication?

The short answer is "any actual, potential or perceived stakeholder", which in turn begs the question "who are the school's stakeholders?".

Schools operate in extraordinary wide networks of stakeholders – students, parents, teachers, non-teaching staff, the board, alumni, neighbours, the local council, state and national governments, government authorities and bureaucrats, local and wider businesses (especially those on whom the school depends, such as bus companies, catering companies and recruiting organisations), the media, banks and financial institutions, and ultimately the general public. In the same way that Jesus taught everyone is our neighbour, anyone and everyone can be an actual or potential stakeholder in a school.

Ideally, all these stakeholders need to have a consistently positive – even enthusiastic – view of the school's character, integrity, efficiency, mission and values. The more advocates a school has, the easier it is to advance and flourish. As I found in every school where I was Principal, the most powerfully positive advertising a school can have is the enthusiastic stories told by parents while they are chatting beside a sports field or at children's birthday parties about the school's love for and impact on their children.

The consequence of this is that a school's branding must accurately reflect the positive identity and character of a school to a very widespread, diverse and dispersed network of stakeholders. Achieving this begins with getting the mission and vision right, then infusing these authentically through the school so that everyday practice matches the rhetoric.

As organisations like Apple and Coca-Cola understand, effective branding may (and should) look simple, but it reflects profound philosophical thought, effective practice, and deep authenticity.

Insight 15

Can a school be a real community?

We often hear the expression "our school community". It sounds warm and embracing, but do we really understand what is meant by that expression beyond the positive emotional feelings it evokes?

The word "community" originally comes from the Latin *communitas*, meaning "shared in common" or "public spirit". However, the way we use the word "community" has shifted quite radically in recent decades.

This became clear to me a few years ago. I was in the Highlands of Papua New Guinea attending a multi-day "sing-sing" (large dance festival) in Wabag, a small town in Enga province. Groups from most parts of Papua Guinea had come to Wabag for the sing-sing, with each group decorated in the ceremonial dress of their region to perform their traditional dances in accordance with their long-standing customs. Each group had its own cultural identity, including its own language,

as Papua New Guinea contains 835 (or 12%) of the world's 7,000 living languages, many confined to an area no wider than the mountainous valley where the speakers live.

In Wabag it became obvious to me that this sing-sing was a vibrant expression of what "community" meant in pre-modern times. Each community was geographically coherent and sustained by a shared commitment to a common set of values, beliefs and experiences that were passed on through families. There was a consensual commitment to a set of rituals and ways to behave towards others in the community, and possibly also a consensus about how those outside the community were to be perceived. Traditionally, therefore, "community" was the expression a set of mutual obligations that a person was born into; it was central to their individual and group identity.

Today, the term "community" is often – even usually - used in a wider incarnation. These days, for example, we freely talk about "the disability community", "the online gaming community", "the LGBTQI+ community", "the activist community", "the tech community", and even "the plane spotting community", among many others.

Does this wider use of the word "community" dilute the force of the word? Some would certainly argue so. It is true that 'modern' communities which are based on common or special interests are usually centred on coherent ideas that bring people together. However, they are not communities in the deeper, traditional sense of the word as their members generally don't live together in close proximity, but rather the "communities" are collections of people who share a common interest or common trait.

Unlike traditional communities, some of these communities may even be ephemeral as members come and go as they please. This apparent freedom contrasts strongly with communities in the traditional sense because the customary sense of mutual obligation has become diluted or is missing entirely.

In the modern sense, then, we tend to describe everyone who shares anything in common or whose lives intersect in any kind of meaningful way a "community". Reciprocal obligation is no longer required, and expectations of roles or beliefs are not a prerequisite for belonging. This is especially evident in industrialised or post-modern societies where individualism and personal freedom have overtaken the duty-focussed priorities of collective obligations. Individualism is largely incompatible with the traditional concept of "community" which, by definition, involves some restriction on personal liberty.

So, how realistic is it for any school in today's world to claim the students, teachers, parents and alumni associated with the school comprise "the [insert name of school here] community"?

One key factor is the depth of connection between the people who function in the school. An authentic community demands strong relationships based on mutual obligations. If the interactions within the school are mainly transactional in nature, with a narrow focus on academic grades, maintaining discipline, attending meetings, providing value for money, and so on, the school probably should be seen as an "institution" rather than a "community". If a few voices (such as the senior management) carry excessive weight and influence compared with students, teachers and parents, then the school's claim to be a "community" may be more aspirational than actual.

A school CAN be an authentic community in the modern sense of the word, but only if it fosters deep relationships based on mutual care for one another and, of supreme importance, a 100% shared commitment to the Mission (enduring purpose) of the school. Sadly, many schools refer to themselves as "communities" more as a branding term in their marketing than a genuine reflection of the deep, mutually obligatory bonds that operate at every level at every minute of every day within the school.

Now, think about the school where you are involved – do you think it is fair to identify it as an authentic "community"?

Insight 16

Chinese mice do not eat cheese

I have heard it said that an elephant is a mouse designed to government specifications.

Schools have always been required to adhere to government compliance regulations. Most people working in schools would agree that the burdens of compliance and accountability are growing relentlessly. Many of the requirements may seem onerous, but this is not always the case.

In 2015, the New South Wales Education Standards Authority introduced a requirement that all Responsible Persons (board members and senior leaders) in independent schools must undertake at least four hours of professional development with a NESA-approved training provider. This requirement was subsequently revised to 12 hours over each three-year period.

This was a brilliant initiative. In the US (where I served my fifth and last headship), a similar requirement has existed for many years, and schools where this requirement is ignored lose their accreditation and therefore cannot send their graduating students to college or university. I found that as a general rule the quality of school board governance in the US is generally first-rate, and arguably – on average – better than I have experienced in any of the other countries where I have worked or evaluated boards for accreditation or approval purposes.

Professional development for board members is a sound investment in a school's future given that:

- Research shows that effective governance enhances student outcomes and raises staff morale.
- Sound governance is necessary for stability and community confidence.
- Good governance provides legal and ethical protection for everyone involved.

Despite overseas experience, this initiative by NESA represented quite a cultural shift for many NSW school boards which were unaccustomed to investing time and resources on their own development. It remains an alien concept elsewhere in Australia where similar government requirements have not been introduced and thus no such professional development is undertaken – to the detriment of the schools in those states I would argue.

The situation reminds me of a mouse I encountered when I was living and working in Hong Kong a little over a decade ago.

One morning, I discovered that there was a mouse in my office. Determined to show my competence in solving the problem, I went to the local market and bought a little wire mesh cage. My plan was to trap the mouse alive using a piece of cheese as bait.

A few days later, the cheese had still not been touched and I was becoming a bit worried because the mouse was obviously still scampering around my office.

One morning, after the cage with the cheese had been lying untouched for about a week, one of the school's maintenance staff came in to do some repairs, and he happened to see the mouse trap. He looked at me and said very seriously with a waggle of the finger "Chinese mice do not eat cheese".

Okay, it is commonly known that Chinese people do not like cheese. My PA told me that people of Chinese ethnicity can't stand the smell of it and to them the taste would be like sun dried rooster's feet or fermented seaweed to a Westerner (trying to help me imagine such a thing). However, it had not occurred to me that Chinese mice might not like cheese as well.

And then I thought about it. If there was no cheese in the average Chinese home, then even a reasonably intelligent mouse might have trouble figuring out that it was supposed to go into the cage to eat something it never encountered before.

There had to be a reason that the mouse had not been enticed into the cage, so I asked the man from the maintenance department what a Chinese mouse might prefer to eat. "Fish" he said confidently, "with soy sauce".

I had never thought of a mouse eating fish or that a mouse might prefer it with a little dash of soy sauce. In fact, that would have been the last thing I would have thought of using. As the maintenance man went out the door he added "Mice like a little ginger on their fish".

And so, I replaced the cheese with a little left-over fish laced with a touch of soy sauce and, of course, some shredded ginger. Finding this more to his liking, the mouse was caught just a few hours later.

We all know the expression the expression "When in Rome do as the Romans do", which in its Chinese version is "When visiting a village, ask how the villagers do things".

The mouse did not like cheese because he (or maybe she, I didn't ask) had never tried it. He (let's assume it was a 'he') had decided he didn't like it but had never experienced it. If the mouse had been told by his mother or father or teacher that cheese was dangerous and therefore avoided it, that would make sense. However, without any knowledge or understanding of cheese, the mouse had decided not to try it.

I hope you can see the light-hearted point I am trying to make here. Boards may not be accustomed to engaging in professional development (whether required by government authorities or not), but it makes no sense to reject the idea on the basis of comfort, precedent, resources or 'other priorities' without seriously first considering its benefits.

When I was in Hong Kong, I had what I thought was a very good mouse trap. However, as long as I continued believing it was good, I was prevented from making an excellent mouse trap.

Eventually I reached the point where I came to others for advice, and through that I achieved excellence – as I am sure the mouse would testify to you today if it had survived.

In the same way, I hope that as a school leader or board member you will always be open to seeking the advice of others - especially those who are politically neutral and have no 'skin in the game' - as you strive for the heights of excellence. There is no better way to maximise the value of your efforts as you seek to make your great school even better.

Please make it a priority to invest in your own professional development.

Insight 17

Civility and respect on school boards

We should assume that there will be disagreements when school boards meet. Disagreements are actually a good thing; they should be welcomed and embraced because they (usually) indicate that serious questions are being asked in an effort to discern the best way forward for the school's future.

However, disagreements can become destructive if they degenerate into personal attacks or descend into conflicts between people rather than conflicts between ideas. When respect between board members breaks down, the board's operations can become seriously dysfunctional.

It is essential for board effectiveness that disagreements are handled in ways that honour the fundamental respect that is due to each person as an equal member of the board. Even fierce disagreements must be conducted according to the moral requisite of civility.

Civility is much more than being polite or courteous. To act with civility is to remove ego from discussions and relationships, refusing to take offence or taking something personally when another person disagrees with you. In other words, reacting angrily in a discussion is to become uncivil.

There may be times in wider society when a lack of civility might perhaps be justified, such as when a group of oppressed people who have been subjugated for aeons cry out angrily for justice. However, it would be an extremely unusual, almost unimaginably rare school board meeting where a situation arose that would justify uncivil behaviour. As a rule, civility should be the assumed moral framework under which every school board meeting functions.

And yet, it isn't always so.

Most school leaders and board members have experienced situations when inappropriate passion has taken over a board discussion or two (or three) (or more). Anyone who has experienced this will know that such lack of civility NEVER aids the process of rational decision-making. Never!

I think two authors provide especially useful insights into civility as a framework that can enhance the dynamics of school boards.

In her book *Mere Civility*, the Oxford political theorist Teresa Bejan defines civility as "a conversational virtue that is meant to regulate the deliberations of free and equal citizens". This definition represents a sound basis for school board dynamics, allowing space for passion and deeply held values while also regulating the words we use, even when board members who are "free and equal" disagree.

Professor of Philosophy at Vanderbilt University and author of *Sustaining Democracy*, Robert Talisse, describes civility as a knotting, or bundle, of three virtues: public mindedness (what is best for everyone, not just the speaker), reciprocity (a genuine exchange between people in which a speaker expects to be heard and to be answered), and transparency (engaging in public conversation in a manner that is intelligible to others who are listening, even if they don't agree with you – making an argument that has a reasonable chance of being persuasive to a diverse audience with whom we share a common future).

If we accept these views of civility, we immediately see a contrast between the way a school board should function and the negative role modelling that is often provided in contemporary politics. Politics in many parts of the world increasingly raises the stakes of any issue to the level of an existential crisis, making the issue insoluble as common ground becomes almost impossible to find. "Your climate policy will make farming areas of this country uninhabitable". "Your industrial relations policy will send this country back a hundred years". "Your defence policy will make us a target for a nuclear attack". The result is extreme divisiveness as the public must navigate an ocean of false dichotomies that preclude civility.

How can board members avoid the slippery slope towards uncivility? Ideally, it requires board members to have the wisdom to restrain themselves voluntarily in order to retain something that is much more valuable than the immediate point being discussed – that is, the effectiveness of the board. This has been likened to a marriage relationship in which one or the other partner might be able to say something or "pull a trump card" to score a "win" in a disagreement, but chooses not to do so in order to preserve long-term trust in the relationship. As the Swedish-American philosopher and ethicist Sissela Bok wrote in her book *Lying*, "**whatever** matters to human beings, trust is the atmosphere in which it thrives".

For such trust and civility to function effectively, consensus and commitment are required affirming that every board member is "free and equal", and that the board's authority is collective, being practised only through a formal process of judicious decision-making. If these foundations are accepted and mutual trust has been established, then respect and civility among board members should be an inevitable consequence.

Insight 18

Codes of Practice for School Boards

I know it's a generalisation, but in my experience, the typical member of any school board is passionate about the school and its purpose, well-meaning and committed, but also time-impoverished and generally untrained for the tasks and duties they are required to perform.

Most new board members address their lack of preparation for serving on the board in one of two ways. Either they bring insights from their experiences on other boards (if they have such experiences), or they sit quietly, observe others in the room, and slowly absorb and then adopt the practices of those around them. The approach of emulating others will, of course, only work well only IF other board members are functioning competently and professionally with a complete appreciation of their duties and obligations – otherwise, the sad alternative may be self-perpetuating incompetence.

The process of onboarding new board members is critically important, which is why most boards engage in a formal orientation process. This usually includes input from an independent, external professional who is qualified and competent in explaining the purpose and implementation of 'best practice' in school board governance.

Whether board members are new or experienced, a common danger which emerges on school boards is that members will become complacent over time, creating their own comfort zones of inertia or short-cuts. This process is usually stealthy and insidious, and thus difficult to recognise from within, and even more difficult to challenge.

The best defence against complacency and inertia on a school board is scheduling regular board performance reviews by an independent, external professional. However, there are internal controls that a board can also establish to withstand poor practice, one of which is adopting a Code of Practice (sometimes called a Code of Conduct).

A Code of Practice is a set of written guidelines issued by an organisation (in this case, a school board) that specifies ethical stan-

Creator: Nuthawut Somsuk | Credit: Getty Images/iStockphoto

dards that must be adhered to by its members. It is common 'best practice' for organisations to develop, publicise and adhere to a Code of Practice, and indeed Optimal School Governance has its own Code of Practice. Many school boards make continued adherence to the Code of Practice a condition of continuing membership and require members to sign an annual declaration to that effect.

A school board's adherence to a code of practice is essential for ensuring ethical governance, transparency, and accountability in decision making. A well-defined code establishes clear expectations for board members and promotes integrity, professionalism, and consistency in their roles. It fosters trust among stakeholders – students, parents, teachers, and the wider community – by making a public commitment to fairness, inclusivity, and student-focussed policies. Additionally, a code of practice provides a framework for resolving conflicts, guiding ethical dilemmas, limiting aberrant behaviour, and maintaining legal compliance, ultimately enhancing the board's effectiveness in achieving educational excellence and organisational efficacy.

Although I could provide sample codes of practice here, it would not be prudent because every school's code of practice needs to be specifically crafted for the school, reflecting its unique ethos, enduring purpose, legal framework, and key priorities. Typically, however, a school board's code of practice will establish a formal framework for ethical practice, commit to high standards of conduct, and specify the ways in those high standards will be implemented by both board members and the employees of the school. Its effectiveness can be enhanced by reminding board members of the importance of their code of practice by asking them to agree to it and sign it annually.

So, if your board does not yet have a Code of Practice, it should develop one as a priority. If a Code Practice does already exist, make sure its contents are known by getting board members to agree to it annually in writing, and then ensure it is always adhered to by all board members without exception.

Insight 19

Committees

Most school boards have committees, but not all board committees operate well. Furthermore, not all committees contribute to the efficiency or effectiveness of the board. At their most extreme, some school boards are so afraid that committees may destabilise the school that they choose not to appoint any committees, thus encumbering the entire board with having to deal with every facet and detail of the school's governance.

At their best, committees disperse the detailed work of the board, both in terms of time and personnel. Committees can interrogate the viability and detail of proposals before being brought to the board for approval. The typical outcome of a healthy committee structure is shorter board meetings that can focus on 'big picture' strategic goals rather than minutiae and detail, usually leading to decisions that are based on evidence and data rather than emotions and opinions.

Another benefit of committees is that they provide the board with the opportunity to "try out" prospective board members, exploring their skills set, capacity to work with others, punctuality, energy, commitment, and so on. This can be done without surrendering any of the board's authority as the usual 'rule' is that with just a few specific exceptions, committees are usually not empowered to make decisions. Committees consider data, evidence, and alternative propositions to form recommendations which are brought to the board for approval.

Recognising that committees should be delegated powers that enhance rather than undermine the Board's authority as the supreme decision-making body of the school, it follows that committees make recommendations, not decisions. Of course, the board may delegate 'convenience' powers to a committee, such as approving payments within prescribed limits at various stages of a building program, but it would be dereliction of its duty for a board to delegate substantial powers to a committee. Consider, for example, the power to approve the budget – no. The power to appoint a new Principal – no. The

power to dismiss a Principal – no. The power to monitor and direct the school's academic and co-curricular programs – no. The power to award a building contract – no.

From a legal perspective, the Board always retains full authority as the school's supreme decision-making body, and Board members carry the legal responsibility for the integrity and consequences of all decisions made at the governance level. Many references support this view (even without referring to my own book on school board governance), and here are seven examples:

"It is the board, and only the board as a whole, that makes policy decisions, but it accomplishes its work through committees and task forces". DeKuyper, MH (2007) Trustee Handbook: A Guide to Effective Governance for Independent School Boards, n.p.: NAIS. P.17.

"In Australia and the US, the board is responsible for the overall governance, management and strategic direction of the organisation. It is also responsible for delivering accountable corporate performance in accordance with the organisation's goals and objectives. Committees, on the other hand, make recommendations for action to the full board, which retains collective responsibility for decision making". Tumarkin, S (2021) Do board committees hinder decision making? Sydney: UNSW. https://www.businessthink.unsw.edu.au/articles/board-committees-decision-making

"A committee is created to provide counselling and advice for the board or to handle a task on the board's agenda. Any recommendations made by a committee need to be approved by the board, but remember, the board is not obligated to go with committee suggestions. Committees are more effective when their charter and scope of work is clearly defined by the board". BoardSource (2022) *Do we really need board committees?* Washington DC: BoardSource. https://boardsource.org/resources/really-need-board-committees/

"The reason for a subcommittee's existence needs to be clearly defined together with broad guidelines as to how it will function and operate. In principle, subcommittees are established to examine, test, review, and explore designated issues and the chairman of the committee reports back to the main board, providing details and recommendations for board consideration and/or, where appropriate, approval". Stein, D (2016) "Governance as a Corporate Discipline" in LeBlanc, R (ed.) *The Handbook of Board Governance: A Comprehensive Guide for Public, Private and Not-for-profit Board Members.* Hoboken: Wiley. pp.83-84.

"A governing board's responsibility is to create an integrated set of values that, taken together, cradle or encompass the nature of the organization. Proper governance is not a piecemeal endeavour... Consequently, board committees, when they are needed to assist the board in decision making, should do pre-board work, not sub-board work... In this process, the committee's job and the board's job are sequential and separate". Carver, J. (2006) *Boards that Make a Difference (4th ed.),* San Francisco: Jossey-Bass. pp.228-230.

"It is clear that the board may delegate its role only to the extent that it is confident it can demonstrate in a court of law that members are performing their duties with due care and diligence. Since the board is ultimately responsible for all of the actions and decisions of an organisation, board members must exert sufficient control over delegates to ensure that the legal obligations of the board and of individual directors are being met". Keil, G., Nicholson, G., Tunny, JA & Beck, J (2012) *Directors at Work: A Practical Guide for Boards,* Sydney: Thomson Reuters. p.383.

"In order to ensure governance consistency, it is recommended that the board develop a policy on delegation for inclusion in the (Constitution) as well as a formal delegation of authority policy". Keil, G., Nicholson, G., Tunny, JA & Beck, J (2012) *Directors at Work: A Practical Guide for Boards,* Sydney: Thomson Reuters. p.389.

So, what committees might the board of a school consider forming? The short answer is "it depends on the school". Large schools tend to have more committees than small schools, and new schools tend to have fewer committees than well-established schools because of the wide range of tasks required in establishing a new school.

The most common and highly recommended committees for schools are a Finance Committee (to oversee financial matters, including the annual budget) and a Governance Committee (to handle the board's internal processes, including succession management, board member performance reviews and regular board evaluations).

Other committees that are commonly found in schools include a Building and Grounds Committee (or Capital Works Committee) and an Executive Committee (comprising a handful of the most senior board members who are empowered to make certain decisions between board meetings). Also common are short-term committees that are established for a particular purpose such as a Strategic Planning Committee or a Head Search Committee.

Less common committees found in some schools include a Fundraising Committee, an Admissions and Marketing Committee, a Financial Aid Committee, a Policy Oversight Committee, a Risk and Procedures Committee and an Education Committee. Education Committees can be a blessing or a curse depending upon how they are populated and their terms of reference (this may require a full article at some stage).

The effectiveness of any board committee will largely depend on its leadership. Committees of school boards are usually chaired by a board member who has a capacity to manage meetings in an orderly manner rather than (necessarily) any particular professional skills set. The

Chair is thus the person who delivers the committee's reports and recommendations on behalf of the committee to each board meeting. The remaining committee members may comprise a mix of other board members, senior staff of the school, parents, and external friends of the school.

It is essential that boards review the leadership of their committees regularly, and preferably on an annual basis. If a board has a weak or mediocre leadership, it must be corrected quickly for the sake of the board and the entire school. It is also important that the board review and reiterate the terms of reference for each of its boards on an annual basis to ensure efficiency, relevance and close alignment with the school's mission statement, vision statement, and the priorities of the current strategic plan.

There is value in maintaining a balance between continuing and new members on board committees. Continuing members provide institutional memory while new members bring fresh ideas and perspectives. Presuming that the composition of board committees is reviewed annually, it may be unwise simply to call for board members to volunteer for the committee of their choice, as this discourages turnover and therefore reduces efficacy. Organising committee membership by volunteering may be good from a social perspective but it is unlikely to generate optimal performance.

Alec Issigonis, designer of the original Mini (the car, not the skirt), famously said "a camel is a horse designed by a committee". No school, even one situated on the Arabian Peninsula, requires a metaphorical camel. If followed carefully, the advice offered here should guide schools towards a committee structure that improves the school for the board, its staff and its students.

Insight 20

Common pressures on school boards

I have been working with school boards in various ways for almost four decades. I have been a member and Chair of school boards, an observer of school boards when working as a Head of School, an evaluator of school boards during accreditation and appraisal visits on behalf of several authorities, and for the past 12 years, I have been a consultant to tens of school boards in many nations of the world.

During this work, I have seen school boards encountering many challenges and problems, but there are four pressures that seem to recur more often than most:

1. **Maintaining a mission-centred, strategic board focus.**
2. **Aligning board culture and senior management practice.**
3. **Planning adequately for board and senior management succession.**
4. **Implementing effective risk management.**

It is only possible to examine each of these at a general level in a brief article such as this because every school's situation has unique forces and elements. At the risk of unseemly self-promotion, that is why wise school boards seek support from independent, experienced, politically neutral consultants such as myself, preferably before irritating or sub-optimal pressure points become toxic (poisonous to the school's culture and/or internal operations) or radioactive (explosively contagious negative impacts beyond the school gates).

1. **Maintaining a mission-centred, strategic board focus.**

A school's Mission is its enduring purpose. Its Vision is the agreed priority area (or areas) to focus on in order to work towards achieving the Mission over the next few years. Many school boards are so focussed on the urgency of their legal and financial fiduciary duties that they fail to devote sufficient quality time to developing and then monitoring the school's strategic progress. This can be expressed in

several ways such as excessively long board meetings that don't follow a tight agenda, poorly structured discussions, excessively detailed papers containing information that focuses on matters which are unrelated or poorly related to governance, and ineffective use of committees as a means of channelling detailed analysis of minutiae away from board meetings.

Boards that have addressed this pressure point tend to adopt one or more of the following techniques:

- Set aside one or two days each year for a 'retreat' to focus on the mission, vision and strategy, as well as building stronger bonds of understanding among board members, and between board members and the senior management of the school.
- Incorporate mid-year board performance reviews into the board calendar, and stick to the scheduled dates.
- Avoid re-litigating discussions and decisions that were settled in previous meetings.
- Use board committees for detailed discussions that will bring specific options and recommendations to the full board meeting.
- Review policies and procedures on a regular, scheduled basis.

- Require that board papers are readable, concise, focussed on governance issues, and address strategic priorities. Board papers should include meaningful performance data such as reliable Dashboards, and employ a 'traffic light' system to set priorities:
  - Items with a green traffic light are for the information of board members and do not require discussion.
  - Items with a yellow traffic light require a discussion but no decision.
  - Items with a red traffic light require a discussion and a decision.

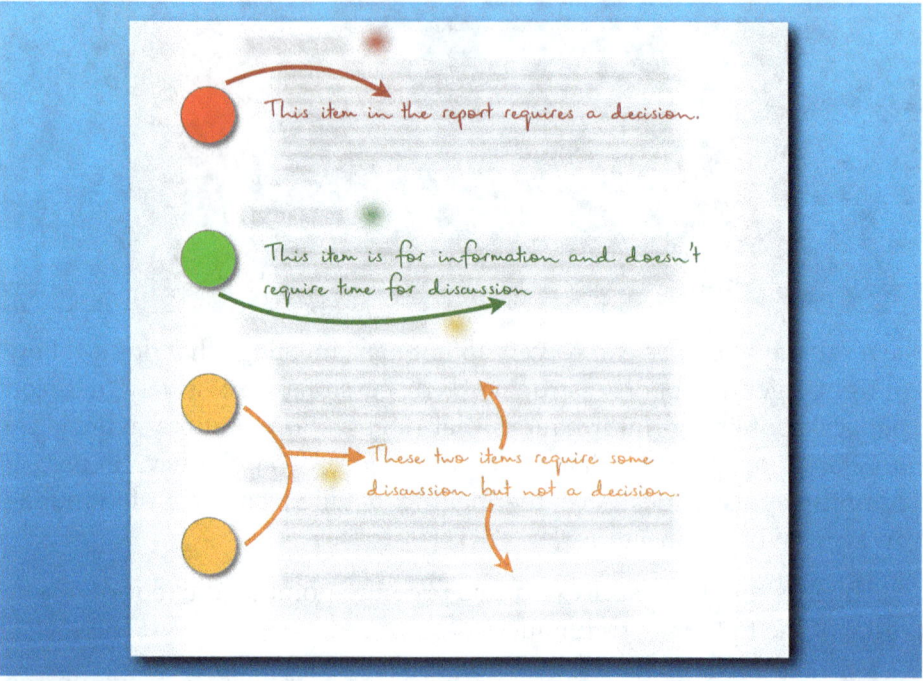

2. **Aligning board culture and senior management practice.**

The most common cause of governance crises in schools is a souring of the relationship between the Board and the Principal. As explained in Insight 104, the Board's role is governance, whereas the Principal's role is management. Board members should (almost) never become involved in operational tasks, while the Principal must respect the Board's authority to determine the direction (Mission) of the school. When the roles of governance and management become blurred, dysfunction is inevitable. Similarly, if communication between the Board and the Principal breaks down, there will be a serious disconnection between the Board's intent and what is happening in the school. When this happens, discord and confusion often arise and the

Principal may lose awareness of the Board's priorities, while at the same time the Board might find they are receiving reports from the Principal that fail to address its areas of interest.

The ideal balance is achieved when the Principal and senior management are simultaneously challenged and supported by the Board. Attaining this goal requires professionalism both on the part of board members and senior managers, and more importantly, an atmosphere of mutual trust and open, transparent communication. The Principal and senior managers must be open to new challenges, but board members collectively must take care only to challenge ideas, strategies, and options – never to attack individuals.

Conflicts of ideas are healthy for school boards; conflicts between individuals are not.

3. Planning adequately for board and senior management succession.

Many school boards struggle to attract motivated people who embrace the school's Mission while also possessing skills that are useful to the Board. Sometimes, this relates to the restriction placed upon many school boards that its members may not receive any remuneration or honorarium for their service, even though the demands of time and effort required of members of school boards are growing relentlessly. In other cases, the difficulties arise because the school is located in an area where relatively few residents possess the skills required to serve on a school board, or perhaps the board has a restrictive set of eligibility criteria based upon factors such as gender, religious faith, or membership of certain organisations.

Many boards seem to have particular difficulty in recruiting younger board members. Perhaps this is understandable as people in their 20s and 30s are typically in the life-stage of caring for young children and/or building their careers. Consequently, many boards have an over-representation of older retired and semi-retired members who may be highly competent (and usually are), but at the cost of diverse perspectives from younger demographic groups.

There are certain "rights" and "wrongs" when speaking with prospective new board members. For example, it is wrong to say things like:

- The time commitment is not onerous. The board doesn't meet that often and a lot of times you can 'just phone in'.
- We're really desperate to find board members.
- The other board members are terrific and lots of fun.
- Yes, there are meetings to attend, but.......... *[A parent who works as a therapist once told me that every time you insert the word BUT into a sentence, you invalidate every word of the sentence that precedes it, such as "I love you, but..."].*

There are also some questions you wish you could ask, but you probably shouldn't, such as:

- Can you assure us that you won't ask any really stupid questions at a board meeting?
- Do you really like to hear yourself talk?
- When someone says something you disagree with, do you either sigh or roll your eyes?
- How many times in the last month have you been on a conference call, hit the MUTE button, and checked your e-mail?
- Will you commit to agreeing with absolutely everything I say?
- Do you tend to assume that someone is doing a terrible job until proven otherwise?
- Do you care if you are late?

On the other hand, there are questions you should ask:

- What do you know about our school?
- Why are you interested in committing your time and energy to us?
- What do you think are the characteristics of a great board member?
- Board members bring experience, wisdom, strategic thinking, and their contacts list. Can you tell us about yours?
- What kind of autonomy do you have over your calendar? There will be meetings between board meetings, and occasional other events like board training sessions.
- When can you come to visit our campus, meet the Principal and the students, and get a feel for the work we are doing?

4. **Implementing effective risk management.**

The importance of risk management in schools has grown sharply over the past few decades. In part, this reflects higher expectations of schools' obligations to provide safe and healthy environments for their students, staff and visitors. However, in more than a few cases, the obligations are fuelled by lawyers' threats, government compliance requirements, and fears of reputational damage through social media posts.

Quite rightly, schools everywhere are now required to have comprehensive policies on managing risk that are implemented through operational risk management frameworks and tracking. The risk management policy will typically include a definition of risk and a classification of the various risks faced by the school, together with a statement on limits of acceptable risk. The operational risk management framework will usually include risk likelihood–consequence matrices that are put into practice through a spreadsheet or other documentary monitoring framework that allows regular reporting to the Board of risks that have been identified, progress made towards reducing or eliminating the risk, and the current areas of continuing risk.

RISK LIKELIHOOD

Likelihood Rating		Description
1	Rare	The likelihood of this risk is very unlikely.
2	Unlikely	The risk is not likely to occur in normal circumstances.
3	Possible	The risk could occur at some time. (History of a single occurrence).
4	Likely	The risk will probably occur in the circumstances present (Every 1-2
5	Almost certain	The risk is expected to occur regularly (Every year).

RISK LIKELIHOOD x CONSEQUENCE

Risk Rating	Action
Low Risk (1-4) – Tolerate	Monitor for change. No direct action required at this stage.
Medium Risk (5-10) – Threat	Monitor and evaluate the controls. Investigate possible actions.
High Risk (12-16) – Transfer	Review practices to achieve short-term risk reduction. Restrict activity if required.
Extreme Risk (20-25) – Terminate	High likelihood of an injury or major event. Immediate response required. Stop activity immediately. Review controls and only restart if new controls or work method employed. Evaluate management procedures at a suitable later date.

RISK CONSEQUENCE

Consequence Rating		Description
1	Insignificant	An event, the impact of which can be absorbed through normal activity.
2	Minor	An event, the consequences of which can be absorbed. Management effort is required to minimise the impact.
3	Moderate	A significant event which can be managed under normal circumstances by the relevant staff.
4	Major	A critical event which, with a high degree of Executive and staff time and effort can be endured.
5	Catastrophic	A catastrophe with the potential to lead to the collapse of the School. School Board time and effort will be required. Staff will be diverted from their usual duties for significant action.

RISK REGISTER TEMPLATE

Likelihood	Consequence				
	Catastrophic 5	Major 4	Moderate 3	Minor 2	Insignificant 1
Almost Certain - 5	Extreme 25	Extreme 20	High 15	Medium 10	Medium 5
Likely - 4	Extreme 20	High 16	High 12	Medium 8	Low 4
Possible 3	High 16	High 12	Medium 9	Medium 6	Low 3
Unlikely - 2	Medium 10	Medium 8	Medium 6	Low 4	Low 2
Rare - 1	Medium 5	Low 4	Low 3	Low 2	Low 1

Some additional information on risk management is provided in Insight 88. It is difficult to generalise or recommend a generic policy or set of practices for risk management because the environment and circumstances of every school are different. However, the one important common universal factor is that every school must have a robust risk management framework which the board monitors regularly to ensure thorough compliance and a safe, healthy environment for everyone involved with the school.

Not having a robust, effective risk management strategy in place is perhaps the biggest risk that any school and its board can create for itself.

Insight 21

Communicate to persuade

Implementing effective change in schools depends not only on having well-founded, worthwhile ideas, but also on the ability of the school's leadership to communicate proposals persuasively. The power to shift perspectives, inspire action, and implement meaningful transformation lies in mastering the art of persuasion through communication.

This is not a new issue. Not surprisingly, there is a long history of influential thinkers recognising and offering advice on this truth. By drawing on these timeless principles, school boards and senior managers can enhance their communication strategies to make their voices heard and move the school forward in ways that will enhance achievement of the Mission, Vision and Values.

Aristotle's Three Forms of Persuasion: Ethos, Pathos, and Logos

Originating in 4th century BC Ancient Greece, Aristotle's framework of public speaking remains one of the most enduring guides to persuasive communication through effective rhetorical appeals. He identified three essential modes of communication, each of which is required as a component of persuasion:

- **Ethos** is an appeal to the authority, reliability or credibility of the speaker. Trustworthiness, which arises from sound ethical consistency, is an important measure of a speaker's reliability as a source of information, something that is essential if their words are to be believed and accepted.

- **Pathos** is the appeal to a listener's emotions. A message will be more compelling to a listener if it appeals to shared values, fears or aspirations. Pathos is not only affected by the attractiveness of the content of a message, but also by the way in which it is delivered – the charisma of the speaker, the tone used in delivering the message, and other techniques which appeal to the audience's emotions.

- **Logos** is the logical appeal of the message. Logical appeal arises from the facts, data, information and evidence provided by the speaker, together with the use of rational arguments to support the claims being made. Clarity is a key element of logos because the same facts that may make the speaker appear knowledgeable and well-informed may be confusing for a different audience, or worse, be regarded as misleading or inaccurate.

Effective communicators skilfully balance all three of Aristotle's rhetorical elements, creating messages that resonate intellectually and emotionally while maintaining credibility.

Confucian Rhetoric: Persuasion Through Ethical Influence

Although persuasive communication was not a central concern of the ancient Chinese philosopher, Confucius (孔子), Confucian philosophy does emphasise the use of rhetoric to persuade others using speech that is grounded in sincerity, moral integrity, and the pursuit of harmony. Unlike the more adversarial rhetorical traditions that were prevalent in Europe at the time, Confucian communication seeks to build consensus rather than to win debates. In some ways, Confucius' emphasis on ethical persuasion aligns closely with Aristotle's "ethos", as credibility and moral character are seen as being essential to

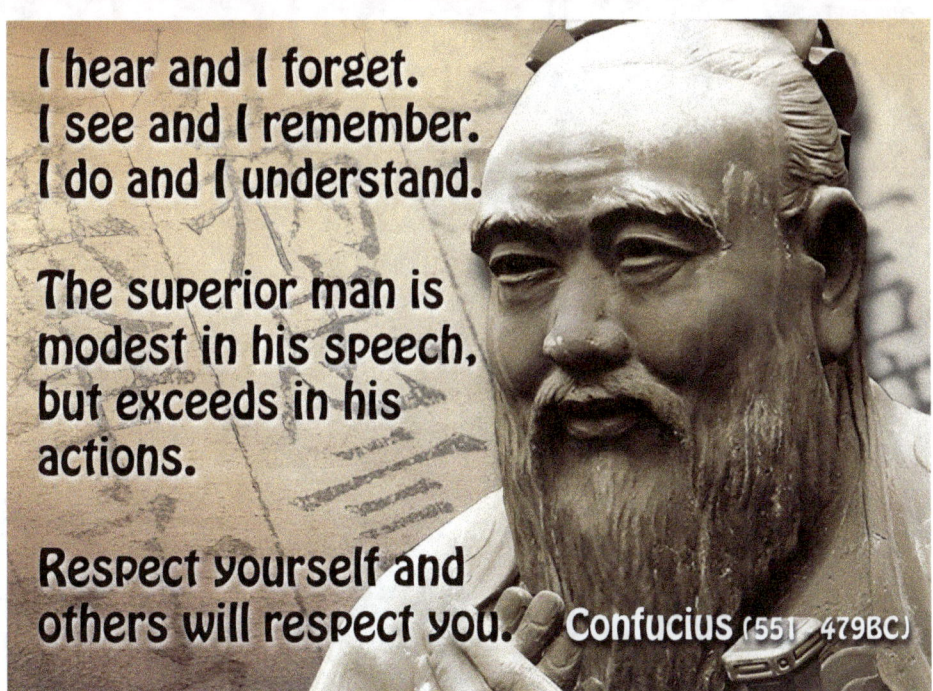

persuade others. By fostering trust and demonstrating genuine concern for the wellbeing of others, Confucius' felt that communication should inspire loyalty and enduring influence over those who listen.

Cicero's Rhetorical Framework: The Five Canons

In about 84 BC, the Roman statesman and orator Cicero wrote a treatise called *De Inventione* which included a systematic approach to rhetoric that he termed the "five canons of rhetoric":

- **Inventio (Invention)** emphasises the importance of developing sound arguments that are relevant to the issue at hand and thus persuasive to the listeners. This involves having a deep familiarity with the content of the subject matter which allows the speaker to draw upon data, illustrative examples, logical arguments and ethical considerations to communicate a compelling case.

- **Dispositio (Arrangement)** refers to the importance of structuring ideas effectively. Cicero's recommended approach is to begin a speech with introductory comments to establish rapport with the audience, and then follow this with a statement of factual information, an expansion of the principal points, reasoning and evidence to establish proof of the argument being presented, a

refutation of possible counter-arguments, finishing with a conclusion that summarises and highlights the main points.

- **Elocutio (Style)** involves choosing language that resonates to ensure clear communication. Cicero encourages the use of similes, metaphors and analogies – tailored and adapted to the specific audience – to enhance the appeal of the speech for listeners.

- **Memoria (Memory)** was seen by Cicero as an important component of effective communication. Cicero valued the ability to memorise a speech and retain the key points to delivery rather than relying on notes because it allowed the speaker to engage more directly and powerfully with the audience.

- **Pronuntiatio (Delivery)** was the final canon according to Cicero as he noted that verbal communication is most effective delivered with confidence and clarity. Cicero emphasised the importance of using voice modulation, facial expressions, gestures and body language to emphasise content and convey emotions.

Cicero thus underscores the importance of preparation and organisation in persuasive communication, arguing that by carefully crafting messages that are both logical and engaging, speakers can guide their audience towards agreement with clarity and impact.

Jesus Christ's Teaching: the Power of Parables, Questions, Authority and Compassion

When we observe the spectacular, prolonged, ongoing growth of the Christian faith across the world over the past two millennia, it seems easy to make a case that Jesus may have been the most effective speaker and teacher in history.

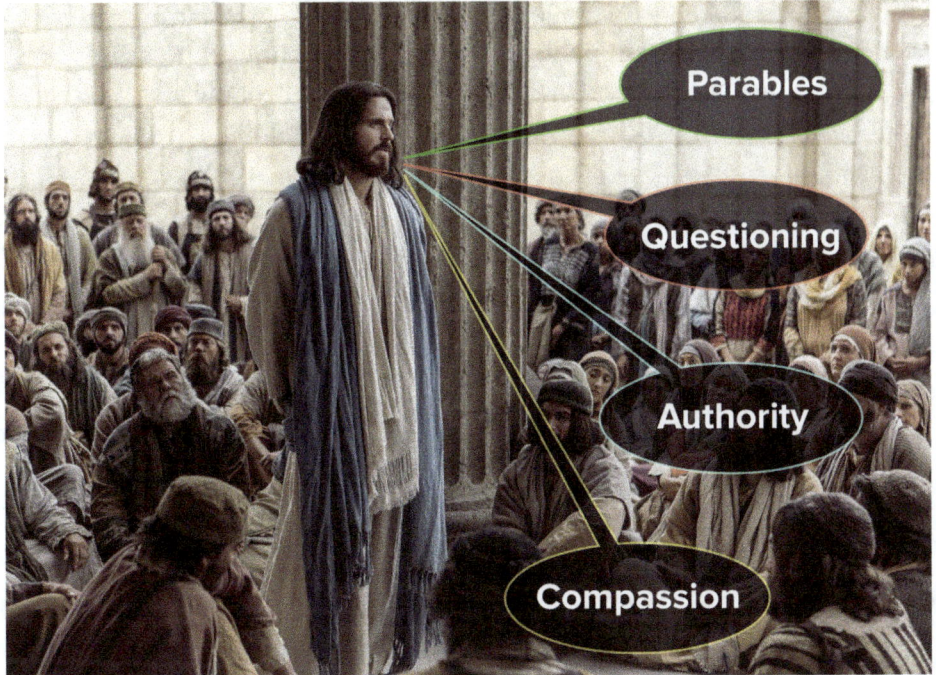

Jesus Christ spoke persuasively through the use of parables, which were simple yet profound stories that conveyed deep spiritual truths (Matthew 13:3-58). These parables, such as the Good Samaritan and the Prodigal Son, used relatable, everyday situations to teach complex moral and theological lessons. Following Jesus' example of speaking in parables in Matthew 13 and elsewhere, we can identify five tips for effective communication:

- Simplify the message (vv.3, 10-13): make it clear, repeat it often, and focus on the familiar.

- See the person (vv.1, 2, 9): know the audience and its needs, don't try to impress.

- Seize the moment (vv.2, 14-17): Recognise teachable moments and receptivity.

- Show the truth (v.54): Be sure your own life lends credibility to your words.

- See the response (v.51): Evaluate the ensure the audience understands and can respond to you.

Because Jesus' parables were engaging and easy to understand, they resonated with people of all backgrounds. Additionally, parables encouraged self-reflection, allowing listeners to draw their own guided conclusions rather than feeling forced into accepting a message. This technique of encouraging individual discernment made his teachings more personal, authentic, memorable and consequential.

Another technique Jesus used was asking thought-provoking **questions**. Like Socrates, instead of providing direct answers, he often answered questions with another question that challenged his listeners' assumptions and invited deeper reflection. For example, when asked whether it was lawful to pay taxes to Caesar, he responded, "Whose image is on the coin?" (Matthew 22:20), leading his listeners to think critically about their own beliefs. By engaging people in this way, Jesus encouraged active participation in the conversation, making his teachings more personal and persuasive, and in many cases, irresistible.

Jesus also spoke with great **authority** and **confidence**, distinguishing himself from other religious leaders of his time. The Gospels frequently note that people were astonished at his teachings because he spoke "as one having authority", and not as the scholars and teachers of the day (Matthew 7:29). His confidence was not based on validation from others but on his deep relationship with God and his knowledge of divine truth. This unwavering conviction inspired awe, trust and admiration, compelling many to believe in his message. Unlike the Pharisees, who relied on rigid interpretations of the law, Jesus emphasised the spirit of the law, demonstrating wisdom that surpassed human understanding.

Finally, Jesus' persuasive power was rooted in his **compassion** and **sincerity**. He genuinely cared for those he spoke to, healing the sick, comforting the afflicted (and afflicting the comfortable!), while also spending time with society's outcasts. His love for people made his words more credible because they were backed by action. Jesus' ability to connect personally with his audience made his teachings not only persuasive but also transformative, leading countless individuals to follow him and adopt his message of love and salvation.

Quintilian's Education of the Orator: The Ethical Speaker

Frontispiece of a 1720 edition of the *Institutio Oratoria*, showing Quintilian teaching rhetoric.

He who speaks evil only differs from he who does evil in that he lacks opportunity.

Quintilian was a Roman educator and rhetorician who lived from 35 to 96 AD. He believed that a great speaker must not only be skilled in persuasion but also be a person of virtue. Like Confucius and Jesus Christ, he emphasised the importance of **ethical rhetoric** in persuasion, arguing that an effective orator must also be a virtuous person. His concept of ethical speaking was rooted in the belief that persuasion should be grounded in truth, integrity, and moral responsibility.

Quintilian was convinced that people's speech should not be used to manipulate or deceive, but rather to guide audiences towards just and reasonable conclusions. For Quintilian, the ideal speaker was not only skilled in argumentation and eloquence but also committed to upholding ethical principles in both speech and personal conduct.

The central focus of Quintilian's philosophy was the idea that a speaker's credibility, or *ethos*, plays a crucial role in persuasion. He believed that an audience is more likely to be convinced by someone who is recognised as being honest, knowledgeable, and morally upright. This notion is highlighted by his famous definition of an orator as being "a good man speaking well". By embodying ethical values, Quintilian argued in his 12-volume textbook *Institutio Oratoria* that a speaker fosters trust and establishes a strong connection with the audience, making the arguments conveyed more compelling and effective. In contrast, those who rely on deception or manipulation may achieve short-term success but ultimately risk losing credibility and influence.

Ignatius Loyola's Advice: Strategy, Diplomacy, and Integrity

Just over 480 years ago in December 1545, the Council of Trent began its proceedings in Italy to address the challenges posed by the Protestant Reformation that was underway in Europe at the time. The aim of the Council was to clarify Catholic doctrine and reform the Church. Pope Paul III, who convened the Council, recognised a need for theological expertise and therefore asked Ignatius Loyola, founder of the recently formed Society of Jesus (Jesuits), to provide three men to serve as theologians to the three papal legates presiding over the council.

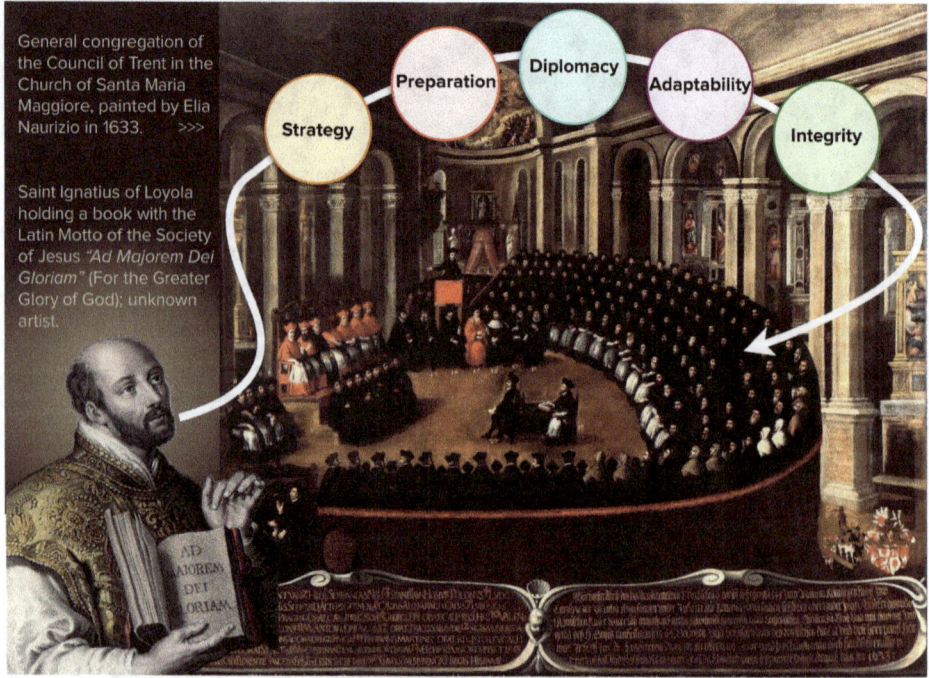

General congregation of the Council of Trent in the Church of Santa Maria Maggiore, painted by Elia Naurizio in 1633.

Saint Ignatius of Loyola holding a book with the Latin Motto of the Society of Jesus *"Ad Majorem Dei Gloriam"* (For the Greater Glory of God); unknown artist.

In response to the Pope's request, Ignatius appointed several men to serve as theological advisors. Before they left Rome in early 1546, Ignatius gave them strategic advice in the form of instructions on how to communicate persuasively in meetings at the Council. His advice emphasised **preparation, diplomacy, adaptability, and integrity** –

qualities essential for influencing others without compromising one's principles. His advice focussed on four instructions:

- **Be Slow to Speak**: Ignatius emphasised the importance of being slow to speak and to listen carefully to understand the meaning, inclinations, and wishes of those who do speak. After having listened to others, they should be in a better position to understand when to speak and when to remain silent.

- **Consider All Sides**: He advised them to consider the reasons underpinning both sides of any matter under discussion, and to do so without showing any attachment to their own opinions. By doing this, they should be able to avoid causing dissatisfaction to anyone else in the meeting.

- **Humility and Sincerity**: When speaking, Ignatius urged them to offer their opinion with the greatest possible humility and sincerity. They should never quote others as supporting their opinion without their explicit prior permission, especially if the people being quoted have political, religious or financial importance. Everyone in the meeting should be treated equally and they should never develop alliances with others at the meeting.

- **"Salvo meliori iudicio"**: When they do speak, Ignatius instructed them always to end their statements with the words "salvo meliori iudicio" (which means "with due respect for a better opinion"), thus showing openness to other perspectives.

This advice may be 480 years old, but it remains sound and relevant today for school board meetings. The Jesuits became known as "the schoolmasters of Europe" in the 16th, 17th, and 18th centuries due to their extensive network of schools and their prominence as scholars, scientists, and educators, and they continue to run schools and universities around the world that are currently education about one and a half million students.

The Jesuits' educational work has continued for almost five centuries following a consistent philosophy of educational formation and discernment. Therefore, it seems wise to consider the wisdom of Ignatius' advice as a timeless model for school leaders as they navigate complex discussions, demonstrating that persuasion is not just about winning arguments but about modelling wisdom, discernment and humility.

Modern Political Oratory: The Power of Clarity and Conviction

Effective political orators in the modern era share several key traits that enable them to captivate audiences, inspire movements, and shape the future – precisely the skills that school boards and principals require. Trying to build a list of the most effective political orators of recent times is inevitably a controversial task, but my "top 12" would include (in alphabetical order of surnames) Winston Churchill, Mahatma Gandhi, Mikhail Gorbachev, Václav Havel, Adolf Hitler, Martin Luthur King Jr, Nelson Mandela, Barack Obama, Margaret Thatcher, Leon Trotsky, Gough Whitlam, and Malala Yousafzai.

One of the most fundamental qualities they all possess is the ability to articulate their message with **clarity and conviction**. Whether through fiery speeches, poetic rhetoric, or measured reasoning, these leaders communicate in a way that is both persuasive and memorable. They also understand the power of **storytelling**, often using personal anecdotes, historical references, and vivid imagery to create emotional connections with their listeners. Additionally, they possess a deep **awareness** of their audience, tailoring their tone, language, and delivery style to resonate with different demographics and cultural contexts.

Another shared strength among these orators is their ability to project **confidence** and **authority**. Whether through Churchill's resolute war-time speeches, Obama's smooth and charismatic delivery, or Thatcher's unwavering firmness, these speakers exude a presence that commands respect. Many of them also employ **rhetorical techniques** such as repetition, parallelism, and rhetorical questions to reinforce their messages. For example, Martin Luther King Jr's "I Have a Dream" speech is remembered for its rhythmic use of repetition, while Hitler's powerful oratory was marked by escalating cumulative intensity that built emotional momentum. Moreover, all of these speakers understood the significance of timing and cadence, knowing when to pause for dramatic effect or accelerate their delivery to energise the crowd.

Despite these common characteristics, each orator has (or had) their own **distinctive style** contributing to their effectiveness. Churchill's speeches, for example, were deeply rooted in classical rhetoric, filled with powerful metaphors and historical references that evoked British resilience. Hitler, on the other hand, relied on emotional manipulation, theatrical gestures, and a soaring intensity to stir nationalist fervour. Obama's style is marked by a combination of intellectual eloquence, personal warmth, and an ability to make complex ideas accessible. King's rhetorical power stemmed from his preacher-like delivery, rich with Biblical references and moral urgency, while Mandela's and Havel's speeches emphasised reconciliation, forgiveness, and unification of a fractured society.

Thatcher's oratory was defined by her steely resolve and assertiveness, which reinforced her image as the "Iron Lady". Gandhi's effectiveness as a speaker did not come from grand oratory, but rather from his quiet, deliberate, and morally persuasive discourse that emphasised nonviolence and truth. Trotsky, who was known for his sharp intellect, used logic and revolutionary zeal to rally crowds, while Whitlam's speeches blended wit, passion, and an infectious, sweeping vision for social progress. Lastly, Malala Yousafzai, though a young speaker, follows in the tradition of passionate moral persuasion, using her personal experiences and measured tone to advocate for education and gender equality.

School principals and board members should be heartened by the **oratorical diversity** of political speakers which highlight the fact that effective communication is not a one-size-fits-all formula that can be achieved (to mix metaphors) by a single silver bullet. Rather, political oratory shows that effective communication is a blend of personal strengths, historical context, clarity, conviction, and audience perception. Whether through impassioned delivery, logical arguments, or sheer moral authority, each of these political speakers found their own unique way to inspire, persuade, and lead.

Modern Psychological and Business Communication Theories: the Science of Influence and Persuasion

Modern psychological and business communication theories are very popular in the corporate world even though they tend to be simplistic **derivatives** of the classical approaches described above. Whereas classical techniques of persuasion rely heavily on the spoken word – oratory and rhetoric – modern business persuasion relies on a more diverse set of persuasive techniques including **video, social media, and advertising**. With the increasing bureaucratisation and corporatisation of many schools, these communication theories are gaining traction in some schools where school leaders and board members are either unaware of classical approaches to oratorical persuasion or else want to be seen to be embracing the "latest bright new shiny object".

One of the most influential of these contemporary frameworks is Robert Cialdini's **six principles of influence and persuasion**: reciprocity, commitment and consistency, social proof, authority, liking, and scarcity.

Reciprocity suggests that people feel obliged to return favours, making them more likely to comply with requests. **Commitment** and **consistency** highlight that individuals prefer to act in ways that align with their past behaviours and beliefs. **Social proof** builds upon the tendency of people to follow the actions of others, particularly in uncertain situations, while **authority** emphasises the power of expertise and expert credibility in persuasion. **Liking** shows us that people are more inclined to be persuaded by those they find agreeable or similar to themselves, and **scarcity** builds on FOMO (the fear of missing out), making limited opportunities more attractive.

Beyond Cialdini's principles, modern business communication theories stress the importance of emotional appeal and storytelling. Research in psychology indicates that messages which evoke **emotions** such as joy, fear, or excitement tend to be more persuasive than purely

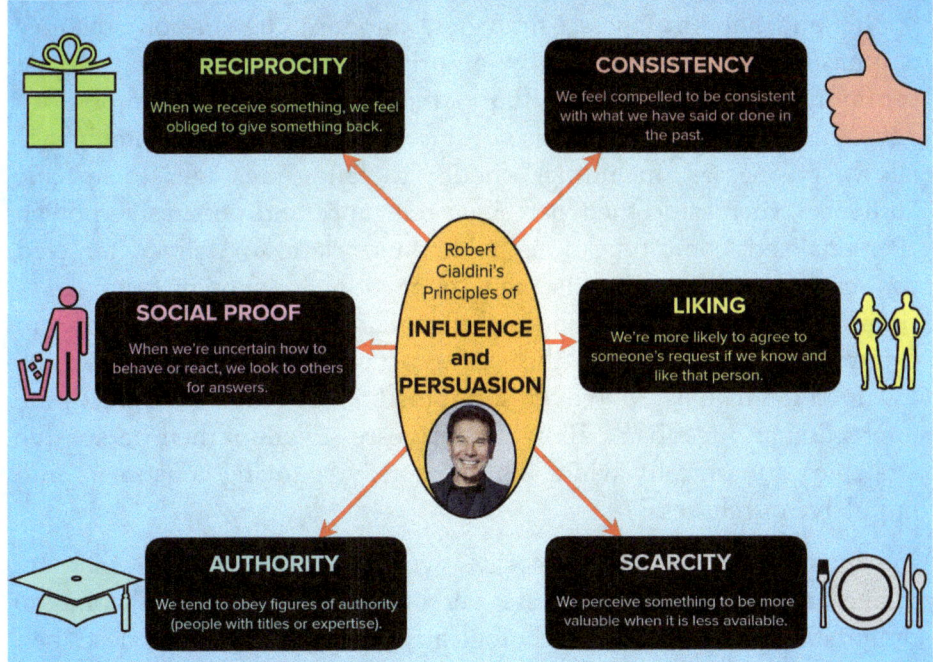

logical arguments. Businesses and marketers use storytelling and narratives to create a connection between their audience and a product or idea, making the message more memorable and powerful. Psychologists maintain that because storytelling engages an audience at an emotional level that (they hope) builds trust, narratives are a powerful aid in influencing decisions in business negotiations, marketing campaigns, and leadership communications such as initiating a policy or strategic change in a school.

Another key approach used in the corporate world to persuade others involves framing and priming. **Framing** refers to how information is presented to shape perceptions. Studies show that people react differently depending on whether they are risk-averse or risk-hungry when a choice is framed as a potential benefit or a way to avoid risk. **Priming**, on the other hand, subtly influences listeners' responses by exposing them to certain cues beforehand. For example, using words associated with reliability and trust in a promotional poster advertising a parents' meeting can lead potential attendees to regard the event (or the school) as being more dependable than they might otherwise think. Techniques such as these help to shape (or manipulate) decision-making while avoiding overt coercion, making them highly effective (if at times deceptive).

In addition to these strategies, modern persuasion theories emphasise the role played by **algorithms** in personalising digital communications, something that Aristotle and his contemporaries never had to consider. The rise of 'big data' and artificial intelligence allows businesses, including schools, to tailor messages to specific audiences, increasing their perceived relevance and persuasive power. Personalised communications which use data to deliver targeted content (including advertisements), have been shown to make a significant difference in enhancing engagement and conversion rates in commercial settings, and the same psychological impacts can be assumed for schools. Moreover, social media platforms enable real-time interaction and feedback, allowing businesses to adapt their persuasive strategies dynamically while simultaneously seducing consumers into impulsive purchases.

Consultants in the corporate world often maintain that by integrating non-verbal (or less verbal) techniques which combine pragmatic business and psychological principles like those described above, businesses (including schools) can craft highly effective persuasive strategies to influence their clients' (i.e. parents') behaviour, their employees' motivation, and the public perception of the organisation.

I'm not confident that Aristotle, Confucius or Cicero would be persuaded by those corporate consultants' arguments.

Insight 22

Conflict resolution and mediation

Wherever two or more people congregate, some degree of conflict is almost inevitable. Schools are especially prone to conflict. This is because schools are places of high emotional and intellectual investment in the welfare of children and the future of our society.

A conflict of ideas is actually a very healthy thing, because it means alternatives are being examined, refined and chosen through a process of discernment that is achieved by applying the collective wisdom of a diverse, well-meaning group of people who share a common goal.

If the conflict of ideas degenerates into a conflict between people, then a far worse situation arises. When such conflicts occur at very senior levels in a school, such as among board members or between the Board and the Principal, then the conflict may quickly become toxic.

Given the inevitability of conflict and the destructive impact it can have on any school, sometimes suddenly and without warning, it is essential that board members and senior leaders are equipped to recognise it and deal with it quickly and effectively at an almost visceral level.

As a starting point, it should be acknowledged that everyone in a school community has a right to be treated with respect and dignity, and everyone also has a right to articulate their argument about they believe it is best for the school. Having said this, the problem with many conflicts is that both sides are looking for a "winner takes all" solution, which immediately works against listening to the points of view that others are expressing. That's a problem, because there are always reasons with at least some validity that those with opposing points of view hold those views.

Perhaps the most contentious conflicts that occur in schools arise when there are disagreements between the Principal and the Board. When handled poorly, such conflicts can have devastating impacts on entire school communities (not to mention the Principal and the Board members) that may take a decade or two to heal.

This is where sensitive, mature, well-managed conflict resolution and mediation become highly significant.

Conflict resolution and mediation are not the same thing. Conflict resolution is a fairly broad term that encompasses various methods and processes used to manage and resolve conflicts. It can include mediation but also involves other approaches such as negotiation, arbitration, litigation, and more. Conflict resolution methods can be collaborative or adversarial, depending on the specific approach chosen.

Mediation is a specific form of conflict resolution that involves a neutral, independent third party, known as the mediator, who assists the conflicting parties to find common ground and reach a mutually acceptable resolution.

How might mediation assist in a conflict between a Principal and the Board, perhaps the most sensitive and challenging scenario that either the Board or the Principal will ever face? The goal of mediation in such a situation would typically be to open up transparent communication, address concerns, and explore possible resolutions before resorting to termination. Ideally, the mediation would involve eight calm, equable stages:

1. **Selection of a Mediator:**

A neutral and trained mediator, often with experience in education or employment matters, is selected. This person should be acceptable to both the Board and the Principal.

2. **Voluntary Participation:**

Both parties, the Board and the Principal, must voluntarily agree to participate in the mediation process. It is essential that both parties are willing to engage in good faith.

3. **Preparation:**

Before the mediation session, the mediator may meet with each party separately to understand their perspectives, concerns, and desired outcomes. This allows the mediator to be well-informed about the issues at hand.

4. **Joint Mediation Session:**

The mediator conducts a joint mediation session with both parties present. During this session, each party has the opportunity to express

its concerns, interests, and perspectives. The mediator facilitates open and respectful communication.

5. **Identification of Issues:**

The mediator helps the parties identify the key issues contributing to the conflict. This may involve discussing specific incidents, communication breakdowns, or policy violations.

6. **Exploration of Solutions:**

The focus shifts to exploring potential solutions that could address the concerns raised by the Board while also addressing the needs and concerns of the Principal. This could involve discussing performance improvement plans, professional development opportunities, or other measures.

7. **Agreement:**

If an agreement is reached, it is typically documented in writing, outlining the terms and conditions that both parties have accepted. This agreement might include specific actions, timelines, and any conditions for ongoing employment.

8. **Implementation and Follow-up:**

Presuming an agreement has been reached, there may be a follow-up process to ensure that both parties are fulfilling their commitments.

The mediator may check in periodically to assess progress and address any issues that arise.

Of course, mediation may not always lead to a resolution, and termination could still be considered if an agreement cannot be reached. Nonetheless, there are deliberate strategies that can be implemented to increase the probability of a successful outcome for everyone involved.

The author Kenneth Cloke suggests that there are three categories of questions that could be asked in any discussion to resolve a conflict.

Category 1: Questions that have one single correct answer. Who is the oldest person in the discussion? Who is the youngest? Who is the tallest? Who is the shortest? Who lives the closest to the school? Who lives the furthest away? Note that once given, these responses can be arranged in order of size or importance.

Category 2: Questions that have one single correct answer for each person. How old are you? Where do you live? How tall are you? Note that these responses can NOT be arranged in order of size or importance because each person is an individual.

Category 3: Questions that have multiple correct answers for each person. What issues are you are facing, regardless of your age? What does your height mean to you? What did your height mean to you when you were growing up? What do love about where you live? What do not love about where you live? Note that these answers are fluid and flexible.

Cloke believes that most significant issues in our world fit into this third category, but unfortunately, most negotiations stay within the realms of category 1 or category 2. This suggests that effective conflict resolution is more likely to occur when interlocutors take the time to build their relationships and understandings of each other as people.

Therefore, although they may not at first seem central to the conflict at hand, some useful questions that both sides in a conflict negotiation might ask are:

- What life experiences have you had that have led you to feel so deeply and passionately about this issue?
- What question would you most like the other person to ask you right now?
- What price have you paid for this conflict?

Questions like these (and many more) can help us to understand the other people we are dealing with in a negotiation. Such questions help each participant to step back from dogmatism which, as we saw above, is a huge barrier to securing a win-win outcome.

What are the signs of a deteriorating conflict negotiation or mediation? If one or both parties to the conflict want the other side simply to go away, to surrender, to admit they were wrong, to disappear, or to give up, that represents a very poor, low-level solution.

A better, higher-level solution becomes possible when both sides discover that the way the other side feels about a solution is more important than what they actually want. Any party in any conflict needs to feel that their interests are being respected, acknowledged, and that the other side is seeking a solution that will work for them. I have helped mediate many conflicts in schools where what one side or the other says they are asking for isn't really what they want; it is a proxy for their true priority.

Mediators do not impose a solution, but they intervene in a conflict to break the intense attachment to a bargaining position that often afflicts the people who find themselves to be deeply entrenched in the conflict. The mediator provides a release from the "fight or flight" reflex that many people experience when they are thrown into a conflict situation.

Mediators remind those in a conflict that there is almost always a 'third solution' waiting in the wings; there are multiple 'middle grounds'. The first, most unsatisfactory middle ground is 'mutual trauma', 'mutual destruction' or 'mutual exhaustion' – clearly sub-optimal middle ground. The second middle ground is compromise or settlement where each side wins something and loses something. The third middle ground is collaboration, consensus, and resolution of the underlying issues that caused the dispute. There is also a fourth (but rarer) and higher middle ground, which occurs when all parties can transcend (rise above) the reasons that led to the conflict.

This fourth pathway represents the way to achieve a sustainable, enduring outcome which elevates the participants beyond mediation and into what is known as 'restorative justice'. Achieving this is seldom easy because it requires people to talk openly and honestly about significant, profound issues with people they probably don't trust. In other words, restorative justice requires a high order of skill, maturity, transparency, and perhaps resilience on the part of everyone involved.

Perhaps the most powerful observation I have encountered about the qualities required to achieve restorative justice through mediation are the words of Martin Luther King Jr, who said (in a speech in Washington DC on 6th February 1968): "I'm not a consensus leader. I do not determine what is right and wrong by looking at the budget of (my organisation). Nor do I determine what is right or wrong by taking a Gallup poll of the majority opinion. **Ultimately a genuine leader is not a searcher for consensus but a moulder of consensus**".

I am indebted to Kenneth Cloke, some of whose ideas I have drawn upon in preparing this article. Kenneth Cloke is co-founder of Mediators Beyond Borders, based in Washington DC in the United States. His book *Resolving Organizational Conflicts* is a useful resource for schools that wish to investigate conflict resolution and mediation more deeply.

Insight 23

Conflicts of Interest

A member of the school board is working for a company which has a side business running after-school coaching clinics that compete with the school's own support programs.

A member of the school board is in a romantic relationship with the principal's spouse.

A member of the school board is showing favouritism to a supplier by allowing them to short-circuit the normal bidding process.

An employee of the school is using the school's database to send e-mails to parents advertising their spouse's business.

A member of the school board has made a very substantial donation to the school's building program and is now demanding regular input to influence the day-to-day operations of the school.

These (and thousands of other potential situations) are examples of conflicts of interest. A conflict of interest arises when a board member's personal or financial interests interfere, or appear to interfere, with their duty to make impartial decisions for the benefit of the school. These conflicts can take many forms, from awarding contracts to businesses owned by relatives, to making decisions that financially benefit a board member's own ventures. When such conflicts are not disclosed or managed properly, they erode public confidence and may even result in legal consequences or the invalidation of board decisions.

Conflicts of interest fall into four broad categories: financial, competitive, romantic or relational, and confidentiality. Unfortunately, they are a fairly common source of problems in schools, especially on school boards.

Conflicts of interest are illegal in many (but not all) countries. They are addressed in the laws and regulations of many countries, including almost all international bodies, most European Union member states, the United States, the United Kingdom, Australia and Canada. While many other countries recognise the importance of addressing conflicts of interest, they don't necessarily criminalise them.

In many countries, conflicts of interest are treated as administrative misdemeanours. This means that the laws governing conflicts of interest usually have relatively low standards of proof, and so the penalties for non-compliance are likely to be less severe than the consequences for related criminal offences. In some countries, organisations and individuals are simply expected to identify, declare, and manage conflicts of interest. It should be noted, however, that the regulatory bodies and accreditation agencies which set standards for schools usually take a stronger stand against conflicts of interest and demand that they be handled according to prescribed policies and procedures.

As discussed briefly in Insights 3 and 44, transparency and accountability are of central importance in addressing conflicts of interest. For example, if a board member owns or is associated with a construction company bidding on a school building project, that board member must be required to declare this interest and abstain from any discussions or votes related to the contract.

Schools (and their boards) are expected to adopt and enforce comprehensive policies and practices to handle conflicts of interest. These should include clear definitions of what constitutes a conflict of interest, detailed procedures for disclosure, and strict rules for recusal from discussions on related matters during board meetings. Training sessions on ethics and transparency are important as part of the induction program for all new board members, and they should be repeated for all board members periodically. An example of a basic, abbreviated Conflicts of Interest Policy is shown below.

 **CONFLICTS OF INTEREST** – *Sample Policy*

Introduction

The Board of [Name of School] is committed to high standards of ethical conduct and accordingly places great importance on making clear any existing or potential conflict of interest.

Purpose

This policy has been developed to provide a framework for all Board Members and Senior Managers ('Responsible Persons') in declaring conflicts of interest.

Definition

A Conflict of Interest arises in any situation where there is potential to undermine the impartiality of a 'Responsible Person' due to of the possibility of a clash between the person's self-interest and/or their loyalty to another person or organisation on one hand, and to their duties to the School Board on the other.

Policy

The Board places great importance on making clear any existing or potential conflicts of interest. All such conflicts of interest shall be declared by the 'Responsible Person' concerned and documented in the Board's Conflicts of Interest Register.

A 'Responsible Person' who believes another 'Responsible Person' has an undeclared conflict of interest should specify in writing the basis of this potential conflict.

Where a 'Responsible Person' has an actual, perceived or potential conflict of interest, that 'Responsible Person' shall not initiate or take part in any Board discussion on that topic (either in the meeting or with other 'Responsible Persons' before or after the Board meetings), unless expressly invited to do so by unanimous agreement by all other members present.

Where a 'Responsible Person' has an actual, perceived or potential conflict of interest, that 'Responsible Person' shall not vote on that matter.

The Board may supplement the definition of conflict of interest if it so wishes, in which case the same procedures shall apply.

'Responsible Persons' are not barred from engaging in business dealings with the School, provided that these are negotiated at arm's length without the participation of the 'Responsible Person' concerned.

All 'Responsible Persons' must sign an annual statement declaring conflicts of interest, and these statements shall be retained for seven years.

Transparency is essential for handling potential conflicts. To this end, it is good practice for all board members to sign an annual declaration of their actual, potential or perceived conflicts of interest as an outward sign that they are aware of the policy and have considered any changes to their previously stated positions. These declarations should be kept on file in case of challenges to board decisions or questions from registration and accreditation authorities.

CONFLICTS OF INTEREST
Sample Annual Declaration

Name of 'Responsible Person' _____

This annual questionnaire must be completed and signed by our board members, officers, key employees, and other persons with substantial influence over financial decisions in accordance with the Conflict of Interest Policy. The responses include not only a description of relationships that could result in reportable transactions, but also the amount(s), if any occurred.

BUSINESS TRANSACTIONS: The following is a list of all entities:

a. in which I have a financial interest (directly or indirectly) through business, family members, or investment, which, during the year, may have a transaction or arrangement for the purchase of goods and services or payment of compensation, with the School or with any entity or individual with which the School has an interest.

b. in which I am an officer, director, manager or influential person, if I anticipate that such organisations will do business with the School in the coming financial year.

Please describe the nature, dates, and amounts of each business transaction that I anticipate will occur: Respond N/A if you have no transactions to disclose:

_____

LOANS, GRANTS OR AWARDS: Describe any loan(s) to or from you or an entity in which you or your family have a financial interest and the School. Include the purpose of the loan, original principal amount and balance due. Enter N/A, if none.

_____

List the name of any person related to you (including you) that did or will receive a grant or award or other assistance from the School during the year. Enter N/A if none.

_____

OTHER TRANSACTIONS: The following is a description of all business transactions involving the School in the past fiscal year (1) in which I had a financial interest (direct or indirect) or (2) that involved an entity or organisation in which I hold a position as an officer, director, manager or other influential person. Provide a brief description of each transaction and a description of your interest in the transaction. Enter N/A if you have no transactions to disclose.

_____

In completing this questionnaire, I have reviewed the School's conflicts of interest policy and hereby agree to comply with the policy to assure that the Board complies with NESA Regulations.

Signature of 'Responsible Person' _____ Date _____

If an undeclared conflict of interest is discovered after a decision has been made, school boards must act promptly and transparently to rectify the situation. This could involve rescinding contracts, conducting internal investigations, or even removing board members from positions of influence. Legal advice should be sought to determine the appropriate course of action, especially if laws may have been violated. Boards must communicate clearly with their stakeholders about their response to such conflicts to rebuild trust and demonstrate accountability.

Ultimately, avoiding and addressing conflicts of interest is not just a matter of compliance – it is a cornerstone of effective and ethical governance. School boards must remember that they are stewards of the resources they control, and members must always place the school's interests above all else when they are making decisions about the school in board meetings. By taking proactive steps to prevent conflicts of interest, responding swiftly if and when they arise, and modelling ethical behaviour, school boards can fulfil their mission with integrity and earn the trust that is essential for their effective service to the school's community.

Insight 24

Consensus building – six approaches

It can happen when a school board meets, and it can happen just as easily in a meeting of teachers or senior management. A proposal is being discussed, and a consensus is proving elusive. The chair of the meeting is reluctant rush the issue to a vote because doing so will inevitably alienate a significant number of participants.

It seems that the days of making easy, clear-cut decisions may be over in today's increasingly polarised society. As James March and Chip Heath note in their book *A Primer on Decision Making: How Decisions Happen*, arriving at a decision in a meeting of people with different perspectives can involve varying appetites for risk-taking or risk-aversion, the leader's personal charisma, the dynamics of giving and taking advice, the organisational politics surrounding the decision, the ambiguity of information provided, perceived external pressures, and the vested interests of stakeholders – among many other variables. Board chairs and Principals today must negotiate varying points of view, navigate ambiguity, and lead their constituents to favourable outcomes.

In the discussion of any proposal, there are certain key questions which must be answered, either implicitly and taken for granted, or explicitly if substantial disagreements emerge. Among such core questions are "How does this proposal reflect or enhance the school's Mission and Core Values?", "Why is this issue important to you?", and "How does this issue affect the school's principal focus, which is the welfare of our students?".

When disagreements arise, strong emotions may come into play. When this happens, meeting leaders (such as the Board Chair or the Principal) must perform an important role, which is to lower the emotional stakes of the discussion. Sometimes this can be achieved by breaking down a larger issue into smaller parts, although on other occasions the best approach may be to adjourn the meeting for a while to give everyone a rest and rehydration break.

When disagreements seem more substantial or difficult to resolve, there are several more formal approaches that can be helpful. There are several frameworks that I have found especially effective in building a consensus.

Gradients of Agreement

The "Gradients of Agreement Scale" was first developed in 1987 by Sam Kaner, Duane Berger and the staff of Community at Work in San Francisco, USA. It has since been translated into Spanish, French, Russian, Chinese, Arabic and Swahili for use in large and small organisations around the world.

GRADIENTS OF AGREEMENT SCALE

1	2	3	4	5	6	7	8
Endorse	Endorse with minor concerns	Agree with reservations	Abstain	Stand aside	Disagree but willing to go with majority	Disagree with request not to be involved with implementation	Can't go forward
"I like it".	"Basically I like it".	"I can live with it".	"I have no opinion" or "I don't have enough information".	"I don't like this, but I don't want to hold up the group".	"I want my disagreement noted, but I'll support the decision".	"I don't want to stop anyone else, but I don't want to be involved in implementing it".	"I need to continue the conversation".

Adapted from the Community at Work Gradients of Agreement Scale described in *The Facilitator's Guide to Participatory Decision-Making*.

The idea behind Gradients of Agreement is that issues are rarely clear-cut yes/no matters. Rather than forcing meeting participants into one of two polar opposite positions, Gradients of Agreement offers a framework to identify and label degrees of support or opposition for any proposal being discussed.

This process usually lowers the intensity of emotional commitment for those people who self-identify towards both ends of the scale, thus opening a way forward to arrive somewhere closer to a negotiated broad consensus.

If and when a decision is required, a vote can proceed on the basis support in any of the first seven categories in the Gradients of Agreement Scale, although it is preferable to have a significant number of votes in Categories 1 and 2 for any significant decisions or are matters that will require a broad team of people to implement.

Six Thinking Hats

The "Six Thinking Hats" was first developed in 1985 by the prolific Maltese author and business consultant, Edward De Bono. It is a model to encourage conflict-free parallel thinking to solve complex problems and proposals that assumes the human brain thinks in six different directions. The model allocates a coloured hat to each type of thinking, and then asks groups within a meeting to imagine wearing each hat in turn together for an equal amount of time while discussing the issue at hand from the perspective of the hat with that colour.

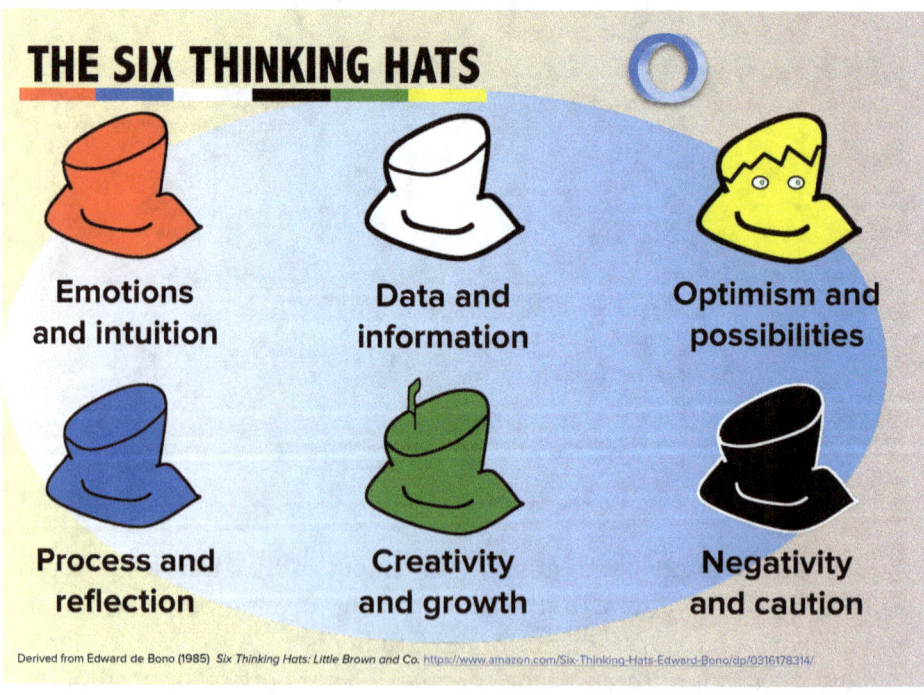

Red is intended to reflect emotion and passion. When wearing the red hat, the group focusses on their initial, immediate, quick emotional reactions to the issue being discussed, asking questions such as "how do we feel about the issue?", "what are our gut reactions and emotions?", and "what does our intuition tell us about the issue?".

White is intended to represent a blank sheet of paper. When wearing the white hat, the group focusses with a neutral mindset on the data and information required to address the issue, asking questions such as "what are the facts?", "what information is available?" and "what information is relevant?".

Yellow is intended to represent sunshine and optimism. When wearing the yellow hat, the group focusses on positive outcomes and possibilities, asking questions such as "what are the positive, constructive points?", "what are the benefits and advantages?", and "how can we make it happen?".

Black is intended to remind us of dark, threatening storm clouds. When wearing the black hat, the group focusses on the challenges and difficulties of the proposal, asking questions such as "what are the risks and dangers?", "what problems might be encountered?" and "what cautions need to be identified?".

Green signifies growth and creativity. When wearing the green hat, the group brainstorms creative opportunities, asking questions such as "what creative potential is there to do something new and different?", "what potential is there for growth and movement?" and "using some lateral thinking, what new aspects can be identified?".

Blue signifies the over-arching sky above us. When wearing the blue hat, the group focusses on organisation, planning, integration, control, oversight and reflection. The group tries to draw together the insights gained while wearing the other five hats, forming coherent conclusions, monitoring and reflecting on the processes used.

Groups that have used the Six Thinking Hats report that decisions often seem to make themselves as people work co-operatively with each other in parallel. The process gives weight to diverse opinions and views, and balances optimist-pessimism, rational-emotional dimensions, and so on. For those so inclined, Six Thinking Hats also provides a framework that encourages lateral thinking and creativity.

The Delphi Technique

The Delphi Technique, which is also known as the Delphi Method or ETE (Estimate-Talk-Estimate) is a structured communication technique that was developed in the 1950s by Olaf Helmer and Norman Dalkey at the RAND Corporation to achieve consensus among experts. In essence, it involves multiple rounds of anonymous surveys or questionnaires, where participants provide their opinions independently. The experts are allowed to adjust their answers in subsequent rounds on the basis of how they interpret the "group response" that has been provided to them. Since multiple rounds of questions are asked and the panel is told what the group thinks as a

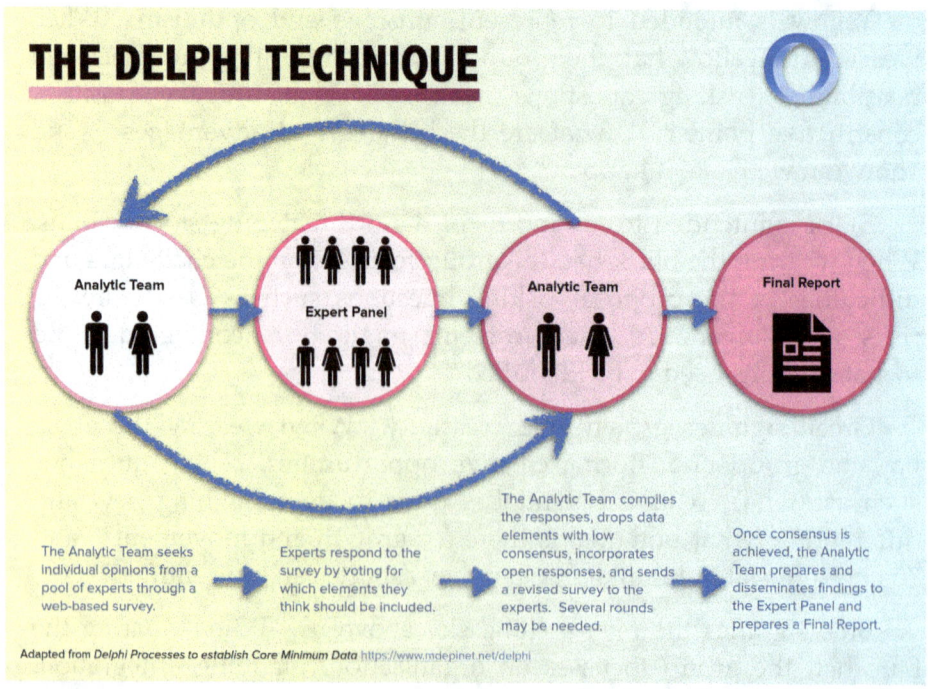

whole, this iterative process continues until a clear consensus emerges. The anonymity of responses minimises the influence of dominant voices and reduces groupthink, making it particularly useful in high-stakes decision-making and complex problem-solving scenarios.

Although a powerful technique, the Delphi Method is too complex and time-consuming to be used to build a consensus in the context on an individual board or staff meeting. The Delphi Technique has been used by schools and larger educational institutions for curriculum development, strategic planning, and policy formulation. It has been found to be especially useful when building new cross-sector agreements by bringing together diverse perspectives from educators, bureaucrats, politicians and industry leaders.

Consensus-Oriented Decision-Making (CODM) Model

The Consensus-Oriented Decision-Making (CODM) model was developed by Tim Hartnett in 2010. Somewhat similar to Quaker-based consensus, it is a seven-step process that helps groups navigate decision-making while ensuring that all perspectives are considered. The steps include framing the issue, having an open discussion, exploring options by identifying underlying concerns, developing a proposal, refining the proposal to select a direction, reaching a final

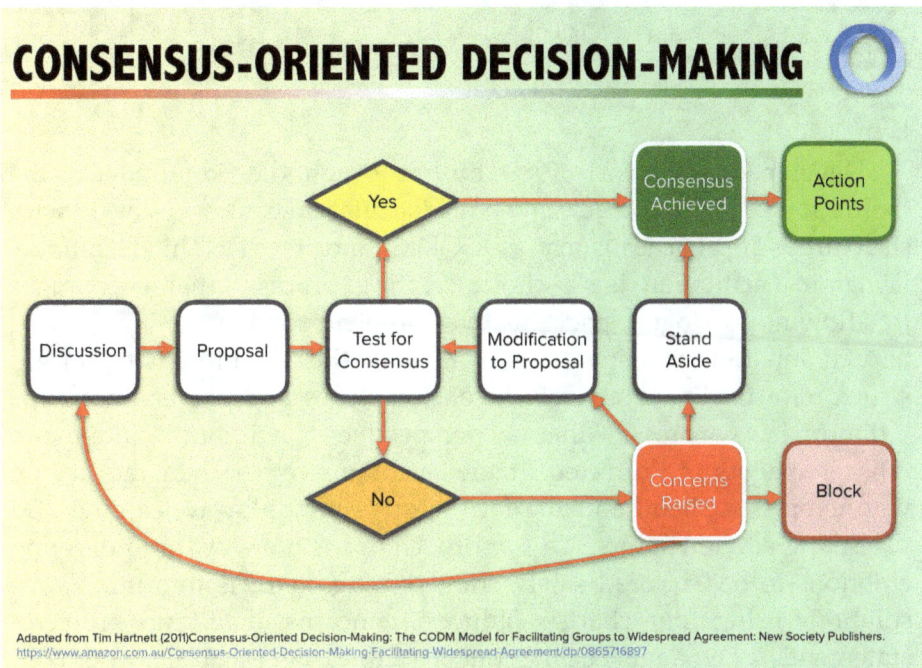

Adapted from Tim Hartnett (2011)Consensus-Oriented Decision-Making: The CODM Model for Facilitating Groups to Widespread Agreement: New Society Publishers.
https://www.amazon.com.au/Consensus-Oriented-Decision-Making-Facilitating-Widespread-Agreement/dp/0865716897

agreement, and implementing the decision. This model emphasises inclusivity, constructive dialogue, and mutual understanding, making it a valuable tool for teams seeking to reach agreement without alienating minority viewpoints. CODM is particularly effective in schools where a focus on the Mission (the school's enduring purpose) drives the direction of decision-making.

Dynamic Facilitation

Developed in the early 1980s by Jim Rough, the Co-founder of the Centre for Wise Democracy, Dynamic Facilitation contrasts starkly with structured approaches such as CODM and the Delphi Technique. Dynamic Facilitation is "a choice-creating process" that encourages free-flowing dialogue and creative problem-solving while guiding participants toward a shared resolution. Rather than following a rigid structure, a facilitator actively listens, captures key points, and helps individuals express their perspectives without judgment. Disagreements are directed at the facilitator rather than the person who expressed them, and the facilitator responds by welcoming and validating all viewpoints. This approach opens the way for underlying emotions to be explored safely, transforming conflicts into innovative solutions using four charts: solutions, concerns, data, and problem-statements. Dynamic Facilitation is said to be especially useful in situations where participants have deeply entrenched opinions or emotional stakes in the outcome.

Yarning Circles

For thousands of years, "yarning circles" have been used in Australian Aboriginal and Torres Strait Islander cultures to solve disputes, learn from elders, build respectful relationships and pass on cultural knowledge. People in other indigenous cultures, especially in North America, have used similar techniques in what is generically referred to as the "Circle Process" to promote equal participation and deep listening.

The technique is simple and highly effective when participants approach it with an open mindset. Those involved in wrestling with a decision sit in a circle which symbolises equality and inclusivity. Participants take turns speaking, often using a talking piece such as a stick to ensure only one person speaks at a time. Yarning circles emphasise respectful dialogue and listening to others, ensuring that everyone has an opportunity to speak and be heard. This method fosters respect, patience, and thoughtful consideration of diverse perspectives. The Circle Process is particularly effective in community settings, conflict resolution, and school gatherings (including board

meetings) where building trust and fostering a strong sense of shared purpose are key goals.

A final thought – insisting on consensus is misguided

Many school boards like to make decisions by consensus rather than having to put motions to a vote. Agreements reached by consensus generally indicate that board members are united behind the decision that has been made.

A few boards insist that EVERY decision is reached by consensus and will not allow a resolution to be passed until consensus is achieved. This is poor practice and should be avoided because it effectively gives any dissenting voice the power of veto. If a school board comprises 11 members, ten of whom wish to pass a resolution at a meeting, it would be absurd to allow one oppositional member to over-ride the wishes of the other ten members.

Consensus means everyone agrees. A practical alternative when consensus seems impossible to achieve is consent. **Consent** means that board agrees to move forward unless someone sees a risk that is so significant that is extends beyond an "I don't like it" risk to the level of a "this might seriously harm the school" risk.

Every school board has procedures to resolve issues by **voting** if and when required. If consensus or consent are both unachievable, then good practice demands that the issue be resolved with a vote.

Insight 25

Converting congeniality into collegiality

Sadly, several boards that I have worked with over years have been plagued by persistent conflict and a lack of mutual respect among its members. Members of such boards understandably crave civility and congeniality.

However, surprising as it may seem, such boards need to be careful what they wish for. Congeniality is not always a good thing, especially for school boards.

In contrast to the boards I mentioned at the beginning of this article, most school board members are – like most of the staff who work in schools – positive, friendly, generous, supportive considerate, and even sacrificial people. Typically they enjoy working with each other and they share a sense of common purpose.

Surely an agreeable, convivial environment such as this must be the ideal, right? Well, not always.

Schools where the dominant cultural priority is comfort are seldom schools where students or teachers are stretched or encouraged towards excellence. If the comfort and happiness of students, for example, is a key priority, then they may not be reprimanded when they fail to complete their homework or apply themselves wholeheartedly to their studies or their co-curricular involvement. Similarly, teachers may consciously or unconsciously avoid conflict with students by inflating their grades to give an artificial illusion of excellence. Moreover, teachers who are uncomfortable with this or some other facet of their colleagues' work will be unlikely to raise objections for fear of causing conflict.

A similar dynamic can operate within school boards for whom conflict is anathema. Conflict avoidance can prevent important clarifying questions being asked, and it can railroad decision-making through unspoken pressure to reach a premature consensus. Conflict of ideas and the contention between competing alternatives, argued with dispassionate clarity and personal respect of course, are essential for effective board dynamics and decision-making.

In short, congeniality may be a recipe for mediocrity. This is because congeniality focuses on the wrong priority. Congeniality emphasises each individual's comfort above the goals and priorities of the school as a holistic community. It may be counter-cultural to say it these days, but individuals in a school are there to serve the ideals and purpose of the school as an educational instrument, not vice versa.

The risk of opening up this issue within a board or a school is that it can quickly become polemical and polarising. The reality is that change in a school, whether through the board or the management, is only achievable when there is a functional balance between the needs of the individual and the needs of the school.

Ideally, individual needs and school needs are complementary as the leadership and staff of the school embrace its mission, purpose, values and priorities. Shared values and priorities represent a collegial approach where the school and every individual within it look out for each other's needs. In such situations, change doesn't have to come about through "steamroller" tactics or even persuasive "buy-in", but through a shared desire to make a positive difference and achieve better outcomes arising from an honest and respectful discussion.

When board members and/or the staff in a school fiercely protect their "comfort zones", the apparent congeniality that is often a source of self-congratulation may simply be smothering the healthy conflict and discussion that ought to emerge to be happening. Without it, effective change that advances the school from good to great will be impossible. It is widely known that "good" can be the enemy of "excellent", but so too is complacency.

Schools and boards with complacency-dominant cultures often suffer from the delusion that conflicts, tensions and disagreements are toxic and must therefore be avoided at all costs. The reality is that only conflicts which are poorly managed are toxic – dealing with conflict respectfully, focussing on the issues and not the personalities, actually builds community rather than undermining it.

Disagreement, tension, and respectful debates over competing ideas are essential to achieving effective and sustainable change in a school. Paradoxically, when board members and/or school staff seek to protect their individual comfort zones, prioritising harmony above exploring options, it actually leads to the stress, apathy, frustration, mistrust and resentment that those people are seeking to avoid.

Another way of viewing this situation is to understand that short-term peace is a high price to pay for long-term mediocrity and ineffectiveness. This is not an argument for insensitivity, bloody-mindedness, or as some refer to it, brutal honesty – it is a call for collegiality.

When I use the term collegiality, I mean collaborating with a high level of shared responsibility – for the school as an educational organisation with a clear purpose and ethos, and also for every individual person within the school community.

In a 2012 article in *Independent School* titled "Getting to No: Building True Collegiality in Schools", the US educator Robert Evans wrote that "to flourish, collegiality requires a foundation of shared commitment to appropriate candour in the service of collective growth". In other words, although candour may cause conflict, such conflict is not only healthy but necessary if the school and the individuals within it are to flourish.

How, then, do we rise from congenial to collegial? Once again in the words of Robert Evans, "the building of true collegiality is a journey, an ongoing exploration of teaching and learning". Collegiality is not so much a destination but a new lens through which we view and appreciate the school and the people within it.

Insight 26

Courage

For at least 2,500 years, courage has been seen as a virtue. The famous Greek philosopher, Aristotle, viewed courage as the marker of moral excellence, noting that it was the virtue which moderates our instincts toward recklessness on one hand and cowardice on the other.

Aristotle believed that a courageous person fears only those things that are worthy of fear. In other words, courage means discerning and thus knowing what to fear, and then responding appropriately to that fear.

The brilliant British comedy series "Yes Minister" took a different, much more pragmatic and cynical view of courage. When Sir Humphrey Appleby (as Permanent Secretary for the Department of Administrative Affairs) thought his minister was about to make a big error, he would raise one eyebrow and say, "that would be a courageous decision, minister". In Sir Humphrey Appleby's world, courage was not a virtue, as the following exchange demonstrates:

Sir Frederick 'Jumbo' Stewart: There are four words to be included in a proposal if you want it thrown out.

Sir Humphrey Appleby: Complicated. Lengthy. Expensive. Controversial. And if you want to be *really* sure that the Minister doesn't accept it, you must say the decision is "courageous".

Bernard Woolley: And that's worse than "controversial"?

Sir Humphrey Appleby: Oh, yes! "Controversial" only means "this will lose you votes". "Courageous" means "this will lose you the election"!

(Yes Minister, 1980, The Right to Know)

It seems that courage may be going out of fashion. At face value, schools seemed far more innovative and open to courageous experimentation in the 1960s, 1970s and 1980s. These days the general rule seems to be to play safe, achieving the often-mediocre outcomes set by external bureaucrats which are measured by standardised testing and dreary, excessively quantitative questionnaires whose only justification is so-called "accountability".

Of course, courage should not be reckless; it needs to be based on sound research and experience. One of my "heroes" in education is the brilliant German educator, Kurt Hahn, who was instrumental in establishing the United World Colleges, the Duke of Edinburgh Award, Outward Bound, Round Square, Gordonstoun School in Scotland, Schule Schloss Salem in Germany (in partnership with Prince Max von Baden), and indirectly, the International Baccalaureate (IB).

In a speech in 1965, Kurt Hahn spoke about achieving the right balance between sound experience and experimentation in these words:

"To make my meaning clearer I will recall a conversation, which the late founder - the real founder of the Salem School - Prince Max of Baden had with a visitor. His enthusiastic guest asked him the following question, "what are you proudest of in your beautiful schools?" He said, 'I am proudest of the fact that if you go the length and breadth of the schools, you will find nothing original in them. It is stolen from everywhere, from the British public schools (you call them private schools), from the Boy Scouts, from Plato, from Goethe'. Then the enthusiastic guest turned to him and said, 'But oughtn't you to aim at being original?' Then Prince Max rather abruptly answered, 'Well, you know, it is in education like in medicine, you must harvest the wisdom of the thousand years. If you ever came across a surgeon who wants to take out your appendix in the most original manner possible, I would strongly advise you to go to another surgeon.' (From Kurt Hahn's Address at the Founding Day Ceremony of the Athenian School 21 November 1965 Danville, California).

One of Kurt Hahn's (many) enduring legacies is the global network of 18 United World Colleges (UWCs), probably the gold standard of international education today. The UWC movement was established in 1962 with the opening of Atlantic College in Wales, initially to build peace at the height of the Cold War by bringing together 16–18-year-olds from around the world (and from both sides of the Iron Curtain) into boarding schools to build bridges of understanding. The concept was arguably more than courageous – it was audacious. The selection of students was (and still is) conducted on the basis of merit, with the vast majority receiving either full or partial scholarships raised through National Committees worldwide.

It is difficult to see the type of courage that established the UWCs at work today – the courage to build a world-wide network of schools based on a set of philosophical ideals, independent of students' ability to pay.

There are rare exceptions, and their rarity makes them notable. For example, the school where I serve as Board Chair, Djarragun College, was established more recently according to an altruistic philosophy not unlike the UWCs. Seeking to overcome discrimination, lack of opportunity, disempowerment, unemployment and erosion of culture, the school provides subsidised education for disadvantaged Australian Aboriginal and Torres Strait Islander students. Many of these students have no alternative access to education because of their remote location, poverty, family situations, violence, or quite commonly, a combination of several or all these factors.

Schools such as the United World Colleges or Djarragun College are rare exceptions in today's educational world. Perhaps this explains why it is so hard to find courage mentioned in newer books on educational leadership. It is easy to find extensive discussions on risk (usually as something to be minimised), but not courage.

Literature suggests that courage is required of soldiers, athletes, corporate leaders, and (notwithstanding Sir Humphrey Appleby's machinations) a few rare politicians. However, courage is rarely mentioned as a positive attribute of school leaders or their governing boards. This seems to be an absurd omission. It is hard to imagine any school leader or board getting through a month, let alone a year, without having to make decisions that demand courage. Sometimes this requires the courage to make important but necessary decisions that will distress some constituents. In more extreme cases (which are increasing in frequency in some places), it may include the courage to deal with physical violence, verbal attacks, character assassination, social media rumour-mongering, or direct challenges to the school's essential mission, purpose, or identity. In the wider context, courage for school leaders and boards includes standing up to changing societal values if these conflict with the school's firm values position or mission.

Perhaps surprisingly, it also takes immense courage to be humble. It takes courage to admit that you are not always right, especially when you in a leadership position in a school. Similarly, it takes courage for school board members to admit that they can't always anticipate every possibility, that they can't solve every problem, that they can't control every variable, that they can't always be congenial, that they will make mistakes and, indeed, that they are mere mortals. It takes courage to admit these things to others, and even more courage to admit them to yourself.

In a 2020 article for Harvard Business School, Matt Gavin wrote "A deep and abiding sense of courage is a quality that separates good leaders from great ones. Research shows that professionals who demonstrate courage in the workplace not only perform better, but influence their peers to act with bravery and drive organizational success". In my mind, this highlights the importance of school leaders and boards working effectively in close, creative, courageous partnership. Neither the United World Colleges nor Djarragun College could ever have become successful without close working relationships between governance and management, working together towards shared, unified goals with the courage to stay focussed on achieving their ambitious goals in the face of significant obstacles and powerful opposition.

Irrespective of the amount of courage an individual possesses, not everyone is in the position of courageously starting an international network of schools or a school which focuses on closing the gap between Indigenous and Non-Indigenous communities. How, then, should a school leader (and a board) exercise courage in the everyday environment of a typical school? Some suggestions are as follows:

1. **Lead passionately by example**

Leaders are people that others follow. People follow leaders they respect, and respect flows from "walking the talk". In other words, people respect those who show servant leadership by only asking others to do what they would be prepared to do themselves. Leading by example also requires passion if the leadership is to be effective. Passion flows easily when someone is committed to their objectives and believes sincerely in their importance. It follows from this that authenticity is required to lead by example and exude infectious passion.

2. Think strategically

Every action taken in a school – courageous or not – should be strategically coherent in enhancing the school's mission (enduring purpose), vision (strategic priorities) and values (ethical position). In one of my own headships, I recall having to summon up the courage to announce to the staff one morning that during its meeting the previous evening, the board had resolved to establish a cemetery in the school grounds for the burial of those "who loved the school dearly". Making that announcement was my duty, but not one that moved the school forward strategically. A strategic plan provides an excellent foundation for coherent, focussed, mission-driven, courageous, decision-making.

3. Take 'acceptable' risks

The word "acceptable" is not intended to be a weasel word here. Different school communities, school leaders and school boards vary in their risk appetites, whether the risk is financial, strategic, operational, or philosophical. Courage means taking well-considered actions right up to the limit of risk acceptability, but not beyond – that is what is meant by 'acceptable' risks.

I love this quote by the US writer, Elaine Welteroth: "I realised that if we aren't vigilant, we can move through our entire lives feeling smaller than we actually are – by playing it safe, by unconsciously giving away our power, by dimming our radiance, by not recognising there is always so much more waiting for us on the other side of fear".

Those words – living on the other side of fear – would be a great motto for school leaders and their boards as they work together to chart an exciting strategically-focussed future for the school in a way honours its history, mission, purpose, vision, values, ethos, and philosophy.

Courage is a not a legal requirement of school leadership or board governance, but it is an immense help in making leadership and governance more effective.

Insight 27

Dealing with poorly performing employees

Having served for over three decades in various senior positions of school leadership, including as Principal and Board Chair, I agree with innumerable colleagues of mine over the years who have claimed that school leadership is the best job in the world. Every day is different, and every day presents a variety of new and often challenging ways in which you can help form young lives and shape the future of our society.

However, there is one aspect of school leadership which I know is not relished by school leaders – dealing with poorly performing employees. One key task of leadership is helping other people to be successful, so leaders often feel a sense of their own failure when an employee is seen to be performing poorly.

I think one reason that most school leaders may see poorly performing teachers though this lens is that so many school leaders have a strong people-pleasing inclination. This is significant, because as I have often commented, **the secret of success is complex, but the secret of failure is very simple – it is trying to make everyone happy**.

I realise this is a huge generalisation and that there are exceptions, but I stand by my claim that most effective school leaders are people-pleasers – not to the extent that they are ineffective in achieving a vast array of tasks and goals, but people-pleasers nonetheless.

Irrespective of whether a school leader is a people-pleaser or not, no-one relishes the idea of terminating a poor performer. It is telling that no school leader I have met has ever said "I wish I had waited longer to fire that person".

An effective school is one that educates its students, just as an effective hospital is one that cures its sick patients. An under-performing school employee is a barrier to meeting the needs of the school's students, and as every good school places the needs of its students at the centre of its identity (irrespective of its mission), it follows that the issue of poor employee performance must be addressed. The reputational risk to the school of ignoring poor performance by an employee is substantial, especially in this age of widespread use of 'democratised' social media.

Moreover, poorly performing employees can erode the effectiveness and the working culture of a school so quickly and so destructively that allowing them to continue their current practice is like leaving a malignant cancerous growth in the human body untreated.

In these difficult situations, the first thing that a school leader needs to remember is that the school's mission – its enduring purpose – matters more than any personal discomfort. If an employee is diluting or slowing the achievement of the school's mission, then for the good of the school, either their performance must change radically or else the poorly performing employee must be removed – the mission is the 'true north' foundation upon which all decisions must ultimately rest.

Every school has its own contractual structure with distinctive conditions and clauses, so it would be imprudent for me to offer detailed advice here that might conflict with a school's legal situation. However, there are several significant general principles that can be stated.

Within the context of the school's mission, any under-performing employee must be given a fair chance to address any shortcomings that have become evident. This involves passing on specific feedback, preferably based upon a confidential performance review undertaken by a competent, neutral external agent. This feedback should be done transparently on the bases of quantitative evidence and data, not personal feelings or relationships. Feedback should not be judgemental, but rather it should provide whatever information is needed to identify shortcomings and develop a strategy that will address them within the framework of the school's mission. The employee then has the freedom to use that information as they wish – perhaps they can develop a pathway that will turn around their poor performance, or maybe not.

If a poorly performing employee can't turn around their performance, they have a right to know this as soon as possible, at which point the employee may be offered the option of moving to other employment where they might be more successful. It is important to remember that all staffing appointments in schools are match-making exercises, and just because a person struggles to succeed in advancing the mission of one school does not mean that they can't be successful elsewhere.

It can be helpful to remember that in many (and maybe most) situations where an employee is seen by the school's leadership to be under-performing, the employee is often quite miserable, perhaps even to the point of feeling 'trapped' in their current situation. I have ex-colleagues who remain friends today who had to be managed out of their employment but who soon found themselves in a far happier place that was a better fit for their skills, priorities, and personality. (That didn't make the separation any easier at the time for either of us, of course).

I have known school leaders who sometimes tolerate poorly performing employees for far too long on the basis that they need somebody (anybody?) to fill a particular role, or they worry about filling the vacancy that will be created. I know this is easier to say than to remember in the midst of such turmoil, but I have always found that **it is better to have a good vacancy than a bad appointment.**

Insight 28

Debating skills: a secret weapon for effective school board chairs

For many years, I coached high school debating. I loved seeing my students undertake research into topics they had never previously thought about and then formulate rational, well-justified, and usually persuasive arguments to support or negate a given proposition. My students needed to use language precisely, concisely and unambiguously with a clear understanding of every single word's meaning. They needed to understand that eloquence is a powerful aid to communication, but it is no substitute for the effectiveness of a sound argument. They needed to understand the difference between reasoning and emotion, the difference between evidence and anecdotes, and the difference between truth and consensus.

My inexperienced debaters thought that the aim of debating was to win an argument. With practice, experience and deeper insights, my students learned that the aim of debating is actually to discern and then communicate **truth** so that others will understand it, and perhaps even be convinced by it.

A VINTAGE YEAR IN DEBATING! N.S.W. STATE CHAMPIONS, G.P.S. FIRSTS & SECONDS CO-PREMIERS, WINNERS OF G.P.S. LAWRENCE CAMPBELL ORATORY, CATHOLIC SCHOOLS' CHAMPIONS — SENIOR & YEAR 10, INDEPENDENT SCHOOLS' CHAMPIONS — YEAR 9 1988
Second Row: P. Baume, J. Kevin, J. Greiner, C. Pagent, S. Dermody, D. Hazard, M. Henry. First Row: P. Birmingham, A. Korbel, R. McNamee, A. O'Keefe, K. Lynch, S. Hall, R. Gett. Seated: P. Henville (V.C.), Mr. G. King, R. Curran (Capt.), Mr. A. Hall (Debating Master), Mr. M. Dredge, Mrs D. Wedesweiler, Dr. S. Codrington Absent: Fr. A. Walsh S.J.

Can you see where this heading with school boards? Sound debating is based on clarity, logic, and respect. A debater must present arguments in a clear and structured manner, using logical reasoning and credible evidence to support the claims being made. Active listening is crucial to understanding opponents' arguments and responding effectively. Rebuttals should ideally focus on dismantling the opposition's points with reasoned counterarguments rather than personal attacks. Additionally, a good debater remains respectful, engaging in civil discourse and acknowledging valid points when appropriate.

When I see school boards in action, it is clear to me that very few board members have ever learned the skills of debating. That doesn't concern me because school boards need to comprise people with a wide array of different skills and perspectives. However, having observed many school boards in action, I have come to the conclusion that the skills of debating can be extremely useful for chairs of school boards.

The role of a school board chair requires strong leadership, effective communication, and sound decision-making abilities. Debating skills such as logical reasoning, persuasive communication, and the ability to think on one's feet, are essential in making the chair's role more effective. With practice, these skills enable the chair to navigate complex discussions, build consensus among board members, and advocate for policies that serve the best interests of students, teachers, and the community. By incorporating the skills of a good debater, the chair can ensure that meetings remain productive and focussed, making it far more likely that decisions will be based on well-reasoned arguments rather than emotion or bias.

One of the key debating skills that benefits a school board chair is critical thinking. According to the Foundation for Critical Thinking, critical thinking can be defined as "self-guided, self-disciplined thinking which attempts to reason at the highest level of quality in a fair-minded way". The Foundation expands this definition by saying "Critical thinking is the intellectually disciplined process of actively and skilfully conceptualising, applying, analysing, synthesising, and/or evaluating information gathered from, or generated by, observation, experience, reflection, reasoning, or communication, as a guide to belief and action. In is based on universal intellectual values that transcend subject matter divisions: clarity, accuracy, precision, consistency, relevance, sound evidence, good reasons, depth, breadth, and fairness."

This is relevant to school board meetings which often involve discussions on implementing the strategic plan, budgeting, program oversight, and policy development, all of which require careful analysis. A chair with strong debating abilities can objectively evaluate different perspectives, identify logical inconsistencies, and ensure that board decisions are based on sound reasoning. This skill allows the chair to facilitate discussions which are not only fair but also focussed on the core values of the school as expressed in the Mission and Vision, leading to more coherent, intentional governance.

Moreover, debating fosters strong persuasive communication, an important trait for a school board chair. The chair must often present and defend policies, negotiate with board members and other stakeholders, and address concerns from parents, educators, and the wider community. The ability to construct clear, well-supported arguments helps the chair to garner support for initiatives and to articulate the rationale behind difficult decisions. Effective persuasion also helps in resolving conflicts and uniting the board around common goals, ensuring that decisions are met with greater acceptance and co-operation.

Another benefit of debating skills for the board chair is the ability to manage and moderate discussions efficiently. Board meetings can become contentious, with members holding opposing views on sensitive topics such as curriculum priorities, the awarding of contracts, and financial initiatives. A board chair who has experienced or has been trained in debating competitions understands how to structure discussions, maintain order, and ensure that all viewpoints are heard while preventing unnecessary conflicts. The ability to ask pointed questions, summarise key points, and steer conversations back to relevant topics should ensure that meetings are conducted respectfully and productively.

Finally, experience in debating competitions helps the chair remain adaptable and composed under pressure. School boards often face unexpected challenges, ranging from emergency funding shortages through changing government compliance demands to controversies involving school policies or actions. The ability to think quickly and respond effectively to difficult questions or criticisms is essential for maintaining confidence and authority. By employing debating strategies such as anticipating counterarguments and using evidence-based responses, the chair can handle crises with professionalism and ensure that the board maintains credibility and public trust.

Two debating techniques have particular value for school board chairs. One is to constantly ask the question "what is the best argument for the other side?". Although some debaters feel the purpose of debating is simply to destroy the other side, it isn't. Adopting a highly polarised, blinkered, one-eyed perspective might (sadly) work in political discourse or when supporting one's sports team, but it is (rightly) futile in debating competitions, and it should similarly hold no sway in a school board meeting. The search for truth will always be more grounded when the reasons underpinning both sides of an argument are articulated and understood.

A second debating technique that helps school board chairs is to ask "even if…" questions. By adopting the strategy of asking an "even if…" question, a debater hypothetically concedes a point or definition made by the other side, but then argues that even if that point were to be accepted, their overall case still fails.

YEAR 8 DEBATING

For example, imagine that the Principal has brought a recommendation to the board to approve loosening some of the onerous risk management procedures for off-campus activities on the basis that the teachers believe the requirements are stifling effective learning in fieldwork activities. One of the board members is a lawyer who is used to getting his own way by invoking "the legal risks" inherent in almost every proposal that is brought to the board, including this one, relying on the timidity of other board members to challenge any argument which is said to have a legal dimension attached to it. A heated debate ensues because several other board members want to encourage creativity through 'hands-on' learning.

They trust the judgement of the teachers who claim that the children's education is suffering because of excessive restrictions.

Depending upon the board's overall risk-appetite or risk-aversion, the chair could intervene with an "even if…" provocation such as this: "Even if we accept that there are legal risks in loosening these procedures, should we also recognise that there are educational risks in keeping them too rigid? Our teachers, who are closest to the students, have made clear that over-regulation is already harming learning. As a board we understand there are reputational risks if we fail to provide the rich, hands-on education that our school prospectus promises. Are we as a board prepared to say that avoiding every hypothetical legal issue is more important than fulfilling our student-centred Mission and Vision?".

This approach should help to validate the competing concerns of all board members while steering the discussion toward the broader 'big picture' goals of governance that should be the board's focus, making it easier to build consensus and move forward with a decision.

Of course, it is unrealistic to demand that debating skills and experience should be a pre-requisite of becoming chair of a school board. Nonetheless, it is helpful to recognise that mastering debating skills empowers a school board chair to lead with confidence, balance diverse perspectives, and drive productive discussions toward meaningful decisions. By applying techniques such as structuring sound and rational arguments, listening actively, and strategically using rhetorical tools such as "even if…" propositions, a chair can foster a culture of respectful debate while avoiding unproductive conflict. These debating skills not only help navigate complex issues but help ensure that every voice is heard and that decisions are made with clarity, transparency, balance and conviction.

The decisions, actions and policies of today's school boards shape the future. A school board chair who embraces the art of debate can inspire collaboration, enhance growth towards achieving school's Mission and Vision, and thus ultimately champion the best interests of the school's students and its community.

Insight 29

Deconstructing school governance

Deconstruction has become quite a buzz-word in recent years. It seems that almost anything which people regard as important has the capacity to be deconstructed – novels, ideas, artworks, philosophies, religions, language, political movements, bad arguments, family structures, systems of education, desserts, and so on.

First developed by the French philosopher Jacques Derrida, deconstructionism seeks to critique established structures by pulling them apart to demonstrate their incompleteness or incoherence. Derrida's writings are famously dense and inaccessible (which suggests they might benefit from deconstructing). The essence of his approach begins from the premise that the words we use are culturally determined, oppression-reinforcing, imprecise and inadequate reflections of the reality we are seeking to describe and analyse, and his philosophy proceeds from there towards its seemingly predetermined conclusions.

I expect that very few school board members have ever studied either Derrida or deconstructionism in detail, and my advice would be to leave things that way if personal sanity and any sense of optimism are valued.

Why, then, am I raising it here?

In my experience, not all deconstruction is explicit or intentional. Unintentional deconstruction can be highly destructive for school boards and the schools they govern, and it is therefore important to know what it is and to recognise it.

Sound, sustainable, effective school governance follows an accepted, time-honoured structure. Among the pivotal principles of sound governance are respecting the boundary between governance and management, fulfilling a range of fiduciary and non-fiduciary duties, acting in accordance with its constitution and policy manual, maintaining clear ethical, legal and financial standards, setting and consistently adhering to a clearly articulated mission, vision and set of values/principles, respecting confidentiality while communicating effectively, supporting its CEO (the Principal), and so on.

By definition, deconstruction means breaking down. For both legal and operational reasons, none of the pivotal principles of sound governance described above should ever be deconstructed, but this is not to say that everything a board does should go unchallenged. After all, practices are not the same as principles. For example, boards which function in a tightly closed manner may consider giving a voice to staff, students, parents, alumni, or other groups – provided doing so does not dilute the board's authority or autonomy. In practice, this might mean (as an example) opening up the board's advisory committees to these or other constituencies. This would be an example of intentional, managed, conscious deconstruction.

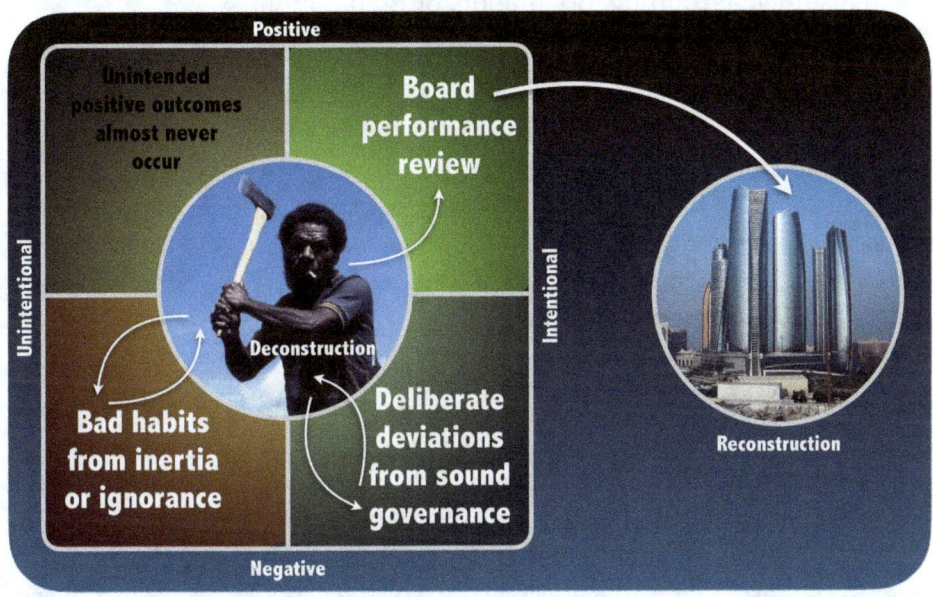

Board deconstruction can be either intentional or unintentional, and it can have both positive and negative impact.

I recall being told about a key member of one board who apparently announced (before I had begun working with that school): "Yes, I know that boards are supposed to govern and leave operations to the staff, but I quite like getting involved in the operational side of things. So, hear me say this – I'm going to keep doing it". This was a board that lost its Principal and imploded shortly afterwards because of the micromanagement of this and other similarly intractable board members. It was a clear example of conscious deconstruction that violated the sound principles of governance, and it was catastrophic for the school. It should have been nipped in the bud by a strong board chair with the unanimous support of the entire board.

Unconscious deconstruction is both more common and usually far more insidious than conscious deconstruction. It occurs when well-meaning but untrained board members slip into bad habits because of inertia, ego, or a simple lack of explicit training in effective governance. The board doesn't mean to violate the principles of effective governance, but it does so unknowingly because its members have never explicitly reflected on what they need to do to add meaningful value to the school. It's almost never the result of malicious intent. Rather, it's the consequence of busy, passionate, well-intentioned people being placed in important positions of responsibility with insufficient training, orientation, or preparation.

In such cases, **intentional positive deconstruction** can be used to rectify the situation. Any board that undertakes a process of re-examining its practices and priorities in the light of 'best practice' will discover benefits it never knew existed. In such cases, deconstruction in the form of an independent board performance review will reveal the dross, uninformed practices and inefficiencies that are working to diminish the board's effectiveness and efficiency. Such intentional, positive deconstruction is like a necessary pruning that provides a foundation for RE-construction – the opposite of deconstruction.

So why don't all boards engage in regular, independent performance reviews to deconstruct 'the old' and then consciously reconstruct 'the new'? For some boards, the reasons are emotional or relational – they don't want to expose the shortcomings of certain members. This is a common but weak reason because few boards would ever tolerate under-performance of the school's paid employees on such grounds. Research shows that school boards have a huge influence on the student outcomes, the staff morale and the community reputation of their schools, so the inclination by some boards to bury their inadequacies is short-sighted in the extreme.

Another reason that some boards don't engage in performance reviews is that they are reluctant to spend money on themselves. Although this argument may seem superficially noble at first ("the students need resources more than we need professional development"), it short-changes the students and the staff because it diminishes the board's capacity to work effectively to provide the resources, the funding, the facilities, and the environment for the school to flourish and reach its potential. Under-investment in the board is one of the most savage forms of under-investment in many schools.

It may not be Derrida's idea of deconstruction, but **performance appraisals and reviews for school boards are essential tools in ensuring accountability, transparency, and continuous improvement.** These assessments help identify strengths, weaknesses, and areas for growth, enabling school boards to make informed decisions and engage in a process of continuous improvement of adapting to the evolving needs of students, staff, and the wider community.

By regularly evaluating their performance, school boards can enhance their effectiveness, demonstrate their commitment to educational excellence, and foster a culture of accountability that ultimately benefits everyone in the school's community.

Insight 30

Developing antifragility in every school

In Insight 7, I explored the concept of **antifragility** — the ability not just to withstand challenges but to grow stronger through them. Unlike resilience, which helps you bounce back to your original state, or robustness, which endures stress without change, antifragility thrives on disruption and adversity.

A fragile person may break under the strain of physical, emotional, or financial hardships. A resilient person recovers and returns to their baseline. However, antifragile people do more — they adapt, flourish, and use adversity as a springboard for growth.

Fostering antifragility is not just a noble aspiration for schools — it is really a **fundamental objective of every school**. Regardless of a school's ethos, vision, mission, or demographic, preparing students to face and grow from adversity must form the heart of authentic education. Anything less leaves students unprepared for the complex, unpredictable world they will step into after graduation.

Nassim Nicholas Taleb, who first coined the term "antifragile" in 2012, wrote that "antifragility is a common property of complex systems that are designed (by evolution, and sometimes by people) to function in a world that is unpredictable". The human immune system is often cited as the ultimate example of antifragility, as it requires exposure to dirt, parasites, and bacteria to strengthen.

Psychologist Dan Gilbert argues that a similar dynamic is required for developing one's psychological immune system. Jonathan Haidt elaborates on this, describing it as "the capacity of a child to handle, process, and get past frustrations, minor accidents, teasing, exclusion, perceived injustices and normal conflicts without falling prey to hours or days of inner turmoil".

Jonathan Haidt further describes the disastrous effect of creating a sense of entitlement in a child:

"A carton of eggs is fragile, if you bang it around it breaks. But bone is anti-fragile. If you bang it around it gets stronger, and if you don't bang it around it gets weaker. Children are anti-fragile. They have to have many, many experiences of failure, fear, and being challenged. Then they have to figure out ways to get themselves through it. If you deprive children of those experiences for eighteen years and then send them to college, they cannot cope. They don't know what to do. The first time a romantic relationship fails or they get a low grade, they are not prepared because they have been rendered fragile by their childhoods".

Exposure to risk-taking, experiencing setbacks, accepting losses, waiting patiently, and recognising the needs of others as important are vital to developing antifragility — and by extension, a sound educational foundation.

However, many teachers are now telling me that they are increasingly frustrated by the growing impact of "gentle parenting" on young students. Gentle parenting, also known as "conscious parenting," aims to cultivate compassion and emotional self-awareness. It emphasises validating children's emotions and addressing the root causes of their frustrations, usually avoiding punishment or negative consequences. While invariably well-intentioned, teachers of young children in schools are finding this approach can lead to children entering school unprepared for boundaries, unable to cope with perspectives that are not their own, and easily frustrated by consequences — in other words, fragile.

This dynamic presents a significant challenge for educators. Developing antifragility in students becomes arduous when children have not been exposed to the foundational experiences that build it. Compounding this issue, many school leaders report that even teachers themselves are showing reduced resilience. They cite evidence such as increasing stress-related leave, unmet deadlines, and rising absenteeism to highlight declining resilience among educators.

Teaching is inherently demanding and requires a high degree of resilience, if not antifragility. To cultivate antifragility in students, teachers must model it themselves.

The circle completes itself here: students can only grow through learning from mistakes, consequences, and challenges. Shielding them from failure — whether by removing the consequences of poor decisions, avoiding tough conversations, or censoring opposing viewpoints — undermines their growth. Without such experiences, students will enter adulthood ill-equipped to handle its inevitable difficulties.

In that context, I love this extract from the speech given by the Chief Justice of the US Supreme Court, John Roberts, at his son's high school graduation ceremony in 2017:

"From time to time in the years to come, I hope you will be treated unfairly, so that you will come to know the value of justice. I hope that you will suffer betrayal because that will teach you the importance of loyalty. Sorry to say, but I hope you will be lonely from time to time so that you don't take friends for granted. I wish you bad luck, again, from time to time so that you will be conscious of the role of chance in life and understand that your success is not completely deserved and that the failure of others is not completely deserved either. And when you lose, as you will from time to time, I hope every now and then, your opponent will gloat over your failure. It is a way for you to understand the importance of sportsmanship. I hope you'll be ignored so you know the importance of listening to others, and I hope you will have just enough pain to learn compassion. Whether I wish these things or not, they're going to happen. And whether you benefit from them or not will depend upon your ability to see the message in your misfortunes".

School boards play a critical role in bringing a school's mission, vision, ethos, and philosophy to life. This responsibility makes it imperative for board members to support their Principal and senior management in actively fostering a culture of antifragility within the school community. By championing risk-taking, reframing mistakes as opportunities for growth, and encouraging students and staff to learn through the natural consequences of their actions, they create an environment where genuine learning thrives.

Whenever he came across a student who thought certain standards or expectations were beyond reach, the great German educator Kurt Hahn would tell that student "your disability is your opportunity; there is more in you than you think". Hahn rightly believed that it was essential that students develop innate strength and overcome their innate defeatism in the face of challenges – in other words, they must develop antifragility.

Antifragility is the cornerstone of building resilience and adaptability through challenge. As Nelson Mandela famously said, "Education is the most powerful weapon which you can use to change the world." However, this "weapon" of education will be impotent whenever schools settle for the ease and comfort of accepting fragility rather than embracing the transformative challenge of forming antifragility.

Insight 31

Disagreeing agreeably on school boards

Some school boards with which I have worked have never experienced a single word raised in anger. Other boards function with a fear that if a certain member attends, or a certain combination of members attend, a flare-up is almost inevitable.

When people of passion and conviction come together on school boards, some conflict is bound to happen. Provided the conflict of ideas remains respectful and does not degenerate into a conflict between people, this conflict is healthy because it means alternatives are being thoroughly explored and interrogated in a collective search for truth – or at least, the best possible solution to a shared problem.

Well, usually.

The sad reality is that not all school board conflicts are as positive or as productive as my earlier paragraph suggests. Personalities and tempers may intrude, and indeed philosophers have for centuries identified a quarrelsome nature to be a vice rather than a virtue. The French philosophers Antoine Arnauld and Pierre Nicole identified a quarrelsome nature as "malformed egotism", and no doubt many school board members who have found themselves in heated arguments on boards would agree.

Arguments undermine positive board dynamics because of attendees' common natural reactions when they find themselves in adversarial situations. Polemical disagreements often cause people into harden their stances – they stop listening to others' reasoning, they cease reflecting on their own arguments and instead blindly reiterate their own position almost as a matter of personal honour. If this attitude reaches the point of simply dismissing what others are saying, the board's meeting dynamics are likely to break down irredeemably.

When this happens, two equally negative consequences become probable. On one hand, a board member may believe something so completely, so passionately and so fundamentally that he or she becomes incapable of processing what others are saying to the contrary. Alternatively, it may happen that the board member is utterly resistant to the idea of having to back down simply because of the reputational damage they imagine might result. (A third, hopefully less likely variation of this second consequence is that the board member so detests, or looks down upon, the character of their interlocutor that he or she just cannot bear the thought of sharing the same viewpoint as that person).

All three consequences reflect the vice of hubris that arises from the egotistical bias of inflated self-belief. As George Sand famously said, "vanity is the quicksand of reason". Anger, distemper, and vanity are all powerful barriers to understanding the reasons underpinning a person's truth position.

The underlying issue here is that the way some board members go about disagreeing is often subconsciously driven by ego. Specifically, their driving force is whatever will make them look good or whatever is best for them, rather than fulfilling their primary fiduciary duty which is to promote whatever is best for the school.

Many commentators claim that ego is an inevitable driver of the human condition; they claim it is human nature to be motivated by ego. However, having worked with school boards in many cultures and countries around the world, I have concluded that this is not universally true; Western societies may be peculiarly focussed on driving people in an ego-centred direction. An effective contributor in

Western societies tends not to be seen as a person who has received ideas and understandings from others, but rather as someone who has formed their own original opinions, often irrespective of their factual bases, and who can then use these opinions to their own advantage. (And as we see in debates over issues such as climate change, vaccine effectiveness, and other less global political issues, opinions in The West do not necessarily have to be grounded in scientific evidence to gain widespread currency).

By contrast, societies in Africa, the Middle East and Asia, together with Indigenous cultures in Australia, the Americas and elsewhere, give great respect to knowledge (including myths) that has been tested and has endured the test of time, and which is consistent with experience and evidence. It follows from this that respect is given to people who convey such knowledge, which helps explain the huge difference in respect shown to scholars and teachers in those societies compared with Western Europe, North America, and other Westernised societies. I believe it is no coincidence that school boards in non-Western societies generally tend to work respectfully and harmoniously, even when disagreements arise, whereas boards in economically wealthy Western societies are more likely argue through the lens of ego.

One of the problems I have observed with some school boards (in Western countries) is that when disagreements occur, the board member who seems to be "winning" the debate starts to demand that the "loser" signify this in what may be a humiliating manner. For example, the "winner" may press for some act of recantation that will result in a loss of face for the "loser". That would never happen in (say) Asia where I worked for many years. Perhaps the lesson for Western school boards is that the ethics of disagreement should include showing grace to those with whom you disagree through some combination of tact, flattery, and even willing acceptance of some of the (perhaps minor) points they have been making.

How then might I advise school board members how to disagree more agreeably, and thus more productively? I would begin by suggesting that all board members should take a short course in logic so they can tell the difference between a sound and an unsound argument, knowing some rules for 'thinking well' and avoiding seductive errors of unsound reasoning. Board members should be invested in thoroughly understanding the reasons underpinning both their own opinions and the opinions of others.

Agreeable disagreements should be embraced because they can reveal important confusions in our own position, thus clarifying our own thinking while simultaneously advancing the wider group's search for truth. Disagreements go well when everyone has been trained to engage in positive, productive communication so that each person understands the 'rules' for effective engagement. Disagreements go poorly when these virtues are replaced by vanity, anger, deafness to others and egocentric hubris.

There is a lovely quote I heard recently from Waleed Aly on one of my favourite podcasts ("The Minefield") which captures very well the humility required to disagree agreeably: **"I've never entered an argument without wishing that the truth was on the other person's tongue, because that way I would learn something"**.

Insight 32

Diversity enhances effective school board leadership

"It is not our differences that divide us. It is our inability to recognise, accept, and celebrate those differences".

I love this quote by US writer Audre Lorde that appears above the Library entrance on the United World College's Dover Campus Library in Singapore.

The message is intended to inspire students, but it should equally inform every school's board composition and leadership style.

Differences of opinion among school board members are common, and indeed, conflicts are to be expected. More significantly, they should be welcomed and embraced. The whole point of having a board is to explore and respectfully consider a diverse range of opinions and suggestions. After all, if every member of a board held the same viewpoint on every issue, you may as well have a board of just one person.

A diverse board will always be better positioned to consider a wide range of perspectives than a board whose members share similar demographics such as age, gender, and cultural background.

Therefore, it is perhaps even more important that boards seek to secure a balanced range of decision-making and enquiry skills (rather than occupational skills) among their members. Effective school boards tend to recruit members who:
- are open-minded and willing to consider new ideas.
- have a sense of curiosity, who seem to find everything interesting, and are thus willing to ask questions.
- are inspired and driven by the mission.
- have a balance of perspective and expertise.
- have good networks and connections.
- can fill needs on board committees.
- have leadership potential (for succession planning) and
- are neither "too busy" nor "too important" to contribute effectively.

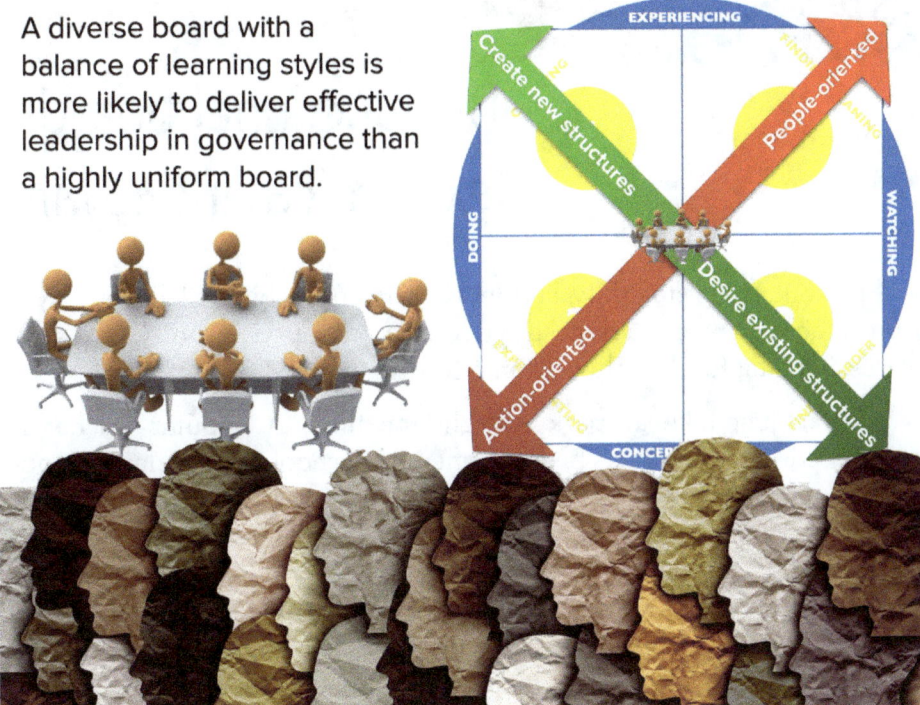

A diverse board with a balance of learning styles is more likely to deliver effective leadership in governance than a highly uniform board.

We know that different people prefer to engage through four foundational learning styles:

- People who search for meaning (and thus ask "Why?")
- People who search for order (who ask "What?")
- People who like to experiment (and ask "How?")
- People who love to create (and ask "What if?").

Of course, everyone operates through a mix of these different styles, often at different times and in different situations. Nonetheless, everyone has their preferred ways of learning, and **high-functioning boards ensure that all four learning styles are proportionally represented.**

Insight 33

Dysfunctional boards: exit, voice and loyalty

It can happen stealthily, suddenly, or relentlessly. Whichever way it comes about, it's always destructive to a school community. In some cases, it's fatal for the school. I'm referring to board dysfunction.

It can just take a spark to light the fire. A popular teacher is dismissed. A student has been maimed in a school fight. A large donor exerts undue influence. A board member starts giving direct instructions to teachers. Allegations of historical abuse emerge. A newspaper reporter or a blogger with an axe to grind starts a public campaign. Two board members have a violent disagreement away from the school at their common workplace or church. Parents think a board member may be benefitting financially from a board decision. The list of possibilities is very long.

In response to the emerging crisis, board solidarity fractures, confidentiality shatters, resolve weakens, and the board's failing reputation becomes a widely known issue, exacerbating the problem. The school's reputation is damaged, enrolments decline, staff morale plummets, academic results fall, and the board becomes paralysed by overly frequent but ineffective meetings to deal with the backlog of crises.

I'm speaking here in generalisations, but everything I've listed (and much, much more) has happened with school boards I have been brought in to assist.

When a school board becomes dysfunctional, life invariably becomes very difficult (and busy!) both for the Head of School and the members of the board. It is said that in these situations, board members (and the Head) essentially have three options. These options are "Exit, Voice and Loyalty", which is also the title of a classic 1970 book by the German-American economist and political scientist, Albert Hirschman.

Hirschman's thesis is that members of any organisation – whether a business, a political party, a nation or a school board – essentially have

two possible primary responses when they perceive that the organisation is encountering a decline. They can either exit (withdraw from the relationship), or, they can voice (attempt to repair or improve the relationship through communication of the complaint, concern, grievance or proposal for change). Hirschman then argues that the individual's level of loyalty will affect the decision whether to exit or to voice – high loyalty reduces the likelihood of exit while increasing the likelihood of voice.

When faced with board dysfunction, board members and the Head of School can leave (exit) or speak up for change (voice). Hirschman also explores a third option, which is loyalty (conform and carry on). Whichever choice is made carries its own risks and potential benefits, both for the individual and for the organisation, making it crucial to assess the situation carefully before deciding on the best course of action.

Let's explore the merits of each of the three options.

One option in a board crisis is for the Head of School to resign and seek employment elsewhere and/or for board members to step down. This is the "exit" option, which as the diagram above shows is active but destructive. Nonetheless, if the dysfunction of the school board is so significant that it is impacting the school's ability to function effectively, leaving may be the most realistic decision. In cases where board decisions or inaction hinder student learning, create an unhealthy work environment, or place the senior leaders in a position where they are unable to fulfil their professional responsibilities, the "exit" option may protect both their career and personal wellbeing. On the other hand, this option also means deserting the school community, abandoning the students and staff who may be negatively affected by the board's ongoing dysfunction.

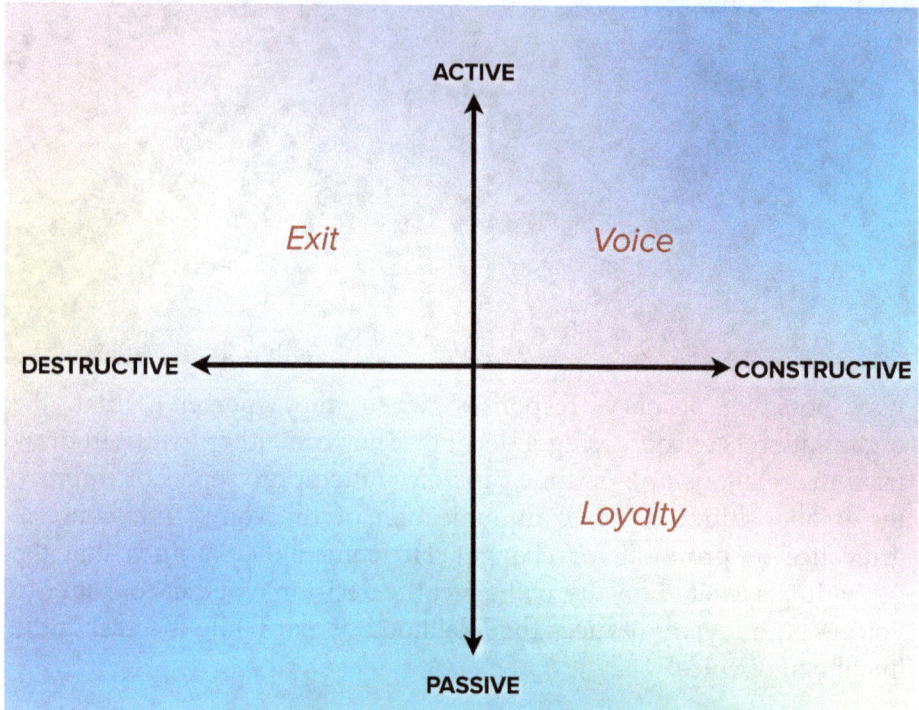

The second option is "voice" in which board members and/or the Head of School speak up and push for change – an action that is both active and constructive. This approach demonstrates strong leadership and a commitment to the school's mission. By being a strong advocate for better governance, transparency, and improved decision-making, a board member or Head of School has the potential to influence positive reforms. On the other hand, this option carries significant risks, especially during a crisis or if there is a majority view on the board that is resistant to feedback or more comfortable with inertia than reform. In such situations, the Head of School or the vocal board member may face retaliation, strained relationships, or even job loss. Despite the challenges, however, speaking up is often the most ethical choice, as it places a priority on the needs of the students, teachers, the wider school community, and perhaps even the school's future viability.

The third option is also constructive but it is passive when compared with "voice". This option is "loyalty" where the Head of School and/or board members simply conform and continue working within the constraints of the dysfunctional board. Some Heads of School may choose this path to maintain job security, avoid conflict, or attempt to achieve small improvements from within the system. Although this approach may provide some level of stability and avoid conflict, it can also lead to frustration, compromised professional integrity, and a failure to address the underlying or systemic problems. Over time, remaining passive in the face of dysfunction may contribute to the school's decline and negatively affect students and staff.

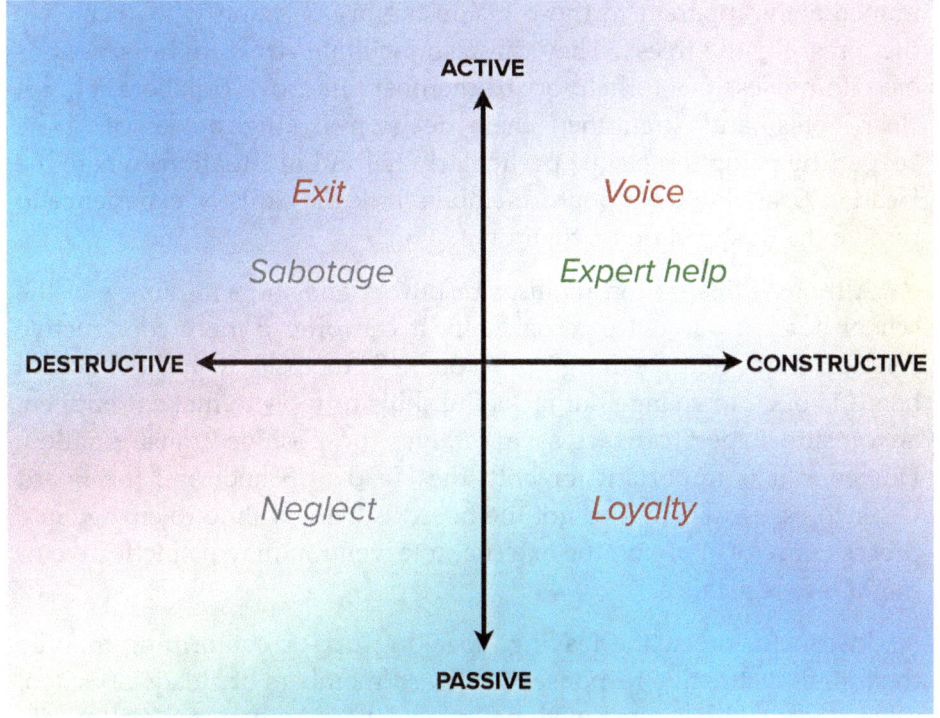

Although Hirschman focussed on the three options of "exit", "voice" and "loyalty", board members and Heads of School realistically have three additional options available to them if the board becomes dysfunctional – "neglect", "sabotage" and seeking "expert help".

Although I have witnessed "neglect" and "sabotage" in some schools as responses to board dysfunction, neither approach can be recommended as both are inherently destructive – indeed, even more destructive than "exit".

The option of "expert help" is worth considering as an effective, active, constructive response to board dysfunction. This solution overcomes the emotions, the political biases and the factionalism that often accompany board dysfunction. The "expert help" option can be highly effective in cases where internal efforts to resolve the issues have failed or where there is a need for an unbiased perspective to guide the process of improvement.

Bringing in an independent expert – such as a mediator, consultant, or facilitator – can help provide a neutral, objective viewpoint on the root causes of the dysfunction. Independent, external experts can assist in identifying communication breakdowns, governance challenges, structural or constitutional problems, and conflicts that may not be immediately apparent to those inside the organisation who "can't see the forest for the trees". They can also facilitate structured discussions or training sessions to help board members improve collaboration, set clear goals, and strengthen their decision-making processes. The "expert help" option can be particularly helpful in situations where the Head of School and/or board members lack the skills or experience to resolve the dysfunction on their own.

Although this option requires resources and the willingness of the school board to accept external help, it can offer a more constructive solution than mere "exiting" or "voicing". In cases where the school board is open to change but lacks the skills or tools to make it happen, an outside expert can act as a catalyst for positive transformation. However, it is important for both the Head of School and the Board Chair to assess whether or not the board is truly willing to engage in a process of reform; if not, the external intervention may be ineffective or might face resistance.

In conclusion, while leaving, speaking up, or conforming may be the initial, instinctive responses for board members of Heads of School when faced with a dysfunctional school board, they are really only partial solutions at best. Seeking external expertise should be considered as an effective option that can calm the waters, relieve the pressures, build an effective long-term solution to the dysfunction, and establish a firm foundation for the school and its entire community to flourish for many years into the future.

Insight 34

Effective boards

If a hospital cures its patients, it will be judged as being a good hospital. Other factors will of course be considered before forming this judgement, such as the quality of facilities, the ideological approach taken, and whether or not the staff are friendly and communicative. Notwithstanding these factors, the hospital is likely to be judged primarily on its effectiveness in fulfilling its basic core function, which is to heal the sick.

For the mainstream community, schools are appraised in the same way. The quality of facilities must be adequate, the philosophical approach must be acceptable, and it helps when the faculty and staff are personable, helpful, and caring. Irrespective of these factors, however, very few people would claim that a certain school is 'good' – or excellent, exceptional, or outstanding – if it is failing in its core purpose of achieving strong, sustainable student outcomes.

Different schools will prioritise 'student outcomes' in different ways. For some schools, academic results will be the primary focus. For others, it might be producing well-rounded students. For other schools, the priority might be highly ethical students, or students who follow a certain worldview or faith position.

Many Trustees (Board Members) believe that achieving excellent student outcomes is exclusively the task of the faculty and staff, under the direction of the Head. However, the research shows that Boards also have an important role to play.

This is not a new discovery. In a landmark study published in 1997 by Goodman et.al. data were gathered through 132 interviews to investigate the relationship between School Board effectiveness and student achievement. The study found that schools with 'high quality governance' tended to have higher student achievement as measured by lower dropout rates, higher percentages of students going on to university, and higher average aptitude test scores. Subsequent research has continued to reinforce these findings. For example, a 2011 study concluded that "effective school boards focus on policy issues that impact on student achievement and instruction".

Given that high performing School Boards appear to raise student achievement, what can Boards do to improve their effectiveness, and thus help the students in their school?

Fortunately, the answers are quite clear. Effective Boards understand the difference between governance (their role) and management (the Head's role). Effective Boards make decisions that focus on student needs. They have efficiently conducted, focussed meetings that are supported by annual or biannual goal-setting retreats. They have a supportive relationship with the Head. Effective Boards work in a spirit of mutual trust and respect.

And importantly, effective Boards ensure that their effectiveness is sustainable by seeking regular external input and by evaluating their own effectiveness on a regular basis using neutral external advisors.

References:

Goodman, RH, Fulbright, L & Zimmerman, WG 1997, *Getting there from here: School board-superintendent collaboration: Creating a school governance team capable of raising student achievement*, Educational Research Service & New England School Development Council, Arlington.

Johnson, PA 2011, 'School board governance: The times they are a-changin'', *Journal of Cases in Educational Leadership*, vol. 15, no. 2, p. 98.

Insight 35

Effort grades boost student outcomes

One of the challenges that is often shared by school leaders and their boards is ensuring that every student is reaching his or her full potential in every area of their formation – academic, physical, spiritual, and so on. Traditionally, academic prizes were used as a prime motivator, but of course only the top few percent of students can ever dream of receiving one of these prizes, which suggests their value as a motivating influence on students is marginal at best.

During four of my five school headships, I introduced an initiative which proved to be extremely effective in motivating students. Indeed, in the words of many of my colleagues, it completely transformed the learning culture of the school.

The initiative was a very simple one. Every school already included grades for "Effort" or "Application" on their student reports, but none of them treated the effort grade as seriously as the academic mark achieved for each subject. Consequently, neither the students nor the parents placed much emphasis on the effort grade. The simple initiative was to treat the effort grade as being more significant than the mark achieved.

The thinking behind this change was that only a few students could ever achieve marks of, say, 90% and above. However, every student was capable of gaining an "A" for Effort if they were working to their full capabilities. In other words, a student who was getting a mark of, say, 55% might deserve an "A" for Effort if they were working their heart out. Similarly, a student who was receiving a mark in the high 80s might only deserve a B or a C for effort, or even a D if they were coasting and not applying themselves seriously to their work.

A key element in this initiative was coming to a common understanding among all teachers of what was required for the award of each Effort Grade. In other words, Effort Grades should be criterion-based. The criteria used in each of the schools where I was Head varied to suit their different demographics, but they were similar to this:

A EXCELLENT SUSTAINED EFFORT
- A highly motivated, always punctual student who submits all work on time.
- Frequently makes a positive contribution in class and participates actively.
- A highly developed work ethic and consistent striving towards goals.
- Homework is always done and to the best of his/her abilities.
- Always comes to class well organised with appropriate materials.

B CONSISTENT, VERY GOOD EFFORT
- A motivated, punctual student who submits most work on time.
- Makes a positive contribution and participates well.
- Good work ethic and ability to set goals.
- Homework is almost always done and to the best of his/her abilities.
- Almost always comes to class well organised with appropriate materials.

C REASONABLE EFFORT
- Usually a motivated, punctual student but not working to potential.
- Sometimes lacks self-motivation and participation.
- Work ethic could improve but some goal-setting is evident.
- Homework is usually done but not always to the best of his/her abilities.
- Usually comes to class reasonably organised with appropriate materials.

D UNSATISFACTORY EFFORT
- Lacks sustained motivation and is often late in submitting work.
- Shows little interest in studying or participating in class.
- Does not work independently or set goals of achievement.
- Homework is done inconsistently and often below his/her abilities.
- Sometimes comes to class disorganised without appropriate materials.

E UNACCEPTABLE EFFORT
- Often disinterested in learning.
- Unco-operative and disruptive in class.
- Does not work without supervision.
- Homework is rarely completed satisfactorily.
- Frequently comes to class poorly organised and without appropriate materials.

Teachers assess Effort based on consistent, demonstrated patterns of learning. They do not base their judgements on isolated incidents. There are no restrictions to the number of Effort grades awarded in a course. Effort grades are awarded on the basis of actual student learning profiles, not quotas. It is important to note that the Effort grades relate to the learning process and the content relative to an individual student's ability, irrespective of actual achievement of marks. Low performing students should be and are capable of receiving an Excellent grade if their approach to learning in the classroom and their performance in completing homework is high.

The introduction of this simple change meant that parents became aware of their children's progress relative to their own individual capabilities and potential, not just in relation to the rest of the class or grade.

An important element of this initiative was following up the Effort Grades in reports. Students who received straight "A" grades for Effort in every subject were awarded a "Gold/ Exemplary Certificate" at a full school assembly to which parents were invited. Students who received straight "A" grades with one "B" received a "Silver/ Distinguished Certificate", and students who received straight "A"s with two "B"s received a "Bronze/ Commended Certificate". These assemblies quickly assumed huge importance in the school community, with parents taking time off work so they could attend. The assembly was followed by a morning tea (or afternoon tea as appropriate) for the award winners and their parents, with food and drinks situated on tables in a location where all the students who had not received awards had to walk past without stopping on the way to their next class.

Important follow-up also occurred for students at the other effort of the effort range. Any student who received three "D"s or one "E" grade on their report was interviewed by me as Principal, had a letter written home, and was followed up by the year co-ordinator. If those poor efforts continued, then for the sake of the welfare of the individual student, we raised questions about whether or not they should continue at the school, asking whether the school was able and effective in meeting the student's needs. Moreover, out of concern for students having difficulties, on a weekly basis Heads of Departments and Year Co-ordinators discussed with me as Principal those students who were causing them concern, academically or otherwise. I was told that few other schools expressed their concern for the individual needs of each student in such intense, some would say time consuming, ways – but it worked.

Insight 36

Empathy enhances leadership

Empathy is the ability to understand and share the ways other people are feeling emotionally. As I write in Insight 37, empathy is thus a basic requirement of caring for others and acting towards them appropriately and compassionately.

Many people confuse empathy with sympathy. In a TED Talk recorded in 2010 that has had more than 62 million views, Dr Brené Brown explained the difference very clearly:

- **Sympathy** is when you see someone as being in a deep hole while you remain on higher ground and talk to them from above. The sympathetic person may also simply try to put a silver lining on the other person's situation instead of acknowledging the person's pain.
- **Empathy** is when you feel with the person, climbing down into the hole to sit beside that person, making yourself vulnerable to connect with them in a sincere manner. The empathetic person will recognise the other person's struggle without minimising it.

Psychologists Daniel Goleman and Paul Ekman have recognised that there are three types of empathy: cognitive, emotional, and compassionate. They describe the differences in this way:

- **Type 1 : Cognitive empathy:** "Simply knowing how the other person feels and what they might be thinking; sometimes called perspective-taking."
- **Type 2 : Emotional empathy:** "When you feel physically along with the other person, as though their emotions were contagious."
- **Type 3 : Compassionate empathy:** "we not only understand a person's predicament and feel with them, but are spontaneously moved to help, if needed."

Most empathetic people are quite good at the first two types of empathy, which involve understanding the other person's feelings (type 1) and metaphorically putting themselves in their shoes (type

2). The third type of empathy, which involves demonstrating care through action, is less common. Many people can put themselves in the shoes of another person (type 2) without actually caring (type 3), but in reality, this may mean little more than the efforts of an effective advertiser or salesperson who is seeking to manipulate people.

On the other hand, people who can show type 3 empathy, which is authentic care and concern for others, behave very differently from those who limit themselves to types 1 and 2.

In general, leaders in schools (including board members) who are loved and respected are those who demonstrate empathetic concern towards others (type 3). Their care for others inspires members of the school community who reciprocate by responding with loyalty towards them. Daniel Goleman has reported that when teachers and students in schools are asked to identify which leaders they love and which they hate, one of the biggest differentiators is the extent to which leaders demonstrate type 3 empathy.

From time to time back in the days when I served as a school principal, I would try to set aside time at least once every year to become a student for the day, usually in either Year 9 or Year 10. In other words, I would follow a student's timetable and participate in everything that a student would do on that day. I found this exercise to be extremely helpful in keeping me grounded and understanding the everyday experiences of my students, therefore serving as a foundation for genuine empathy.

I would try to sit towards the back of the classroom because I knew that was where trouble-makers liked to sit. In a highly varied day I might study the profile of a sand dune, answer some questions that were being asked (I think) in French, construct a mind-map, learn the difference between mensuration and menstruation, help to grow some plant seedlings, analyse Freud's theory of human nature, tuck in my shirt intuitively when I heard there was to be a uniform inspection, and successfully solve some maths problems that I seem to recall involved wildlife parks and chicken wings.

I remember the huge range of emotions I experienced one day while I was a Year 9 student for the day. There were times when I felt anxious, such as when called upon to give an answer to the class. There was the sense of achievement in finishing a particularly challenging Maths problem – with the help of some of my new Year 9

friends. There was the chill I felt when I thought I was about to be blamed for another student's talking. There was the admiration and humility I felt when listening to an excellent group presentation by other students. There was the embarrassment when I was asked if I had completed my homework and I had to respond honestly 'not for more than 30 years'. And there was the simple hunger – waiting for the bell – as lunch time approached, followed by the genuine joy of joining the queue at the canteen to buy a chicken burger, capped off by joining a game of handball and demonstrating to the students how a self-proclaimed 'expert' plays the game.

I concluded that Year 9 students at my school worked hard, but not as hard as their Principal. I also found that Year 9 students at my school had lots of fun, and maybe even more fun than their Principal (at least when the deadline for writing my board report was imminent).

It is easy to see how empathetic leadership is important for school leaders – the Principal, senior and middle managers, and every classroom teacher – because schools are complex communities of people with different needs, vulnerabilities, challenges, and aspirations – all of which require understanding and empathy.

I think the same principle applies at least as strongly for members of the school board, even though their work is more remote from the everyday life of the school. Achieving empathy may be more challenging for board members than other school leaders because not all board members necessarily share the lived experience of the people they are serving. For example, we can assume that every board member attended school at some time in the past, but that may have been many decades ago when the educational world was very different from today. In any case, most school board members will have never worked in a school or any kind of educational environment, and more-than-likely not even in a not-for-profit organisation with all the unique cultural quirks that this entails. Not having any shared lived experience with staff and students in a school places a distance between school board members and their community, building a barrier to empathy.

The consequence is that many school board members are somewhat detached from type 3 empathy (their ability to care) because they lack accessibility to the people and environment they are governing. This is not an argument for student or staff representation at board meetings, but a plea for school board members to visit the school from time to time when it is fully operational, meet and chat informally with staff and students, and hopefully even visit the communities that send students to the school in the case of boarding schools.

Simple strategies such as these are important and effective ways to help board members understand how and why their work is important in transforming students' and staff lives (type 1 empathy) which can - and should – progress to the critically important type 3 empathy. Board members must be in touch with their purpose in a meaningful way if they are to be effective and add value to the school they are serving.

Insight 37

Empathy shapes school culture

According to an extensive web survey I undertook last month, the most commonly used adjectives to describe school boards are (in descending order of frequency):

1. Effective
2. Ineffective
3. Transparent
4. Accountable
5. Responsive
6. Progressive
7. Conservative
8. Collaborative
9. Divisive
10. Visionary

I found it disappointing that "empathetic" did not appear in that list. Having worked with many school boards and leaders, I have come to realise how important it is for boards and leaders to demonstrate empathy if they are to function effectively, and how this can impact their entire school community.

This is especially so when contentious issues are under consideration and tempers begin to rise. It is important to remember that the opposite of unproductive anger is not artificial calmness, it is genuine empathy.

Empathy *[noun]*: the ability to understand and share the feelings of another.

Empathy should always be one of the key defining characteristics of any school culture, and it flows from the school's board and leaders.

Let's explore the importance of empathy in a little more depth.

On a morning just over ten years ago when I was working as Head of a large school in the United States, I was walking north along 13th Street in Philadelphia from my hotel to the venue of the NAIS conference I was attending. On my way, I crossed a wide street known as Market Street. It was not the corner in the photo shown below, but it looked very similar.

I bent down to talk to him, but although he was lying face down on the street, I could see that he seemed to be unconscious.

To my amazement, no other pedestrian stopped.

I was worried that when the traffic lights changed, cars would start moving and the drivers might not see him lying on the road. I stood up and called out to passers-by to help me move him to the side of the road. A couple of men came across, and as we started to lift him up together, he regained some consciousness, so we helped him walk to the side of the road as we kept an eye open towards the movement of the cars which had begun swerving around us at unnervingly high speed. We helped him sit down and we stayed with him for a while to make sure he was okay, which fortunately, he was.

I was telling my daughter about this incident a few days later, and her immediate response was "Dad, why didn't you upload a Facebook post about it?".

To be honest, writing a Facebook post was probably the furthest thing from my mind at the time. Upon reflection, however, I started asking myself what kind of message I would have posted, because the staggering aspect of the experience from my perspective was not that a man had collapsed in front of me on the roadway, but that no-one else stopped to help. Where was the empathy?

Before my experience in Philadelphia, I would never have imagined a situation in which no pedestrian would stop and help an elderly man who had suddenly collapsed in the street. Was my experience in Philadelphia an example of the self-centred individualism that is said to typify western societies (and especially the United States) according to some foreign commentators?

Interestingly, there is well-established research evidence that helps to answer that question. In 1973, two researchers (JM Darley and CD Batson) conducted an experiment in a seminary to try and find a link between personality types and the likelihood of helping others in an emergency. It has become known as the "Good Samaritan experiment", although its more grandiose and official title is "A Study of Situational and Dispositional Variables in Helping Behaviour".

Whatever one's religious stance, Jesus' parable of the Good Samaritan presents an interesting model for relational behaviour. Why did the priest and the Levite pass by the man who was lying injured beside the road after being attacked? Were they just in a hurry and occupied by their busy thoughts and priorities? Despite the ethnic antipathy of the era, why did the Samaritan stop? Was he in less of a hurry – or did he possess some virtues that the others did not?

In their experiment, Darley and Batson proposed three hypotheses: (1) People thinking religious, 'helping' thoughts would still be no more likely than others to offer assistance, (2) People in a hurry will be less likely to offer aid than others, and (3) People who are religious because of what they can gain from their religion will be less likely to help others than people who are religious because of the intrinsic value of the religion or who are searching for meaning in life.

To conduct the experiment, Darley and Batson had the seminarians complete a questionnaire, after which they were told to walk across to a different building to complete the procedure. Before they left the building, one group was told they would have to prepare a talk about seminary jobs, while the other group was told that they would need to prepare a talk on the parable of the Good Samaritan. Within each group, there were two sub-groups, one of which was told the task was urgent while the other was given no message about urgency.

On the pathway between the two buildings, both groups encountered a man slumped in an alleyway. He moaned and coughed twice as each group of seminarians approached him; maybe he was hurt, or maybe he was drunk. The seminarians were observed and rated on a 5-point scale:

0 = failed to notice the victim as being in need

1 = perceived a need but did not offer aid

2 = did not stop but helped indirectly (told the aide upon arrival)

3 = stopped and asked the victim if he needed help

4 = after stopping, insisted on taking the victim inside, and then left him

5 = refused to leave the victim, or insisted on taking him somewhere

The results were, I think, fascinating. As I would have expected, the how hurried the seminarians were did have a major effect in whether or not they were willing to stop and help the victim. Of greater interest, however, the task they had been given did not affect their willingness to stop, even when their task was to prepare a talk on the parable of the Good Samaritan.

Overall, 40% offered some help to the victim. In 'low hurry' situations, 63% helped, compared to 45% of 'medium hurry' situations and 10% of those in 'high hurry' situations. There was no correlation between the religious types and helping behaviour.

I think it would be fascinating exercise to relate this experiment to people's behaviour in schools, including at the board and leadership level. **After all, the actions and the empathy shown by school boards and leaders flow through to have a huge impact upon the culture, morale, and cohesion of the entire school community.**

Does the 'hurry' that board members and school leaders sometimes feel to make a decision or finish a meeting reduce the empathy they might otherwise feel for those who will be affected by the decision? Does any discussion on finances consider the human impact that 'difficult but necessary' cutbacks might have on the staff or students who are affected?

I wonder what the outcome would be in your school if the students were to participate in a similar experiment to that conducted by Darley and Batson – it could provide a fascinating measure of their empathy.

And I wonder also if the distribution of their parents would indicate a greater or a lesser willingness to stop and help than their children would show.

As the Austrian psychotherapist Alfred Adler said, **"Empathy is seeing with the eyes of another, listening with the ears of another and feeling with the heart of another"** – to which I would add, empathy creates connection, compassion, and community, three essential elements of any effective school.

Insight 38

Ethics for school boards and leaders

It goes without saying that almost all boards act ethically. And those few boards that are falling short ethically MUST lift their game for a myriad of legal and other reasons that can be summarised in one word – risk.

However, although all boards strive to act ethically, there is a surprising lack of consensus on what constitutes ethical behaviour.

We've got to draw a line on unethical behaviour and then get as close to that line as possible.

When the word 'ethics' is used generally in everyday conversations, it is often equated to similar concepts such as morality, virtue, and goodness. For school boards and leaders, what constitutes ethical behaviour in practice may become more nuanced and less clear-cut.

Ethics represents one area where it is helpful for board members and school leaders to step back from time to time, look at the big picture, re-examine their own positions, and ask the question "what do WE really mean when we claim that we act ethically?".

A basic understanding of the three broad theories of ethics can be very helpful in answering this Big Question (with sincere apologies to my readers with degrees in philosophy for the highly abbreviated summary of ethical theories in the following three paragraphs).

Some ethicists argue that ethics is essentially a matter of doing your duty and fulfilling your obligations. This is known as **duty ethics**, or the **deontological approach**, advocated by the German philosopher Immanuel Kant. Kant claimed that everyone has three core motivations for doing good: (1) you expect something in return, (2) sympathy, and (3) duty. He claimed that actions have moral value only if they arise from duty. In other words, the end does not justify the means; purity of motive is all-important.

A second approach is **utilitarianism**, which is closely related to **consequentialism**, in which the ends do justify the means. In other words, it is the consequences or results of actions and policies, that determine whether they are good or bad, right or wrong. In utilitarianism, there is one and only one supreme moral principle - we should seek the greatest happiness for the greatest number of people. Maximise happiness! Happiness = good. Unhappiness = bad.

A third approach is **religious ethics**. The world's religions are sources of moral insight and guidance to millions of people. In the case of theistic religions, ethics flow from revealed truth from divine sources. Many believe that the "Golden Rule" - treat others as you want to be treated - is a common factor in many religions. Christian, Jewish and Islamic ethical approaches are the opposite of utilitarianism, in that rather than measuring goodness by the care we give to the largest number people, goodness is measured by the care we give to the most vulnerable.

School boards and leaders set the tone and the quality of ethical standards that permeate the entire organisation. These ethical standards define the school's moral compass, what is considered acceptable and not acceptable, and what is considered to be "good" and "bad". It is ethical standards of honesty and integrity that help define the school's identity and its standing among its stakeholders and within the wider community.

It follows from this that schools should articulate their code of ethics (which may also be called a code of practice) and make it widely available in an open, transparent manner, such as on their websites.

For the ethical stance of school leaders and boards to be effective, it is worth articulating to one another which ethical approach (or balance of ethical approaches) is underpinning discussions, meetings, policies and, perhaps most importantly of all, the mission and strategic vision.

Insight 39

Euphemisms and jargon are enemies of effective school leadership

I wrote about Boeing's use of the term "quality escape" in Insight 13. Boeing used that term to describe the manufacturing fault which resulted in a section of the side of an Alaska Airlines Boeing 737 MAX blowing away from the plane while in flight. It is fair to say that using the term "quality escape" was an attempt to reduce the scale of the manufacturing fault in the minds of the general public.

Politicians seem to love euphemisms. Ever since Winston Churchill re-labelled "lies" as "terminological inexactitudes" in 1906 and "freedom fighters" became confused with "terrorists" depending upon who was making the speech, politicians have used euphemisms with exuberance. The economy isn't in recession, it is undergoing a necessary restructure or a period of disinflation. We didn't destroy heritage wetlands, we re-classified them as scrublands before bulldozing them.

I love Bernard Woolley's euphemistic quip in the brilliant British political satire 'Yes Minister' when he responded to news that his line manager may have breached security in a conversation with a newspaper reporter. His response was: "Oh, that's one of those irregular verbs, isn't it? I give confidential security briefings. You leak. He has been charged under section 2a of the Official Secrets Act".

In the corporate world, euphemisms are often seen as helpful when trying to manage a crisis. Desperate managers hope they might soften the impact of bad news or deflect blame away from themselves.

This hope is not entirely without foundation as euphemisms are widely used in everyday language, not just in crises. Thus, we speak of the 'rest room' instead of the 'toilet', 'landscape management' instead of 'clear felling' of a forest, 'passing away' instead of 'dying' and 'pleasantly plump' or 'shapely' instead of 'fat'.

Military forces have used euphemisms for decades. They talk about "neutralising" an enemy when they mean "killing". They refer to "friendly fire" when they have accidentally killed their own troops, "servicing a target" when they drop bombs on it, "strategic redeployment" when they mean "retreat", and "inoperative combat personnel" when they mean "dead soldiers".

In the corporate world, we hear of "personnel changes" rather than layoffs or job cuts, "rightsizing" rather than downsizing the workforce, "revenue enhancements" rather than price increases, "ethical lapses" rather than fraud or corruption, and "enhancements" when retail products are reduced in size or benefits removed.

When euphemisms obscure clarity of meaning, they descend into jargon – words or expressions that are difficult for others to understand. Many Australians will remember a former Prime Minister, Kevin Rudd, who was a master of jargon, referring to "detailed programmatic specificity" in a speech to a visiting German delegation headed by their Chancellor, Angela Merkel. The context was a declaration that "it is unlikely any progress will emerge from the Major Economies Forum (MEF) by way of detailed programmatic specificity". Unsurprisingly, the German press never managed to translate that phrase, and no native English speakers found they were able to offer meaningful assistance.

It seems that the use of jargon is expanding in society. Recent examples I have come across include:

- "As we prepare for the next major bull cycle, it has become clear that we need to focus on talent density across the organisation to ensure we remain nimble and dynamic" *(Binance Australia)* really means "we are about to fire some of our staff".

- "Humaneering is an emerging applied science with the goal of maximising the actualisation and achievement of individuals, groups, organisations, institutions and other complex systems dependent on human effectiveness" *(Institute of Management Services)* means something like "people are important".

- "We will increase our talent velocity" *(McKinsey)* means "we will train our staff in new skills".

- "Our tax technology automation solutions enable organisations to increase efficiencies and de-risk manual processes, thereby freeing up group tax and finance functions to focus on value accretive tasks rather than repetitive processes" *(PwC)* probably means "our tools will free up time for other tasks, or for reducing staff numbers".

- "I have the utmost confidence in our processes and our systems to not let any of the consultants enter any problematic intersection of those contracts or those arrangements interfering with or having that problematic intersection with a criminal investigation" *(Australian Federal Police)* means something like "the consultants won't be getting any information from us".

It may sound self-evident, trite and even tautological, but the point of communication is (wait for it) – to communicate. Schools need to communicate simply and clearly so that their students and their community grasp the message that is being conveyed. Therefore, it follows that no school would ever use jargon such as this. Or would it?

Unfortunately, much of the professional language that is legitimately used in schools every day may unintentionally come across to some (or many) parents as unintelligible jargon. Terms that many parents struggle to understand include formative assessment, metalanguage, flipping the classroom, differentiated instruction, norm-referenced assessment, rubric, explicit instruction, phonics, STEAM, Essential Learning Standards, scaffolding, closed questions, Socratic seminars, ATAR scores, and many more. It is quite appropriate that educators use such terms in their professional conversations, but they should never assume that such terminology will be understood by non-professionals without substantial explanation.

I would love to say that in contrast with jargon, schools don't engage in euphemisms. However, that isn't true either.

Several decades ago, teachers' comments on students' reports were often brutally honest. These days in most countries, teachers' comments are invariably positive and encouraging, even when students' performances are unsatisfactory (a word that is almost never used on students' reports). Rather than writing "below expectations", teachers are more likely to write "needs improvement" or "developing skills". Rather than writing "needs to pay attention in class" or "misbehaves and doesn't accept correction", reports are more likely to show "has some focus challenges" or "highly sociable". "Constantly late submitting homework" is more likely to be described with "works at his own pace".

I remember a real situation in a school where was I working when one student's end-of-term report had a string of teachers' comments that read "very quiet in class", "needs to contribute more during class discussions", and "if all my students were like him my job would be a dream". The student had left the school at the end of the previous term but all his teachers had felt the need to write something positive, even for a student they were no longer teaching!

While euphemisms (and to a lesser extent jargon) are often used with the intention of softening language or presenting information in a more positive light, they can have harmful consequences when used in schools:

1. **Lack of Clarity and Transparency:** Euphemisms can obscure the true nature of a situation, leading to a lack of clarity and confusion over expectations, policies, and decisions.

2. **Undermining Trust:** When individuals perceive that euphemisms are being used to mask or downplay negative aspects, trust in leadership or institutions may be eroded.

3. **Employee or Student Distrust:** Teachers and students may feel disrespected or patronised if critical issues are not communicated in a transparent, honest, straightforward manner, and this can lead to a deep sense of distrust.

4. **Impacts on Morale:** Euphemistic language can sometimes be employed to try and hide or minimise challenging situations, such as staffing reductions or cuts to academic programs. Such attempts at minimisation may have the opposite effect, inflaming the situation by failing to acknowledge the adverse impacts on individuals.

5. **Ineffective Problem Solving:** In educational settings, effective problem-solving requires thorough knowledge and a clear understanding of issues. However, euphemisms can hinder the clear identification and thus resolution of problems by disguising their true nature.

6. **Missed Opportunities for Improvement:** Effective schools are learning environments where honest, respectful feedback is essential for improvement. When euphemisms are used in performance evaluations or educational assessments, the areas requiring improvement may be obscured, thus hindering personal and/or organisational growth and advancement.

7. **Reduced Accountability:** Euphemisms may be used to shift blame or responsibility away from specific actions or decisions, masking under-performance by responsible personnel and thus informally sanctioning mediocrity and sub-standard performance.

8. **Negative Impact on Culture:** Euphemisms can contribute to a culture of avoidance, where difficult issues are not openly discussed or addressed, thus stifling the healthy and transparent organisational and educational conditions required to nurture the formation of young lives in a school.

In summary, while euphemisms may be employed to navigate sensitive topics, their overuse or misuse in schools and businesses can impede effective communication, damage trust, and hinder the resolution of challenges. Clear and transparent communication is generally more conducive to a positive and constructive environment.

Insight 40

F-shaped reading can help digest reports efficiently

Being a member of a school board or a school's senior executive involves lots of reading. I recently heard of an educational board that had just over 3,000 pages of pre-reading for its monthly meeting.

An essential part of every board member's Duty of Care is the legal obligation to be reasonably well informed and to participate in decision-making. These duties demand reading and understanding the meeting papers. Likewise, School Principals who make a point of signing every student's term report will have many hundreds of pages to read and digest in that one task alone, even before they start reading their subordinates' regular reports, letters from parents, proposed policies and procedures, formal complaints, daily e-mails and all the professional reading that Principals need to understand and manage the rapidly changing educational environment.

Inevitably, board members and school leaders find they benefit from techniques to help them cope with the huge volume of required reading they face. One common – and often sub-conscious – technique is F-shaped reading.

What is F-Shaped Reading?

Eye tracking research reveals that most people scan printed pages, web pages and computer screens in various patterns, the most common being in the shape of the letter 'F'. This means that most people scan the words at the top of a page first, usually getting to end of a headline or sub-heading provided it is not too long. Having scanned the heading, readers commonly move down the left-hand side of a page before moving to the right again when they come to a sub-heading or a line that attracts their attention for some reason.

This pattern of reading forms an F-shape, or in languages that read from right-to-left, a mirrored F-shape.

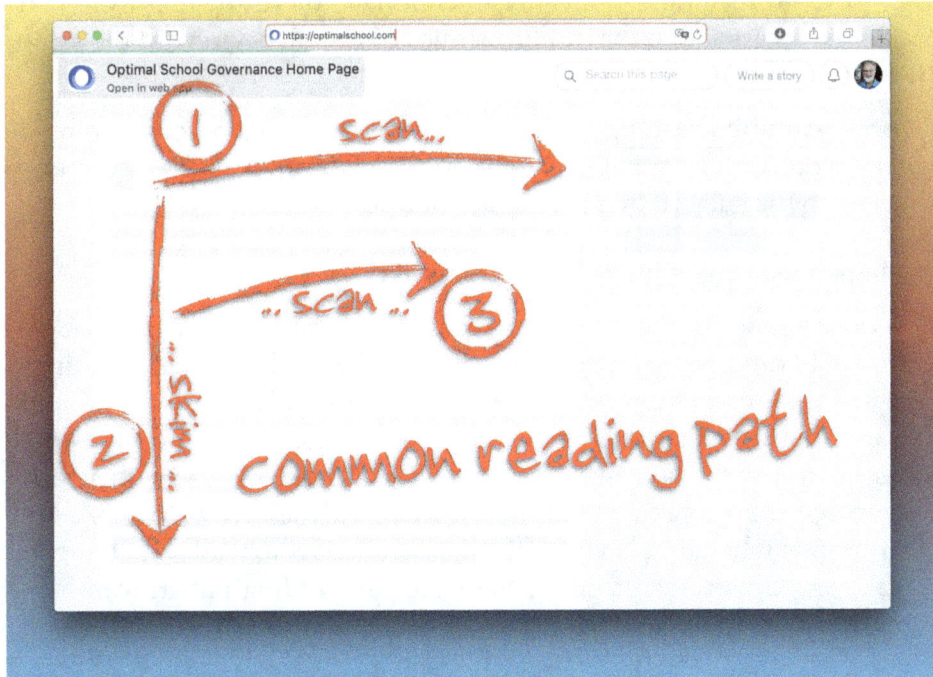

Implications of F-shaped reading

F-shaped reading means that the first lines of text on any page tend to receive more attention than the subsequent lines of text. Furthermore, the first few words at the left-hand end of each line of text receive more attention than words at the other end of the line.

Perhaps that's the approach you are taking when reading this page.

Other reading patterns

Although F-shaped reading is the most common pattern, no-one should assume that everyone follows this route. Among other recognised patterns are the following:

• Leopard spot reading – the reader skips large sections of text while looking for something specific in a seemingly random manner, such as a key word, or bold text, or numbers rather than words, or something specific such as an address or phone number.

• Cake layer reading – the reader scans headings and sub-headings while completely skipping any text or paragraphs between these headers.

- Bypass reading – the reader intentionally omits the first words on each line by assuming that multiple lines of text all begin with the same word or stem.

- Committed reading – the reader takes the time and effort to read every word on every page, usually as a reflection of high motivation, interest in the subject, or a keen sense of duty.

F-shaped reading helps readers and writers

Understanding the F-shaped reading pattern is useful for people who write reports. Knowing that the headline and early sub-headings are likely to receive the most attention, these should be expressed and set out in a way that retains the reader's interest. Doing so raises the likelihood that the text away from the "F" will also be read rather than skimmed. Sub-consciously, busy readers will be trying to make up their minds whether it is worth the time and effort to read something in detail, and thus understanding the F-shaped reading pattern can help both writers and readers alike.

On the other hand, the danger of F-shaped reading is that large portions of potentially important content may be missed by a reader simply because of the way a page is set out. This is a particular danger when reading e-books or other text which has a flexible format on a tablet or mobile phone because the targets of "F-pattern" reading on such devices become unpredictable.

Overcoming the challenges of F-shaped reading

The Nielsen Norman Group in Delaware (USA) has undertaken quite extensive research on F-shaped reading and has developed a helpful set of antidotes to overcome the shortcomings:

1. Include the most **important points in the first two paragraphs** on the page.
2. Use **headings** and subheadings. Ensure they look more important, and are more visible, than normal text so users may distinguish them quickly.
3. **Start headings and subheadings with the words carrying most information**: if users see only the first 2 words, they should still get the gist of the following section.

4. **Visually group** small amounts of related content – for instance, by surrounding them with a border or using a different background.

5. Present important words and phrases in **bold text**.

6. Take advantage of the different **formatting of links**, and ensure that links **include information-bearing words** (instead of generic 'go', 'click here' or 'more'). This technique also improves accessibility for users who hear links read aloud instead of scanning the content visually.

7. Use **bullets** and **numbers** to call out items in a list or process.

8. **Cut unnecessary content**.

Concluding thoughts

Humans are not machines, and their behaviour is not always predictable. The Harvard Rule of Animal Behaviour states "You can have the most beautifully designed experiment with the most carefully controlled variables, and the animal will do what it damn well pleases". The same seems to apply to school board members when they are confronted with a massive bundle of papers to read. To quote the words of the New Zealand nuclear physicist Ernest Rutherford, "The only possible conclusion that the social sciences can draw is – some do, some don't!".

Therefore, we should never assume that every School Principal and Board Member will follow the F-shaped reading pattern when preparing for important meetings. Nonetheless, evidence suggests that a solid majority will follow an F-shaped reading pattern, depending upon individual factors such as motivation, time pressures, personal goals, layout of the formatting and text, and the content they are reading.

Knowing this, report writers can optimise the content and layout of their documents to help readers find and assimilate important content quickly.

Insight 41

Face-to-face or remote?

During the global COVID-19 pandemic, stay-at-home orders in many countries changed the way people work. Workers and students in most internet-equipped countries (together with many school boards) quickly adopted video conferencing and webinars as a substitute for face-to-face meetings and in-classroom teaching. In just four months, one platform (Zoom) saw its number of meeting participants rise from 10 million per day in December 2019 to over 300 million per day in April 2020. Large increases were also reported on other platforms such as Microsoft Teams, Google Meet and Cisco Webex.

Although it was often grudgingly acknowledged that online meetings "were better than nothing, I suppose", meeting on screens rather than in-person proved to be very challenging for many participants. Countless users complained of 'Zoom fatigue', suffering mental and physical exhaustion after spending multiple hours each day sitting and relating to others on screens. Some of the problems were so pervasive that they became memes – "You're on mute", "How do I share my screen?", "I think your daughter has enabled a setting that turns you into a cat", and of course, wearing a shirt and tie above the waist but running shorts below.

There is evidence (see Karl et.al) that webinars and video conferencing privilege high-status and more outspoken attendees in meetings and online classes, they obscure non-verbal cues and body language, and according to Gupta they disadvantage some women who find themselves interrupted and spoken over during meetings. Moreover, it is well known that working from home (which is made possible by online meetings) removes opportunities for relationship building through impromptu meetings and the creative solutions that often arise from chance encounters.

Despite the inherent shortcomings of the format (often exacerbated by lousy wi-fi connections), many employers (including some school boards) see financial benefits in the switch to remote meetings. Travel, office, and workspace costs are reduced or shifted onto employees, students or clients, and the need for expensive real estate is reduced. Leaders of some schools and workplaces speak glowingly of the benefits and intimate that the changes should and/or might become permanent.

One example of this that I know about is a tertiary institution in Australia that has recently converted all its teacher training programs from face-to-face lectures and tutorials into online reading and assignments supplemented by a single two-hour online Zoom class once per fortnight. Clearly, the diverse role modelling and personal interaction that used to be experienced by these aspiring teachers is now impossible, a sad consequence of society's new capacity to cut staffing costs through greater use of remote technology.

If the aim of accessing screens for work or study was simply to soak up content in the form of data and information, then I think the platform could work well PRESUMING (in a pandemic context) that some content is better than no content. However, once we try to convince ourselves that we are genuinely engaging with people or authentically communicating with others by means of these artificial technologies, then we are deceiving ourselves.

In answer to a question at last year's Simone Weil Lecture, the ethicist Scott Stevens described screens as a 'moral prophylactic' in that they give us the sense that we are getting close to other people while not getting close enough to challenge us or cause any danger to us. Engaging with others on screens, he suggests, gives the illusion of doing something meaningful when we are actually not doing anything that is significantly meaningful at all.

Having conducted many online workshops, lectures and meetings during the COVID pandemic, I now refuse to teach or lead workshops via platforms such as Zoom because the experience is so deficient compared with face-to-face encounters – although I do still reluctantly agree to chair and participate in board and committee meetings remotely. When I organise or host such meetings, there are some simple rules I expect:

- The online meeting must be the sole focus of every participant, so no-one should multitask (such as checking e-mails) during the session or allow interruptions by passers-by.

- All attendees should remain on 'mute' while not speaking and avoid interrupting others by raising a hand to create a queue. (Zoom has a waving function that can be monitored, but physically raising your human hand also seems to work well).

- Commit to civility and mutual respect.

- Commit to real breaks, not just the 5-minutes to stretch legs and have a quick toilet break variety.

- No single online session should last more than 90 minutes (unless there is unanimous agreement to an extension for exceptional reasons).

Why am I now reluctant to host workshops or teach remotely online? The simple answer is that I believe it is a sub-optimal way of interacting and therefore shows disdain for the time and effort spent by the participants. The more complex answer explains why I believe this is so, and why it is important for board meetings and gatherings of school leaders to be conducted in person wherever possible.

Everyone knows the impact of being in the presence of another person. We know that the presence of the other person is indispensable

to whatever it is – the words, the ideas, the feelings – that are passing between the two of you. We know this because we are human beings who have inherited the cumulative sum of hundreds of generations of social skills.

Although some people are better at this than others, we all know and understand body language - the various forms of communication that pass over somebody's face, the uncomfortable twitches or the words that are never uttered. We recognise the flash of recognition in somebody's eyes that tells us 'I understood what you just said'. We know the tiny wince of pain, barely suppressed, that says "you're transgressing onto sensitive territory". We know the ways that hurt can be registered without those words being spoken.

In an age of growing reliance upon screens for remote communications, many people seem to have come to the point of seeing close personal proximity as an annoyance or a nuisance. Perhaps this stems from a sense that when you are in the presence of another person, greater expectations and demands are placed upon us.

The psychoanalyst and media scholar Sherry Turkle gave a powerful example of this phenomenon in her 2016 book called "Reclaiming Conversation". She described a crisis she was having with her students at MIT. She described how she would write to her students posing a question, asking them to make an appointment to come and see her so they could discuss it. She found that the students would make up every possible excuse so they could never meet, preferring instead to communicate exclusively through e-mail.

Turkle realised that what was terrifying her students was the vulnerability of having to be in the physical presence of another person and therefore possibly being exposed as 'not quite their best selves'. When communication is by e-mail, the students can edit, manicure, and dress up their ideas up so they are presenting the very best version of themselves, probably appearing far more articulate than they really are in person (especially if they are using AI tools such as ChatGPT). Having come to this realisation, Sherry Turkle insisted "it's the office or nothing".

This is the same rationale I have for "it's face-to-face, or it's nothing". Effective outcomes demand nothing less.

We now exist in an age of screens. Although I appreciate the benefits, I think we are worse off overall for it. The more that teaching takes place on screens rather than face-to-face, the more we are losing something incalculable. Of course, the genie is out of the bottle, but in acknowledging that, I believe we should never use remote on-screen learning as a substitute for being in the physical presence of others.

References:

Gupta AH (2020) It's not just you: In online meetings, many women can't get a word in. *The New York Times*. https://www.nytimes.com/2020/04/14/us/zoom-meetings-gender.html.

Karl KA, Peluchette JV & Aghakhani N (2022) Virtual Work Meetings During the COVID-19 Pandemic: The Good, Bad, and Ugly. *Small Group Research*, 53(3): 343-365.

Stephens, S (2022) 'We do not breathe well': Tending the moral conditions of our common life, *The Simone Weil Lecture on Human Value*, Melbourne: ACU. https://www.acu.edu.au/about-acu/events/2022/november/annual-simone-weil-lecture.

Turkle, S (2016) *Reclaiming Conversation: The Power of Talk in a Digital Age*, New York: Penguin Random House.

Insight 42

Finance officers should be on tap, not on top

"School boards have only one employee, and that is the Head of School".

I first heard this somewhat quirky expression a decade or so ago while I was Head of a large international school in the United States. It doesn't mean that that the Head of School (or Principal, or Director, or whatever term is used to describe the school's CEO) is paid from a separate bank account than the rest of the staff. It means that that the Board directly delegates duties to only one person – the Head – and only one person – the Head – is directly accountable to the Board. In other words, the Head of School is the only official conduit between the Board and the school.

Why did articulating that quirky sentence become necessary? Why was it necessary to state the obvious fact that the Head of School (CEO) is the board's only employee?

The short answer is "finance officers".

Finance officers in schools are known by many quaint and idiosyncratic terms – bursar, accountant, CFO, financial controller, and so on. Because school boards are rightly concerned about financial health, school accountants often find that they have fast access to board members' ears (and hearts), especially on boards that comprise several professional accountants. If this line of communication not handled appropriately, it can undermine the Head's authority. Some school accountants not only know that this is true, they like it and they cultivate it. That is why the expression is so important: "School boards have only one employee, and that is the Head of School".

In any school, finances are a means towards achieving goals. Finances are not ends in themselves. The reason any school exists is to fulfil its mission – its enduring purpose – which usually means a focus on educating its students as effectively as possible.

Financial management is one of the important factors in achieving the mission. Other pivotal factors include the quality of the teaching staff, the facilities, the leadership of the Head, the nature and quality of the curriculum, and so on. However, if the mission ever becomes secondary to financial outcomes, then the school drifts and will quite possibly fail.

As I have often seen in my work with schools, schools that focus on their mission and educational excellence usually find that the finances take care of themselves, whereas schools that focus primarily on the finances find that their education suffers, which in turn leads to failing finances. It's a paradox – focussing on finances leads to poor financial outcomes, whereas focussing on the students and their education leads to strong financial outcomes.

Having said this, it is important to remember that not all Finance Officers are equivalent – the job descriptions of Finance Officers can vary widely from school to school. Some Finance Officers perform as CFOs, whereas others are more focussed on day-to-day operations:

	The CFO	**The Controller**
Perspective	Spends most time looking forward.	Spends most time looking backward.
	What will the next quarter look like? Next year? The year after that?	How did we do last month? Last quarter?
	What are our goals and how do we get there?	How did actual results compare with budget?
Interaction	Deals extensively with people outside the school.	Deals primarily with people inside the school.
	Deals with lenders, business partners and the board through the Head as CEO.	Supervises the accounting staff, interacts with department heads.
	The financial face of the school	Deals with some outsiders such as auditors.
Background	Comes with a variety of previous professional experiences.	Comes from an accounting background.
	In addition to accounting, this may include commercial banking, investment banking, treasury and other finance areas.	
Personality	Must have a high level of self-confidence and excellent communication skills.	Less likely to be an exceptional communicator.
	Needs to be able to discuss financial matters with a non-financial audience.	Has self-discipline, plus organisational and analytical skills.
	Should be articulate, confident and comfortable in front of a crowd.	Not expected to make speeches.

adapted from the work of David Greenbaum, CEO at OnPlan.co

Irrespective of their specific role, however, it is important for Boards and Heads to ensure that the appropriate lines of authority, delegation and communication are never short-circuited. Finance officers may have a special relationship with the Board, but this must never undermine the pivotal, unique authority of the Head of School.

Finance officers should be on tap, not on top.

Insight 43

Firing an employee humanely

In Insight 27, I wrote about the difficult challenge faced by boards and school leaders when they need to deal with poorly performing employees. It is essential to understand relevant policies and appropriate procedures, but it is also important to acknowledge that every situation is likely to have unique components that can muddy the purity of the process.

Consider this hypothetical situation, which is based on a true story although the names and titles have been changed. Let's imagine that you were an internal applicant for the position of Principal in your school, and you were successful. You are now the new Principal.

Unfortunately, one of your colleagues (Kim – a unisex name so you aren't tempted to draw any gender stereotypes) also applied and was unsuccessful. Kim seems unperturbed and remains outwardly friendly to the staff in general, but you have no difficulty seeing that that Kim is inwardly seething with anger at the apparent injustice of the decision. Kim treats you civilly but coldly.

You decide to diffuse the situation and re-build your working relationship, so you give Kim some additional leadership responsibilities and a more elegant professional title – Senior Director of Curricular and Co-curricular Integration.

Kim has a new sense of power and authority, but quickly begins to misuse it. Kim starts to undermine you by making disparaging comments to the staff about you behind your back, and even seeks out some board members to convey (confidentially and with a heavy heart, of course) "the staff's concern" about the direction you are taking the school as its new Principal.

Through these actions, Kim's professional unworthiness to be appointed Principal is being demonstrated both to you and the board that appointed you. In the months ahead, Kim misses deadlines, fails to answer your e-mails, is absent from your regular meetings, shows declining overall performance and effectiveness, and yet strides around the school campus with all the airs and authority that befit a Senior Director of Curricular and Co-curricular Integration.

Soon collateral damage begins to surface as a consequence of Kim's attitude. One of the stars of the school's teaching staff, your Head of Mathematics, announces he is leaving to go to a competitor school, confiding to you that his main reason is that he can no longer work with Kim. You soon learn of similar decisions by other young staff who the students admire and respect, and who have huge potential as future educational leaders.

Meanwhile, Kim's poor performance is increasing your workload as Principal as you seek to 'plug the gaps' and overcome deficiencies in Kim's work. Many of your own priorities have to be delayed as you fight to keep the school functioning effectively.

You KNOW that Kim needs to go but you feel the timing isn't 'quite right' – even though you have heard the old adage a hundred times: "No manager ever says I'm glad I waited so long to fire that person". After all, you tell yourself, there are so many things that Kim hasn't documented that a departure now could cause administrative chaos.

The other complicating factor is that you are a nice person. Like most school leaders, you are a people pleaser. You want to make other people happy. And like many school leaders, you are so busy making other people happy that you forget to include yourself.

However, the good news is that one day you have a revelation – you read an article on the Optimal School Governance website (actually, this article!) that shows you a way to fire-sack-dismiss-terminate Kim humanely and compassionately.

Step 1: Let an under-performing employee fail.

This may sound counter-intuitive and contrary to your view of leadership, but the alternative is either for you to cover for the shortcomings of the employee (which reduces both your professional effectiveness and the performance of the school as a whole), or else other people in the school have to take up the slack. Either way, it is an unsustainable strategy. It is better for the person's shortcomings to be visible so you can document them; if you continue to cover up the shortcomings, then you can't document them.

Step 2: Initiate a performance review.

Performance reviews should seek documented input from a diverse group of people who have a variety of working relationships with the person being reviewed. If conducted effectively, a performance review will provide the most significant, balanced evidence to support your intended dismissal of a non-performing employee. However, for this to be so, it the Review should be conducted by a politically neutral external expert with no "skin in the game" who can report honestly and fairly without fear or favour. When the report has been completed, issue a copy to the employee and request a written response to its findings.

Step 3: Get expert advice.

It is important to get external expert advice from a lawyer and/or an HR expert before initiating any action that may be contested legally.

Step 4: Have counselling support on hand.

Even with the best of intentions and the purest heart, severance meetings sometimes become adversarial, contested and a source of grief

and anguish. Having a trained counsellor on hand (but out of sight) who has been thoroughly briefed on the situation may provide much-needed support following the meeting.

Step 5: Bring a support person.

When you schedule your meeting with the person in question, don't hide the topic (i.e. you intend to follow up their performance review) and give them explicit permission to bring a support person if they wish. Equally importantly, you should have a support person with you, partly to act as a witness to the conversation in the event of a subsequent dispute, but also because it will give you the courage that you may need during the meeting. Surprisingly, I have heard about many of these meetings where the Principal "feels sorry" for the under-performing employee and they still remain on the staff at the conclusion of the meeting. That outcome is far less likely if you have a support person with you to keep you 'on script'. (One Principal tells the story of terminating an employee who became so angry that she – the employee – began to dribble uncontrollably, and then told the Principal that her husband had a heart condition and this action was going to kill him. The Principal recalls that having another person sitting there helped greatly during both the meeting and the long debriefing session that followed the meeting).

Step 6: Be direct, stick to the facts, keep it short, agree on timing for 'The Announcement', and walk the employee out the door after offering counselling support.

Being a school leader is hard, and few tasks are more confronting than having to dismiss an employee. However, with a genuinely compassionate attitude, a sense of fairness and justice for the entire organisation, sound externally-generated documentation and thorough preparation, this difficult task can be conducted in a way that serves the greatest good for everyone involved.

In the end, if an employee is a poor fit for your school, you are not really being a "good people pleaser" by struggling to make the dysfunctional situation work. It is far better – and more humane – for everyone if you can give your (soon-to-be-ex) employee the opportunity to find a better fit for their talents and skills set elsewhere.

Insight 44

Free riding

Why should I vote when it is most likely that my vote will not make any difference to the outcome? Why should I pay my taxes when they are an insignificant droplet in the national budget? Why should I switch off my lights when doing so will have a negligible impact on climate change? In other words, why should I not 'free ride' on the decent actions of others?

These wide-ranging questions have direct relevance to the dynamics of school board meetings through the concept of 'free riding'. Before we can understand the relationship between school boards and free riding, we should first explore the concept of free riding more deeply.

The Free Rider problem arises because there are some issues and situations where the scale of collaboration is so large that the contribution of any individual is negligible. In such situations, although an individual may very much want a particular outcome, the reality is that one person's input has almost zero impact. Therefore, from the individual's point of view, it seems entirely rational to Free Ride.

Global warming is a great example of free riding. At a planetary scale, we understand if everyone collaborated to reduce harmful emissions, if we stopped cattle raising (which generates more global warming greenhouse gases than all the world's transportation, as measured in carbon dioxide [CO_2] equivalent) and stopped cultivating rice (which also produces enormous quantities of greenhouse gases such as methane and nitrous oxide), we could achieve some extremely desirable outcomes.

And yet, at the scale of the individual, it makes no practical difference whatsoever to global warming whether I, for example, leave my light turned on or not, or whether I choose to eat rice for dinner. The same arguments could be made about paying taxes, contributing to trade unions, or voting. It seems to be a genuine philosophical paradox. People collectively want a certain outcome, but at the individual level, it is actually more rational to enjoy the benefits of the sacrifices others make without sacrificing personally to achieve the desired outcome.

Does this mean that Free Riding might be morally offensive? If 100 people walk across a lawn in a single track, it will probably kill the grass. But if one person walks across a lawn, there will be no discernible impact. Therefore, which pedestrian committed the offensive act that tipped the balance and started to kill the grass? This is similar to the age-old philosophical question of 'how many grains of sand are needed before we have a pile of sand?'. There is clearly a cut-off point, but in reality it is impossible to define, or even know. It seems absurd, for example, to define a pile of sand as comprising, say, 500 grains of sand or more, and then try to justify convincingly why a collection of 499 grains could not be a pile - this is the problem of vagueness.

In the situation of global warming, a similar situation can be said to exist. It is most unlikely that the emissions from one coal-based power station make any significant difference between the earth warming or not. There is a threshold of impact beyond which changes will occur, but it is a vague band, and our collective fear seems to be that perhaps we may be approaching that threshold, if we are not already there. And yet, anyone can reasonably say that their light bulb, or their power station, or even all the power stations in their own country, are unlikely to make much difference, given the enormous scale of the issue.

Does it therefore follow that people are free to act in a way that is environmentally unfriendly? In Kantian ethics, which supports 'the Golden Rule', the solution seems easy - I should act in a way that I want all others to act. Since I don't want others to leave their light bulbs on, then neither should I. Or, to express it a little more formally, Kant would argue that in deciding whether a certain action is ethical or not, we need to ask ourselves "what would be the consequences if everyone did it?", and the answer to the question should govern our behaviour. If the answer to the question is something inherently bad, such as chaos, anarchy, extinction or disaster, then quite simply, we shouldn't do it! In reality, of course, it is never as easy as this.

In a book published in June 2008, Richard Tuck claimed that when considering free riding, we should probably differentiate between those cases where the threshold of making a difference is genuinely vague (such as building a pile of sand or global warming) and those situations where there is a clear point at which a difference or a change occurs, even though any individual's actions might be miniscule, such as voting. When I vote, and if I have supported the winning candidate, then mathematically it is actually quite likely that my vote was part of the bundle of votes that helped to determine the outcome. I know personally that this was so in a recent election where I was registered to vote in the country's most marginal electorate, and the final result came down to just 143 votes. In that case, all but the last 143 votes helped to get the candidate elected, so to say that these votes were inconsequential would be absurd. My vote may not have been necessary to affect the outcome, but in conjunction with the votes of others, it would have been sufficient to affect the result.

It is sometimes argued from a moral or religious perspective that we do have a duty to act in a certain way even if others are not acting similarly or towards the same goal. If we were to ignore the religious or cultural element of this argument, then the sense of duty of the individual would become much more questionable. If everyone else is not acting in a way that will achieve a certain goal through collaboration, but without collaboration the goal will not be achieved, then pragmatically it becomes irrational or even preposterous for an individual NOT to go with the majority and Free Ride. This suggests that the argument of Darwinists such as Richard Dawkins that morality is not rooted in religious beliefs may be simplistic at best, and downright wrong at worst. In practical terms, though, the apparent rationality of Free Riding certainly highlights the importance of collaborating and networking with others if genuine results are to be achieved, rather than claiming for example, that having changed our light bulbs, then we have "done our bit" to address global warming!

I have been thinking about the Free Rider problem following some of my recent work with several school boards where I have been focussing on the dynamics of their board meetings and other interactions, especially as they relate to self-interest versus the common good.

In Insight 59, I note that although there is no universally ideal size for a school board, there is a 'sweet range' that is neither too small nor too big. When a board has too few members, there is a risk of burnout due to excessive pressures upon the small number present. Furthermore, the range of perspectives available during discussions on small boards is artificially blinkered. On large boards, arriving at a consensus position can become frustratingly difficult and protracted, and board members may feel they don't need to contribute or even attend board meetings because there are others who will rise to the need.

This is where free riding can become a problem for a board.

A board's authority is collective. The board only has power when it meets and makes collective decisions (whether by consensus or majority). When the board is not meeting, no individual board member (with the possible exception of the Board Chair through delegated powers) has any official authority whatsoever over the school.

In this sense, school boards are counter-cultural in that societies around the world are increasingly valuing self-interest over collective responsibility. This is not a new trend (it was discussed at length by Machiavelli in the early 1500s), but it is accelerating.

However, there is no place for self-interest on school boards. Members have a duty to place the school's interest at the centre of their decision-making, even if (and especially if) it conflicts with self-interest, or the interests of friends, family, associated organisations, and so on. That is why it is essential that schools have robust policies on conflicts of interest and related parties transactions.

On a larger board, a dissenting board member can employ the free rider principle to make a 'protest vote' against a popular proposal with the clear expectation that their one vote will not affect the outcome. Free riding is far more difficult on a smaller board. Irrespective of the size of the board, however, once a vote has been taken and a decision is made collectively by the board, a dissenting board member MUST adhere to that decision. Indeed, every board member has a duty to support board decisions in public, the only alternative being to resign from the board if the decision represents an irredeemable conflict of principle or conscience.

The free rider principle reminds us that when one member disagrees with a majority position while it is being considered by the board, voting against the proposal usually doesn't change the outcome of a vote. Therefore, no harm is done in expressing a contrary viewpoint, especially if it creates a worthwhile discussion despite its ultimately fruitless outcome – provided the dissenter does not subsequently undermine that decision outside the board meeting. This is one reason that it is normally inadvisable to record the names of dissenters in board minutes, or to record any names against the individual arguments made during a discussion at a board meeting.

So to return to the 'free rider' problem – the dilemma I now have in my own mind is why should I write a long article if it is unlikely that my words will make any difference to any outcome?

The answer, I hope, is that this article will serve to improve the dynamics of board meetings among more than just a few of my readers.

Insight 45

Generational differences affect educational leadership (in MEDCs)

A few years ago, I visited a makeshift settlement of the nomadic Mursi people in the Omo Valley near the border between Ethiopia and South Sudan. As I was undertaking field research for a Geography textbook I was writing at the time, I did some preparatory reading and learned that my journey was "not for the pusillanimous". I also read that this "is a two-footed leap into true African wilds. You'll battle roads that eat Land Rovers for brunch, wage war with squadrons of mosquitoes and tsetse flies, and sweat more than you thought humanly possible."

Because of the time of year, I didn't encounter any mosquitoes, but (by law) I did need to have an armed guard travel with me as an escort. I asked, half-jokingly, whether the armed escort was for wild animals or hostile people, and I was told "for hostile people, of course", as though such a response should have been self-evident.

Needless to say, not many outsiders choose to visit the Mursi people. However, those who know me well will understand when I say "it was a fabulous experience that I will never forget".

Life for the Mursi people today is barely different from the way it was 500 years ago. The women still wear their distinctive lip plates, education still focuses on traditional story-telling by the elders, rites of passage such as 'korda kôma', 'jônê chibin', the 'donga' and lip piercing remain timelessly unchanged, and ceremonial duelling (a form of ritualised male violence) remains popular among the unmarried men.

The absence of electricity (and the internet) means Mursi parents never have to stop their children playing video games or watching TikTok videos. Younger Mursi people never order food online for home delivery. In the absence of birth control, young women are having children at about the same age as their mothers did, and their grandmothers before that, and their great-grandmothers, and so on.

'Generational change' is an almost meaningless term for the Mursi people and for thousands of other societies around the world where time-honoured traditions continue to define daily life.

The same cannot be said for more globalised societies. In the MEDCs (More Economically Developed Countries), generational change is so rapid that we identify each generation by a name and a list of (highly generalised) characteristics:

- **The Greatest Generation** (born 1901-1927) is (or was) characterised by resilience, duty, self-sacrifice, patriotism, and a strong sense of collective spirit.
- **The Silent Generation** (born 1928-1945) is shaped by the experiences of the Great Depression and World War II, and characterised by traditionalism, loyalty, and a strong work ethic.
- **Baby Boomers** (born 1946-1964) were born during the post-war baby boom, and tend to value hard work, success, and loyalty to institutions.
- **Generation X** (born 1965-1979) is known for independence, adaptability, and scepticism, shaped by technological advancements and cultural shifts.
- **Millennials** (born 1980-1994) are often seen as tech-savvy and socially conscious people who prioritise work-life balance, diversity, and innovation.
- **Generation Z** (born 1995-2012) has been completely raised in a digital age, and so is marked by technological proficiency, individualism, relativism, political polarisation, sexual fluidity, and a global perspective.
- **Generation Alpha** (born 2013-2029) represent the youngest generation, with early indications of being technology-immersed, socially aware, and never having experienced a world without strong interconnections.

Unfortunately, there is a growing tendency in MEDCs to label generations other than one's own using derogatory terms like "clueless boomers" or "lazy millennials". Like all stereotypes – racial, religious, national, neighbourhood, gender – the labels are almost always inaccurate because they over-simplify and negate individual people's character by grouping unlike individuals into amorphous categories.

The innate character, personality and upbringing of every individual person matters greatly when defining each person's identity. Nonetheless, it isn't surprising that 'big picture' differences do emerge from generation to generation (in MEDCs) due to external, objective influences such as historical events, communications, pandemics, wars, macroeconomics, migration, technology – the list is long.

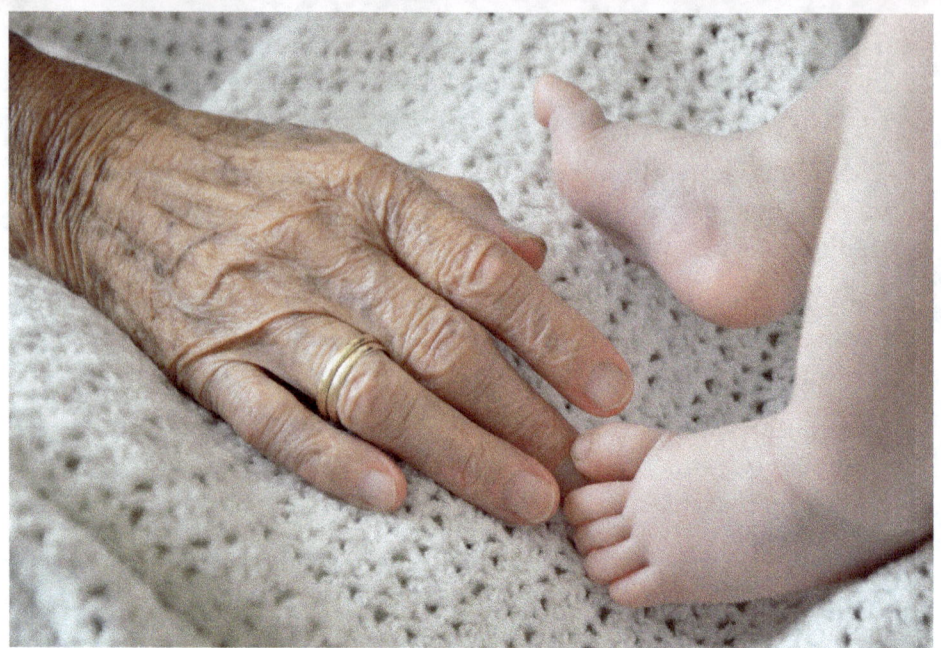

What makes a boomer a boomer, a silent a silent, or a millennial a millennial?

A recent book by Psychology Professor Jean Twenge titled *Generations* makes a strong case that technology is the consistent, fundamental factor leading to generational change. Although the data in her book is heavily US-centric, the case she makes is clearly applicable to MEDCs in general. She traces the cumulative impact of technological innovations such as the radio in the 1930s, television in the 1960s, personal computers in the 1980s, laptop computers and the internet in the 1990s, mobile phones in the 2000s, social media in the 2010s and generative artificial intelligence in the 2020s.

During most of the twentieth century, these changes resulted in increased accessibility to information, more widespread dissemination of popular culture, easier connectivity, rising aspirational materialism, and greater democratisation of publishing rights. In more recent years, the impact has shifted into more negative territory and now includes blurring of work and personal life, growing mental health issues, less integrated family life, increasing political polarisation, job displacement, spread of misinformation, greater sensitivity to personal image, rise of the precarious gig economy, and a stronger sense of being "always connected". Jonathan Haidt's recent book *The Anxious Generation* affirms this hypothesis with compelling, deeply worrying, research-based evidence.

Perhaps the most significant overall macro-consequence of generational change in MEDCs is rising individualism combined with declining personal resilience. This is demonstrated by strong negative correlations between chronological age on one hand, and mental health issues, cyberbullying, individualism, aspirational materialism, declining respect for authority and reduced sense of duty on the other.

Twenge claims that changing technology use is the dominant factor in causing this generational transition. She states (on page 39):

"As the technological leaps of the post-war era accelerated, individualism grew: TV allowed people to see others' perspectives and experiences, jet and space travel made the rest of the world seem closer, and the shift away from manual labour opened up more job opportunities for women. Gradually, an emphasis on individual rights began to replace the old system of social rules organised around race, gender, and sexual orientation."

Television created an environment of high expectations though the glamorous way it portrayed the world, especially through mass advertising. The rise of the internet has amplified this trend to a deafening level, particularly through the widespread embrace of social media. It is not difficult to understand how such significant technological changes in a short period of time (evolutionarily speaking) would lead to significant generational differences.

Understandably, generational differences are a common topic of discussion among teachers in schools. These discussions may be humorous, or perceptive, or a deep expression of frustration, or most frequently, a combination of all three. This is to be expected because teachers are almost invariably members of a different generation to the students they teach, and therefore everyday surprises, annoyances and misunderstandings can be expected to become an obligatory part of the teaching experience.

Generational differences in classrooms are fairly well understood. Less well understood – and even less frequently acknowledged - is the impact of generational differences between the school's leadership and the staff, or between the school's board and the leadership.

What tensions could arise between a school's leadership and the staff, or between the board and the Principal, when there are significant generational gaps? Might generational differences lead to conflicts and misunderstandings when unstated assumptions and expectations are never articulated? I have no trouble thinking of six possibilities:

1. **Communication styles.** In general, younger staff members prefer digital communication whereas older leaders tend to favour more personal face-to-face interactions. It is easy to see how misunderstandings can arise if these preferences are neither acknowledged nor accommodated.

2. **Work-life balance and personal resilience.** The research is clear that younger generations place a higher priority on work-life balance and are more determined to protect their off-work time than older generations often expect. Younger people are more likely to demand flexible working arrangements which may conflict with the highly organised environments of schools. Statistics show that declining personal resilience is increasingly expressing itself in MEDCs when staff unilaterally take stress leave when they feel they are being asked to do too much work or turn up for duties at inconvenient times.

3. **Technology use and integration.** Younger staff are often keen to embrace the perceived efficiency benefits of technology, while older staff and some school leaders are less comfortable with expensive innovations that they fear may erode autonomy, confidentiality and personal responsibility.

4. **Respect for Leadership and Authority.** One of the most significant generational shifts in recent decades has been the declining respect for leadership and authority among younger people. This trend shows in declining religious observance and escalating cynicism for (usually elderly) politicians in an increasingly polarised environment which is less and less tolerant of contrary points of view. The challenge for schools is that the same attitudinal shift may overflow into the working environment of schools as frustration over older political figures morphs into a generalised intolerance of older people in positions of authority. Younger staff often prefer collaborative, inclusive, flat leadership styles, while older leaders are often more inclined towards traditional hierarchical structures that operate through an assumed sense of duty. Younger staff members tend to value – and expect - participatory decision-making, while older leaders may prefer more authoritative approaches that might be labelled "top-down". When misunderstandings and contradictory assumptions underpin a school's decision-making processes, strained relationships and debates over authority structures are inevitable. Similarly, misalignment of expectations may occur when there is a generational gap between the Principal and board members. In such situations, power struggles and conflicts are highly likely to emerge if the implications of generational differences are not acknowledged and articulated.

5. **Expectations Regarding Recognition and Feedback.** Younger staff members tend to expect and appreciate regular feedback and acknowledgment, while older leaders may have grown up in an era when constant praise was neither expected nor emphasised. Consequently, older managers may struggle to understand (and therefore satisfy) the seemingly insatiable appetite for constant praise and acclamation demanded by younger staff members.

6. **Approaches to Change Management.** Throughout history, younger people have tended to be more adaptable to change, whereas older people (including school leaders and boards) may place greater emphasis on the value of tradition and established practices. As with unstated assumptions in any area, unstated assumptions regarding change management are likely to result in resistance and conflict.

None of this is new. In about 1274, Peter the Hermit preached a sermon that included this reflection:

"The world is passing through troublesome times. The young people of today think of nothing but themselves. They have no reverence for parents or old age. They are impatient of all restraint. They talk as if they alone knew everything and what passes for wisdom with us is foolishness with them".

Much earlier, the Greek philosopher Aristotle (384-322BC) stated:

"They [young people] have exalted notions, because they have not been humbled by life or learned its necessary limitations; moreover, their hopeful disposition makes them think themselves equal to great things –8 and that means having exalted notions. They would always rather do noble deeds than useful ones: Their lives are regulated more by moral feeling than by reasoning -- all their mistakes are in the direction of doing things excessively and vehemently. They overdo everything -- they love too much, hate too much, and the same with everything else".

Even earlier, the Greek philosopher Socrates (469-399BC) stated:

"The children now love luxury; they have bad manners, contempt for authority; they show disrespect for elders and love chatter in place of exercise. Children are now tyrants, not the servants of their households. They no longer rise when elders enter the room. They contradict their parents, chatter before company, gobble up dainties at the table, cross their legs, and tyrannise their teachers".

The solution to generational tensions and misunderstandings in schools is to employ a range of staff who represent as many generations as possible and to appoint Board members from several generations.

Generational diversity in senior leadership and board governance will almost always create a more tolerant, empathetic, dynamic, humane, inclusive and effective decision-making environment that not only reflects the world's diverse and rapidly changing MEDCs, but also equips its students with the diverse skills required to function effectively.

Paradoxically, traditional societies such as the Mursi have understood and valued the importance of multi-generational understanding for centuries.

References:

Haidt, J (2024) *The Anxious Generation: How the Great Rewiring of Childhood Is Causing an Epidemic of Mental Illness.* London: Allen Lane.

Twenge, JM (2023) *Generations: The real differences between Gen Z, Millennials, Gen X, Boomers and Silents – and what they mean for America's future.* New York: Atria Books.

Insight 46

Getting Governance Right: Advice for new schools

At its best, effective governance can provide a strong foundation and clear direction for a school to flourish and reach heights that other schools simply dream about. At its worst, poor governance can destroy a school by fermenting mistrust and insecurity, destroying morale (and careers), creating a toxic environment that prevents students ever reaching their potential. It is a sad reality that many of the issues that arise in schools stem from well-intentioned but poor or ineffective governance. Governance is one area that schools MUST get right.

Poor governance is often the last shortcoming to be addressed in an under-performing school. This is because many boards and their individual governors are reluctant to self-analyse or accept criticism. It is easier for governors to blame others or spend money on professional development for managers and teachers than to face the challenge of self-improvement. Having said that, by far the preferable pathway is for a board to establish itself with clear objectives, policies and practices that should prevent the issue of poor governance ever arising.

The board's work of governing a school is a collective, or group, responsibility. Boards only have power and act authoritatively when they meet together and make formal decisions. Outside a meeting, no governor has any formal authority beyond that of any other citizen or parent, as governors do not govern a school as individuals. However, when a board meets, either in person or through remote means, its decisions become binding. The board is ultimately responsible for the legal compliance, financial viability and philosophical direction of the school. In order to achieve these ends, boards are invested with all the authority they need to enable a school to function effectively, including the most important of all their tasks, appointing the Head.

It is impossible to over-emphasise the importance of a positive, professional relationship between the board and the Head. This relationship should operate in a spirit of teamwork and genuine partnership where the board's role is governance, complementing the Head's role of management. Governance (the board's responsibility) is setting the mission, vision, financial base and direction of the school, while the role of management (which is led by the Head) is to ensure that the board's goals and directives are implemented effectively. In effect, the Head is the CEO (Chief Executive Officer) of the school, with all the authority and accountability this implies. Ideally, governance and management respect each other's boundaries and work coherently together to achieve common goals that will enhance the welfare of students, teachers, parents and staff to the greatest extent possible.

The power and authority of governance should be clearly separated from the power and authority of management. Congruence of purpose and clear communication are thus vitally important. The board delegates all day-to-day and operational matters to the Head, and through the Head to the management team that is responsible to the Head. In return, the Head is accountable to the board for the achievement of the board's goals and directives. A strong Head and a strong board working together in partnership is a formidable combination to achieve effective outcomes for a school.

The board's key functions in governing the school are:

- creating, sustaining and continually reviewing the mission statement, which is an expression of the school's enduring purpose;
- selecting, appointing, supporting and evaluating the Head of School, who is the one and only employee with direct accountability to the board;
- providing the resources required by the school to function effectively under the school's management;
- ensuring the school complies with all legal regulations and statutes;
- establishing general policies in areas that affect the school's viability, reputation and direction; and
- managing the board's own business such as meetings and annual evaluations.

It follows from this that the single most important relationship in a school is that between the Head and the Chair of the Board, because this relationship is the interface between governance and management. When the board is not meeting, the Chair is the conduit of communication between the board and the Head, and through the Head, to the school.

The Head-Chair relationship works best when communication is frequent, frank and open. Depending on local conditions, meetings may occur in person on a regular (say, weekly) basis, or perhaps by telephone or video chat such as Zoom, FaceTime, etc. Head-Chair meetings should be conducted on a 'no surprises' basis, so that any significant incident which may have occurred in the school, or any potential threats facing it, are known by both the Chair and the Head prior to a board meeting and prior to information being released publicly through media outlets or social media.

Although the Head-Chair relationship should be close, it must also remain professional. The Chair and the Head must not become so close that other board members become jealous or feel disempowered.

Schools are not like most businesses. Parents and teachers can become very passionate about their children's education, which leads to the danger of short-circuiting of communication channels. A school can have only one Head, and the Head is the only official channel for communications between the board and the school. Although CFOs normally attend board meetings and have a close relationship with the Board Treasurer, their primary line of accountability is to the Head, and governors must never allow a CFO (or any other employee) to undermine the Head's authority with the board. Similarly, governors who were appointed by outside organisations, parents or alumni, owe a primary duty of loyalty to the board. They thus have a responsibility to respect the confidentiality of board meetings and always to make decisions that are in the school's best interests.

Boards become collectively dysfunctional when the boundaries between governance and management are blurred, when communication ceases to be full and frank or has become short-circuited, or when seeds of mistrust are sown. When disagreements arise between the board and the Head, it is important to remember that the board always retains ultimate authority. The board hires the Head, but it can also dismiss the Head. A Head can never dismiss a board.

In situations of disagreement, the board can either direct the Head or dismiss the Head. The Head has a duty to support, follow and implement the board's collective decisions, and if this proves impossible for whatever reason, the consequence is to resign. Conversely, the board has a duty to support the Head publicly at all times, and if it cannot do this, then there are few alternatives other than dismissing the Head. It is said that very few Heads survive their third Chair because of the changing directions of new board leadership. Anecdotally, about 70% of Heads do not leave their positions of their own volition or on their own terms. This represents a failure of effective governance, although of course public relations are usually handled well for the sake of the school's stability and reputation.

Most school boards comprise highly dedicated, idealistic men and women who are passionate about the school's success. Governors are

often time-impoverished, but it is almost impossible to find any school governor who does not strive towards achieving the very best for their school. And yet, boards can and do become dysfunctional over time, either collectively or because of individual problem trustees. One of the reasons that board governance goes awry is that even good boards create their own comfort zones over time without realising it, as governors slip into cosy patterns of operation, form alliances, adopt conflict avoidance strategies or appoint an insufficiently diverse membership. Significant dangers arise when boards do not rigorously and dispassionately self-evaluate or fail to analyse the performance of each governor regularly in a critical manner.

In a new school, it is important to ensure that board structures and operations are established soundly in accordance with established best practice. When a school board's governance becomes sub-optimal, it is wise to call in a neutral outsider to help before the situation becomes desperate. Perhaps governors and/or the Head can identify the changes that would enhance the board's effectiveness, but that doesn't mean the governors, and especially the Head, should initiate or activate these necessary improvements. Whatever the outcome of any process of board reform or enhancement, someone will probably feel aggrieved, and it is preferable that any blame be directed to an outsider rather than to the Chair, the Head or a governor. A good rule in change management is to try not to burn political capital unnecessarily.

An even better rule is to avoid the need for uncomfortable change by getting governance right from the very beginning.

Insight 47

Good. Fast. Cheap.
Can schools have all three?

School leaders and the members of school boards are almost invariably individuals with a huge generosity of spirit. Unless they have been seriously misinformed, very few people have ever entered teaching as a profession because they think it will make them wealthy, and even fewer serve on school boards for personal gain. To work in education is to serve others before oneself. It is a vocation, not just a job.

As a generalisation, school leaders and the members of school boards also tend to be some of the most idealistic people in our society. Perhaps that is to be expected, because the future of our society is quite literally in the classrooms, corridors and playgrounds of today's schools (in the absence of a global pandemic, that is). School boards, Principals and teachers are performing one of the world's most important jobs – building our future – and that is not a comment I make lightly.

Perhaps unexpectedly, there can be a downside to this idealism, this generosity and this desire to make our world a better place. The downside is that individual and collective passion and enthusiasm may outstrip the capacity to achieve the high aspirations that people in education almost invariably set for themselves.

This sometimes presents a challenge when a new Strategic Vision is being developed. A good Strategic Vision should spring from and reflect the ethos and mission of the school, be achievable, be ambitious and contain an element of 'stretch', it should contain criteria for determining success, and be concise.

When developing a new Strategic Vision, School Boards and Principals understandably can get very excited about the wonderful things that start to emerge on the horizon. One danger that can arise amidst the excitement in any school that is trying to "stretch" its resources (and frankly, that is every school!) is to want everything to happen quickly, cheaply and to a high standard.

Realistically, that is an almost impossible target that is setting up the school and its new Strategic Vision for failure. As the diagram

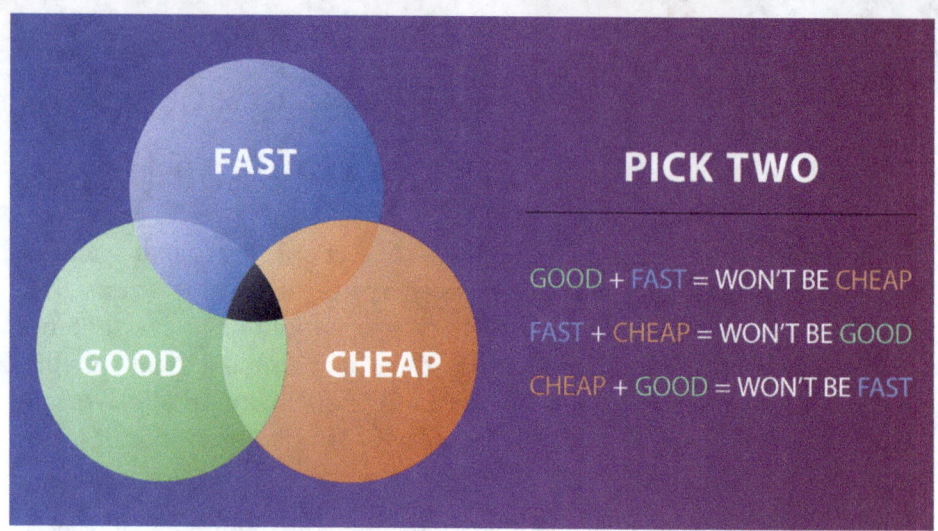

suggests, from the tripartite goal of good-fast-cheap, you have to pick two of the three.

If the outcome is to be both good and cheap, it won't be fast.

If the outcome is to be both fast and cheap, it won't be good.

If the outcome is to be both good and fast, it won't be cheap.

This compromise is a harsh reality that is often lost in the enthusiasm and idealism of planning a school's future. It demands a thorough examination of priorities so that when the inevitable compromises are required, decisions made reflect a consensus of priorities.

"Isn't it possible to have all three?" is the inevitable question, or as the headline to this article expresses it: "Good. Fast. Cheap. Can schools have all three?"

Experience and Betteridge's Law suggest that the answer must be "no".

Insight 48

Governing is not the same as governance

Most board members and school principals are aware of the fundamental difference between the board's role (governance) and the principal's role (management). Both roles are important components in the leadership partnership, and it is essential that the respective roles are never confused or blurred. This is discussed in Insight 104.

On the other hand, the difference between governance and governing is less clearly understood by many school board members.

In its essence, school governance focuses on power, developing the philosophical framework for the institution, overseeing implementation and achievement of philosophical and strategic goals, and taking responsibility for legal, financial and other fiduciary duties.

On the other hand, governing focusses more on operational processes. The process of governing involves implementing and enforcing certain rules and norms, ensuring compliance, and supervising the work of others. In this sense, it could be argued that implementing the processes of governing (as opposed to governance) is the responsibility of management.

Because governance concerns power, it also involves accepting responsibility. That is why school boards are ultimately responsible for everything that happens in a school – bad as well as good. This may seem a bit unfair at first, given that boards are supposed to oversee the school's operations without becoming directly involved in the day-to-day operations (which would be governing, not governance).

Of course, it is not really unfair because the board has all the power it needs to ensure completely effective operations in every area of the school. We know the board has this power because it is the board which appoints the one key person – the Principal – to whom the responsibility (and thus the accountability) is delegated to ensure everything in the school is done to the high philosophical, ethical, legal, financial and quality standards required by the Board. This explains why the relationship between the board and the Principal is by far the most critically important relationship in the school – it is the link between governance and governing.

In accepting responsibility for the power it has, boards need to be prepared to be scrutinised and held accountable for decisions they have made. This can take many forms depending upon the constitutional structure of the school. Some school boards report to regular (though often infrequent) gatherings of stakeholders, such as parents, alumni and staff – always with the Principal in attendance of course. Other school boards report directly only to the school's owner, whether this is a company, a church, an NGO, an individual, the government or some other organisation, usually at an Annual General Meeting (AGM), although sometimes through other reporting channels. Boards of schools that accept government funding and/or which require external accreditation or registration will, of course, also have reporting obligations to those authorities.

Whatever reporting mechanism is used, and whatever structures are in place, two key concepts are essential for both governance and governing – honesty and transparency. This is not dream-like idealism; it is essential. If either honesty or transparency is lost in a school, that school's future will almost certainly spiral downwards to become precarious at heart-breaking speed.

Insight 49

Handling disrespectful remarks

The famous painting above by Danish artist Wilhelm Marstrand shows a scene from Miguel de Cervantes' famous 17th century novel, *Don Quixote*. In the novel, the nobleman Don Quixote recruits a simple farm hand named Sancho Panza as his squire. Without giving away too many spoilers, there are many lovely examples of discussions between Don Quixote and Sancho Panza in which (to quote Salvador de Madariaga) "Sancho's spirit ascends from reality to illusion, while Don Quixote's declines from illusion to reality".

One such discussion includes the barbed compliment shown in the overlay to Marstrand's painting above. Sancho is telling Quixote that his words have been the manure that has fertilised the dry soil of his intellect: "Some of your Grace's wisdom has got to rub off on me, for land that's dry and unfruitful will give you good crops if you put on enough manure, and weed it, and till it. I mean, your Grace's words have been like manure spread on the barren ground of my dry and uncultivated mind" (*Don Quixote*, Part 2, Chapter 12). This comment is both a compliment and a sneer. Sancho Panza is telling Don Quixote that he has benefitted enormously from his conversations and adventures with him, but at the same time, he is essentially telling Don Quixote that he is 'full of it' (the 'it' being manure).

Unlike Sancho Panza's and Don Quixote's interactions, schools should be places where the bests ideals of behaviour and speech are modelled consistently by adults. Students should expect to be treated fairly and respectfully by teachers, and teachers should have the same expectations of each other, their line manager, their Principal, and the Board.

Anyone who has ever worked in a school or served on a school board will have experienced occasions where this ideal deviates from reality. Encountering subtle yet disrespectful comments in the workplace can be challenging, and they often take the listener by surprise. Disrespectful remarks, often disguised as jokes, sarcasm, or casual observations, will often create discomfort, undermine confidence, threaten workplace morale, and erode the school's (including the board's) sense of unity and purpose.

An underhanded comment which may seem polite or innocuous at face value can also contain a hidden meaning, one which usually has a negative connotation. Examples in a school situation might be something like:

"It must be nice to be the Deputy Principal's favourite. You can show up late whenever you want."

"That's a really interesting way to approach that task. It's not the way I would have done it, of course."

"I'm not sure how you won that Teachers' Award, but congratulations."

"That's a colourful outfit. Do you think your students will take you seriously when you show up wearing it?"

Addressing comments such as these effectively requires a combination of assertiveness and professionalism. Here are some tactical responses to handle such situations with grace and authority based on the work of UK Consultant Psychiatrist in Neurodevelopmental Disorders, Dr Neetu Johnson.

1. The Mirror Response

One effective way to address a disrespectful comment is by reflecting it back to the speaker. Asking **"How am I meant to respond to that?"** directly calls attention to the inappropriate nature of the comment and shifts the discomfort back to the speaker. This approach redirects the direction of the conversation without either escalation or retraction, thus encouraging composed self-awareness and prompting the speaker to reconsider the words used.

2. The Therapist Approach

Encouraging self-reflection can be a powerful tool in diffusing inappropriate remarks because it can lead to backtracking. A response like **"How do you feel when you say that to me?"** invites the speaker to examine their motivations and the impact of the words chosen. This approach often leads to the individual reflecting, and then retracting or reconsidering their statement, fostering a more respectful dialogue.

3. The Expectation Challenger

Disrupting the intent behind a comment can be an effective way to reveal its inappropriateness. Asking **"What response were you hoping to get?"** forces the speaker to analyse their true intentions. This technique shifts the focus of the conversation by exposing the underlying negativity, thus discouraging and disempowering any additional negative comments.

4. The Professional Redirect

Maintaining a focus on professionalism can help steer the conversation away from drama and negativity. A response such as **"Let's focus on finding solutions instead"** signals that you are not willing to engage in 'unconstructive' discourse. This approach reinforces a culture of respect and efficiency by redirecting the discussion productively towards a focus on finding solutions.

5. The Clarity Seeker

Individuals sometimes make remarks without considering their implications. Responding with **"Could you explain what you mean by that?"** compels the speaker to break down and elaborate their comment, often revealing the inappropriateness of the comments made. This method encourages clarity and accountability, deflecting negativity while discouraging vague, disrespectful statements.

6. The Boundary Setter

Establishing clear professional limits is essential for fostering a respectful work environment. A straightforward response such as **"I prefer to keep our discussions constructive"** sets a firm professional boundary. This statement communicates the idea that negative or unproductive remarks will not be entertained, reinforcing a culture of professional respect.

7. The Power Pause

Silence can be a powerful tool in communication. **Simply maintaining eye contact and pausing** after a disrespectful comment can have more impact than any verbal response. The strongest response may be not to respond! This approach signals confidence and composure, highlighting the awkwardness of the situation without engaging in conflict.

Of course, trying to address inappropriate comments without the help of others will not always be successful, and further action may be required by approaching a line manager or even filing a formal complaint.

Nonetheless, by responding to disrespectful comments with respectful professionalism, individuals can maintain control over their workplace interactions and set the tone for constructive and respectful conversations. Establishing these communication strategies not only fosters a positive professional environment but it also reinforces and models personal confidence, authority, and care for others – in other words, leading by example.

Insight 50

Hat, haircut or tattoo

James Clear, author of the popular book *Atomic Habits*, describes three types of decisions using the metaphor "hat, haircut or tattoo":

"Most decisions are like hats. Try one and if you don't like it, put it back and try another. The cost of a mistake is low, so move quickly and try a bunch of hats.

Some decisions are like haircuts. You can fix a bad one, but it won't be quick and you might feel foolish for a while. That said, don't be scared of a bad haircut. Trying something new is usually a risk worth taking. If it doesn't work out, by this time next year you will have moved on and so will everyone else.

A few decisions are like tattoos. Once you make them, you have to live with them. Some mistakes are irreversible. Maybe you'll move on for a moment, but then you'll glance in the mirror and be reminded of that choice all over again. Even years later, the decision leaves a mark. When you're dealing with an irreversible choice, move slowly and think carefully."

Clear's metaphor provides a powerful framework for school boards. Many decisions made at the governance level in schools involve choices between short-term initiatives, medium-term structural decisions, and long-term cultural shifts.

A "hat" represents a temporary, easily reversible decision such as piloting a new digital learning platform for a semester. If it doesn't work, the Board and the Principal can simply remove the "hat" and try something else.

A "haircut" suggests a more significant but still reversible decision, like introducing a new timetabling model. Undoing this change would take time, but the original decision to introduce the new timetable would not have to have been permanent.

A "tattoo" represents a fundamental, usually irreversible shift such as deciding to build a new classroom to provide additional teaching capacity in the school.

The "hat, haircut or tattoo" metaphor encourages a school board to be intentional and transparent about the weight and permanence of its decisions. For example, when a board considers rebranding its logo or renaming the school, it must recognise this as a "tattoo" as it is a decision which goes to the heart to the school's values and identity.

"Tattoo" decisions such as this demand a profound level of investigation, consultation, and thoughtful discussions.

On the other hand, introducing a new communications app for parent-teacher interactions might only be a "hat", being useful to try but certainly not something that defines the school's identity. By categorising decisions in this way, school boards can manage risk, align resources appropriately, and maintain trust with stakeholders who want to know whether a change is temporary or transformative.

The "hat, haircut or tattoo" metaphor also helps board members to maintain a strategic mindset which empowers them to lead with clarity and purpose. It should foster a culture of reflection, where board members don't simply ask "What will be the immediate impact of this decision?" but rather "What does this decision say about our long-term future?" This medium-to-long term lens helps boards to avoid reaction-ary policy making and instead encourages a more strategic approach to governance. This is especially important during times of crisis, such as responding to a pandemic, when distinguishing between a "hat" (temporary safety protocols), a "haircut" (hybrid learning models), and a "tattoo" (establishing a distance learning support facility) helps the board to act swiftly while maintaining long-term vision.

Ultimately, the "hat, haircut or tattoo" metaphor is a simple but helpful tool that can equip boards with the perspectives required to navigate seemingly complex decisions, ensuring their decisions use resources wisely to serve both present needs and future generations.

Insight 51

How frequently should your school board meet?

I was Principal of five schools in four countries over 25 years. Two of those schools had monthly board meetings, or more accurately 11 meetings per year as there was no meeting during the long summer break. Two other schools' boards met eight times each year, which represented two meetings per term. One school's board met four times per year (twice per semester).

The boards that met monthly typically had meetings that lasted between five and seven hours. Meetings of the boards that met eight times per year typically lasted about four hours. The board that met four times per year always had meetings that lasted for precisely 2 hours 15 minutes (10:00am to 12:15pm – several members would stand up and leave at 12:15pm even if someone was speaking at mid-sentence so they would not be not late for their lunch appointment).

I'm sure you can see the pattern here. Schools that meet more frequently have longer meetings than board that meet less frequently, counterintuitive though this may seem.

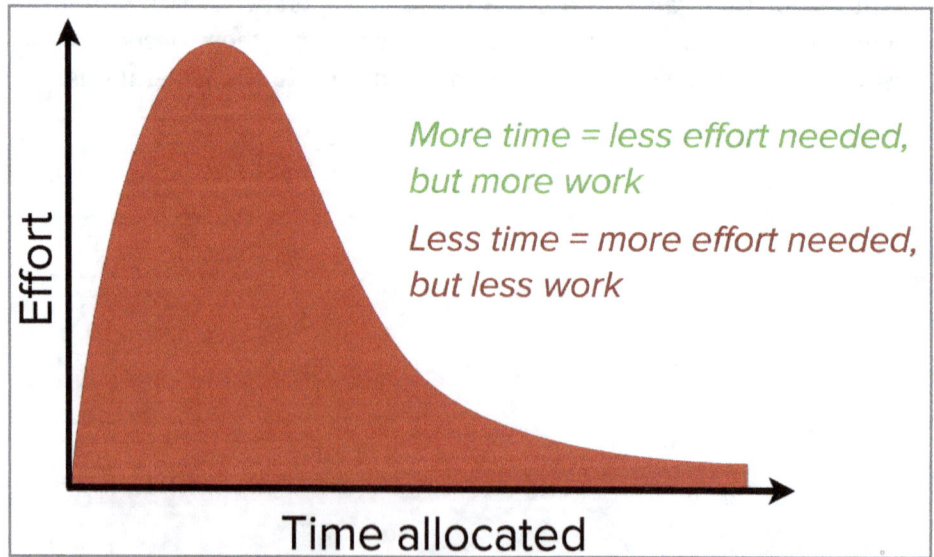

This suggests that Parkinson's Law may be true – that the amount of work in a school board meeting expands to fill the time available. This can be expressed in several alternative ways – the Stock-Sanford claim is that "If you wait until the last minute, it only takes a minute to do". Mark Horstman said that "Work contracts to fit in the time we give it".

There is no single rule for the ideal frequency and duration of a school board meeting – every school is unique, so every school has different needs.

Inevitably, young schools usually require more board meetings than older schools, simply to deal with the process of establishing the school, developing policies and procedures, planning building programs, and so on.

I can also personally verify that attendees' productivity declines after about four hours, irrespective of the quality of Chinese takeaways or microwaved pizzas that are provided at the meeting.

I believe that for most schools, monthly meetings are probably too frequent. We can see this by considering the cycle underpinning monthly meetings. Consider the cycle of (say) the October board meeting, scheduled for the first week of the month:

3rd week of September: The Chair starts to think about the agenda, and the Principal starts to write the report.

4th week of September: The Principal's board report is complete, presentations are ready, guest presenters have been arranged, and all the documents/materials have been distributed to members via e-mail, via a secure website or platform, or (sometimes, even today) as a pile of paper.

1st week of October: The day of the board meeting arrives. The board meets, and the Principal basks in the glow of appreciative feedback.

2nd week of October: The Principal sends out a follow-up e-mail to the board with answers to any questions that arose during the meeting, and begins to implement decisions made by the Board and delegated to the Principal during the meeting.

3rd week of October: The monthly board meeting planning cycle starts all over again.

In between this flurry of activity, the Principal is expected to do everything else that is involved in running the school – conducting meetings with the management team, meeting with parents, conducting tours with prospective parents, writing policies and documents, leading collective staff meetings, conducting assemblies, appointing, supporting and evaluating staff, handling crises, ensuring compliance with government regulations and accountability requirements, leading the process of change management and reform to ensure the success of initiatives, picking up rubbish in the playground (not a joke!), actually caring for the welfare and educational formation of the students, and fulfilling all the duties and tasks delegated by the Board. (Note that this is just an indicative list – it is certainly not an exhaustive one!).

As you have probably gathered, I am not a big fan of monthly board meetings. They CAN work, but only if the problematic consequences can be addressed effectively. What are the challenges to be addressed?

Challenge No.1 – The Principal spends so much time planning for the board meeting, including writing up the report, and then following up the decisions made in the board meeting, that it can be difficult to find sufficient time to perform the role description (i.e. do the real job of running the school). Given the timeframes listed above, when can the Principal focus on student and staff welfare, think strategically, evaluate potential initiatives, and so on?

Challenge No.2 – Monthly board meetings tend to follow highly predictable, routine structures, because there is little time to consider creative alternatives such as inviting staff visitors to share the challenges they are facing, inviting outsiders to provide governance-related professional development for board members, etc.

Challenge No.3 – High frequency meetings permit discussions to drift into operational matters that are really the purview of the management team, whereas less frequent meetings exclude time for such distractions, meaning that the board focuses exclusively on governance matters – as it should! At its worst, having excessive time at board meetings can invite micromanagement by the board on issues such as the quantities of homework given to students or the quality of food in the cafeteria to the neglect of generative strategic thinking.

Challenge No.4 – Some boards meet monthly to avoid having committees. The common thinking behind this idea is that every member of the board should be fully involved in every facet of board business. This is a recipe for long meetings that deal with minutiae, often spending extended periods discussing issues in which several members have neither the expertise not the interest to contribute. It is generally far more efficient to allow committees to "get into the weeds" and then bring well-considered recommendations to the full board meeting for approval.

How might we address these challenges?

Having made the point that every school is unique and every board's needs reflect this uniqueness, I would encourage boards that meet monthly to consider meeting less frequently. Board members invariably want to 'add value' to the organisation. They are also almost always time impoverished. Therefore, to maximise the impact of the time board members contribute, and to give the Principal the time and flexibility to perform their job effectively, I recommend that boards consider meeting twice per term (eight times per year), or bi-monthly (six times per year).

If the experiment works and the board finds it is achieving better results and staying 'on task' by spending less time, everybody wins. It might even lead to consideration of meeting just once per term (four times per year), assuming of course that time is also set aside for an annual strategic thinking retreat.

Insight 52

I can't believe we used to …

I follow the social media feeds of Graeme Codrington, a well-known and highly respected South African professional speaker who may (or may not?) be a distant relative of mine. His often-provocative discussions are invariably stimulating and thought-provoking as well as entertaining and informative. During his keynote presentation at the Professional Speaking Association annual summit last year, he posed an intriguing question: "What can we imagine saying in the future, when we look back, to complete the sentence 'I can't believe we used to …'"?

As an educator who began working in schools in the 1970s, and whose own experiences as a school student spanned the 1960s (and a little beyond), my brain immediately started flowing with answers to his question as it applies to schools, all based on my own first-hand experiences. For example, I can't believe we used to …

- Allow smoking in the staff room and in the playground for teachers on duty.
- Cane boys for being late to class, having their shirts out, or not having their socks pulled up properly.
- Forbid female staff from wearing red dresses because it might excite the boys, or shiny shoes because the students might see inappropriate reflections.
- Humiliate misbehaving students by making them wear a pointed dunce cap and sit on a stool in the corner.
- Make boys swim naked in the school's pool because the filtration system couldn't handle lint from their swimming costumes.
- Require girls to kneel in a line with their hands behind their backs at the front of the stage to check the length of their skirts.
- Turn a blind eye to students insulting one another using racist, sexist, ableist or ethnic slurs.
- Construct metal playground equipment on hard, concrete surfaces without any overhead shade.

- Spend (waste?) countless hours of classroom time getting students to perfect their cursive handwriting.
- Require students to dissect dead frogs in biology classes.
- Schedule compulsorily gendered subjects (cooking for girls, woodwork for boys) and allocate students to subjects by ability (Latin for the bright students, Geography for the so-called less intelligent).
- Organise the school library using handwritten or typed catalogue cards.
- Have class sizes of 42 (my experience as a 1st year teacher in the late 1970s) or 84 (some parts of China today).
- Prohibit Physical Education teachers entering the staff room on the basis that they were not academic staff.
- Pretend that there is such a thing as values-neutral education.

Following my reflection on the past, I was ready to turn my mind to Graeme Codrington's question – "What can we imagine saying in the future, when we look back, to complete the sentence 'I can't believe we used to …'"? I imagined myself as a commentator on education in, say, 2065, and I could see myself claiming "I can't believe we used to….":

- Rely so heavily on standardised testing.
- Organise schools with rigid, inflexible timetables.
- Treat mental health as a peripheral issue.
- Be so confused about the levels and direction of appropriate use of technology.
- Provide students with food we knew to be unhealthy in the cafeteria or tuck shop.
- Allow students to claim pride in their identity or appearance rather than their achievements.
- Treat teachers with minimal respect even though their work is the key to forming the future of our society.
- Surrender the school's innovation and creativity to the demands of government bureaucrats with little to no educational background imposing mediocre outcomes-based specifications.

and perhaps most significantly of all:

- Think that schools can achieve their potential without periodic independent external culture reviews, or that school boards can function effectively without regular professional development on governance and periodic performance reviews.

We know that values in societies around the world are changing rapidly. Ideas that were once acceptable are no longer acceptable, and practices that were once taboo are now widely accepted. For example, the top-rating television series "Succession" could not have been made in the 1970s, just as "All in the Family" and "Fawlty Towers" could not be made today, all because of changing views of the types of language that were (or are) acceptable.

When you reflect on today's schools and education, how do YOU think people 40 years from now will complete the sentence "I can't believe we used to … '"?

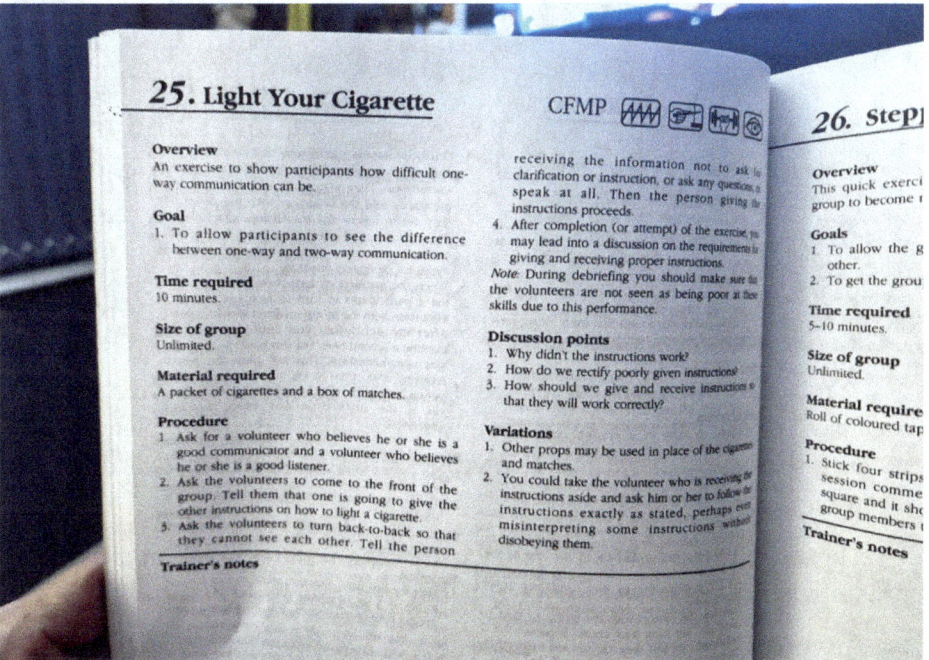

Remarkably, this training book for senior executives was only published about 20 years ago.

Insight 53

Idealism and pragmatism in school leadership

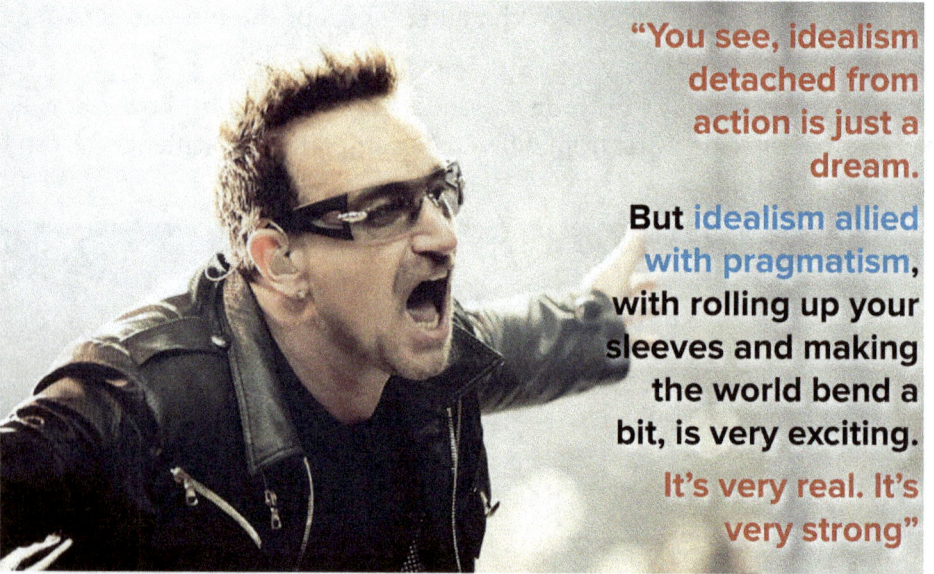

"You see, idealism detached from action is just a dream. But idealism allied with pragmatism, with rolling up your sleeves and making the world bend a bit, is very exciting. It's very real. It's very strong"

"You see, idealism detached from action is just a dream. But idealism allied with pragmatism, with rolling up your sleeves and making the world bend a bit, is very exciting. It's very real. It's very strong".

These are not my words, but those of the Irish activist musician and philanthropist, Paul David Hewson, better known as Bono.

Anyone who has worked in schools can easily identify staff who are the idealists on one hand and the pragmatists on the other. School leaders who are idealists will often be criticised for "making life difficult", while those who are pragmatists are likely to be criticised for their apparent "lack of consistency". The one common factor is that every school leader can expect to attract criticism!

In reality, it is far too simplistic to suggest that idealism and pragmatism are opposing virtues that compete to attract the attention of those who work in schools, including members of school boards and the senior management. The psychologist Erik Erikson, who is known for introducing the term "identity crisis", developed an eight-stage theory of psychosocial development that helps us understand why idealism and pragmatism do not fall on a simple two-dimensional spectrum".

Erikson's Psychosocial Stages

Stage	Basic Conflict	Virtue	Description
Infancy 0 - 1 year	Trust vs mistrust	Hope	Trust (or mistrust) that basic needs, such as nourishment and affection, will be met.
Early childhood 1 - 3 years	Autonomy vs shame / doubt	Will	Develop a sense of independence in many tasks.
Play age 3 - 6 years	Initiative vs guilt	Purpose	Take initiative on some activities – may develop guilt when unsuccessful or boundaries overstepped.
School age 7 - 11 years	Industry vs inferiority	Competence	Develop self-confidence in abilities when competent or sense of inferiority when not.
Adolescence 12 - 18 years	Identity vs confusion	Fidelity	Experiment with and develop identity and roles
Early adulthood 19 - 29 years	Intimacy vs isolation	Love	Establish intimacy and relationships with others
Middle age 30 - 64 years	Creativity vs stagnation	Care	Contribute to society and be part of a family
Old age 65 onward	Integrity vs despair	Wisdom	Assess and make sense of life and the meaning of contributions.

Source: https://www.simplypsychology.org/erik-erikson.html

According to Erikson, humans progress through eight stages of psychosocial development from infancy through to old age. At each stage, there is a conflict between two opposing states that shapes the person's personality. Resolving these conflicts satisfactorily leads to virtues like hope, will, purpose, and wisdom. Failure to resolve the conflicts leads to outcomes like mistrust, guilt, role confusion, and despair. Pragmatism can be a person's easy 'short-cut' to dealing with the basic conflicts at each stage of the process. On the other hand, the more difficult process of successfully completing each stage should give rise to a healthy personality based upon integrity.

At this point, I need to indulge in a short autobiographical reflection. For 12 years before I was first appointed as a School Principal, I served as Head of Geography in a Jesuit school in Australia. I didn't fully realise it at the time, but those 12 years were foundational to my professional formation and preparation for later school leader-ship. During those 12 years, I learned by watching, listening and observing the brilliant examples of fine educators who were steeped in a set of traditions, principles, practices, and philosophy developed assiduously during almost 500 years of running schools across the globe.

Of relevance here, one of the many lessons I learned was the importance of remaining steadfast to the values of the school – in other words, maintaining integrity. As incubators of young lives, schools are often messy places behaviourally and relationally. Situations arise that can be dealt with in one of two ways – EITHER speedily, summarily and pragmatically, OR by staying true to the ideals of care and justice for each individual, which means, of course, more slowly and painstakingly.

Every situation I observed in that school was resolved in the second manner – that is, through the lens of idealism rather than pragmatism. In that school, the core values meant something profound, so in practice they were never sacrificed to pragmatism or convenience. I was deeply impressed by this unwavering supremacy of core values, and I adopted the same principle myself during the subsequent decades of my own principalships.

As a school leader, adherence to idealism often meant taking difficult decisions rather than slipping into the easy seduction of pragmatism.

It is not easy to resist the demands of a large donor who insists on interfering with the daily running of the school, but it is important to do so.

It is not easy to discipline the son of a board member who has engaged in gross misbehaviour just a few weeks before his final examinations, but it is important to do so.

It is not easy to withstand pressure from the CFO who is a close friend of the Board Treasurer and wants his best friend promoted into a position for which he is completely unqualified, but it is important to do so.

I could cite many more examples, but you get the point. Heads of School are often confronted by the pressure to act pragmatically when their idealism compels them to act with integrity.

As I have written in Insight 101, values define the identity of any school, and therefore should be the foundation of every action taken in that school. Of course, a school isn't a sentient being. When we talk about the "school's values", we mean the enduring values of the school's founders and current owners, overseen by the Board, and delegated through the Head of School to the staff to be implemented.

Given the supreme importance of a school's values in defining its identity, it follows that wherever possible, schools must have as much autonomy as possible to recruit teaching and non-teaching staff who not only embrace the school's values, but are excited to promote them. In an international school, it is very likely that a teacher who is intolerant of certain cultures or ethnicities will sooner or later undermine the school's mission. In a school that is faith-based, employees who do not embrace that faith would either have to suppress their own beliefs or act hypocritically if they are to avoid undermining that school's mission.

Many schools find themselves with employees who do not authentically embrace the school's values. Maybe they once embraced the values – they will almost certainly have claimed to do so during their job interview – but either their personal values have shifted, or they sense that the school has undergone mission drift. This is where pragmatism may start to dominate or even overwhelm idealism.

In 1962, the former Chinese leader, Deng Xiaoping, famously said "It doesn't matter whether a cat is black or white, as long as it catches mice it is a good cat". It was a powerful appeal to pragmatism that contrasted with his rival Mao Zedong's hard-line ideological purity. In

Mao's view (to paraphrase Deng), the colour of the cat is supremely important; it must be red!

In the everyday busyness of leading schools, it is easy to imagine a Head of School sitting at her desk, surrounded by reports, budgets and unfinished correspondence, looking wistfully through her office window at the vibrancy of children from diverse backgrounds in the playground outside, holding hands, seemingly without a worry in the world. Could there be a sharper real-world contrast between the freedom of optimistic idealism and the prison of pragmatism imposed by extrinsic demands?

Realistically, school leaders (whether board members or senior managers) need to find a balance between idealism and pragmatism. Idealism is futile if it can't be implemented, just as pragmatism is dangerous if it leads to mission drift. I would urge that the mix should not be 50:50, but the balance should be heavily weighted towards idealism if school leaders are to fulfil their duty to enhance the school's mission and values.

The former US Secretary of Defense, Caspar Weinberger, seems to agree with me. In a speech delivered in 1983, he stated "In the end we cannot choose to be prophets without plans, pragmatists without a moral purpose, idealists without some means of preserving those ideals, or enthusiasts for less than the most noble of causes."

It should not surprise you to learn that Casper Weinberger's mother was a teacher.

The photo of Bono used as a base for the lead image on page 248 is by Peter Neill, CC BY 2.0 https://creativecommons.org/licenses/by/2.0, via Wikimedia Commons.

Insight 54

Improving the sustainability of small schools

Few schools are as small or as basic as the one shown in the photo below. Comprising just two small rooms with straw on the floor for matting, no glass in the windows, sheets of corrugated iron for doors, thin bamboo thatching for walls, and having no furniture, this school is administered by the congregation of the tiny Bethel Church, located beside the Wamena-Kurulu Road in Punakul village of Libarek District in the remote Highlands of West Papua (formerly Irian Jaya), Indonesia. I visited on a Sunday, which explains the absence of the school's 30 students despite the presence of the two teachers.

Anyone who works in a small school knows what magical places they can be. Class sizes tend to be small, classroom instruction tends to be individualised, management has immense flexibility to respond to local needs, and the close-knit sense of community is palpable because everyone knows everyone else by sight if not always by name. Many small schools are destined to remain small because they serve the needs of geographically isolated communities or sections within larger communities that have specific social, ethnic, religious, disability or other needs and preferences.

On the other hand, small schools can face significant challenges that are seldom encountered by larger schools. There are often fewer opportunities for career advancement available to the staff for example, and more limited sporting and academic challenges available to the students.

For the sake of a definition, I see a "small school" as one that has 300 or fewer students in a combined primary-secondary setting, or 200 or fewer in a stand-alone primary or secondary setting. Although small schools do not account for a large proportion of overall students' numbers, they do comprise a significant proportion of the total number of schools in most countries around the world, such as 39% of independent schools in Queensland (Australia) and almost the same proportion (38%) of independent schools across the United States.

Perhaps the biggest challenge faced by small schools is the existential challenge of viability – maintaining their existence on a sustainable basis. When I refer to sustainability, my background as a geographer comes to the fore – I define "sustainability" as the capacity to continue functioning in the present form in perpetuity. For a school, sustainability therefore embraces financial sustainability, demographic sustainability, regulatory sustainability, governance sustainability, administrative/ operational sustainability, and sometimes even physical sustainability.

Several of these "sustainabilities" are interwoven, and it is possible to identify five key challenges that most small schools must confront to maintain sustainable viability.

Challenge 1: School fees. For any school that is reliant on income from fees, it is inevitable that fees must increase at least at the general rate of inflation in the wider economy if the school is simply to maintain its financial position. If median school fees are not rising at a rate which at least keeps pace with inflation, then the quality of educational provision must decline (in the absence of new alternative income sources). There is no easy solution to this challenge, although one possibility is to generate new auxiliary revenue sources, such as renting facilities like the auditorium or gymnasium to outside organisations. Another possibility is to add programs for the wider community such as child-care, adult education courses, vacation camps, and so on, that use existing spaces on the campus out of normal hours to offset some operating expenses, and perhaps also create new opportunities to market the school and increase enrolments.

Challenge 2: Staff salaries. Like school fees, staff salaries must remain competitive within the wider "market" for a school to survive. However, statistics in most countries around the world show that over the past decade or so (including the COVID-19 pandemic), staff salaries in schools have not kept pace with the rate of inflation. Under such circumstances, it is little wonder that many schools are struggling to attract and retain a high-quality staff, and this is especially so for small schools in remote areas. Solutions are difficult to find. Some school boards have considered entering into consortium agreements with other nearby small schools to try and pool staff, but difficulties with scheduling and travel often seem to create insurmountable barriers. Other school boards have considered forming consortium agreements with other schools to cover services such as health care, salary sacrificing benefits, child-care, and grounds maintenance to free up resources that can be diverted into competitive salary and benefits packages for staff. Unfortunately, to the best of my knowledge, there have been no effective, long-term, sustainable examples of this concept in practice.

Challenge 3: Financial planning. It is good practice for every school to develop forward-looking (say, five-year) financial plans. Such planning is especially important for smaller schools that have less "fat" or "wiggle room" (to use two non-technical but widely understood terms) than larger schools. Boards must have data-based financial information if they are to achieve an appropriate balance between income on one hand, and recurrent and capital expenditure on the other. Despite their evident importance, many small schools seem not to have developed these plans, or if they have been developed, they aren't adequately updated and maintained, arguably because the school's leadership is so busy addressing more immediate needs. The sad reality is that well-kept financial records, accurate minutes of meetings, and records of leadership team meetings are notably absent in schools which have become non-viable and are thus forced to close. The solution here is fairly straightforward – do not neglect financial planning at either board or management level, even in small schools. Develop, maintain and use a workable five-year plan, and eventually work towards developing a sound 25-year financial plan.

Challenge 4: School facilities. When finances are tight, it comes as no surprise that small schools struggle to find sufficient resources to expand, renovate, or even maintain their current facilities. Pressure on boards increases as deferred maintenance become more and more urgent and difficult decisions must be made about which projects are to be made a priority and which are to be delayed further or abandoned. The pressures become increasingly acute as the school matures and its facilities age and deteriorate. Clearly, school facilities must be maintained in good order for legal, health and safety reasons (not to mention aesthetics). Young schools must resist the temptation not to set aside funds for future maintenance or to short-change depreciation in the annual budget. Schools that are heavily in debt or do not have deep reserves of funding might consider renting facilities until they are able to build up their financial reserves. Having said that, it should be remembered that owning infrastructure does provide the potential to generate extra revenue by renting school facilities to outside groups.

Challenge 5: Enrolments. For small schools, failure to achieve enrolment targets can quickly create a life-or-death situation. Even minor fluctuations in enrolment numbers represent large percentage changes for small schools, with consequent implications for fee income, staffing requirements and government support. For such schools, it is essential to have a clear understanding of the school's mission – its enduring purpose. Why was the school started and why is its continued existence important? Which students' needs can be met more effectively by THIS school than any other? If the school's mission can be articulated clearly to community, then enrolments are much less likely to decline, all else being equal. Clearly, meeting enrolment targets is critically important in meeting financial targets, which in turn are the means of ensuring the school's continuing viability. Most small schools present a compelling value proposition to parents – a value proposition based on its mission and a caring learning environment where every student is treated as an individual who is loved, known and valued. The best advice to maintain enrolment numbers is to make sure everyone knows what the school stands for, what it offers for the students entrusted into its care, and to make sure every promise made to parents is fulfilled abundantly.

Insight 55

Intentional Cultural Change

Culture is created; it is not an accident. That doesn't mean culture is always intentional (unless neglect or inertia can be classified as 'intentions'). Culture is expressed through the ordinary, permissible actions of everyone in the school, not by the aspirational rhetoric of senior management or the ambitions of a strategic plan. Nonetheless, school boards and the senior leadership are ultimately responsible for the culture that pervades 'their' school because they possess all the authority needed to change culture intentionally – if they choose to exercise that authority.

Schools everywhere in the world possess a shared culture that is quite unlike any other type of organisation. The mission of schools is centred on long-term results that focus explicitly on transmitting knowledge and values rather than goals for the next financial statement or appraisal cycle. The outcomes of schools' work may not be seen for several decades, and even then, their value may be easier to describe in words than to quantify in numbers.

Perhaps the most significant distinctive characteristic of schools relates to the people who work in them. In general, teachers share a strong service ethic and desire for job security. They seldom express a thirst for risk and competition. They work co-operatively, but they love autonomy, a characteristic that often require patience and improvisation on the part of school leaders. Staff in schools understandably and justifiably want higher salaries, and yet they react negatively to proposals for merit pay. Teachers share a strong collegial/communal ethic which means their primary motivation tends to be achieving qualitative rather than quantitative outcomes – or to express it in another way, most teachers believe that many things which count cannot be counted.

If we look at the typical classroom in Victorian England shown in the photo on the next page, we see a large class size by today's standards, a rigid seating layout and teacher-dominated instruction. Today's classrooms might have smaller student numbers (in most parts

Classroom in England, 19th century.

of the world), but philosophically they still share many features of classrooms a century ago.

This suggests that change is often difficult in schools. As a father of four children, a grandfather with thirteen grandchildren, and someone who has worked in and with schools for five decades, I feel I am qualified to make this bold statement: the only people who really like change are babies with wet nappies.

Classroom in Ghana, today.

It is said that implementing change is more difficult in schools than almost any other type of organisation with the possible exceptions of families and religious organisations. Teachers invariably demand to know details of "why?", "what?" and "how?" for any proposed change.

Resistance to change in schools can present a significant barrier to reform. Whenever a school board introduces a new strategic plan or the Principal introduces a new policy, change is an inevitable consequence. Change has always been a feature of education, but today's challenge for school leaders is ensuring that change is intentional, deliberate, directional, supportive of the school's mission and vision, while also being sensitive to different viewpoints and predispositions.

Unless a school is conducted in a dictatorial, authoritarian manner, managing what is often a complex process of change can be a daunting proposition for the school's governing body and senior management. In any change process, there are usually five types of people involved:

- **Innovators** – people who are ahead of change and who address the future.
- **Change agents** – people who seek knowledge and understanding; the executors.
- **Pragmatists** – people who want practical skills and focus on utility and application.
- **Sceptics** – people who demand "show me" and thus address unasked questions.
- **Traditionalists** – people who honour and value the past, and thus appreciate the school's core values.

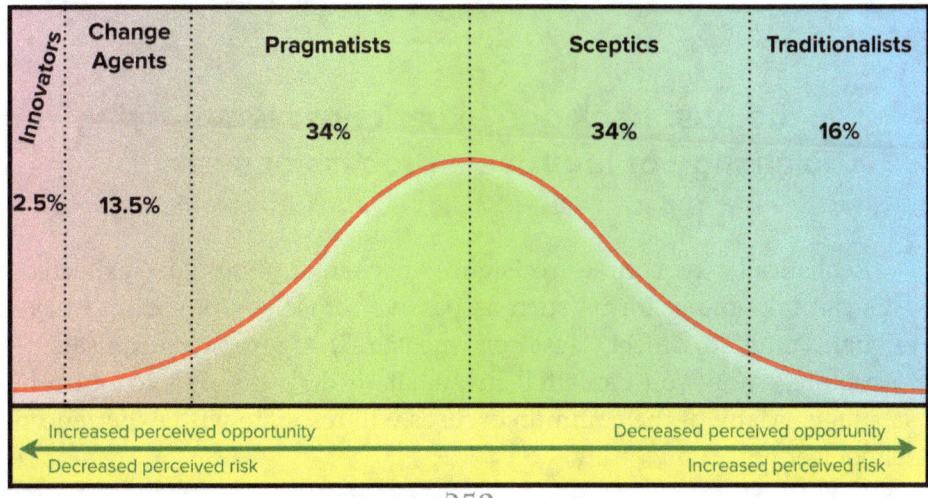

My anecdotal research shows that the proportion of these types of people is fairly constant in school irrespective of their location, size and philosophy, as shown in the graph at the foot of the previous page.

It is important that people in all five groups are provided with opportunities to express their viewpoints and be heard by those in the other groups. Those people who are in the red range of the graph must not ignore those who are in the blue zone. Similarly, those in the blue zone must not be allowed to shoot down those in the red zone.

Change will be most effective if key roles are allocated to the optimists and evangelists (those in the red zone) provided the procedural rule is followed that all ideas must be considered with respect, based on the assumption that the underlying motive of everyone involved is to do whatever is best for the students in the school.

Resistance is the pushback one experiences when trying to change or improve a process or system.

Realistically, of course, resistance to change should be expected. This can take many forms such as passive refusals – "We didn't have enough time to meet, test or measure", aggressive refusals – "Absolutely not! You can't tell me what to do", through to outright sabotage. Many of the common excuses will resonate with experienced school leaders:

- "Our students are not as bright as theirs…"
- "That's fine for them, but it won't work here – we're different."
- "But we don't have the (you name it)."
- "You're changing the fundamental nature and direction of the school I love".

Resistance can be the result of many factors:

- Fear (of the unknown, of being overwhelmed, of change itself).
- Mistrust (of the Administration, of the Board, of the Opinion Leader or Change Agent).
- Lack of information (not enough information provided to "prove" the value of the proposed change).
- Complacency (can't see the benefit of the change, not enough tension for change).
- Lack of incentives (inertia, reluctance to surrender the comfort zones that have been created over the years).

The lesson for school boards and leaders is that if they wish to implement significant deliberate change, such as introducing a new strategic plan, or a new organisational structure, or a new curriculum, then that change is more likely to be effective if everyone in the school community shares a common understanding of the proposed change. In other words, school boards and leaders should do everything they can to be transparent and ensure that there is "common knowledge" and understanding. As explained in Insight 61, "shared knowledge" allows space for individuals to harbour ill-informed views and habits that resist change, but "common knowledge" does away with this limitation. "Common knowledge" achieves this because at its best, it builds a pathway to replace destructive prejudice with enlightened consensus.

The key to appreciating and harnessing this power of "common knowledge" is understanding that effective collaboration requires a stronger consensus than "shared knowledge" can ever provide. "Common knowledge" is pivotal in enabling effective change because unlike "shared knowledge", it can foster a cohesive sense of community where every participant – teacher, administrator, student, parent – arrives at a shared understanding of the goals, strategies and values underlying the proposed changes.

Although "common knowledge" is a powerful tool in implementing effective change because of the consensus it generates, it is of course not the only factor. As I argue in my book "Optimal School Governance", effective change requires vision, skills, incentive, resources and an action plan in addition to consensus (or "common knowledge"). If any one of these factors is missing, then the change is likely to fail, as the diagram below illustrates.

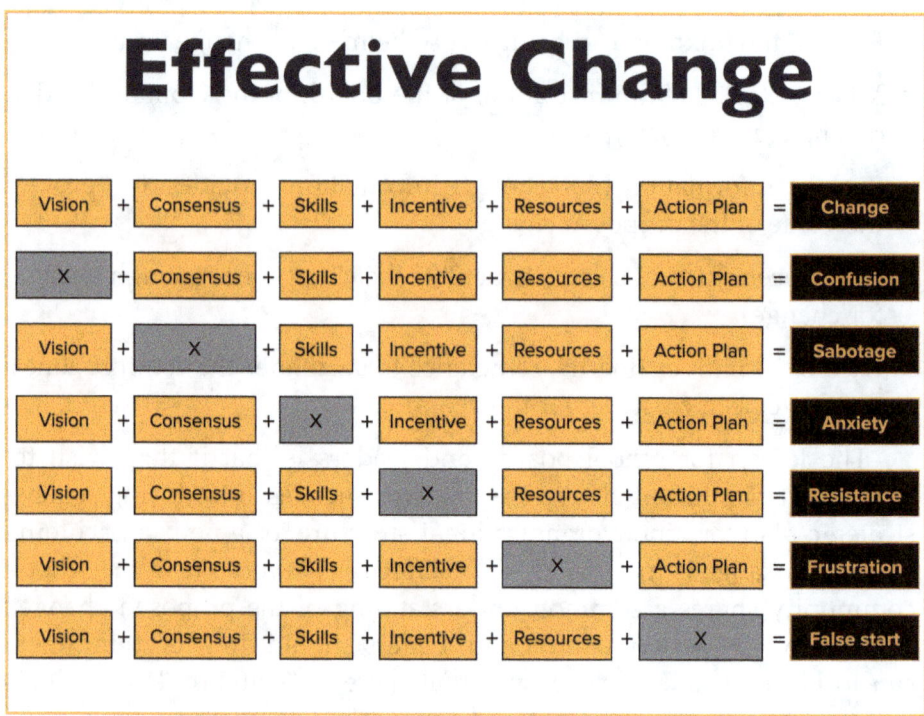

Understanding how to manage and direct change in a school is one of the most important insights that members of school boards and senior management can possess as it is the key to creating an intentional school culture.

Insight 56

Interim headships

Many school boards, and indeed many teachers, students and parents, view interim headships as an inconvenience. Interim Heads are usually appointed as a last resort when a Principal departs suddenly and unexpectedly, leaving insufficient time for an orderly search and recruitment process to appoint a permanent replacement. However, Interim Heads may also be appointed if the Board has identified a very strong candidate to be the next Head but that person will not be available for contractual or other reasons for another year or so.

Whatever the situation, school boards will want to reassure the school community that the best aspects of the school experience will continue unabated despite the departure of the previous Principal. Honest, reassuring, transparent communication from the board to both the school's internal and external communities is therefore of paramount importance.

Although sudden vacancies are sometimes handled internally by appointing a senior member of staff to serve as Acting Head, this usually results in a highly disruptive domino effect of cascading responsibilities that results in stress and excess workload for the entire management team, and even beyond the management team to include many of the teachers and non-teaching staff.

Therefore, many boards bring in an external Interim Principal, often a recently retired Head from another school. Such appointments have the benefit of bringing in the wisdom and experience gained from performing the "top job" without the flow-on impact of disrupting the established roles of the rest of the management team. Moreover, unlike an internal acting appointment, an experienced external Interim Head will have no reason to distort decision-making with an eye to future job security or promotion. This means that the period of an Interim Head should not be "interim" for anyone apart from the Interim Head.

School boards tend to adopt one of two highly contrasting, mutually exclusive approaches to interim headships. In countries such as the UK and Australia, Interim Heads are usually instructed by their boards not to make any key decisions, but simply maintain operations. This approach is designed to give the incoming Principal as much freedom and discretion to set direction as possible when they arrive.

In US schools, on the other hand, a very different approach is more common. Interim Headships are seen as an ideal opportunity to clean up long-standing problems such as staffing or curriculum issues in the school so that the new Head can begin with 'a clean slate', making changes without first having to lose political capital by making important but polarising decisions. In other words, the Interim Head can clean up the school without worrying about eroding their political capital because they know they will be leaving at the end of the year, hopefully with the school in a better position to move into the future.

On balance, I advocate the second (US) approach as being preferable for most schools. Of course there are limits to the reforms an Interim Head should make. It would not be expected that an Interim Head would, for example, move to make a single-sex school co-educational. Nonetheless, with guidance from a well-informed board that genuinely has the school's mission, vision and values at the heart of their decision-making, a reforming Interim Head can provide the ideal environment for a new Head to arrive at the school.

Insight 57

International experience benefits everyone — students, staff and boards

As long ago as the 1950s, the term "Third Culture Kids" (or TCKs) was being used to describe children and young adults who are raised or spend their formative years in a culture that is different from that of their parents or their own nationality. The term gained widespread use after the publication of David Pollock's and Ruth Van Reken's classic book *Third Culture Kids: Growing Up Among Worlds*.

Given unabated globalisation over the past century or so, it is understandable that there has been extensive research into the impact of living abroad, both for adults and children. The evidence points overwhelmingly towards positive impacts for individuals who spend time living overseas – enhanced creativity, greater tolerance and understanding of others, reduced intergroup bias, career success, more self-concept clarity, and so on.

In some ways, this evidence is surprising. Many transitional experiences such as relationship breakups and job changes tend to lower confidence and self-concept, but the opposite seems to be the case with international moves despite the initial discomfort that many people experience. This suggests that living overseas is an unusual, and perhaps unique, transitional experience insofar as it tends to raise self-awareness, self-confidence and achievement.

This was tested in a 2018 study by Hajo Adam and four others published in the journal *Organizational Behavior and Human Decision Processes* (and later heavily summarised in *Harvard Business Review*). Their extensive study established that the growth measured in emotional intelligence, self-awareness and self-confidence is primarily driven by how long a person has lived abroad, not where.

While this research is of particular interest (and encouragement) to international schools, there are important lessons and implications for every school, and indeed for every school board. To understand this point we should first explore the benefits and challenges of spending time living abroad.

BENEFITS

- **Expanded worldview.** Adults who have lived abroad are more likely than others to understand that there is more than one way to view new situations. This applies even more strongly to children who have lived overseas during some or all of their formative years.

- **Multi-dimensional view of life.** Open-minded people who have lived in internationally diverse communities or in several countries usually come to appreciate the value of solving problems using a variety of approaches that they have observed in different cultures.

- **Inter-personal sensitivity.** People who have been immersed in other cultures develop skills of interpreting others' emotions, body language, societal norms and cues more adeptly, more sensitively and thus more accurately. In words that were used often in one of the international schools where I was Principal, "you simply can't hate a person you know".

- **Cross-cultural sensitivity and adaptability.** The experience of living as a minority individual in another culture usually raises cultural intelligence with a consequent growth in capacity to function comfortably and effectively in a wide range of ethnic, national and organisational cultures.

- **Linguistic ability.** Living overseas often expands a person's ability to learn foreign languages, interpret different terminology and 'tune into' different accents. Expanding linguistic proficiencies is important because language is the organisational framework through which our thinking occurs – expanded linguistic abilities therefore widen the potential for new pattens of thinking and problem-solving.

CHALLENGES

- Frustration upon return. People who have expanded their worldview by living abroad can become frustrated by the comparative naivete, narrow-mindedness, inward-looking worldview and perhaps even ethnocentrism they perceive after returning to their home country.
- Confused loyalties and identity. Children who have spent their formative years immersed in other cultures can struggle with developing their political and values positions because they have been exposed to so many alternatives. This can especially apply when young adults move between collectivist and individualist societies.

International mobility is thus a both a challenge and an opportunity that applies to all schools, not just international schools.

Schools that accept TCKs must be aware that in spite of any apparent self-confidence they may exhibit, children who are moving internationally are undertaking a major life-change that involves leaving behind friends, relationships and familiar surroundings. They are taking on a new life where almost everything may initially be alien, and the move will almost never have been their decision to make.

Such students may need special care and attention as they settle into their new surroundings. Of course, the effort will be worth it, both for the student and for the school. The school especially benefits because TCKs bring maturity, perspectives, experiences and histories which benefit not only their fellow students but also the teachers and any other adults in the school who are open to listening and learning.

Equally important is the question "how can the board benefit?". There is a massive body of research establishing that boards benefit from having a diverse mix of members. The simple reason is that homogeneous thinking and decision-making almost never drives innovation. Having members with a variety of backgrounds and experiences will inevitably provide a rich mix of perspectives that will bring choices and new alternatives that are unlikely to have been tabled in a room with largely uniform board.

Historically, people have looked at diversity through moral, racial or political lenses. Tolerance, acceptance, and inclusivity have been widely seen as moral imperatives – 'the right thing to do'. Indeed, diversity has emerged as a legal requirement in many school environments. Notwithstanding the moral imperative, I believe we should also consider the pragmatic benefits of diversity – how diverse ways of thinking and seeing problems lead to better practical outcomes.

Relating this specifically to school boards, we must acknowledge that the way we think in groups is different to the way we think as individuals. Collective wisdom exceeds the sum of its individual parts – that is the strength of boards. It follows from this that the more diverse the group, the more diverse the input will be, thus raising the efficacy of the group.

Interestingly, most people express a strong preference for working in groups of like-minded people. They also rate more diverse groups as being less effective (probably because the individuals are less likely to get their own way in a group with fewer other similar-thinking individuals). However, despite the greater discomfort felt by the participants, groups of people that comprise a mix of ages, genders, occupations, nationalities, religions, backgrounds and experiences are far more likely to find effective creative solutions to problems than less diverse groups.

The ideal for school boards is therefore to maximise mission effectiveness by actively seeking creative "diversity of thought". It is important to understand that a contest of ideas and thinking styles within a homogeneous group does not represent diversity of thought. Indeed, working within a homogenous board is likely to create complacency about the lack of diverse representation.

True diversity of thought comes from diverse identities and experiences, along with an inclusive culture that emphasises openness, commitment, transparency, and accountability.

Research by John Quigley, for example, showed that every time the size of a city is doubled, the average IQ of that city increases by 4% and the average productivity of each worker rises by up to 27%. In his book "The Diversity Bonus", Scott Page refers to this research, arguing that these changes occur because of the increased power generated by bouncing ideas off one another in a more diverse population.

Every so often, all school boards should ask themselves the Big Question: "How can we be more productive together?" I suggest that part of the should ensuring the board has members from different backgrounds and life experiences, including especially international and intercultural experiences.

By not actively seeking diverse composition, school boards miss one of the easiest and most potent opportunities to improve their effectiveness.

References:

Adam H, Obodaru O, Lu JG, Maddux W & Galinsky AD (2018a) The shortest path to oneself leads around the world: Living abroad increases self-concept clarity. *Organizational Behavior and Human Decision Processes*, 145:16-29.

Adam H, Obodaru O, Lu JG, Maddux W & Galinsky AD (2018b) How living abroad helps you develop a clearer sense of self. *Harvard Business Review*: 2018-05-22.

Leblanc R (2016) *The Handbook of Board Governance*. Hoboken: Wiley (see pp.49-55).

Page SE (2017) *The Diversity Bonus: How great teams pay off in the knowledge economy*. Princeton: Princeton University Press.

Pollock, DC & Van Reken, RE (2017) *Third Culture Kids: The Experience of Growing Up Among Worlds*, Boston: Nicholas Brealey Publishing.

Quigley JM (1998) Urban diversity and economic growth. *Journal of Economic Perspectives*, 12(2): 127-138.

Rhode DL & Packel AL (2014) Diversity on corporate boards: How much difference does difference make? *Delaware Journal of Corporate Law*, 39: 377-425.

Insight 58

Interviews

Interviews are an integral component of recruiting senior personnel in any school. This applies especially when Boards appoint a new Principal in which multiple interviews are not uncommon. Interviews are also a vital part of the process when a Principal appoints new staff. Interviews are usually also a step in the recruitment of new board members, although surprisingly this isn't a universal practice.

Of course, interviews are never the only step in a school's recruitment process.

The first step for most candidates in a recruitment process is responding to an advertisement or an approach from a third-party recruiter by submitting a resumé, or curriculum vitae (CV). There are many divergent viewpoints about what comprises a good CV (which may be a good topic for a future article?). However, the general consensus is that a good CV is visually appealing, easy to read, tailored to the specific job requirements, congruent with the school's mission/philosophy, includes a strong personal summary, contains a comprehensive work experience section, shows relevant education and skills, is error-free, and is easily verifiable.

A good CV can be thought of as an entry application. It should attract sufficient interest and attention that it results in an invitation to attend an interview, preferably face-to-face, especially for senior positions. Even face-to-face interviews have their limitations, which is why no offer of employment should ever be made without first conducting due diligence checks, including thorough reference checks – confidential spoken conversations with referees, not just relying on written open or 'public' references which have almost no value whatsoever.

Interviews for senior positions usually involve a fairly standard set of often unimaginative questions which are posed uniformly to all short-listed applicants, questions such as:

- How do you envision involving teachers, students, and parents in decision-making processes at our school?
- Can you share your approach to addressing underperforming teachers and supporting their professional growth?
- How do you plan to foster a positive and inclusive school culture for students and staff?
- How do you stay informed about current educational research and best practices, and how do you incorporate that knowledge into your leadership style?
- Can you describe a specific challenge you faced as a principal (or deputy, or whatever is the current position held) and how you approached resolving it?
- How do you build and maintain positive relationships with community stakeholders, including local businesses and organisations?
- Can you share your philosophy on the role of technology in education and how you envision integrating it into our school's curriculum and operations?
- How do you plan to address issues of equity and diversity at our school?

- Can you describe your approach to budget management and resource allocation?
- How do you envision collaborating with teachers and staff to set and achieve academic goals for our school?

Of course, questions such as these all have inherent merit, but perhaps the most significant value of these (and similar) uniform questions is seeing how much humour or personality applicants can infuse into their answers to help the interview panel stay awake.

With that in mind, I recommend trying to insert less predictable, more original and creative questions into the mix, like some of these 12 examples:

- **How would you describe yourself in one word?** This question forces the applicant into extreme conciseness by restricting the response even more tightly than Twitter's original 140 characters. Nonetheless, that single word will try to encapsulate everything that applicants feel is significant and relevant in defining themselves. Having said that, the important thing is not really the single word provided for the answer – you already know it will be both flattering and expressed with humility. Rather, the important thing is the manner in which the applicant responds to the question, with better applicants taking the time to think and reflect carefully before responding.

- **Give us fair warning – what is your most significant weakness or area where you will need support?** Although a handful of delusional applicants will not admit to any shortcomings, many applicants will try to identify a shortcoming that is intended to please the interview panel, such as 'being a workaholic' or 'being neither a big picture person nor a details person, but a mix of the two'. Better applicants will be willing to share their individual vulnerabilities in response to this question with a refreshing level of honesty and openness.

- **What is the last thing you've learned in your current job?** This is a nuanced variation on a commonly asked related question: What is the most important thing you've learned in your current job? An applicant who has prepared his or her answers for the interview may still answer the more common question rather than the one which was asked, but the key point for the interview panel should be whether or not the applicant has an active, continuing curiosity and passion to learn. Better applicants will be able to describe and analyse a very recent experience, not something from a more distant past.

- **Who has been your most significant role model or mentor?** In addition to giving applicants an opportunity to acknowledge the importance of others in their personal and professional formation, their responses to this question will reveal something of the ideals and leadership style to which they aspire. Better applicants should be able to relate insights gained from their own personal relationships and experiences rather than more generic responses such as 'Nelson Mandela', 'Mother Teresa', and so on.

- **Tell us about our school.** An interview panel should expect that all short-listed applicants have performed thorough due diligence and undertaken extensive research on the school where they wish to work. Better applicants will demonstrate that they are well versed in the school's mission/philosophy, its history, its fundamental statistics, its general reputation and any recent crises or controversies that have been reported in the press.

- **Tell us all the reasons that led you to leave your previous job and take up your present position (the one you would be leaving if we were to offer you this role).** Many applicants will have prepared a response to the standard question "why would you want (or be prepared) to leave your current position?" However, discussing the realities of their previous move should reveal insights into the applicant's values, drivers, motivations, ambition, expectations, loyalty, tolerance for frustration and appetite for risk.

- **How long are you willing to fail in this job before you succeed?** This question takes most interviewees by surprise because of the obvious inherent assumption that not everything a school leader does is initially successful. Weaker applicants usually try to side-step the question because they are unwilling (or do not want to be seen) to acknowledge failure. Alternatively, other weaker applicants may waffle through a largely meaningless, vague response that is designed to make the interview panel feel good while providing little or no substantive answer to the question. Stronger applicants will acknowledge that setbacks occur and provide personal anecdotes of such setbacks from their own experience before proceeding to explain how they would analyse the reasons for the setback, consult appropriately, and then persist for however long it took to achieve the goals that had been set.

- **Tell us something which you believe is true that almost nobody agrees with you about.** Effective school leadership demands people who are not afraid to speak their minds and who can do so while showing unwavering respect towards others with whom they may disagree. This question is designed to explore originality of thinking together with an applicant's courage in speaking up in a difficult context. Better applicants will reveal original, perhaps even counter-cultural thinking, and explain the reasons or evidence that support their thinking, doing so in a manner that shows respect both for competing ideas and the people who hold them.

- **What is today's most interesting news story?** Many applicants will be surprised by this question, but school leadership demands an up-to-date understanding of the world within which the school exists and the challenges its students, parents and teachers face. Weaker applicants will fumble for an answer, perhaps even acknowledging that they were so busy preparing for the interview that they haven't caught up with that day's headlines. Better applicants will have no trouble engaging with some item in that day's news and explaining with some passion why they find it interesting. Many school leadership situations require a capacity to engage in small talk, and the manner in which an applicant engages with this question is likely to reveal a great deal about their capacity for engaging in animated small talk.

- **Think of an imaginary day that has just been the highlight – the number one experience – of your entire working life in schools. You're driving home and your emotions are a mix of ecstasy, elation and euphoria. What was it about that working day that made you so happy?** This question is designed to reveal the true passion, motive and enjoyment for the applicant's work. Needless to say, people who are doing things that they love to do will achieve goals and transform a school environment far more effectively than those for whom their job is a chore. It is the contrast between a vocation and a job. Better applicants are likely to really enjoy answering this question as they cannot hold back their excitement.

- **What makes you really special?** This is a variation of the fairly standard question "what are your main strengths?". By asking the question in this way, the applicant is really being invited to provide a holistic view of themselves that embraces not only professional skills but personal qualities such as integrity, worldview, energy, life balance, and so on. Better applicants will convey a passion for education and its potential to transform young lives while also emphasising the importance of life-work balance and family life.

- **What did you not get a chance to include on your resumé?** By definition, any CV or resumé is a highly condensed summary of the applicant's education, experience, career, writings, and so on. The format of CVs and resumés dictates that what is omitted may be the most interesting and potentially relevant points, even if they are anecdotes that don't lend themselves to being listed in point form. Better applicants will use this question to provide a passionate and original insight into themselves that may even become the compelling factor in selecting the successful applicant.

As mentioned above, the interview is just one component of the selection process for a new school leader, board member, or middle/senior manager. It is, however, arguably the most important single component. Whether this is the case or not, it is vitally important to maximise the effectiveness of the interview.

It is hoped the questions and advice in this article help you achieve this. However, interview effectiveness means much more than just finding the right interview questions – it means learning how to listen and interpret applicants' responses appropriately in order to find the stand-out person you need – the one individual who will be the ideal fit for the school to take it into the future.

Insight 59

Is there an ideal board size?

One question I am often asked when I conduct workshops is whether there is an ideal number of members for a school board. The short answer is "no, every school is different and must come to its own conclusion about what works best for its particular situation".

However, this leads to a more important question: "what factors should determine the ideal size of OUR school board?".

A useful starting point when considering this question is Brooks' Law. Originally arising from the software development industry, Brooks' Law states "adding personnel to a late project makes it even later". According to Fred Brooks, who developed this idea in his 1975 book "The Mythical Man-Month", when an incremental person is added to a project, it makes the project take more, not less time. This could be paraphrased as "most people simply cannot effectively manage complex relationships".

Although this is, of course, an over-simplification, it describes the counter-intuitive reality that adding more people does not always mean work gets done more quickly. The reasoning behind this thinking is that as the number of people grows linearly, the complexity of communication increases exponentially.

In the diagram at the top of the next page, it can be seen that increasing a board from three to four members adds just one extra person, but effectively doubles the number of lines of communication that must be managed. Similarly, if we had a board with five members and doubled its number to ten, the lines of communication would increase by 450% from 10 to 45.

It is said that we (i.e. most people) are capable of having tight relationships with about five people, and slightly less intense relationships with an additional 15 or so. We can relate this to the size of sporting teams which rarely have more than 15 members.

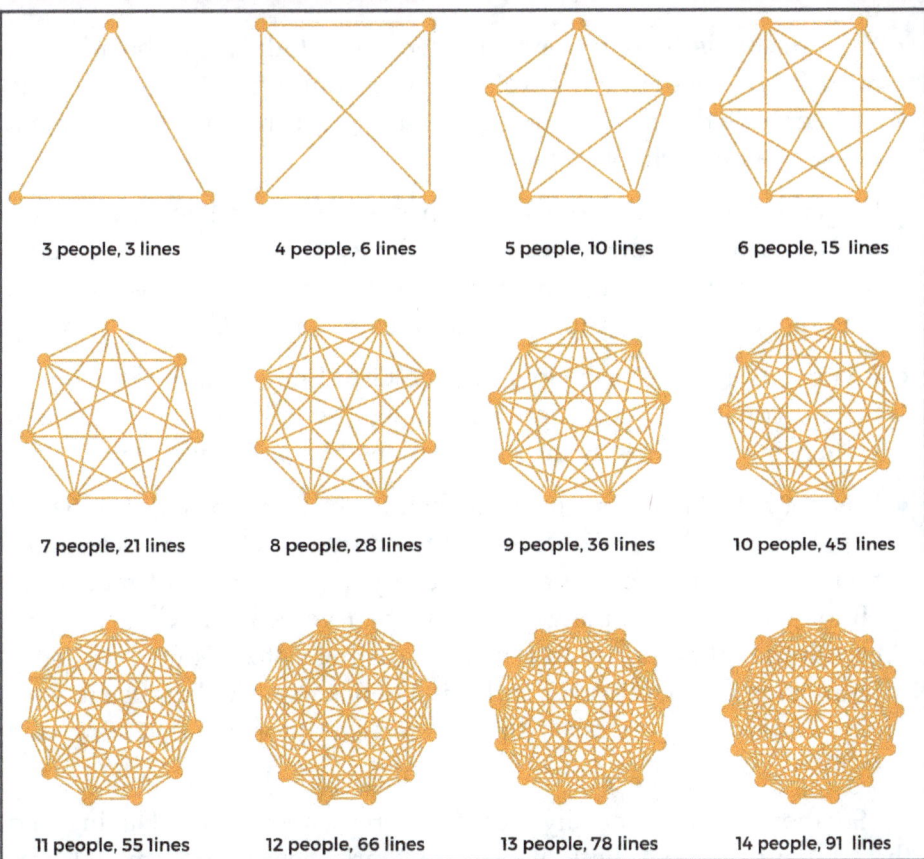

This suggests that small boards will usually be more effective than large boards because communication will probably be more direct and less prone to misunderstandings.

On the other hand, small boards can lead to burnout among members when there are too few people to handle the duties and obligations required. This assumes, of course, that every board member is making an active contribution, as burnout can also arise when a larger board has several 'chair warmers'. Indeed, 'chair warming' can be a risk with larger boards because some members may assume they don't have to work hard because there are so many other people around. Thus, burnout can be a risk with both large and small boards.

There are other factors influencing the ideal size of a board for any particular school:

- Boards with several committees can be smaller than boards with few committees. This is because much of the menial work of governance can be delegated to the committees, allowing the board to focus on decision-making and 'big picture' thinking.

- Young schools tend to have smaller, more tightly run boards that meet fairly frequently (as well as fewer committees) because of the interconnected nature of decision-making during the establishment phase of a new school.
- Larger schools and more established schools tend to have larger boards to handle their greater complexity as well as accommodate the requirements for representation by certain groups such as alumni, parents, governments and/or external church groups, etc.
- It is good practice for boards to have term limits, and if these are in place, conscious consideration must be given to succession management, especially the key positions of board leadership.
- It is not mandatory, but it can be helpful to have an odd number of members whether the board is large or small. Odd numbers make tied votes less likely (provided everyone attends the meetings), although a board can always resolve tied votes if the Chair has the constitutional authority to exercise a casting vote. (Some boards try to function by consensus, but this is rarely successful because it gives every individual member the excessive authority of vetoing any motion).

So, there is no universally ideal size for a school board. Having said that, I have worked with boards that are clearly too small (three members) or too large (24 members) for effective operations. In general boards with (say) 7 to 13 members seem to work fairly well depending on factors such as the experience and competence of the members, and the respect members show each other when attending meetings and between meetings.

This brings me to what is perhaps the most important factor when considering board effectiveness. It is not the size of the board, which is just one, relatively minor factor. It's not even the respect with which members treat each other, essential though this is.

The key factor in enhancing board effectiveness is having a neutral, external person conduct regular comprehensive performance reviews of the board as a whole, identifying the relative areas of strength and shortcomings. Regular (say, biennial) performance reviews enable the board to focus on intentional self-improvement and thus maximise its capacity to achieve its stated mission and vision.

Everything else is really just a footnote to this core purpose of the board – maximising capacity to achieve the stated mission and vision.

Insight 60

It's not fair

Anyone who has worked in schools will be familiar with the claim "It's not fair!". After all, schools are full of children, and any parent will also be familiar with that same three-word combination. It is not only the students who make claims of "it's not fair" in schools, however – it is also heard coming from teachers when they feel aggrieved by a decision made by the board, the Principal or the senior management.

I have met very few school leaders or members of school boards who go out of their way intentionally to make unfair decisions. Indeed, more than in many other types of institutions, most school leaders tend by nature to be harmony-building people-pleasers. Perhaps that explains why they often feel bruised when accused of unfairness. Board members may not be as singularly focussed on pleasing people (especially during times of financial distress), but most genuinely want a school with happy, positive teachers and students.

When considering fairness, it is important that school leaders and boards understand what is really meant by equality and equity. Equality relates to inputs. Equality is achieved when all individuals and groups are provided with equivalent access to resources or opportunities. On the other hand, equity relates to outcomes, and specifically to the notion of all individuals and groups are achieving equivalent outcomes.

However, not all equality is equal. There are two types of equality, formal equality and substantive equality. Formal equality occurs when everyone is treated the same way irrespective of their individual circumstances. Substantive equality occurs when an individual person's circumstances are taken into consideration to address their disadvantage or discrimination when providing resources or opportunities. Substantive equality aims to work towards greater (though not necessarily absolute or perfect) equality of outcomes – in other words, equity.

Formal equality   Substantive equality

When claims of "it's not fair!" are heard in schools, it often reflects a misunderstanding of the difference between formal and substantive equality. Formal equality sounds fair, but as one of my lecturers commented when I was studying education at university back in the 1970s: **"there is nothing so unequal as treating unequals as equals"**.

The difference between formal and substantive equality is important in schools in multiple ways such as providing resources that meet students' varying individual needs, treating staff justly and being honest and transparent when communicating information.

Another common situation that arises in schools where the two forms of equality are often confused is the area of student discipline. Teachers and parents who are unaware of all the facts behind an incident may question decisions that appear to be treating students differently, perhaps demanding formal equality so that consequences are imposed regardless of significant individual psychological, motivational, or other relevant circumstances such as prior warnings, and so on. Situations like that are very difficult for school principals because of the competing need for student privacy on one hand, and the ideal of transparency on the other.

By definition, "fairness" is a relative term. We evaluate fairness in terms of how two people (or groups) are treated in relation to each other. If a school board decided to give the Mathematics staff a 10%

pay rise at the same time as granting the Visual Arts staff a 5% pay rise, the Visual Arts staff will immediately assert "that's not fair". Of course, that assumes the salaries for both groups were the same at the beginning of the exercise. If the Mathematics staff were being paid less than the Visual Arts staff, then an apparently "fair" pay rise of 10% for both groups would result in the Mathematics staff claiming "that's not fair". The two reactions represent the difference between formal equality and substantive equality.

In schools, the situation is usually more nuanced, and thus complex. For example, Heads of Department might receive an annual allowance of (say) $20,000 plus release time of five lessons per week to perform their extra duties, whereas Heads of Student Welfare might receive an annual allowance of (say) $12,000 plus release time of eight lessons per week to perform their extra duties. In such situations, disagreements over "fairness" will commonly arise when remuneration is adjusted because it is never easy to equate financial compensation with time and other allowances.

Some international schools face additional allegations of unfairness when they pay local staff less remuneration than staff hired from overseas. In some ways this reflects the higher costs incurred by foreign staff when moving to another country for work (finding accommodation, buying basic necessities, travelling to visit family in other countries). The differential may also reflect the extra costs required to recruit teachers from elsewhere when the required skills are scarce in the country where the school is located. Where pay differences like this occur, the decision is based on substantive equality. On the other hand, an argument from formal equality would demand that all staff who perform the same roles are remunerated equally, irrespective of their country of origin.

When school leaders and boards examine these matters philosophically, they should understand that the intimate connection between equality and fairness often reflects the role that luck plays through "no fault or choice of their own". Among equally deserving people, making some people worse off than others through no fault or choice of their own is a negative action, because it is genuinely unfair. On the other hand, among unequally deserving people, making someone who is more needy better off than someone less needy, even if the former was worse off through no fault or choice of their own, is a positive action because it is not unfair. Such actions are sometimes colloquially referred to as "positive discrimination".

In an ideal world, none of this should be controversial – and yet, it often is. Some people (including board members I have worked with) claim that fairness and relativities don't matter, arguing that the ONLY thing which matters is the absolute level of remuneration and conditions enjoyed by staff. I have actually heard such board members explain their position like this: "Which would you prefer – a world where you earn $100,000 a year and all your friends earn $50,000, or a world where you can earn $200,000 a year and your friends earn $500,000?". They claim that everyone is better off in the second scenario, even though research suggests most people tend to opt for the first. Clearly, this is an over-simplification, because it assumes many constants such as the equivalent costs-of-living, but such arguments can make for challenging discussions at school board meetings.

Consider one hypothetical example of equality in practice to understand the issues at hand. Caroline is a young teacher in her third year of teaching in a fairly typical school in any More Economically Developed Country (such as Australia, Belgium, Canada, Denmark, etc). Caroline is a healthy single mother who has two young children, works in a restaurant on weekends to earn extra income, and drives a twelve year-old small car. She worries how she can make enough money to pay the rent for her modest two-bedroom house and she has no idea how she will be able to send her children to college on her annual income of $80,000.

Caroline is clearly less affluent than many of the people she sees every day. Like many other teachers in the school, she is less wealthy than many of her students' parents who live in million dollar homes, own two or three new prestigious cars, take expensive overseas holidays and have annual household incomes well over $500,000. Nonetheless, the parents of Caroline's students respect her and really appreciate her hard work, dedication and care that she shows to every one of the children in her care.

When the school's board undertakes its annual review of teachers' salaries, they worry that teachers' salaries seem to be slipping compared to the general population, making it increasingly difficult for the school to be competitive in attracting good teaching staff. They are also concerned to minimise fee increases for parents so that the school does not become too expensive for the school's community. Most board members are genuinely concerned to help teachers like Caroline, not only in absolute terms, but also in terms of how her remuneration compares with the wider community in their well-off society. Nonetheless, some board members who are "high-fliers" in the corporate sector observe that teachers like Caroline do at least have a roof over their heads, indoor plumbing with hot water, a mobile phone, a television and a car.

Some board members who work internationally remark that Caroline and her colleagues aren't living in a war-torn country, or one that is ruled by a dictator, and she has no fear of catching smallpox, tuberculosis, malaria, or diphtheria. She and her children drink safe water, they eat three meals every day and they have a reasonably long life-expectancy. One board member who works in a nearby university remarks that for most of human history, and indeed for the world as a whole today, someone as well off as Caroline would be among the most privileged of all people. Another board member comments that "to put this into blunt perspective, as difficult as it is to be relatively poor in a rich society, it is much worse to have to sit and watch your children die of starvation or disease".

This is where an understanding of the difference between formal equality and substantive equality becomes important in clarifying the discussion. Formal equality may appear fair at an initial, superficial level, but it often results in unequal outcomes. Substantive equality may initially look unfair, but it is more likely (though never guaranteed) to result in more equal outcomes. Although there are powerful reasons to care greatly about absolute levels, relative levels also matter.

Would you agree that it seems unfair, and hence bad, for someone like Caroline to be much worse off than others through no fault, or choice, of her own?

Thanks to the Saskatoon Health Region ©2014 for the base graphic that was adapted for use in this article.

Insight 61

Knowing when it's time to go

Warning: this article bravely ploughs into territory where more timid consultants fear to tread – it discusses school principals and an authoritarian, despotic dictator within the one piece of writing.

As a Cold War Kid, the year 1989 was a heady time for me. I watched in fascination as two immutable alternate universes – East and West – seemed to converge. All my assumptions about the natural order of the world seemed to crumble as the Berlin Wall fell and Communist regimes across Eastern Europe collapsed like dominoes.

I didn't know it at the time, but that period now provides some really important lessons for today's school boards and leaders. Yes, really! Stay with me – unless you are in a hurry and need to go directly to the lessons for school leaders and boards which begin on page 290.

In 1987, two years before the fall of the Berlin Wall, I visited the USSR and then travelled extensively through much of Communist Eastern Europe with my then-young family. We experienced Czechoslovakia, Hungary, Romania, Bulgaria and Yugoslavia under Communist rule. As a consequence of those travels, I could easily visualise the actual places where revolutions were overthrowing dictatorships in rapid succession.

By far the most bizarre Communist country I visited in Eastern Europe at that time was Romania. As soon as I drove across the border from Hungary, I realised we had entered a country with deep problems. I had to steer around an unusual combination of road hazards –huge potholes in the road as well as countless groups of children who would suddenly ran out in front of the car to beg for food.

I had entered a truly weird country marked by poverty mixed with intense fear engendered by the ruthless, hated President Nicolae Ceauşescu, his despised but powerful wife Elena, and their joint use of the colossal secret police force known as the Securitate. At the time of my visit in 1987, the BBC writer and presenter Jacques Rupnik wrote a book titled "The Other Europe" and said this about Ceauşescu's Romania:

Above: a road sign in the town of 30 Decembrie (30 December), south of Bucharest, when I visited in 1987. The sign, typical of hundreds across Romania at the time, means "Our esteem and pride – Ceauşescu – Romania!". The town was re-named 1 Decembrie in 1996, and the same road now is shown below.

"Romanians always refer to 'Him'; even in private they avoid mentioning his name. Just in case 'They' overhear. 'They' stand for the omnipresent and much feared Securitate, the secret police. Ceauşescu's wife is called simply Elena. So with 'Him', 'Them' and 'Elena' you have all you need to know about contemporary Romanian politics."

Perhaps not quite all, because Rupnik then writes a seven-page-long diatribe about contemporary Romanian politics beginning with the words "The Ceauşescu regime is without doubt the most repressive in the Soviet bloc today…" If you are interested, you can read more about the state of Romania under Ceauşescu in the references at the end of this Insight.

Nicolae and Elena Ceauşescu receiving bouquets of flowers from children who have been especially selected to adore the couple.

I am not for one moment suggesting that Nicolae Ceauşescu and his regime resembled any Principal or School I have ever known or worked with. It is in the causes and the process of Ceauşescu's fall from power two years after my visit that lessons are found for today's school leaders.

The Ceauşescus had been universally reviled in Romania for over a decade, but criticisms were only uttered in muted whispers among one's closest and most trusted friends and family. However, as winter enveloped Romania in December 1989 and fraternal Communist regimes collapsed across Europe, something unprecedented happened in the provincial city of Timișoara, some 550 kilometres west of Romania's capital, Bucharest.

On 16th December, a public protest began in response to the government's attempt to evict and reassign a minor but well-loved church pastor, László Tőkés, to a remote rural parish for speaking out about state-restricted seminary enrolments. Public protests were unknown in Ceaușescu's Romania, and the Securitate responded first with tear gas and water cannons, and then with machine gun fire. Events escalated, but of course nothing was reported in the state-controlled media. Nonetheless, most Romanians learned what was happening from clandestine broadcasts by the BBC and VOA and through the country's highly effective verbal grapevine.

Strada Turda, a main road in downtown Bucharest – our lunch stop on 1st August 1987.

As events in Timișoara continued to escalate, Nicolae Ceaușescu decided to give one of his dreary, stage-managed speeches from the balcony of the Communist Party's Central Committee building in downtown Bucharest. And so, on 21st December, about 100,000 people were bussed into the large square in front of the balcony and given pro-Ceaușescu banners and signs to demonstrate their loyalty for the cameras (and the Securitate) – the usual procedure that had occurred countless times in the past. The television cameras were there to beam the rally as a 'live' event.

But this speech turned out differently. After Ceaușescu's first few sentences, murmuring began in the crowd that soon grew into a crescendo of shouts – "Timișoara", "Timișoara", "Timișoara". The microphones picked up the voices. Ceaușescu looked confused and held up his arm to silence the crowd.

Nicolae Ceaușescu, centre, with his wife Elena, delivering his final address to the masses on 21st December 1989 from the balcony of the Communist Party's Central Committee building in central Bucharest.

That is when the live TV feed was cut, denying the television audience the scenes of chaos that ensued. Of course, the cut in transmission revealed much more than it hid. Suddenly, everyone understood what was happening, and across the country people ran out of their homes and into the streets – a spontaneous revolution was underway.

The Ceaușescus escaped the mayhem, but a few days later they were unceremoniously arrested and subjected to a show trial. Then, on Christmas Day 1989, Nicolae and Elena were shot and killed by a very zealous firing squad and close-up images of their bullet-ridden bodies were displayed on national television for all to see.

This is what the same place looked like on my recent visit. The white pyramid now serves as a memorial, pointing upwards to the balcony where Nicolae Ceauşescu delivered his final address on 21st December 1989. The pyramid is inscribed "Glorie martirilor nostril", which means "Glory to our martyrs" as a memorial to the 49 people killed and 500 wounded there on that day.

Why was this sudden mass uprising possible in 1989 after being unthinkable for over a decade? This is where school leaders and boards have lessons to learn – and not because they (usually!) need to suppress a revolution I hasten to add. The key factor that enabled change to occur was a change in the nature of knowledge.

In an article by Julian De Freitas in 2019, **the progression of knowledge from individual through shared to common knowledge** is described. When Romanians were hiding their disdain for the Ceauşescus in private, it remained at the level of 'individual knowledge' and was thus largely passive and ineffective in any practical sense. When they were brave enough to whisper their disdain quietly to trusted others, it became "shared knowledge", which spread information but remained below the threshold for effective change. However, when the crowd in Bucharest began chanting, the shared knowledge suddenly became "common knowledge" and therefore impossible to ignore. As Tim Harford states, "an information cascade had started a revolution; common knowledge was about to finish the job". The reason was that "common knowledge" creates a distinctive cognitive state that empowers collective action.

(Left): "The Genius of the Carpathians" – one of Nicolae Ceaușescu's many personality cult posters from his time as leader. (Right): Ceaușescu's image appeared at the front of most books published in Romania during his period in power. This example was defaced after his fall from power by the owner of the book, a 1983 scientific manual issued by the Ministry of Education and Training. (Both images show exhibits I was able to photograph when I visited the Muzeul Amintirilor din Comunism – the Museum of Memories of Communism – in Brașov, Romania).

I believe there are four important lessons for school boards and leaders arising from the story of Ceaușescu's downfall.

The first lesson relates to the progression of "shared knowledge" towards "common knowledge". If discontent (whether justified or unjustified) is growing towards a Principal, then it is in everyone's interests (including the Principal and the Board) if the Principal plans to retire or move to another school while this discontent remains at the level of "shared knowledge". If action is delayed until the "shared knowledge" becomes "common knowledge", then the situation can escalate suddenly and unpredictably, causing considerable reputational damage to both the school and the Principal's reputation.

This leads to **the second lesson**. Some Principals are genuinely unaware that discontent is escalating either because they are aloof and out-of-touch with the school's staff, parents and students, or because they have surrounded themselves with a servile, sycophantic executive team that never challenges the Principal. The obvious answers to such situations are for the Principal to consult widely, be transparent, listen to advice with true humility and receptivity, know the school community, and assemble a diverse executive team of articulate, professional critical thinkers.

This leads in turn to **the third lesson** from Romania's experience. Discontent towards leaders (of schools as well as nations) is more likely to increase as their time in office becomes longer. One factor contributing to this discontent may be simple boredom or yearning for change (the "it's time" factor), but more commonly it reflects the impact that the leader is having. A good general rule for any School Principal is to remain in office only as long as you are still making effective changes, which usually means no more than a decade. Although every school is different, a decade is about the typical time that "shared knowledge" discontent can shift dramatically towards "common knowledge" discontent.

The fourth lesson flows from this. The best way to protect long-term leaders from the dangers of isolation, complacency and inertia is to conduct regular performance reviews. For politicians, that means facing the voters on a regular basis (Ceauşescu take note!). For school principals, it means undertaking annual appraisals that lead to goal-setting for the coming year, combined with full 360-degree performance reviews during the period before contracts are renewed.

A thorough, planned, confidential, well-executed **performance review** by an independent, politically neutral professional will almost certainly identify the danger signals – declining performance, staff morale issues, lack of support from the board, difficulties in resolving conflicts, loss of passion, increasing isolation and/or stubbornness, persistent challenges, limited professional growth, declining communication skills, health issues, budgetary challenges, personal or family issues, legal or ethical concerns, burnout, community disconnection, vision misalignment – while they are still at the level of "shared knowledge" before they escalate more dangerously into "common knowledge".

Everything that has just been said about school principals should also apply to board members.

If the quality of any board member's "value-added" is declining, it is time to consider vacating the position and allowing a replacement to take the seat – someone who embraces the school's mission and vision with passion, and who has the creativity and energy to make an active contribution.

One additional factor may apply to board members. According to many governance experts, board effectiveness is enhanced when term limits are applied to board members. This is a common factor for both political leaders (e.g. the US Presidency) and school boards, as I have written in Insight 97.

Term limits for school board members can improve board effectiveness because:

- they allow board members to recharge their energy and avoid burnout;
- they provide a mechanism to bring new perspectives, fresh ideas and a variety of skills and talents to the board; and
- they provide a relatively painless framework for the removal of board members who are losing their passion and energy, or who have been poor contributors.

There is no fixed ideal period for term limits that can be applied unquestioningly to every school. This is because every school is at a different stage of its institutional life, has different needs, has varying capacities to recruit new members, and has different approaches to conducting its own board self-reviews and appraisals.

The US author Dennis Miller makes these observations (which I support):

> "It is best to stagger board terms so only a few board members leave each year. You do not want to lose more than one-third of your board at one time. I suggest that the term length be in the two-year to three-year range and that members serve a maximum number of three to four terms. This would ensure that no one board member serves more than 10 years on the board."

We should recognise and reward the dedication and years of service for those who have served with distinction on the non-profit board. However, after serving on a board for 10 years, it is time to allow others to step up and take their rightful place as the next generation of board leaders ready and willing to serve.

I realise that all this may sound somewhat dismal because it has focussed on leadership that has bred discontent. There is a reason for that focus – the American consultant John Littleford recently wrote this about the sad state of Heads' turnover in schools:

> *"Almost eighty percent of all heads of schools are fired. They do not leave of their own volition. Thirty years ago many heads served long terms of office and most left under their own steam. While the job today is more complicated and pressured, and while parents, boards, students, alumni, faculty and community are all more demanding than thirty years ago, there appear to be a number of specific factors which have led to the early termination of heads"*

That statistic may surprise many people, but it does not surprise most school principals, not does it surprise the public relations personnel who draft statements to the school community announcing that the Head is leaving to spend more time with his (or her) family, to travel, for health reasons, to explore new opportunities, to seek new challenges, and so on.

Of course, there is also the other 20% of Heads who make a move because of the "pull factors" of a new school rather than the "push factors" of the existing one. When I read the statistics, I feel very fortunate that I fell into this group when I served as Principal of five different schools over 25 years. Of my five headships, I only initiated an application for the first – the remaining four were all initiated by search companies or school boards that knew of me by reputation, sought me out, made an approach and after a preliminary conversation, strongly encouraged me to apply.

My reasons for "knowing it was time to go" were therefore completely different from the factors described above. Yes, I had my share of cantankerous and self-serving board members, plus a few overly ambitious, less-than-ethical executive staff who were more than willing to spread untruths in the hope of furthering their own career aspirations or avoid being pushed beyond the comfort zone they had erected around themselves in their role. However, none of these was a factor in my wanting to move from any school where I served as Head. (As a parent in one of the schools where I was Principal said to me, "we love the fact that you are not a quitter").

The ceremony farewelling me from Li Po Chun United World College in Hong Kong (China) to take up the headship of The Awty International School in Houston, Texas (USA) in 2011. This was the first event to be held in the new auditorium which was the largest building project undertaken during my headship in Hong Kong.

For me (as a change leader), the usual reason that I thought it was time to move was feeling I had faithfully and honourably achieved the most important reforms required in the school where I was serving, and I could now contribute more to the world of education in a new school with different needs. New challenges have always excited me, with the more difficult-to-achieve challenges always seeming to offer the greatest satisfaction.

I loved being the leader of every school where I was Principal. I never regretted leaving when I did as I invariably felt the time was right to move on to new challenges where my skills could be of even greater use in the service of others.

POSTSCRIPT:

I recently re-visited Romania for the first time since 1987. Today, it is a beautiful, prosperous, confident member of the European Union, functioning effectively under effective "rule of law". It is completely transformed from the dismal, quirky place I encountered in 1987. This is encouraging as it shows how a country (like a school) can recover and thrive from a period of turmoil.

Strada Turda in downtown Bucharest today (the same place shown in the 1987 tram photo on page 287).

The House of the Republic, now re-named the Palace of Parliament, was constructed under Ceauşescu's orders from 1984 to 1997. At 240 metres long, 270 metres wide, and with 12 stories, it is now the world's second largest building.

The only reminders of Ceaușescu today are some museums and the "House of the Republic", a huge extravagant 'palace' that was built on his orders and now dominates downtown Bucharest. Second only to The Pentagon in Washington DC as the world's largest building, the Guinness Book of World Records claims the House of the Republic is the world's most expensive building and the world's heaviest building.

It serves as a sullen warning of the dangerous excesses that suppression of "common knowledge" can bring. Sadly, I think it can also serve as a warning to the boards of schools with long-standing Principals who are approaching retirement and may seem intent on leaving a highly visible legacy of their leadership – perhaps a sports complex, a pool, or a classroom block with their name inscribed on the front – in what is sometimes facetiously termed having an "edifice complex".

The inspiration

This article was originally inspired by an episode of the consistently excellent podcast *Cautionary Tales* by Tim Harford: 'The Rise and Fall of a Megalomaniac', 12 Apr 2024.

References and further reading

Almond M (1991) *The Rise and Fall of Nicolae and Elena Ceaușescu*. Orion.

Behr E (1991) *Kiss the Hand You Cannot Bite: The Rise and Fall of the Ceaușescus*. Villard Books.

DeConici D, et.al. (1989) *Revolt Against Silence: The state of human rights in Romania*, US Commission on Security and Cooperation in Europe article.

De Freitas J, Thomas K, DeScioli P & Pinker S (2019) "Common knowledge, coordination, and strategic mentalizing in human social life". *PNAS* 116(28): 13751-13758 article.

Elliott M (1990) László Tőkés, Timișoara and the Romanian Revolution. *George Fox University Occasional Papers on Religion in Eastern Europe*. 19(5) article.

James A (2014) *Death of the Dictator: the Romanian Revolution of 1989.* article.

Keresztes PK (1985) When Romania turned Bibles into toilet paper, *Wall Street Journal* 14/6/1985 article.

Littleford J (2024) *Leadership Of Schools And The Longevity Of Heads* article.

Pacepa IM (1990) *Red Horizons: The True Story of Nicolae and Elena Ceausescus' Crimes, Lifestyle, and Corruption.* Regenery Publishing.

Rupnik, J (1988) *The Other Europe*. Weidenfeld and Nicholson.

Sweeney J (1991) *The Life and Evil Times of Nicolae Ceaușescu*. Hutchinson.

Insight 62

Language and Communication in Board Meetings

When I was a student in high school, I had a Maths teacher named Ralph Cooper – "Mr Cooper" to his students, of course. We always knew when he was getting angry (which was several times every lesson), as his face turned bright red, his breathing became slow and deep, and he stood silently at the front of the classroom, staring at us in silence while slowly rolling a piece of chalk back and forth in the palm of his open, upwardly turned hand.

These days, we refer to this behaviour as 'body language'. Language and communication are not the same as each other. Language is based on vocabulary and strict rules of grammar (yes, even nowadays) – that is why "Jack hit Jill" is not the same as "Jill hit Jack". These precise rules of language may be subtle, which explains the difference between the Spanish sentences "Mi papá tiene 47 años" (My dad is 47 years old) and "Mi papa tiene 47 anos" (My potato has 47 anuses).

Spanish	English
Mi papá tiene 47 años	My dad is 47 years old
Mi papa tiene 47 anos	My potato has 47 anuses

Imagine two situations, both of which occur in a meeting of your school board:

Situation 1: You are bored with the discussion and, while the Chair is looking away, you catch someone's eye across the table and make a yawning gesture by putting your hand to your mouth.

Situation 2: You are trying to look interested in what a board member is saying and to your horror you find you are starting to yawn.

Both yawns communicate information, and might be termed 'body language', but only the first should really be described as language, because the gesture was intentional.

Board meetings can be notorious for the mis-communication that occurs, especially when well-meaning passions cloud a person's ability (or willingness) to consider other people's viewpoints. In extreme cases, respect for others can break down and heated rhetoric might itself become an issue when attendees fear that their words are falling short of the intensity of their feelings. The American writer Ralph Waldo Emerson once wrote that to speak is to "roast your marshmallows on Vesuvius" – that is, our language is just a pale reflection of the fire within us.

This potential for mis-communication has expanded enormously with the increasing use of conducting meetings online through platforms such as Zoom, Webex, Teams and GoTo Meetings. Even setting aside concerns about poor bandwidth and distracting backgrounds, online board meetings lack spontaneity because of repeated tiny time lags and, more significantly, the loss of much of the body language and eye contact that most people take for granted – and rely upon – to communicate effectively.

There are commonly accepted cultural rules of conversational communication. For example, when I was Head of an international school in Hong Kong, and my board's membership consisted entirely of local Hong Kong Chinese people, I soon learned that the conversational dynamics were vastly different from my experiences elsewhere. When an issue was being discussed, it was usually the younger members who would speak first, and a range of opinions would be expressed. As the discussion continued, more senior members would agree with the emerging consensus, adding some additional weight to the arguments. We knew the discussion was drawing to a close when one or two of the most senior members of the board (who had usually consulted together by telephone prior to the meeting) spoke quietly to the hushed room and revealed the "correct" outcome, at which point everyone around the table would nod in agreement.

In most societies, there are widely (but not universally) recognised rules for conversing, especially regarding the protocols for interrupting other people, or correcting other people's comments.

To take an example from everyday life (as opposed to the more heavily structured situation of a board meeting), when someone asks you for the time, you might reply by saying "it's half past ten" when it is actually 10:28 or 10:32. This helps us understand that some conversations occur in a precise context, which others take place in an imprecise context. In an imprecise context, it is acceptable to round off the time within, say, three or four minutes. On the other hand, in a precise context, such as counting down to New Year's fireworks (or in every conversation with my eldest son), it is expected that you would be very particular in expressing accuracy.

Board meetings are somewhat contrived conversation environments. The rules of conversation are seldom articulated explicitly, which means every member may well come to every meeting with different underlying assumptions about what is acceptable and what is not. It is easy to see how unintended misunderstandings can arise in such situations, especially if the unwritten rules for correcting others hang ambiguously over the meeting.

Some school boards fall into the habit, or the comfort zone, of tolerating sub-optimal meeting dynamics. It may seem easier at the time to let this slide, but inevitably it diminishes the effectiveness of the board's work and ultimately adds to everyone's workload, especially that of the Principal.

Every board – and the school it serves – benefits from the periodic input of a well-informed, external, politically neutral critical friend or mentor.

Insight 63

Language matters

Many people think that our so-called post-truth society only emerged in the last decade or so. This is, of course, untrue. As long ago as the late 1940s when he wrote "1984", George Orwell was aware of the power of language to shape people's thoughts. Change the meaning of words, and you change not only the patterns of thinking, but you impose limits around the ideas that be conceived or conceptualised.

I had a direct personal experience of this, ironically in the year 1984. At the time I was a member of the Geography Syllabus Committee of what was then the New South Wales Board of Senior Secondary School Studies (a great-great-grandparent of what is now NESA).

Syllabus Committee members were (rightly) becoming increasingly sensitive to language that might be sexist. A proposal came to the Committee that the person in charge of the Committee should no longer be referred to as "Chairman". The rationale for this proposed change was that the word "Chairman" identified an elite position of power while also implying that the position would be filled by a man. It was seen to forge a grammatical link between power and gender bias towards males. Rather than introducing an additional sexist term – Chairwoman – the proposal was that the position be re-named "Chairperson".

This led to a vigorous debate (as often happens when changes are proposed in committees, and even in School Board meetings!). A counter-argument was put to the meeting claiming that the "man" component of the word "Chairman" did not designate masculinity, but it derived from the Latin word "manus" meaning "hand", from which we also get the English words "manual" and "manage", as in managing the meeting.

Many members of the Committee conceded that the verb "to manage" was indeed the source of the word "Chairman". Nonetheless, several vocal members argued that even though the word "Chairman" may not have arisen from an assumption of male power, the general public thought "Chairman" implied an exclusively male role, and therefore it should be replaced with a gender-neutral alternative.

However, the situation became genuinely absurdist when one Pythonesque member of the Committee argued that the word "Chairperson" was also sexist, because "son" still implied masculinity, resulting in a debate over whether we should use "Chairperchild", but this was in turn seen by some members as an ageist term implying youth. I sincerely hope your school board meetings never descend to the abysmal level of that Syllabus Committee meeting.

In the end, it was agreed that the role would henceforth be known simply as "Chair", despite some objections that "Chair" implied inactivity because a chair is an inanimate object. So yes, the photo below shows me standing beside the Chair 😄.

Language matters because it is the medium through which we form concepts and understandings. School boards must be sensitive to society's changing use of language. At the same time, school boards must never surrender truth to semantics.

Some current real-world examples illustrate the point.

Whether gender is defined as a binary dichotomy or a point along a spectrum matters when school boards and leaders develop policies relating to issues such as admissions, provision of washrooms, organisation of sports teams, and so on.

When teachers are guiding class discussions, it matters whether they refer to the European colonisation of Australia or the Americas or most of Africa as "settlement" or "invasion", or indeed whether an open debate on this question is permissible or not.

It matters whether we believe the documented evidence that smoking is hazardous to students' health.

It matters whether we believe or reject the arguments that arming staff in a school with guns enhances the safety of the students.

It matters when students don't know the difference between inductive reasoning and deductive reasoning. It also matters when students avoid reasoning altogether and simply draw conclusions on the basis of their intuition (gut feelings). It matters even more when school boards do the same thing.

School boards and leaders inevitably rely on clarity in language because, as Edward Sapir and Benjamin Lee Whorf independently demonstrated, language provides our scaffolding for thinking, understanding and discerning the relative merits of alternative propositions.

Language matters.

Use of the word "Chairman" is discussed in further detail in a footnote on page 423.

Insight 64

Looking in the mirror before joining a School Board

Before stepping into the high-stakes world of school board membership, there is one critical meeting which all aspiring board members must attend first – the one with themselves.

I have often observed that school boards tend to be better at pointing an accusatory finger than holding up a mirror to reflect on their own performance. In other words, boards are often better at accusing others than accepting responsibility. That is why looking into a metaphorical mirror is so important for current and aspiring board members.

Looking in the mirror is not just a metaphor; it represents a necessary moment of self-reflection. Why do you want to serve? Are you prepared for the challenges, conflicts, and responsibilities that come with shaping a school's future? Joining a school board is not about furthering a personal agenda or inflating an ego; it is about commitment, collaboration, and the courage to make tough decisions for the benefit of students, educators, and the community. Before you take a seat at the table, take a long, honest look at the person staring

back at you and ask the serious questions "Are you ready?" and "Are you worthy?".

Some people join school boards because they want to contribute something significant to children's futures. Others may join because of pressure from their friends on the board who are worried about low numbers and the problems they have to raise a quorum. Still others join because of a passion to pursue a single issue that concerns them or because a nominating organisation has put forward their name. Some are motivated to join a school board for personal or family reasons, others for emotional reasons that may relate to loyalty, while a surprisingly small number join for purely rational reasons.

Irrespective of the personal motivation, most people join school boards with honourable intentions and a passionate desire to improve the school. Of course, some board members may interpret the word "improve" differently from others, and that can lead to some robust discussions at board meetings. Occasionally, motivations are less honourable, ill-informed, prejudiced, self-serving, or simply unconstructive. Ego rather than service certainly drives some people to join school boards.

If you are a member of a school board, or if you are considering joining, it can be helpful to hold up a metaphorical mirror and reflect on your own motivations. Your motivation may be noble and focussed on serving others, such as one or more of the following:

- You have specific skills that are lacking on the board at present and which could help the school flourish.
- You care deeply about the school's mission (enduring purpose) and want to have some input regarding its future vision and direction.
- You have a specific project that is important to you, such as a new building or curriculum initiative, and you want to support it.
- You feel you have benefitted from your own education and now want to "give back" to help the next generation of students.
- You have concerns about the school's viability or direction, and you believe you can help turn it around or make it successful again.
- You have the time to commit to a meaningful service activity.
- You have skills in leadership and want to share these skills to benefit others.

Alternatively, your motivation may be more self-serving and personal, such as one or more of the following:

- You are building your professional career, and being a board member would look rather good on your CV while also allowing you to learn new skills and network with other professionals.
- You are a current parent of the school and want to be an insider who knows what is "really" going on so you can have a direct influence on the school's operations.
- You are retired and feel that serving on a school board would give you some focus in life through meaningful work that fits within your flexible schedule.
- You are new to the community and want to make friends.
- You enjoy challenges and feel that service on a school board service might be interesting as you have previously never tried this.
- You are interested in getting a job with the school, and you suspect serving on the board would be a way to get preferential treatment.

If you are interested in joining a school board, or if you have been approached by the board to consider joining, there are several important steps that should be taken. The first step is to find out and develop a clear understanding of the school's mission. One of every school board's primary duties is to develop, guide and implement the mission, which is the school's enduring purpose – the guiding framework that underpins every decision that is made. If you don't embrace the mission, you will not be able to contribute fully to the board, and you will probably experience intense frustration.

Effective school boards comprise members with various skills, talents, backgrounds, and perspectives. Some larger boards create their own skills profile matrix which allows them to reflect upon the present composition as a means towards determining future needs. Therefore, board recruitment is a two-way process in which both the board and the individual need to be satisfied. Being willing and able is not enough; an aspiring board member must fill a need that the board has at a particular moment – a need that is beyond simply 'adding to the numbers'.

It is also important that a prospective board member understands the expectations that the board has of its members. How many meetings are held each year? Is personal attendance required or is remote access acceptable? Is there a Code of Conduct to be signed, and if so, what are its inclusions? What are board's policies on conflicts of interest and related party transactions? Does the board reimburse expenses for attending meetings? What are board members' legal responsibilities and liabilities? These and many other details should be discussed openly and transparently before committing to board membership.

If an invitation to board membership is extended after all the conversations and information sharing have been completed, breathe a sigh of relief and celebrate – but only for a short time, because the hard work and the long hours are about to begin as the joy of serving others in this most important of duties gathers momentum.

In the wise words of Pat Bassett, former President of NAIS (National Association of Independent Schools) from 2001 to 2013: "Being a board member does not allow you a special benefit; it burdens you with a responsibility".

Insight 65

Lying applicants

To the astonishment of (just a few) school principals, it seems that not every applicant for a teaching position is always honest when they submit their application for employment.

Research conducted for the employment agency SEEK found that 36% of applicants confess that they have not been completely honest in their applications. It seems that the untruths fall into four broad areas: (i) the applicant's experience in one or more aspects of the job, (ii) the applicant's formal qualifications, (iii) the salary they have been earning in their current or previous positions, and (iv) their reasons for leaving previous positions or wanting to leave their current employment.

Dishonesty is most definitely not an example of type of role modelling that schools expect from their teachers. In some more extreme cases, lying on a resumé can result in a legal charge of fraud,

especially if the lying is supported by counterfeit or forged documents such as degrees or professional credentials, and/or if the false information appears as part of a signed document. Furthermore, it is clearly illegal for an applicant to deny criminal history, especially in areas such as child abuse and child safety.

So why do so many applicants lie?

It may be because the applicant is simply desperate to get a job to overcome financial or personal problems. It may be because the applicant feels inadequate, especially if applying for a position in a desirable or prestigious school. Related to this motive, it may be because of a real or imagined pressure to meet expectations. It may be an attempt to get an advantage over other applicants.

Lying on applications is also a significant factor for school boards when recruiting a new principal, as applicants for principals' positions have also been known to embellish their applications with false claims about qualifications, experience, or reasons for leaving previous positions. It is one of the reasons that some schools use external consultants when they are seeking to recruit a new principal.

To state the obvious, dishonesty can have serious consequences not only for the individual but also for the educational institution and students in a school that is deceived by the lies presented in the application. Whatever the so-called rationale, lying on a job application is never excusable.

Given the seriousness of getting recruitment right, there are several actions that principals can take when recruiting staff – and which boards can take when recruiting principals – once the initial short-listing has been concluded that can reduce the risks of being seduced by lying applicants. These actions fall into two groups: (i) during the interview, and (ii) after the interview.

DURING THE INTERVIEW

Unless it is absolutely impossible, try to conduct interviews in-person, face-to-face, rather than remotely on a screen. Remote interviews almost always obscure important body language and signs of stress which are important in revealing unease due to lying (as well as other factors). In-person face-to-face interactions make information transfer easier and more natural, enabling everyone involved to make better connections. Without doubt there is a place for remote work, but top management is not one of those places.

If possible, during the face-to-face interview, get the applicant to demonstrate some of the competencies required for the position rather than simply talk about them. For example, require a teacher to teach a demonstration lesson to one or two classes of students in the school, ask to see examples of their own lesson plans and teaching registers, and so on. Similarly, it is entirely appropriate for the board's selection committee to ask short-listed applicants for Principal to deliver a short speech, to be placed in situations where their interaction with students can be observed, and to address and answer questions from a panel of representative members of the staff.

For teacher and principals' interviews, it is often helpful to present real scenarios in the school and then engage in a deep discussion about how the applicant might go about addressing the challenge specified. The areas that could be explored are as wide as the school's activities, but whatever the topic, there should be an in-depth discussion that go well beyond platitudes and engages in real-world problem-solving. In this way, the real (as opposed to imagined or claimed) experience and qualifications of the applicant should emerge.

It is important that style and eloquence are not allowed to obscure untruths or false claims during an interview. Charm can be a helpful asset in education, but it is never a substitute for honesty, truth, and competence. An interview panel should never be afraid of pursuing a robust line of questioning, even to the point of discomfort, especially if lying or cover-ups are suspected. To that end, inserting some less common interview questions such as those outlined in THIS article can be very helpful.

AFTER THE INTERVIEW

No-one – no teacher, no member of the non-teaching staff, and especially no Principal – should ever be employed without first obtaining several (ideally three) confidential reference checks. These days, written 'open' references are generally regarded as useless because of the fear that any negative observations or opinions may be subject to dispute or even legal action by the subject of the reference. References should be confidential and must always include questions about the applicant's work performance and history in the area of child safety. It is essential that anyone appointed to work in a school has no convictions relating to child protection or any previous conduct that precludes working with children. Therefore, reference checking should always include an open question along the lines of "is there any factor I should know about that would preclude employing this person in a school?".

It is increasingly common to include a 'due diligence' check of social media before offering a position to any teacher or principal. This can be a worthwhile step, but principals and boards should also be aware that not everything on social media is accurate, it is often opinionated, and may be the work of jealous colleagues or upset students "letting off steam". The accuracy of information on social media is likely to deteriorate even further in the years ahead as generative AI becomes more widely available and sophisticated. Social media checks should be used only with discernment.

Finally, it is important not to rush the appointment of a new teacher or new principal. As I have often said "it is better to have a good vacancy than a bad appointment".

Insight 66

Making decisions using data

Soon after I completed my fifth and final Headship, I returned to Australia and was asked by a former colleague, "What is your number one take-away after a quarter of a century as a school Principal?" I had to consider not only the schools where I had served as Principal, but also the many others I had visited or evaluated as a member of various accreditation teams. I am by nature a positive person, and yet I eventually replied using an uncharacteristic double negative: "I cannot think of a single school that could not be improved with better Board governance".

That does not mean that most Boards are disastrous any more than it implies that most schools are disastrous. However, it does suggest that most Boards are operating sub-optimally, probably unknowingly, and most likely because of inertia.

My answer surprised my colleague. School Boards and Administrators devote considerable energy and resources to improving student outcomes, raising teacher morale, developing facilities and ensuring sound management practices. However, unless they are deep in crisis, very few school Boards give sufficient time or attention to their own welfare, efficacy, operations or procedures. Even fewer Boards consciously consider the impact of their own 'Board health' on the operations and reputation of the school.

Are Board Members prepared to accept a sub-optimal level in their own operations that they would not tolerate in the school's day-to-day operations?

Having worked directly with hundreds of Board Members, and having been a Board Member myself, I can count on the fingers of just one hand the few Board Members I have met who might place their own interests above those of the school. School Board Members rank among the most sacrificial, public-spirited and generous people I have ever worked with or known. And yet, even with that immense generosity of spirit, Boards can fall into the trap of blaming others when the reality is that their own policies, procedures and processes might be inhibiting the school's effectiveness.

Boards know that they must accept responsibility for the school's finances, legal obligations, risk management, mission, policies, safety, and the appointment and oversight of the Principal, as well as ultimately the school's reputation and its viability. Yet too few Boards seem to appreciate how important their responsibilities to self-evaluate and to be evaluated are for the school.

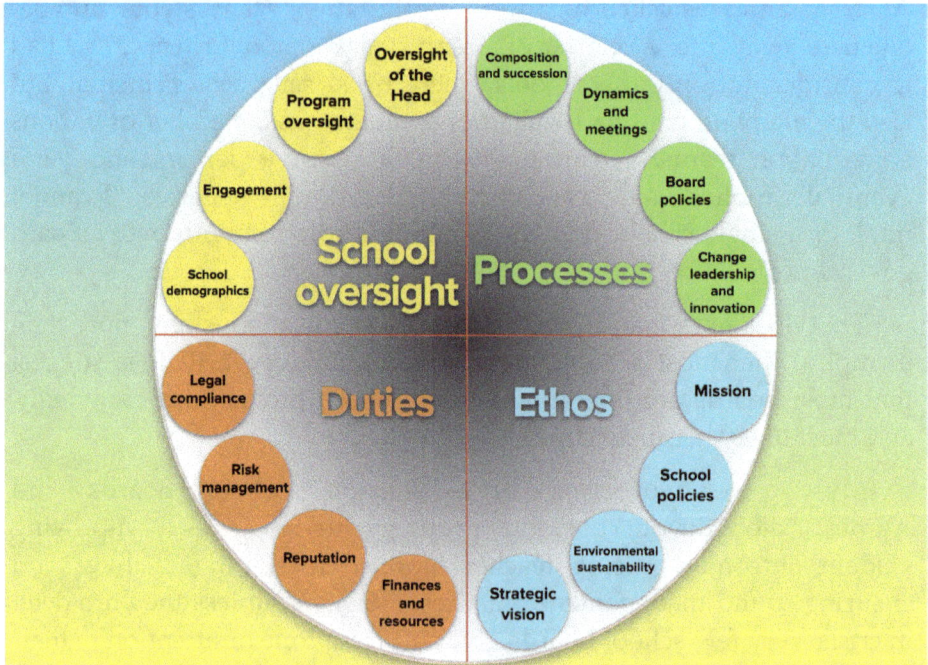

Why is Board evaluation so important? Quite simply, effective Boards that operate according to best practices add value to their school. And Boards can only ensure that they are operating optimally if they can measure performance against clear, impartial criteria. Warm fuzzy impressions simply don't make the grade in today's competitive environment.

In the United States, school Boards routinely monitor their own performance, both through regular formal self-evaluations and independent external consultants. To date, such practices have been less common in the UK, Australia and elsewhere. However, as Boards appreciate the significant impact they have either to enhance or diminish their school's effectiveness, it is imperative that regular Board training becomes the expected norm everywhere.

Insight 67

Making schools green

Thousands of contemporary statistical studies from all parts of the world are conveying an overwhelmingly consistent message – the general population is increasingly concerned about declining environmental quality and sustainability. This trend is strongest among school-aged children and their parents.

In a 2021 survey conducted by the Governance Institute in Australia among 550 board members and senior executives, climate change (together with fallout from COVID-19 and economic instability) ranked as the top responses to the question "What are the three main issues you believe will have the most impact on society and, therefore, your organisation by 2025?".

It is important to note that this survey targeted business rather than education. In contrast to the survey results, many school boards and leaders are yet to appreciate the full significance of this trend for their school. Nonetheless, as a general rule, parents increasingly want schools that practise environmental sustainability and promote care for the environment.

Prioritising renewable energy, installing roof-top solar panels, constructing buildings with biologically green roofs, reducing waste, implementing recycling, using stored rainwater, green cleaning, planting local indigenous trees and shrubs, designing classrooms with natural passive ventilation, and so on, are all attractive factors in the eyes of many parents who are exploring schools for their children.

It seems that many parents (as a highly significant component of the wider population) feel that if our society doesn't take consequential action urgently, then future generations – including their own children – will be left to deal with the devastating consequences of our inaction.

School leaders and boards thus have the opportunity to make a significant impact on the future of our planet through the school's environmental priorities and their implementation. As climate change and environmental degradation become increasingly pressing issues, many would argue there is a moral imperative for schools to consider and hopefully prioritise environmental sustainability as a core component their decision-making processes. When schools implement sustainable practices, they become role models that not only reduce own carbon footprint but also inspire future generations to become environmental stewards.

When I refer to "sustainability", my background as a geographer demands that I use the word in the strict sense – to use a resource sustainably means it is managed in such a way that the resource can be used in perpetuity. Sustainability is arguably the perfect ideal for humans to exercise environmental stewardship of our planet.

Environmental sustainability should be a priority for school boards and leaders for several reasons:

1. **Environmental sustainability benefits students educationally.**

The goal of every school's board should be to provide students with a top-quality education (in whatever way this is defined by the mission and vision statements). However, education is not restricted to the confines of the classroom and the lesson plans that derive from the syllabus. Modelling sustainable practices in a school can not only inspire students to adopt these same practices in their own lives, but can become a 'living textbook' to illustrate, exemplify and enhance studies in subjects such as Science, Geography, Mathematics and even Economics and Business Studies.

2. Environmental sustainability enhances student and staff health.

Environmental sustainability isn't only good for the planet – it also benefits our health. By reducing pollution, removing toxic substances and promoting sustainable practices, a healthier environment is created for students and staff. This can lead to lower rates of respiratory illness, allergies, and other health problems.

3. Environmental sustainability is financially beneficial.

Implementing sustainable practices can also save a school money in the long run (even though some initial, short-term investment may be required). For example, switching to energy-efficient lighting and appliances can reduce energy bills. Installing water-saving fixtures can reduce water bills. Reducing waste can save on disposal costs. These and other savings can be reinvested in the school to improve educational programs and facilities.

4. Environmental sustainability expands community engagement.

When a school promotes environmental sustainability, it almost inevitably leads to engaging with the community in important conversations about the future of the surrounding region. This can in turn lead to greater community involvement in school programs and events, which then can help build stronger relationships between the school and its community in multiple practical ways that enhance opportunities for the students.

A helpful conceptual framework for approaching, organising and implementing environmental sustainability in schools is the United Nations Sustainable Development Goals (SDGs). The SDGs highlight the mutual interdependence of environmental, social and economic sustainability and the ways in which they rely on each other for success.

To summarise, the SDGs are a set of 17 goals established by the United Nations in 2015 to create a globally sustainable future. These goals cover a range of issues, from poverty reduction to climate action, and they provide a framework for governments, organisations and individuals to work towards a better world.

School boards have an important (and arguably unique) role to play in achieving the SDGs, particularly those related to ensuring inclusive

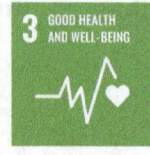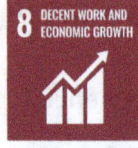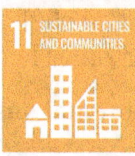

and equitable quality education for all (Goal 4) and developing sustainable cities and communities (Goal 11). By incorporating environmental sustainability into a board's decision-making process, school boards can help achieve both of these goals within the wider, integrated framework of all 17 SDGs.

If environmental sustainability is so important for schools, why do many school boards underestimate its importance? I suggest there are five possible reasons:

1. **Denial of the importance of environmental sustainability**

Some board members may be opposed to environmental sustainability on ideological grounds, especially when a discussion on sustainability becomes conflated with politically contentious debates on topics such as human-induced climate change or elevating poorer people out of their financial poverty.

2. **Lack of awareness**

Some school boards may simply not be aware of the potential significant impact their decisions can have on the environment. They may not have either the knowledge or resources to implement sustainable practices.

3. **Short-term thinking**

School boards often prioritise immediate financial concerns over long-term sustainability. They may not see the benefits of investing in environmentally sustainable initiatives if they don't see an immediate or short-term return on investment.

4. **Perception of environmental sustainability as a lesser concern**

School boards may view sustainability as a secondary concern, believing that their primary focus should be on academic achievement and student outcomes within the ethical ethos of the school.

5. **Resistance to change**

Some school boards may be inherently conservative and thus resistant to change in general (on any issue), or else sceptical of the value of environmental sustainability initiatives specifically. Such board members may believe that the cost and effort of implementing environmentally sustainable practices outweigh the benefits.

Notwithstanding these five factors, and given the positive impact schools can have in shaping our collective and individual futures, what can school leaders and the board do to promote environmental sustainability?

Here are five ideas to get started:

1. **Conduct an environmental audit.**

Start by conducting an environmental audit of the school. This will help the board and the entire school community identify areas where sustainability practices can be improved. This audit can include energy and water usage, waste management practices, recycling opportunities and more. The results of the audit can be used as the foundation to create a sustainability plan for the school.

2. **Establish sustainability goals.**

Using information acquired during the environmental audit and with reference to the SDGs, the school board and management leadership can establish relevant goals and measurable targets for reducing waste, energy consumption, and carbon emissions. These goals can be incorporated into school policies, used as a scaffold to guide decision-making, and provide the basis of strategic KPIs.

3. **Educate students and staff.**

Educate students and staff about the importance of environmental sustainability. Lessons that incorporate the concept and practice of sustainability can be incorporated into the curriculum, and relevant, practical training can be provided for staff. The school can also create awareness campaigns to encourage students and staff to adopt sustainable practices in their daily lives.

4. **Implement sustainable practices.**

There are many sustainable practices that schools can implement, from installing solar panels to reducing single-use plastics. Other strategies might include installing energy-efficient lighting and appliances, using low-flow water fixtures, and composting food waste. Schools can also reduce waste by using reusable plates and utensils in the cafeteria, and by providing recycling bins throughout the school. By adopting these and other practices which promote sustainability, schools can reduce their environmental impact and set an example for the wider community.

5. **Work in partnership with the surrounding community.**

Schools can also encourage community involvement in sustainability efforts. Community partnerships can include working with local businesses to reduce waste, collaborating with community organisations on sustainability initiatives such as community clean-up events, promoting sustainable transport options, and inviting community members to participate in sustainability events at the school.

Environmental sustainability is emerging as an essential consideration for school boards in today's world. By making environmental sustainability a priority in schools, boards and school leaders can educate students, promote health, reduce costs, engage the surrounding community, and help protect the planet for future generations in accord with the UN SDGs.

I encourage school boards, leaders and educators to give genuine consideration to the expanding implications of environmental sustainability for their schools, not only for today but with a clear view to the decades and generations to come.

Insight 68

Managing a crisis

From time to time, all school boards and leaders endure what are politely termed "those days", or less politely – "crises".

It may be a depressing thought, but the philosopher Slavoj Žižek says that crises should no longer be considered as "exceptions" to the normal order, but we should acknowledge that we are now living in a permanent state of exceptions. Martin Amis agrees, calling this "the Age of Vanished Normalcy", while Stephen McAlpine relates this to the growing hostility in society towards Christian education by identifying our era as "Exile Stage Two".

In other words, we are now living and working in an era where exceptions are the norm – to which I respond "what a great foundation to start your next strategic planning session" (yes, sarcasm alert!).

At a national and international scale, Žižek claims our leaders deliberately keep talking about crises as a mask to hide the need to take genuine action. Sir Humphrey Appleby (of "Yes Prime Minister" fame) would have agreed, as he once argued that "politicians like to panic – they need activity; it's their substitute for achievement".

In stark contrast, school boards and leaders do not have that luxury (and neither, it could be argued, should national and international leaders). When a crisis hits, schools – and their boards – MUST act.

Crises are usually unpredictable, and can be triggered by a myriad of causes – the sudden death of a student or a teacher, a blogger or a journalist with an axe to grind, a disgruntled former employee, staff who are upset about the pace of change (which may be too slow or too fast depending on the situation), changes in workload, reductions in benefits, the expulsion of a popular student or the dismissal of a popular teacher, parents' concern about examination results or a perceived lack of sporting successes, a perceived conflict of interest – the list is almost endless.

The spark that triggers a crisis can become a wildfire if a perception grows in the school community that the Board and/or the Principal has mismanaged (or even worse, caused) the situation or incident. The angry voice of a vocal minority can start to dominate the debate, often out of proportion to the original trigger, after which the personalities of the warring parties can start to become issues in themselves.

Every crisis in any school has its own unique factors that must be taken into account when managing the situation. However, irrespective of these differences, it is essential that the efforts of the Board and the Principal are unified and coherent, both privately and in public. The board itself must remain unified and maintain confidentiality having nominated just one person to be the public voice – usually the Principal if it's a school matter or the Board Chair if it is a governance matter, or alternatively both together if a strong sense of unity needs to be conveyed.

As a general rule, there are certain things that should NOT be done in a crisis:

- DON'T make any promises or commitments that can't be kept;
- DON'T enter into a point-by-point campaign of letter writing;
- DON'T write to the group or to the wider school community rashly or in haste;
- DON'T make any public criticisms of any individuals;
- DON'T hold a 'town hall' meeting; and
- DON'T backtrack on an earlier position without a very good reason (such as legal advice)

Schools have been known to take a decade or more to recover from a serious crisis, so crisis management should always be taken very seriously and implemented as early in the crisis as possible.

It will not surprise you to learn that I believe the wisdom of an independent, politically neutral, highly experienced external consultant is not only valuable, but necessary to help guide a school through a process of crisis management.

Insight 69

Measure what you treasure

Nothing is more important for building and maintaining the integrity of an independent school than living according to its founding ethos and philosophy. A school's foundational positions are usually expressed formally though public statements such as the Mission Statement, Vision Statement, and Statement of Values.

So, how can the leadership of a school monitor the extent to which its mission, vision and values are being achieved in practice? Ideally, the answer should be to conduct an assessment that focuses specifically on measuring mission and values performance.

But there's a problem. The tyranny of measurement suggests "if you can't measure it, you can't manage it", and values are notoriously difficult to measure. That is why core values tend to get neglected when schools undertake their traditional performance reviews.

I have addressed this significant shortcoming of traditional school appraisal and performance review processes by crafting an original ground-breaking tool that authentically evaluates a school's performance in achieving its mission, vision and values.

This targeting instrument is the Schools Mission Appraisal Reporting Tool (SMART).

SMART is derived from methodological approaches that were first developed in the field of environmental sustainability, another specialty area in which developing reliable evaluative indicators is notoriously challenging. SMART thus draws upon extensive academic and project-based research into developing values-based measures and applies these to the specific needs of assessing values in schools.

SMART shifts the key question away from "what can be measured using current methods and datasets?" to "what should be measured to ensure progress towards the kind of education that will enhance achievement of the school's mission, vision and values?".

Experience in many schools has demonstrated that what gets measured gets done, and by implication, anything that is left unmeasured is likely to be neglected. SMART offers a solution to this challenge.

THE UNMET NEED IN SCHOOLS

Every school exists to fulfil its unique enduring purpose, usually expressed through its Mission and Vision Statements.

So, how can the leadership of a school monitor the extent to which its mission, vision and values are being achieved in practice? Ideally, the answer should be to **conduct an assessment that focuses specifically on measuring mission and values performance**.

This is a task that is neither easy nor frequently undertaken. As the American Sociology Professor, William Bruce Cameron, wrote in 1963: **"Not everything that counts can be counted, and not everything that can be counted counts."**

Cameron's statement encapsulates one of the great paradoxes faced by educators, school leaders and school boards, which is that **the most highly valued educational outcomes are those which are the most difficult to measure**.

In contrast to Cameron's assertion, an all-too-common saying is **"if you can't measure it, you can't manage it."** For many organisations, this approach has led to 'measurement' becoming a goal in itself, often encouraging managers to take the easy road of focussing only upon those outcomes which are easiest to measure and quantify. Such outcomes seldom focus upon, or even include, a school's founding mission, vision and values.

Most independent schools were founded on the basis of a **strong, coherent values position** that is expressed through its mission and/or vision. Such schools aim to share and develop those values explicitly with their students – it is the school's primary *raison d'être*. It follows from this that **an effective school evaluation, or performance review, ought to focus primarily on the extent to which its values objectives are being achieved.**

Every educator understands the tyranny of measurement. Most school performance reviews are not designed to measure the extent to which its mission, vision and values are being achieved and implemented. Most school performance reviews largely comprise fairly generic, easily measured indicators, even though such variables are at best trivial shadows of the school's fundamental values – mere footnotes to the real purpose and mission.

"Not everything that counts can be counted, and not everything that can be counted counts".

William Bruce Cameron, 1963

THE SMART SOLUTION

SMART is **an original ground-breaking tool** that authentically evaluates a **school's performance in achieving its real purposes** – its mission, vision and values.

Following Research-by-Design methodology espoused by researchers such as Brockwell (2019), the SMART approach is based upon **two key principles**:

- Engaging key stakeholder groups in defining which outcomes are the most valuable, meaningful and worthwhile within the context of the school's mission, rather than uncritically adopting the values and priorities of the commonly used generic measuring tools; and

- Developing multi-level evaluation frameworks that take these diverse views into account through a curated process of choosing and prioritising the significant indicators to be investigated and the most effective ways to assess these indicators.

SMART shifts the key question away from "**what *can* be measured** using current methods and datasets?" to "**what *should* be measured** to ensure progress towards the kind of education that will enhance achievement of the school's mission, vision and values?".

WHAT ARE VALUES-BASED INDICATORS?

"**Values**" is a helpful shorthand term that embraces the beliefs, attitudes and consequent behaviours that are individually or collectively viewed as valuable, worthwhile, important and meaningful within a community that has a shared outlook, such as a school.

The values used in SMART are those which define a school's identity, and these in turn provide the foundation of the indicators and assessment tools used to evaluate performance. Specifically, we can think of values as "the principles and standards that guide behaviour", or "the ethics that contain an imperative for action", rather than mere "judgements about what is important in life" (a common dictionary definition).

It is widely recognised that attempts to measure values by using generic, predetermined constructs are problematic, especially in situations where there are people from several cultural backgrounds (Braithwaite & Law, 1985; Brown & Crace, 1996; Peng, Nisbett & Wong, 1997). SMART avoids these shortcomings by establishing viable alternative criteria to the traditional inflexible benchmarks.

WHY ARE VALUES-BASED INDICATORS IMPORTANT?

We know from experience in many schools that **what gets measured gets done, and by implication, anything that is left unmeasured is likely to be neglected**. Therefore, if a consensus were to emerge that 'values' are not 'measurable', they are likely to be overlooked and therefore diluted, even though they are central to a school's identity and purpose. In turn, **this is likely to contribute to** the marginalisation of a school's founding values, creating an ethical vacuum that is likely to be filled by more easily measurable dominant economic and political narratives.

The **indicators used** in SMART:

- help school leaders assess the values-based intangibles that define the individual school's identity, including identifying culturally defined legacies that are often missed in 'normal' evaluations;
- help school leaders crystallise the authentic values of the school (which often happens during "eureka" moments when the importance of previously overlooked factors is recognised);
- help school leaders communicate what the school offers beyond the usual 'deliverables' to students, parents, staff and the wider community;
- help school leaders capture important skills and capabilities that are seldom seen in conventional assessment approaches (such as how effectively students work in groups, how students relate emotionally to the school's values and thus put these values into action, and the extent to which students and teachers feel empowered to effect positive change);
- help school leaders monitor the extent to which the values of the school overlap with the values of staff and students, and use this information to improve the translation into action of the school's mission, vision and values; and
- following from these points, help school leaders create transformational learning situations in which students and teachers embrace, internalise and act upon the school's values with head, heart and spirit.

THE VALUES-ACTION GAP

Knowledge in itself is usually insufficient to change people's behaviour. Even though people know what they should be doing, they still do not do it. This **"knowledge-action gap"** is common, not only in everyday society, but in educational settings. The inaction or inertia resulting from knowledge-action gaps usually requires a values-action gap to be identified, addressed and overcome, as values tend to be deeper influences on people's behaviour than knowledge.

In numerous situations where strong statements about values are espoused, the sad reality is that many individuals within that community or environment fall short of performing the actions or behaviours implicit in those values. This can be regarded as a **"values-action gap"**.

If the values-action gap is to be addressed in schools, the actionable implications and consequences of the mission, vision and values need to be promoted and amplified through a regular process that uses a different type of performance review than those commonly conducted (which simply focus on easily measured, less significant factors).

SMART **offers a solution to this challenge**.

IMPLEMENTATION OF SMART

Every school has its unique mission, vision and values. Therefore, the process of implementing SMART varies from school to school. Nonetheless, as a generalisation, implementation usually follows an iterative process such as the one shown in the diagram below.

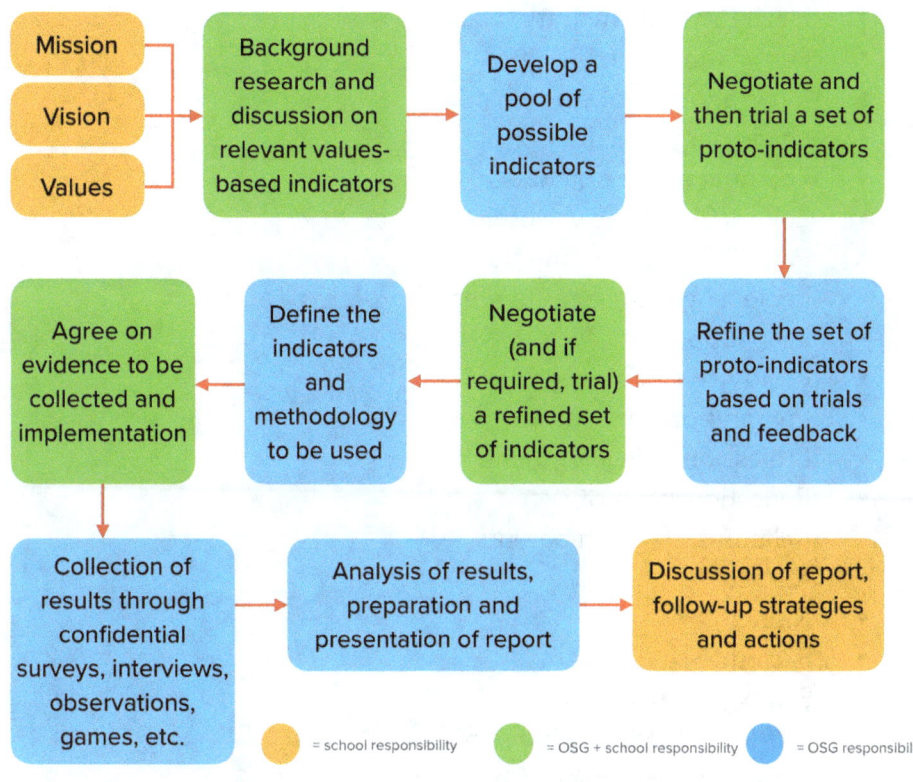

In addition to mission-specific variables, it is expected that many schools would expect also to include more general indicators of ethical practice such as trust, integrity, justice, empowerment, unity in diversity, and care and respect for the community of life.

Value clusters that have emerged in earlier discussions with schools in several countries when exploring Mission-based indicators include (in alphabetical order):

- Academic excellence / examinations performance
- Challenge / risk-taking
- Community action / connection / 'real world' action
- Compassion / caring
- Creativity
- Dialogue / collaboration
- Discipline / behaviour
- Enabling / empowering
- Engagement / initiative / responsibility
- Extra-curricular activities / co-curricular activities
- Financial benefits
- Flexibility / inclusivity
- Fun / humour / silliness
- Integration / holism
- Leadership / facilitation
- Learning environment
- Love / friendship / closeness
- Parenting / guardian role
- Personal goals / employment / progress
- Peer support
- Positivity / happiness
- Preparation / resources
- Professional development
- Reflection / criticality
- Relationships with parents
- Respect
- Rights
- Sacredness
- Safety / security
- Self-knowledge / self-awareness
- Sense of place / roots / heritage

- Service / giving
- Student-centredness
- Transformation
- Understanding

(after PERL, 2014, passim; and Brockwell, 2019; pp.179-180).

Using values clusters such as these, school-specific indicators can be developed using **four criteria**:

1. The indicator draws explicitly or implicitly from the school's enduring purpose (mission), vision (priorities) and values (ethical position).
2. The indicator represents a statement of an ideal or valued reality.
3. The indicator includes a subject (even a vague one such as 'people') and a verb.
4. The indicator is seen by the researcher as potentially 'measurable' or at least pointing towards something that can be evaluated (such as though observation, surveys, and/or qualitative methods such as interviews and focus groups).

Even when using these four criteria, **discernment** is required. For example, a statement such as "students acquire values and competencies different from those of materialistic, technocratic societies" does not provide sufficient detail to identify what the desired competencies might be – it needs to be expressed positively rather than as a deficit.

Brockwell (2019), Sabo Flores (2008) and Burford, Valasco et.al. (2013) offer several **strategies** to help students identify values-based performance effectiveness:

- "The First Thing You Think Of": asking students to write down the first thing that came into their minds when the facilitator mentions certain words, e.g. 'participation', 'community', 'sustainability', and the name of the school itself (c.f. Sabo Flores, 2008, p.52)
- "The 'Yes, And...' Game": encouraging students to create a 'collective story' about the type of future they would like to see for their school, in which each new participant has to acknowledge the preceding contribution by saying "Yes, and…" (c.f. Sabo Flores, 2008, p.56).

- 'Human survey' to assess the extent to which the students feel that key skills are already being put into practice in the school, by asking them to arrange themselves along an imaginary line across the room that represents a scale from 0% to 100% (c.f. Sabo Flores, 2008, p. 50). This has parallels with the 'spatial survey' method that was tested during the ESDinds Project in which participants were required to move into one of three different physical spaces to represent their choice from three possible answers to a question (Burford, Velasco, et al., 2013).

FREQUENTLY ASKED QUESTIONS (FAQs)

1. *Will the results be valid?*

Yes, the results will be as valid as you want them to be. The reality is that no measurement is considered rigorous if it is the only one that is made, so it can be helpful to validate the result by measuring the indicators using more than one method (such as **surveys, interviews, observations, focus groups, document analysis, diaries/logs, scenario analyses, guided visualisations, drama and theatre-based methods, word elicitation, diagram analysis, collective memory work, etc**). Using (say) three different methods to measure and triangulate an indicator would yield a result that is considered rigorous. On the other hand, not everyone requires such rigorous results – a school may simply want a more approximate result or even just 'a rough idea'. The choice is up to each school, depending upon the school's requirements, the time available, how many helpers are available, the budget available, etc.

2. **Does it matter if we don't use questionnaires?**

No, you can use any measurement method that suits the values and demographics of the school. Different measurement methods are listed in bold in FAQ-1 above. Whichever approach is used, we need to make sure:

   a. that everyone really understands the questions in the same way. Could a slightly different emphasis change the meaning of a question? Do we need to pre-test the questions with a small group first?

   b. that students and teachers are not just giving the answers that they think you (or their managers) want to hear. Do they feel comfortable enough to tell the truth? Are there any indicators that are so sensitive that we need to keep answers confidential?

   c. that students and teachers do not just 'follow the crowd' because they are afraid to show their real feelings in front of the group.

   d. that those people with the greatest difficulty making their voices heard, especially from marginalised groups, participate equally. Is anyone reluctant to speak in public, within a diverse group? Are there cultural barriers?

3. **How can we be confident we are using a legitimate system of indicators?**

The values-based indicators used for each school are individually crafted to harmonise with the school's specific mission, vision and values, and then curated to ensure seamless and effective implementation. The underlying framework of developing values-based indicators arises from a formal research project called ESDinds, which was funded by the European Union's Seventh Framework Programme (www.esdinds.eu). It involved academics in social sciences, environmental sciences, indicators and sustainable development, in partnership with four Civil Society Organisations (CSOs).

The method used to develop the indicators was rigorous, and can be found formally written up for academic journals, several of which are listed at the end of this Insight on pages 333 and 334. As described by PERL (2014), an initial set of relevant values and indicators was collected from several CSOs, and analysed using discourse analysis and coding (social science methods) (Podger et al., 2010). The indicators were tested in the field using action research methods (Podger et al., 2013). After several stages of analysis and consultations between CSOs and university researchers, 177 indicators were trialled in real CSO projects in the field. Following further modifications, the refined set of values-based indicators was developed.

THE 'FINE PRINT' OF DEVELOPING VALUES-BASED INDICATORS TO ASSESS A SCHOOL'S PERFORMANCE ON ACHIEVING ITS MISSION

SMART is inspired by the approach used by PERL (The Partnership for Education and Research about Responsible Living) to develop values-based indicators to assess Environmental Sustainability, which is (like values in education) often difficult to quantify.

SMART is a radical adaptation of the methodology of assessing value-based indicators of environmental sustainability to meet the needs of school boards seeking to evaluate their schools' success in achieving their values-based mission and vision statements.

The approach adopted in SMART for the design of the assessment and evaluation is **inductive** insofar as the indicators flow from board members' and school leaders' understanding of the mission, vision and values, in contrast to being derived from a generic evaluation instrument or theoretical framework (which would be a deductive approach). The SMART approach is also **intersubjective** in that it is based upon explicit agreement on the meaning and definition of terminology and the values underpinning them.

Unfortunately, the sad reality is that most schools still use appraisal measures that are neither inductive nor intersubjective. Rather than explicitly basing school performance reviews on the fundamentally important values that underpin the mission and vision statements, and then using assessment and evaluation to track and advance progress towards their achievement, they tend to base appraisals on tradition (what has been historically measured) or convenience (what is easily measured, or what is easily obtainable through consultancies that do not appreciate the importance of assessing mission, vision and values).

IN CONCLUSION

The indicators used in SMART:

- help school leaders assess the values-based intangibles that define the individual school's identity;

- help school leaders crystallise the authentic values of the school;

- help school leaders communicate what the school offers beyond the usual 'deliverables';

- help school leaders capture important skills and capabilities that are seldom seen in conventional assessment approaches;

- help school leaders monitor how well the values of the school overlap with the values of staff and students, and use this information to improve the translation into action of the school's mission, vision and values; and

- following from these points, help school leaders create transformational learning situations.

Rather than relying on simple, generic, easily quantified factors, SMART focusses on the distinctive characteristics that authentically target a school's unique identity – its mission, vision and values. SMART thus overcomes one of the main shortcomings of traditional school appraisal and performance review processes – their neglect of a school's core ethos and values.

References:

Braithwaite VA and Law HG (1985) Structure of Human Values: Testing the Value of the Rokeach Value Survey. *Journal of Personality and Social Psychology*, 49(1): 250-263.

Branson CM (2008) Achieving organisational change through values alignment, *Journal of Educational Administration*, 46(3): 376-395.

Brockwell, AJ (2019) *Measuring what matters? Exploring the use of values-based indicators in assessing Education for Sustainability*. PhD thesis, Wageningen University.

Brown D and Crace RK (1996) Values in Life Role Choices and Outcomes: A Conceptual Model. *The Career Development Quarterly*, 44: 211-223.

Burford G, Hoover E, Velasco I, Janoušková S, Jimenez A, Piggot G, Podger D and Harder MK (2013) Bringing the "Missing Pillar" into Sustainable Development Goals: Towards Intersubjective Values-Based Indicators, *Sustainability*, 5: 3035-3059.

Burford G, Hoover E, Stapleton L and Harder MK (2016) An Unexpected Means of Embedding Ethics in Organizations: Preliminary Findings from Values-Based Evaluations, *Sustainability*, 8: 612-34.

Burford G, Tamás P and Harder MK (2016) Can We Improve Indicator Design for Complex Sustainable Development Goals? A Comparison of a Values-Based and Conventional Approach, *Sustainability*, 8: 861-98.

Burford G, Velasco I, Janouskova S, Zahradnik M, Hak T, Podger D, and Harder MK (2013) Field trials of a novel toolkit for evaluating 'intangible' values-related dimensions of projects. *Evaluation and Program Planning*, 36(1): 1-14.

Campbell RJ, Kyriakides L, Muijs RD, and Robinson W (2004) Effective teaching and values: some implications for research and teacher appraisal, *Oxford Review of Education*, 30(4):451-465.

Chen V, et.al. (2016) Measuring the attitudes of dental students towards social accountability following dental education—Qualitative findings, *Medical Teacher*, 38(6): 599-606.

ESDinds Project (2015) *We Value: Understanding and evaluating intangible impacts of Projects of organisations*. University of Brighton.

Hanushek EA and Rivkin SG (2010) Generalizations about Using Value-Added Measures of Teacher Quality, *The American Economic Review*, 100(2): 267-271.

Harder MK, Burford G, and Hoover E (2013) What Is Participation? Design Leads the Way to a Cross-Disciplinary Framework, *Design Issues*, 29(4): 41-57.

Harris DN (2011) Value-Added Measures and the Future of Educational Accountability, *Science*, 333(6044): 826-827.

Harris DN and Herrington CD (2015) Editors' Introduction: The Use of Teacher Value-Added Measures in Schools: New Evidence, Unanswered Questions, and Future Prospects, *Educational Researcher*, 44(2): 71-76.

Harris DN, Ingle WK and Rutledge WK (2014) How Teacher Evaluation Methods Matter for Accountability: A Comparative Analysis of Teacher Effectiveness Ratings by Principals and Teacher Value-Added Measures, *American Educational Research Journal*, 51(1): 73-112.

PERL (Partnership for Education and Research about Responsible Living) (2014) *Measuring what Matters: Values-Based Indicators*. PERL.

Peng KP, Nisbett RE and Wong NYC (1997) Validity problems comparing values across cultures and possible solutions, *Psychological Methods*, 2(4): 329-344.

Podger D, Hoover E, Burford G, Hak T and Harder MK (2016) Revealing values in a complex environmental program: a scaling up of values-based indicators, *Journal of Cleaner Production*, 134(A): 225-238.

Podger D, Piggot G, Zahradník M, Janoušková S, Velasco I, Hak T, Dahl A, Jimenez J and Harder MK (2010) The Earth Charter and the ESDinds Initiative, *Sustainability Indicators*, 4(2): 297-305.

Podger D, Velasko I, Luna CA, Burford G and Harder MK (2013) Can values be measured? Significant contributions from a small civil society organization through action research, *Action Research*, 11(1): 8-30.

Radinger T (2014) School Leader Appraisal – A Tool to Strengthen School Leaders' Pedagogical Leadership and Skills for Teacher Management?, *European Journal of Education*, 49(3): 378-391.

Sabo Flores K (2008) *Youth Participatory Evaluation*. San Francisco: Jossey-Bass.

Symes W and Putwain DW (2016) The role of attainment value, academic self-efficacy, and message frame in the appraisal of value-promoting messages, *British Journal of Educational Psychology*, 86: 446-460.

Insight 70

Measuring things

In his book *The Art of Doing Science and Engineering*, Richard Hamming wrote "what gets measured gets better, and what's difficult to measure suffers".

In our era of quantitative accountability, measuring finances, assessment grades, strategic goals, learning outcomes, curriculum compliance, demographic changes, admission numbers – and lots more – has never been more important in schools. Of course, it doesn't necessarily follow from this that Hamming's claim of "what gets measured gets better" is true for schools. Nonetheless, the conventional wisdom of many bureaucrats and school boards seems to be that Hamming's words are indeed accurate – measuring things makes them better.

In schools, and elsewhere, great care must be taken in determining what is to be measured and what is not. For school leaders and their boards, this often translates into a set of **KPIs** (key performance indicators) which are regularly presented in the form of **dashboards** – easy to understand visual representations of a variety of statistical data.

Determining the combination of factors which are important to measure is a key decision for school leaders and boards. It is necessary to remember the caution inherent in **Goodhart's Law**: when a measure becomes a target, it ceases to be a good measure". In school environments, this implies that when a measure is chosen to assess people's performance, they will find a way to "game the system".

The classic (non-school) example of this is a nail factory in the former Soviet Union. The goal of the government's central planners was to measure the performance of this (and every other) factory in the USSR, and so the factory manager was given targets (KPIs) based upon the number of nails produced. In order to meet and exceed the targets, the factory manager ordered the factory to produce millions of tiny, useless nails. The central planners reacted by changing the target to measure the total weight of nails produced, and so the manager shifted operations to produce several enormous, heavy and useless nails.

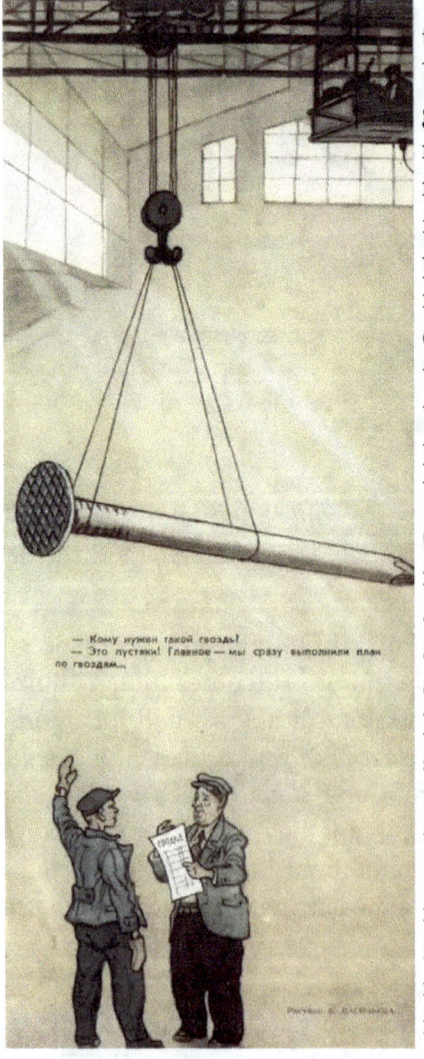

(I have not been able to verify the name or location of the nail factory, and indeed it may be apocryphal. Nonetheless it was celebrated in the cartoon shown on the left that was published in the Soviet satirical magazine *Krokodil* in 1922. The embedded caption translates as "Who needs such a nail?" "That's not important. What's important is that we immediately fulfilled the plan for nails!". Apocryphal or not, I think it illustrates Goodhart's law brilliantly).

It is easy to see how such targets can distort a school's culture. If enrolment targets are set to maximise new admissions, students who are not well suited to the school and who would not previously have been considered suitable are very likely to be admitted. If enrolment targets are set to emphasise high academic standards, sports-oriented and artistic students may be turned away, or even worse, students with special needs might be rejected.

When KPIs are set, it is essential that consistency is maintained, or at least changes are thoroughly discussed and negotiated before being introduced. I know of one school where the board set an ambitious enrolment target – a net gain of 50 students in the coming year - which the Principal had to achieve as a KPI. By the end of the year, there was a net gain of almost 100 students. Notwithstanding this achievement, the board claimed the Principal had failed to achieve the KPI because many of the additional students were from poorer families and were thus entitled to subsidised fees under the school's policies. Consequently, the increase in fees income had been less than the board's treasurer wished, even though income from fees was never mentioned as a KPI. Not unexpectedly, that Principal was soon leading a different school.

An uncharitable interpretation of this Principal's initiative to secure additional enrolments could be to label it as an example of the **Cobra Effect**. The Cobra Effect arises when a well-intentioned initiative backfires and achieves the opposite effect to the one intended. It is named after another possibly apocryphal event in India during the period of British colonisation.

The story is that the British authorities decreed that there were too many cobras around Delhi, so they introduced a cash reward for anyone who brought in a dead cobra. Apparently, this incentivised some enterprising folk to start breeding cobras to collect the bounty. When the British authorities realised what was happening, they discontinued the scheme. This resulted in the closure of the cobra farms and the owners releasing the now-worthless cobras, which bred profusely, thus greatly increasing the number of cobras in the wild.

Whether or not this story is true, there have been numerous documented examples of the Cobra Effect. In Hanoi (Vietnam), a bounty on rats' tails followed an almost-identical track as the cobras in Delhi, while a measure in Bogotá (Colombia) to reduce traffic congestion by restricting each car from driving one day each week

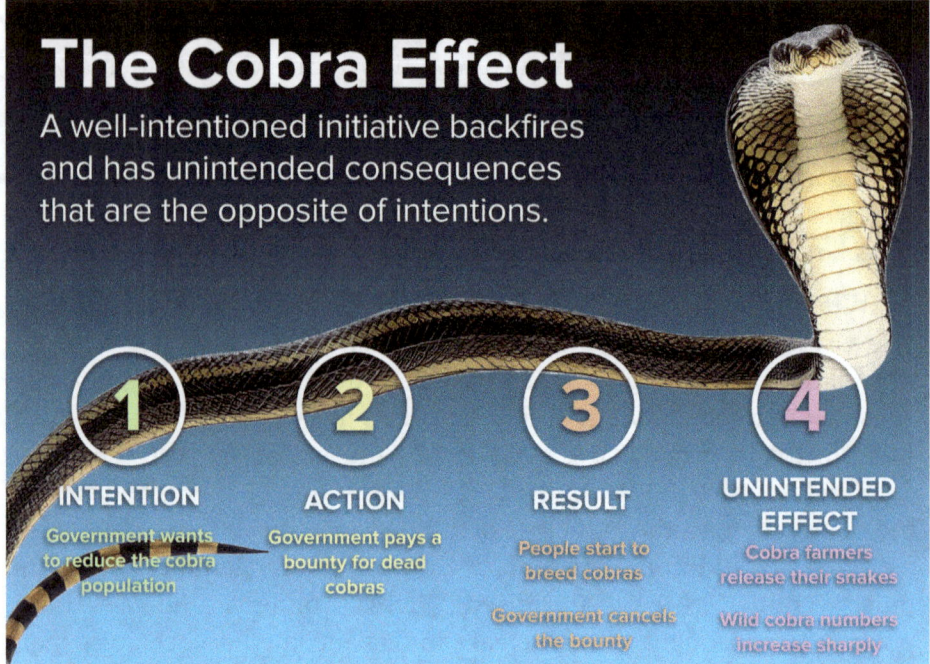

resulted in residents going out and buying second cars, thus increasing traffic congestion.

Unintended consequences like the Cobra Effect also affect schools. I have seen well-intentioned school leaders who conflate student achievement with student effort, and specify additional homework or other requirements such as formal study times to increase students' effort. While this did work for some students, many students simply spent more time in activities that superficially resembled studying (such as quiet daydreaming). The Cobra Effect was operating when students pretended to be studying in ways the school demanded rather than in ways that genuinely worked for them, causing their grades to fall rather than rise. Sadly, many well-intentioned but ill-informed bureaucratic initiatives from government authorities and school boards can result in similar 'Cobra Effect' consequences in schools.

Neither the Cobra Effect nor Goodhart's Law should deter schools from making decisions based on evidence and data – indeed, it would be foolish (and in some cases, possibly illegal) not to do so. Nonetheless, wisdom and prudence are required if Hamming's claim is to be realised so that "what gets measured gets better."

Reference:
Hamming, R (2020) *The Art of Doing Science and Engineering: Learning to Learn*, San Francisco: Stripe Press.

Insight 71

Melting the cultural iceberg

One of the great joys of my current work supporting school boards and principals is visiting the campuses of many fine schools. Having also served as the Head of five schools in four countries over 25 years before focussing exclusively on my current work, I feel I have become quite adept at discerning the **culture** of any school I visit fairly quickly as I start walking around. I refer to this colloquially as "sniffing the mood" of the school.

When I refer to the 'culture' of a school, I mean the authentic, everyday ways in which the school's 'values' are expressed, '**values**' being the beliefs, attitudes and consequent behaviours that are viewed as valuable, worthwhile, important and meaningful within the school.

art, dress, drama, music, food, celebrations, crafts, dance, literature, language

faith, conversation patterns, concept of time, personal space, courtesy, rules of conduct, ways to show respect, facial expressions, non-verbal communication, body language, touching, eye contact, handling emotions, status mobility, notions of modesty, concept of beauty, courtship practices, definition of sin, concepts of humour, relationship to animals, relationship to nature, patterns of superior/subordinate relationships, notions of leadership, tempo of work, concepts of food, ideals of child rearing, theory of disease, social interaction rate, esteem for introversion vs extroversion, notions about logic and validity, nature of friendships, degree of optimism/pessimism, tone of voice, attitudes towards elders, concept of cleanliness, notions of adolescence, concept of justice, incentives to work, patterns of group decision-making, definition of insanity, preference for co-operation or competition, tolerance of physical pain, concept of 'self', concept of past and future, definition of obscenity, attitudes towards dependents, problem solving roles in relation to age, sex, class, occupation, kinship, and so on...

Unfortunately, the significance of a school's culture can easily become diluted. At one level, many schools reduce the concept of culture to being a disparate collection of somewhat superficial outward symbols, such as music, food, art, dress and drama, especially when cultural festivals are celebrated. In the same way that this approach diminishes the richness of the cultures being celebrated, it can blind the school community to deeper facets of the concept of culture – including the '**school's own culture**'.

The concept of the '**cultural iceberg**' can be very helpful in addressing this situation. The idea is a simple one. Only about 10% of an iceberg is visible above the surface of the ocean. As the crew of the Titanic realised far too late, most of an iceberg (about 90% of its mass) is hidden beneath the surface of the water.

In 1976, the American anthropologist and cross-cultural researcher, Edward T Hall, suggested that culture was like an iceberg, and in doing so, claimed that there are two broad components of culture. First, he claimed that the **external, or surface, culture** (which is easily visible) comprises about 10% of the total concept, while the remaining 90%, which is usually hidden below the surface, is **internal, or deep, culture**.

External surface culture (the visible 10%) is explicitly learned, conscious, easily changeable and mainly comprises objective knowledge. On the other hand, internal deep culture (the hidden 90%) is implicitly learned, unconscious, difficult to change and mainly consists of subjective knowledge.

When people first experience contact with other cultures, they usually interact only at the surface level (the visible 10%), which is (to circle back to the metaphor) just the 'tip of the iceberg'. Dealing with the visible 10% of another culture makes a relatively low emotional demand. It remains superficial and fails to engage in deeper understandings, which would require a much more intense emotional load. Remaining at the surface level is rarely, if ever, an effective way to develop authentic intercultural understanding.

The same principle applies when we are examining school culture. Most independent schools were founded on the basis of a strong, coherent values position. These values are communicated through the mission, vision and other documents, and are demonstrated in practice through the behaviours and attitudes that express the school culture on a daily basis.

In today's tense, globalised world, it is essential that schools help to grow international-mindedness among its students. This requires challenging students to engage with the internal, deep facets of other cultures. Cultural celebrations are an important, necessary, highly effective and thoroughly enjoyable beginning, but they are merely a means to set the school community on the right pathway; they are not the ultimate destination.

Cultural celebrations certainly play a very valuable role in raising awareness, but they seldom require deep engagement with other cultures. Deep engagement comes as students are pushed beyond their comfort zones. At this point , I am struggling to encapsulate all the thoughts that are flooding into my head as I write. Let me try and encapsulate my ideas into one single (but very long) sentence...

I believe that deep engagement with other cultures comes when students are pushed beyond their comfort zones to become aware of other world-views in which they consider different political ideals and systems; they appreciate different religious perspectives and how they make an impact on different societies; they understand multiculturalism, cosmopolitanism, citizenship and nationality from various perspectives; they understand indigenous peoples and the concept of ethnicity; they come to appreciate the tensions between national interests and globalisation; they understand the distribution and transfer of both natural and human resources; they can analyse the positive and negative impacts of trade and aid between countries upon people with different attitudes towards materialism; they can conduct a complete and balanced investigation of international efforts to address global environmental concerns and conflict; they understand why peoples from different cultures act differently towards the implications of environmental sustainability; they attain fluency in one or more foreign languages, preferably language(s) from a different language family than their first language, in order to learn the processes and concepts behind others' thought processes and worldviews; they truly understand the different historical and geographical backgrounds of several countries from the perspectives of residents of those countries; they become aware of the social structures within their own country and how these differ from other societies; they can make sense of the impact of resources, wealth and culture on education, women's rights, child labour, child poverty, human trafficking and other issues of international significance; and they fully comprehend the impact of human society on the natural environment, understanding the interplay between sustainability, diversity and environmental impact.

Whew! I hope that is the longest single sentence I will ever write. And yet, it is not exhaustive (even if it is exhausting); it is just - to repeat the analogy - a little more than the tip of the iceberg. Having achieved all the things listed in my long sentence, students will be in a great place to deepen their appreciation of the issues shown beneath the water surface in the iceberg graphic above. Yet even with all these understandings behind them, I suspect many students will still have a lot to learn about other cultures in the years after they graduate, which is precisely why schools must try to instil a genuine passion for life-long learning in each and every one of its students.

Clearly, developing international-mindedness is an ambitious task. It involves far more than mastering the content that is presented to students in the classroom. It requires schools to model exemplary international-mindedness in its policies, its practices, its appointment of personnel, and the way it relates collectively to the rest of the world.

If schools are really concerned to form communities that give life to the school's mission and values position, the school's leadership must challenge the students and staff to engage authentically with the internal, deep facets of their 'school culture'. The external surface culture (the visible 10%) represents an important, necessary, and thoroughly enjoyable beginning, but it ought to be an initial transition step that sets the school on the right pathway – it is neither a sufficient nor ultimate destination in itself.

Insight 72

Mission drift

Imagine a situation where you are in charge of a non-profit refuge shelter for homeless animals. One day a wealthy entrepreneur makes an appointment to see you and offers an ongoing annual six-figure donation if you agree to train four animals every month and release them to perform with a travelling circus.

Would you agree with the proposal? More significantly for the purpose of this discussion, whether you agreed to the offer or not, would you regard this request as an example of 'mission drift'?

What is 'mission drift'? Boston's Harvard University gives us a real example of actual mission drift. Harvard's original mission statement (1636) was "to prepare ministers of upright character". By 1701, this has been modified to read "To be plainly instructed and consider well that the main end of your life and studies is to know God and Jesus Christ." Today, Harvard's mission statement would be quite unrecognisable to its founders as it now reads "to educate the citizens and citizen-leaders for our society through our commitment to the transformative power of a liberal arts and sciences education".

Mission drift occurs when an organisation consciously or unconsciously begins to engage in work that deviates from its core values. Rightly, 'mission drift' is usually used as a pejorative term because it causes confusion and/or lack of authenticity as the mission (enduring purpose) of the school becomes diluted. The school's 'true north' direction and values become compromised.

Mission drift should ring alarm bells throughout any school community where it is seen to be occurring because it indicates that the organisation is veering off course in a way that is likely to damage and/or distract the enterprise. Board members should be especially concerned as they hold the duty to define, monitor and ensure achievement of the mission, vision and strategic direction.

Peter Greer and Chris Horst have written a very helpful book on the subject of mission drift with an admirably easy-to-remember title – the book is called simply "Mission Drift". They describe mission drift as "the unspoken crisis facing leaders, charities and churches", to which I would add "and also some schools".

Mission drift can arise from a variety of causes, but I suggest four reasons dominate:

- **A weak or vague mission statement** : A school's mission statement is a public declaration of its enduring purpose. It defines the unique identity, direction, values and consequent culture of the school. If a school can't clearly fill in these blanks: "We do ___ through ___ in the service of ___," and if the mission statement is too vague, too broad or simply difficult to understand, then it is failing to provide the boundaries required to preserve the school's intentional direction.

- **Ego** : As I write in Insight 91, successful school leadership requires servant leadership. Humility is a prerequisite for effective board membership, and contrary to traditional (though outdated) preconceptions, it is also a requirement for proficient school principals. If, on the other hand, a principal or board members approach their roles with a high sense of self-interest, it is highly likely that 'pet projects' will expand in scope and thus marginalise the facets of the school that express its true identity.

- **The Bright Shiny Object Syndrome** : Schools are almost always highly fertile zones for creative ideas. In some schools, every week or staff meeting seems to propose a new initiative, always advocated with great passion. Such proposals, which are especially prevalent in young schools, invariably are designed to bring benefits, either to students or staff, or both. The problem is, as Jim Collins famously argued, "the good is the enemy of the great". Therefore, the risk arises that a 'good' initiative may be embraced without asking the critically important question – will this initiative enhance the school's mission? If it enhances the mission, it should be explored further, but if not, it should be acknowledged as a worthwhile idea, but rejected because it risks diluting the school's core mission.

- **The temptation of a wealthy donor** : Sadly, experience shows that very few donors to schools have purely altruistic motives. I wish it were different, but large donations usually come with strings attached, and these conditions may have a seductive appeal to convince the board to set aside facets of the school's core mission or professional practices. Unfortunately, large donations often demand sacrificing the purity of one or more aspects of the school's mission and identity, which opens the door to ongoing and accelerating mission drift. Schools must follow the mission, not the money.

It would be tragic if mission drift were inevitable in schools. However, the good news is that it is not inevitable – **there are several effective defences against mission drift**.

- **Know the Mission** : There are several ways that the mission can become the central pillar of decision-making for the board. For example, a statement of the mission and vision could routinely be inserted at the top of each agenda document to serve as a focus or reminder. An interesting exercise might be to set aside a hour or so at a board meeting and begin by asking every attendee to try write down the mission statement as accurately as they can. This exercise could become even more interesting if each board members was then asked to read aloud what they have written. After concluding this exercise with some embarrassed laughter, a great discussion about the meaning and importance of the mission statement should ensue. The discussion could even take the form of completing the sentence "we do ____ through ____ in the service of ____." This exercise might even result in agreement to get together again for a larger block of time to reflect on the importance of defending the mission.

- **Test everything against the Mission Statement** : It is helpful to administer an informal test to evaluate current programs and test new proposed programs in the school (especially if they consume large quantities of key resources such as time, money or staffing). Having developed a mission statement, best practice suggests that there will be a consequent vision statement that identifies the school's current priorities in achieving the mission, supported by a set of measurable strategic objectives. All the school's current and any proposed programs could then be listed, matched to their specific strategic objectives, and then rated on a scale from 1 to 10 on the extent to which each contributes to the mission. Programs that rate poorly on this criterion might be flagged for subsequent discussion!

- **Re-think the way your Mission Statement is expressed** : Although the mission statement is an expression of the school's enduring purpose, the way it is expressed will need to change from time to time to adapt to our society's changing language usage. A 150-year-old school may have once expressed its mission in the form of a Latin motto, but that will hardly communicate effectively today. An effective mission statement should not only be unambiguous, but it ought to be concise and easy to remember. A good test might be whether or not a young teenager can remember it so that if someone asks them "what is special about your school?", their accurate recitation of the mission statement would provide the perfect answer. The bottom line here is that **it is really worthwhile for the board to hold an annual or biennial retreat/reflection on how adequately the current mission statement is articulating the school's enduring purpose to the school community and the general public.**

Insight 73

Muddy puddle or leaking ceiling

When I lived and worked in New Zealand some years ago, a good friend who was a suburban doctor (a General Practitioner, or GP) explained to me that whenever a patient came to see him with a new health issue, he would invariably refuse to prescribe any medication. Instead, he would instruct the patient to wait and see how the condition progressed and come back in 10 days if the symptoms persisted. His rationale was that more than 70% of medical conditions that are brought to GPs heal themselves without intervention within a week or so. By taking this approach, my GP friend was avoiding giving patients medication they didn't need, and for about 30% of his patients, he was receiving income from a return visit that may not otherwise have been made.

The bursar (CFO) of a school in Australia that I worked closely with has a similar attitude. When financial problems arose, his approach was usually to leave them alone – often for months on end – in the hope that they would rectify themselves. Occasionally they did, which gave him intermittent reinforcement that his 'hands-off' approach was working. Eventually, and predictably, some financial problems arose in the school which did not fix themselves, but rather they escalated – which helps to explain why the bursar is no longer employed at that school.

The US speaker and author James Clear described the approach taken by this school bursar and my GP friend as the "muddy puddle" approach. A "muddy puddle problem" is one in which leaving it alone can make it clearer. He contrasts this with a "leaky ceiling problem", which is a problem that becomes worse if it is ignored and left alone.

In brief, muddy puddles can be left until they become clearer, whereas leaky ceilings need urgent attention. To quote James Clear in his own words:

"Some problems are like muddy puddles. The way to clear a muddy puddle is to leave it alone. The more you mess with it, the muddier it becomes. Many of the problems I dream up when I'm overthinking or worrying or ruminating fall into this category. Is life really falling apart or am I just in

a sour mood? Is this as hard as I'm making it or do I just need to go workout? Drink some water. Go for a walk. Get some sleep. Go do something else and give the puddle time to turn clear.

Other problems are like a leaky ceiling. Ignore a small leak and it will always widen. Relationship tension that goes unaddressed. Overspending that becomes a habit. One missed workout drifting into months of inactivity. Some problems multiply when left unattended. You need to intervene now."

For boards and leaders dealing with the typical challenges that arise in schools, resolving the problem effectively could begin by asking this seemingly strange question – "Are we dealing with a leak or a puddle?".

It is an important distinction. When my children were little, they would love jumping into puddles with their friends, splashing the water, stirring up the mud and making themselves filthy. As they jumped more and more in the puddle, the sediment was stirred up more and more and the children became muddier and muddier, making the job of cleaning them up even more difficult. That may be cute (if irritating) behaviour for little children, but it is a terrible metaphor for effective problem-solving in a school. When the children's puddle jumping antics finally finished, the sediment would settle, and the water would become clear.

By contrast, a leaky roof will have greater and

greater consequences the longer it is left unchecked. A slow drip grows into a trickle which grows further to become a steady stream of water. If nothing is done, the paint peels and then the material of the wall of itself may disintegrate. At its most extreme, the building may flood or even collapse – another terrible metaphor for effective problem-solving in a school!

Determining whether to intervene immediately or just wait and observe is an important decision that demands accurate discernment. It is not always easy to distinguish between a "leak" and a "puddle", so the decision depends on the specific problem and its potential impact on students, staff, and the overall school community.

Examples of "muddy puddles" in schools are usually fairly minor issues such as trivial or isolated behavioural issues, temporary academic struggles, or the initial implementation of a new policy, program or organisational structure.

On the other hand, examples of "leaking ceilings" tend to be more significant priorities such as safety concerns, significant or persistent academic decline, severe disruptions to the learning environment such as behavioural issues, and legal or policy compliance issues.

In summary, the decision to intervene immediately (fix the leaking ceiling) or wait (let the muddy puddle settle) depends on the nature and severity of the problem, its potential impact, and the likelihood of resolution without intervention. School boards, leaders, and staff must assess each situation carefully and consider the best course of action to support the well-being and success of their students and school community.

Recognising the difference between the metaphorical 'muddy puddle' and 'leaking ceiling' is a great starting point for wise discernment.

Insight 74

Nailing the Principal's annual performance review

Every board knows (or should know) how important it is to conduct an annual review of the Principal's performance. The conduct of these annual reviews is usually specified in writing in the Principal's contract, the goals are usually negotiated well in advance, and the timing is normally specified with precise clarity. And yet, many Principals with whom I have worked complain that their performance reviews simply don't happen. In a few cases it may be even worse; the review is conducted in ways that are completely inconsistent with their contract or negotiated process.

Board chairs are often busy people – sometimes they are even 'quite important' people. It is therefore not difficult to imagine a situation where the Principal mentions that the review is imminent, the chair promises to get the process underway, but time passes, urgent issues arise, and the performance review slips quietly into the background of the board's thinking. This can become a demoralising scenario for a Principal who is keen to serve the board and advance its priorities but can't do so effectively without a full and frank conversation about the board's thinking and goals.

There are five steps that a Principal can take to ensure an effective annual review takes place while also ensuring they have every opportunity to "nail" the review when it does happen.

Step 1: Make sure the review happens.

No Principal should ever assume that the annual review shall take place as planned or scheduled. It is usually safer to assume that board members are busy people – perhaps almost busy as the Principal! – and therefore they appreciate help in making the annual review happen. One good approach is for the Principal to include it as an item on the agenda for one of the weekly conversations that (should) always happen between a Principal and the Board Chair, thus gently initiating the process a couple of months before the scheduled date.

Step 2: Help develop the review process.

Most boards adopt a fairly flexible, semi-formal approach to annual reviews (unlike the far more rigorous 360-degree appraisals that typically precede end-of-contract renewal negotiations). Although the timing and the Principal's goals for the year will have been established, the precise nature of the process is often more malleable. Some schools handle the annual review as an extended conversation between the Principal and the Board Chair over coffee and biscuits, but it can be more productive and generative if the Principal can guide the thinking towards a slightly more structured process, such as:

- Stage 1: Form a small team of two or three board members (one of whom is the Board Chair as convenor) to conduct the review. This is to avoid criticism that the Board Chair may have allowed personal feelings (either positive or negative) to distort the neutrality of the process.
- Stage 2: Share the Principal's job description with the review panel to use as a basis for the review. If this job description can be formatted into a word processing document with spaces between each responsibility and each attribute, the review panel has an instant evaluation form to use which, helpfully, can also be used as a self-evaluation form by the Principal.
- Stage 3: Presuming a set of agreed annual goals for the Principal's work was determined at the beginning of the year, these goals should

be added to the word processing document identified in stage 2 to complete a comprehensive review form.

- Stage 4: Develop a schedule that allows (a) the Principal's written self-evaluation to be received by the team a week or so before the review meeting, and (b) the meeting (or meetings) to be completed well before the due date.

OPTIMAL SCHOOL GOVERNANCE
Sample Model of a Principal's Performance Review

Leadership Requirements

Professional Practices

	Vision and Values	Knowledge and Understanding	Personal qualities & social skills
Leading operational management	Creates a student-centred environment	Leads organisational practice	Creates an efficient, supportive culture
Developing self and others	Builds capacity	Promotes professional learning	Manages self
Leading improvement, innovation and change	Inspires and motivates	Understands and leads change	Initiates improvement through innovation and change
Leading management within the school	Aligns ethical practices with educational goals	Manages resources	Manages high standards and accountability
Engaging and working with the community	Creates a culture of inclusion	Engages with the community	Collaborates with and influences the community
School-specific criteria	Supporting the School's enduring purpose (Mission)	Fulfilling the role description	Personal characteristics of leadership

- Stage 5: Having received the Principal's self-evaluation, the review team meets (without the Principal) for an hour or two to compare the self-evaluation with the Principal's stated goals for the year and other indicators of performance. Areas of alignment are noted, and areas of difference are identified. The team then agrees on key questions and talking points to raise during the forthcoming meeting with the Principal.

- Stage 6: The review team and the Principal meet in person for a couple of hours or so to discuss the Principal's self-evaluation in the context of the role description and goals for the year. A neutral person (such as the Principal's PA) should be present to take accurate minutes of the meeting. By the end of the meeting there should be a shared consensus of the Principal's strengths and achievements together with agreement on areas for improvement and goals for the coming year.

- Stage 7: The draft minutes from the meeting are circulated by confidential circular e-mail to those present at the meeting, who propose changes if required and then confirm the accuracy of the minutes, also via confidential circular e-mail.
- Stage 8: At the next board meeting and in the presence of the Principal, the Board Chair (as the convenor of the review team) presents a summary of the review team's work and outlines the proposed goals for the Principal for the coming year. The Principal is offered the opportunity to add any comments, after which Board members have the opportunity to ask the Principal, the Board Chair and the review team members any relevant questions. With the Principal present, the Board collectively approves the Principal's goals for the coming year.
- Stage 9: Towards the end of the same board meeting, the Board should meet in Executive Committee (i.e. with only voting members in attendance; the Principal and any other school employees attending the meeting having been asked to vacate the room). In the Executive Committee session, board members are given the opportunity to engage in a confidential discussion, including consideration of any adjustments to the Principal's remuneration for the coming year. The decisions arising from the Executive Committee discussion should be communicated verbally and in writing by the Board Chair to the Principal at the earliest opportunity.
- Stage 10: The Board Chair follows up the Principal's annual review by issuing a public message to the appropriate elements of the wider school community informing them that the Board has conducted its annual review of the Principal. In this message, the Board Chair would usually publicly thank the Principal for efforts made during the year and offer congratulations on several named achievements.

Step 3: Approach the review diligently.

An annual performance review is no trivial matter. Some School Principals may develop a negative attitude towards their Board if they think board members are not seeing the review as an important priority. If this causes a Principal (perhaps understandably) to view the review process (or board members) in a dismissive manner, then a risk arises that the Principal may not participate as actively, as comprehensively, or as punctually as required. Whatever the circumstances, it is in the Principal's best interests to treat the review process seriously and commit to it fully.

Step 4: Keep written records.

The Principal's self-evaluation is a key element in the review process. This is understandable as board members are only intermittent visitors to the school and as such, they are not able to know (or remember) every facet of a Principal's day-to-day work. The Principal's self-evaluation should be supported where possible by data and evidence that helps to build a comprehensive overview of the year's work and achievements, including congratulatory e-mails and messages of appreciation received from staff, students and parents that collectively build and convey a compelling narrative. Most Principals are reluctant to boast, but the annual review is one place where it is appropriate to do so.

Step 5: Approach the review with humility.

Notwithstanding my previous comment about boasting, the attitude with which the Principal approaches the review should be one of humility. In other words, the Principal should follow the advice that is often given to a school's sports teams – be humble in victory, gracious in defeat. In the context of a Principal's annual review, this means accepting compliments without displaying vanity and taking on board (as opposed to challenging) suggestions for improvements or ratings and comments by others that might seem harsh. It is worth remembering that the review is being undertaken by well-meaning people who have (almost always) never been a School Principal themselves and can therefore only begin to imagine the range of day-to-day pressures that the job entails.

The annual performance review should be one of the most valuable and insightful professional experiences for a School Principal. At its best, it is a healthy reality check, a doorway through which the school's future can be re-framed, an occasion to be encouraged and congratulated, and a golden opportunity to re-align with the Board. Unfortunately, some boards fail to realise the potential of the annual performance review, and their lack of commitment to the process results in significant loss to the school, its students and staff, the Board and the Principal.

Whatever the Board's attitude towards the annual performance review, I encourage every Principal to remain optimistic and committed to their role. Our next generation requires nothing less.

Insight 75

Normalisation of deviance

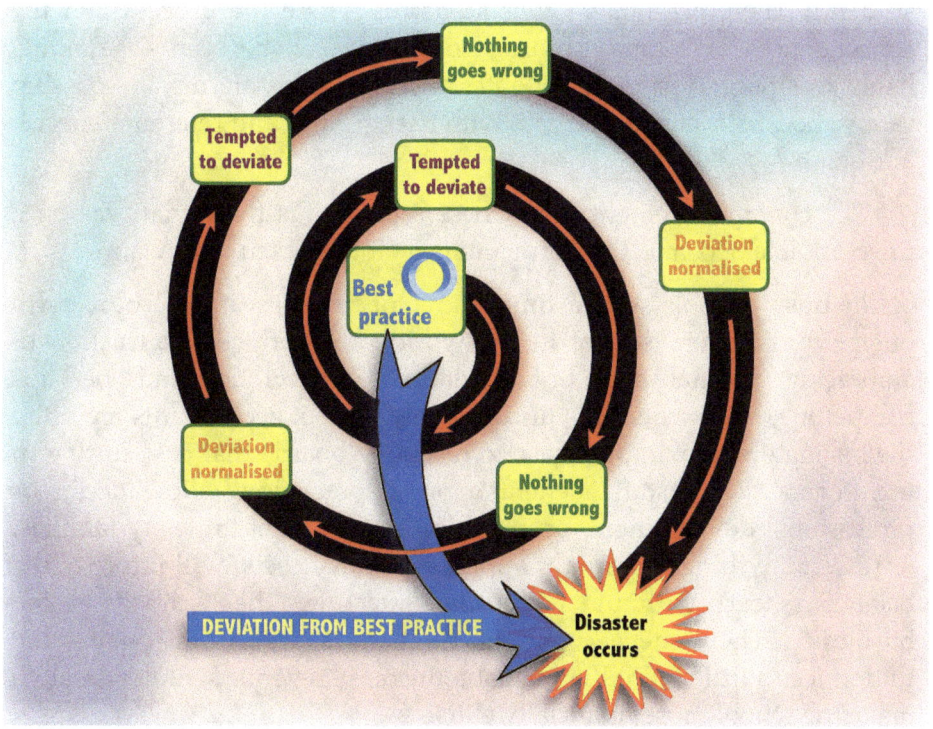

Normalisation of deviance may sound mathematical, and therefore uninteresting to some folk. On the contrary, normalisation of deviance is neither mathematical nor uninteresting. More significantly, it is of huge importance to school boards and leaders.

Normalisation of deviance is the process that occurs when things that were once unacceptable gradually become acceptable. The longer the time that passes without encountering problems, the greater the tolerance for accepting the changed standards.

On a building construction site, for example, a long period with no accidents may lead to complacency which results in less conscientious wearing of hard hats, and eventually widespread neglect of the requirement. Alternatively, a driver who starts ignoring the speed limit and doesn't have an accident or get fined, may start to use excessive speed routinely. A student who starts sharing passwords with others to avoid licensing fees may become overly generous with sharing personal data.

It is easy to see how each of these situations can lead to disaster – a crushed skull on a construction site, a major traffic accident or loss of licence for a driver, or serious identity theft for the generous student. There are many other scenarios where the process and the consequences of normalisation of deviation can be seen – smoking, hand washing, closing farm gates, ignoring fire alarms, by-passing safety checklists, cutting corners with background and reference checks, and so on.

The common element in all these scenarios is that what was once unacceptable becomes the norm and is no longer seen as deviant.

In busy schools where time and money are scarce resources (in other words, every school in the world), the seductive attraction of embracing normalisation of deviation is obvious, and perhaps compelling, even when it is unconscious. School accountants are often the instigators, making the case to receptive boards that cost-cutting in maintenance, or staff benefits, or depreciation allowances, or professional development, or provision of fees relief to needy families, or (insert anything that might appear to reduce costs) will improve the balance sheet without adversely affecting the school's 'core business'. The same accountants might also argue that raising the tuition fees a little more than usual to increase revenue will not "really" make the school more financially elitist.

School boards must be conscious of the cumulative impact of decisions that deviate from 'best practice', and they should firmly resist them. The apparent absence of negative outcomes when corners are initially cut tends to reinforce the behaviours and the decision-making processes associated with normalisation of deviance – by-passing safety checklists, ignoring alarms, overlooking obvious tripping hazards, and so on. However, decisions that compound over time to dilute the school's mission and vision will almost inevitably trigger a crisis or disaster as the cumulative deviations from best practice escalate. Such crises or disasters invariably wind up costing far more than the real or imagined savings gained in earlier decisions that attempted to normalise deviations, especially when reputational damage is included (just ask Boeing).

How can school boards and leaders ensure that they are not surrendering to the temptations of normalisation of deviance?

- Ensure that all board members understand the concept of normalisation of deviance, how it occurs, and what are its consequences.
- Ground every discussion and decision in the school's mission, vision and strategic plan.
- Develop, communicate, and adhere unswervingly to a clear set of policies and processes that are explicitly grounded in the school's philosophy, define acceptable standards of ethical behaviour and compliance, and contain explicit consequences of deviant conduct.
- Foster an environment of openness, transparency, and honest communication, including establishing channels for reporting concerns, malpractice or potential deviations from defined 'best practice' that allow individuals to raise legitimate concerns without fear of reprisal.
- Conduct regular performance reviews of the board, senior management and all staff using a neutral, transparent, widely communicated and well-understood framework.
- Resist pressure to deviate from 'best practice' through (for example) emotional appeals to ignore conflicts of interest, requests to engage in related parties transactions without arm's length safeguards, by-passing proper channels of communication, neglecting regular board and senior management performance reviews, nepotism, overlooking financial or legal mis-steps – in short, anything that falls short of the highest standards of ethical, legal, or financial integrity.
- Attend to any and every health or safety risk as an urgent priority.

Normalisation of deviance can be particularly tricky to avoid when failures are rare yet severe or when they are known but the consequences seem distant, such as smoking. Fortunately, the consequences of normalisation of deviance in schools are far more predictable and therefore easier to avoid – provided school leaders and boards understand the risks they pose. It's really quite simple – avoiding normalisation of deviance within schools just requires the board and leadership to establish a culture of integrity, accountability, transparency, continuous improvement, and adherence to established standards.

Your board can do that, can't it?

Insight 76

Operationalising a strategic vision

An effective strategic vision is one of the most powerful tools the board can have at its disposal for guiding the school towards a better future. Of course, the board's role is not limited to developing and promulgating the strategic vision. Having articulated the strategic vision, the board has a continuing role to play in its implementation and monitoring.

Typically, only small parts of a strategic vision will refer directly to the board's own operations. This is appropriate, as the strategic vision should focus on the school and the benefits that will accrue to the students. Therefore, most of the work to operationalise the strategic vision will fall upon the faculty and staff of the school, under the leadership and direction of the Head.

The main responsibility of the board is to monitor this process of implementation to ensure it is being carried out faithfully and effectively. The board's monitoring will be most effective and inclusive if discussion of the strategic vision becomes a significant and integral component of each board meeting. Indeed, it makes sense to use the strategic vision as the organising framework to structure each board meeting, given that the strategic vision should articulate the key goals and direction for the school in the coming few years. In this way, the strategic vision will provide the board with coherent direction as it performs its central role of governance.

There are **two ways** of ensuring that the strategic vision is kept at the forefront of board members' thinking at every meeting. The first way is to print the vision statement at the top of every agenda. This simple act will help to keep board members focused on the reason they are attending the meeting, and it should help the Chair keep the discussion focused should it begin to wander. With the strategic vision printed on every agenda document, it should be much easier for trustees to ensure that they apply the key criterion for the approval of any new proposal – it must enhance the mission.

In general, there should be **three types of reports** presented at board meetings:

- papers that require a decision to be made;
- papers that require discussion, but not necessarily a decision; and
- reports on progress, background information, and points to be noted.

There is no place for reports that simply talk about how busy someone has been!

This leads to the **second**, and more significant, way in which the strategic vision becomes the focus of every board meeting. At the beginning of each meeting, type (c) reports should all be taken as 'read' during the consent agenda, unless a member specifically asks that the paper be discussed. On that basis, a **board meeting agenda** with a strong strategic focus might look something like this:

- **Attendance, apologies, declarations of interest.**
- **Consent agenda.**
- **Approval of previous minutes.**
- **Matters arising (unless otherwise on agenda).**
- **Correspondence (addressed to the board or having direct strategic implications).**
- **Principal's Report (and recommendations).**
- **Committee Reports, organised by strategic goals that are relevant to their areas (with recommendations).**
- **Finance Report (if not already tabled by the Finance Committee)**
- **A report on each action plan arising from the strategic plan that was due to have commenced by the date of the meeting. (These reports will usually be provided by the Principal, or a member of the Executive under the delegated authority of the Principal).**
- **Professional board development (one item).**
- **A staff presentation on the issues faced in their area.**
- **Check - are there any changes in the strategic environment?**
- **AOB (Any other business).**

This meeting structure should enable the board to operationalise its strategic vision effectively, focussing on the school's direction without deviating tangentially, while at the same time maximising the effective use of trustees' time. Assuming the board is also operating solely within the realm of governance and not interfering in the school's operations, achieving these three points would be indicative of a truly exemplary board.

Insight 77

Overcoming negativity : perhaps your own

Some people are intrinsically negative. Quite simply, negativity is an inherent component of their identity; it helps to define them.

Other people enter the realm of negativity only when major events cause their lives to fall apart in some way. It may also happen when another person causes so much irritation or pain that customary patience and tolerance evaporate. It's probably fair to say that in recent years, the pressures of COVID-19 and other political and social changes have been pushing more and more usually optimistic people towards uncharacteristic negativity.

About 2,500 years ago, the Greek philosopher Socrates famously said that "an unexamined life is not worth living". In other words, if we don't take the time to reflect and learn from life's experiences, then our souls – our true selves – remain stunted and immature.

On the other hand, excessive introspection can have a similar effect, leading to depression and psychological paralysis that not only makes the individual less effective, but negatively impacts on those around that individual – friends, family, co-workers – everyone.

Those in school leadership positions can be especially vulnerable to negative mindsets, especially if they take to heart the inevitable criticism that follows any and every decision they make. After all, every decision affects other people, and even the most positive change will unavoidably disadvantage someone in some way. As a generalisation, school leaders tend to be idealistic people pleasers (school boards less so!), and thus negative mindsets can easily become a common hazard of school leadership.

Here are four practical, and hopefully effective, approaches that may help school leaders overcome negativity.

1. **Take the time to pause and reflect.**

Decisions in schools are rarely required as urgently as most school leaders think. In stressful situations, conscious deep breathing often helps, but there are also occasions when this strategy is inadequate. This is when it becomes necessary to walk away from whatever is happening to a different venue and take a break. Of course, doing so is seldom easy in a school environment, and it demands considerable self-discipline – paradoxically more self-discipline than remaining within the stressful situation! Nonetheless, a physical break promotes clear reflective thought, especially when combined with some physical activity such as walking, swimming or cycling. A chocolate biscuit or two (but never more than that) may also be a big help in overcoming negative thinking.

2. Focus on the things that are going well before pivoting to the problems.

Although it may be easier said than done, a positive, optimistic mindset is a wonderful antidote to negative thinking as it can calm internal conflict and place negativity in proper perspective. Calling a halt (or 'timeout') to whatever events are happening and simply taking the time to reflect – or even better, pray (if prayer is part of your life) – can really help to restore optimism and idealism. A productive thought process could perhaps begin by considering the detrimental things that could easily have happened but didn't, and then try to find things that are genuinely positive. To paraphrase and mix some common aphorisms, 'take time to smell the roses' and thus 'wake up and smell the coffee'.

3. **Make sure expectations are realistic.**

Many school leaders are not only 'people pleasers' (as described above') – many are also perfectionists. School leaders who hold themselves responsible or accountable for unrealistic, perfectionistic excellence – sometimes reinforced or even amplified by their board's ambitious expectations – can easily find themselves feeling frustrated, fearful, anxious or hopeless in the face of hostility or resistance. The tensions faced by school leaders in achieving their own aspirations while simultaneously satisfying others' expectations and demands often lead to turmoil, and in far too many situations, backhanded complaints from others to the school board (to which the Principal is directly responsible). Of course, aspiring to achieve the very best for everyone in a school community, inspiring others through personal example and taking the school to new heights are all admirable and worthy goals, but there are times when leaders need to refocus on achieving a lesser outcome that would satisfy the requirements even if not every facet of the outcome is ideal.

4. **Maintain open conversations with trusted colleagues and friends.**

Loneliness is a strong ally of negativity. Another accomplice of negativity is the need that many school leaders have to maintain an artificially positive public persona even when life and work are not going well. Having a close confidante is almost essential in times of stress and uncertainty – ideally a spouse or partner, but perhaps alternatively a pastor, a long-term trusted friend, or maybe even the board chair if the board-head relationship is of such quality that transparency, frankness and confidentiality have been established.

I should emphasise that this article explores what I call 'garden-variety negative thinking', NOT clinical depression or anxiety. If you think you may be suffering from either of these conditions, please seek professional help, or at the very least, visit a website such as 'Beyond Blue' in Australia, 'Public Health Agency' in Canada, 'Manatu Hauora / Ministry of Health or Mental Health Foundation' in New Zealand, 'NHS National Health Service' in the united Kingdom or the 'National Alliance of Mental Illness' in the United States.

Insight 78

Parents who are board members

Many boards I work with include members who are parents of current students in the school. Other boards specifically exclude current parents becoming board members. A few schools I work with make being a current parent a requirement to serve on the board. 28 of the 38 OECD countries have laws requiring parental participation on the boards of public (government-run) and government-dependent private schools, although independent schools and international schools are usually free either to include or not to include parents as board members.

As with many facets of schools, there are sound arguments both for and against parental involvement on school boards – remembering, of course, that obeying the law is always a persuasive argument!

On the positive side, current parents (almost by definition) are always intensely interested in every broad aspect of the school – its safety, its curriculum, the quality of its teaching and care, its facilities, its cost-effectiveness, even down to congestion in the car park and the cleanliness of the toilets. Current parents are usually therefore very generous with their time and energy, and their expectations and aspirations are high.

On the negative side, parents are clients of the school, and conflicts of interest can arise between the role of governance (representing ownership) and the role of client. For example, every year when the school board considers the level of tuition fees for the coming year, parents have a conflict of interest by simple definition of their role. Moreover, boards may struggle to secure the collective skills they require if (for example) all board members or a majority of board members must be current parents – at the very least it will reduce the diversity of ages and institutional memory on the board.

One danger that parent-heavy boards often experience is that parents can become excessively focussed on the needs of their own child or the children of their close friends, bringing their operational frustrations to a board meeting where the focus should be on governance, not operations. This invariably undermines the Principal's capacity to address situations in the school in a balanced manner as certain issues become amplified in what often becomes a divisive and emotional board meeting where "the squeaky wheels demand the most oil". As I sometimes comment when I conduct board workshops – parents may want to focus on their own children's needs, but boards have a duty to focus on the needs of the future children which the current children in the school will have one day.

Despite the challenges, I have seen boards that include members who are current parents function very effectively. A key to this effectiveness is board members understanding their role and, to draw on imagery developed by Edward de Bono, knowing which 'hat' to wear at different times – their "parent hat" or their "board member hat".

The key to getting this right is remembering that board power is a collective authority. In other words, when the board is not meeting, each parent board member has no more – and no less – power than any other parent. Therefore, like any other parent who has a concern about their child, a parent board member can (and should) approach the teacher or the Principal to address their concern. When they do so, they have no more or less authority than any other parent in the school (despite any sense of intimidation the teacher might wrongly feel). It is at these times that the parent board member should explicitly wear their "parent hat" – and do so with humility.

On the other hand, when the board is in session and meeting formally, the "parent hat" must come off and be replaced with the "board member hat". Like every member in a board meeting, a parent board member's prime loyalty MUST always be to what is best for the institution, not to any outside group or to oneself, which would be a conflict of interest. Furthermore, as the board's function is governance, not school operations, raising matters that are rightly the domain of management (especially ones that affect individual students or staff) should be ruled as 'out of order' by the Board Chair.

Understanding when to wear the "parent hat" or the "board member hat" should be an important element of the orientation (onboarding) process for every new board member, whether parent or not. Every board member must understand the boundaries within which they and every fellow board member must operate. All board members (whether parents or not) have no say as board members in timetabling, teacher allocations, discipline, admissions, tidiness of the playground, or any other aspect of day-to-day operations. Board members are responsible for governance, which means they focus on quite different 'big picture' matters like setting policy, overseeing the school's actions and outcomes to ensure they align with its mission and strategic plan, ensuring the school is financially stable, legally compliant and maintaining accreditation standards, and appointing and then supporting the board's one employee, who is the Principal.

Problems arise when these principles are neglected or forgotten. When I conduct workshops with school boards, I often introduce several hypothetical scenarios to illustrate the grey, messy ways in which problems can escalate. Let's look briefly at two simple scenarios (that I don't use in workshops) as examples.

An issue has arisen that affects a board member's own child

A board member's son is struggling academically in a particular class. The parent suspects it may be related to bullying that the boy has just admitted is also happening, so the parent reaches out to the teacher wearing his "parent hat". It looks as though this process may take a few weeks to understand and then resolve, but throughout this process, the board member must keep the "parent hat" on so his actions are not considered an abuse of power. This means that like every other parent in the school, he should not cut corners and go straight to the Principal, he should not exert pressure for a teacher or another child to be reprimanded, and he must never call upon his role on the board as justification to be heard. The school's normal protocols for communication must be followed. If the issue remains unresolved with the teacher, then the parent may contact the relevant middle manager (such as department or division co-ordinator), still assiduously wearing the "parent hat". In the unlikely event that the issues remain unresolved, then like any other parent, he may escalate the issue to the Principal. At every step of the process, it is important for the parent board member to acknowledge the "elephant in the room" – to be transparent and acknowledge "I know I'm a board member, but I'm speaking to you strictly as the parent of my son". Note that this matter should never be brought to a board meeting, because the Board has no authority to intervene in an operational matter such as this. If the board member did raise the matter of his own son's situation at a board meeting, the Board Chair would have a duty to dismiss it without hesitation.

What is being taught seems incongruent or incompatible with the school's enduring purpose (mission)

A new way of teaching language has been introduced, and a parent board member thinks it is out of step with the school's mission as defined in the strategic plan. Should the parent board member deal with the concern wearing the "parent hat" or the "board member hat"?

Wearing her "parent hat", she can share her concerns with the Languages Co-ordinator. However, in doing so, she should emphasise she is speaking as a parent, not as a board member.

Because the concern extends to alignment with the school's mission, which is the domain of governance, she can also put on her "board member hat" and present her concern privately to the Board Chair (or to the Chair of the Board's Education Committee if it has one). Although board members do not have a role in implementing curriculum, they are expected to oversee quality, ensure policies are being followed, and support the school's Mission. If the Board Chair agrees that there may be some misalignment with the Mission, then the matter of possible school mission misalignment can be placed with due notice on the agenda of a forthcoming board meeting. In such a case, the next step would be for the Board Chair to explore the matter with the Principal before the board meeting to ensure the discussion is well-informed and conducted in a "no surprises" context. In the end, however, the Principal will have the final say on the new languages program as there may be regulatory, accreditation or other reasons that need to be taken into account. Nonetheless, a wise Principal would make such a decision with the full support of the board!

When I conduct board training, I am sometimes asked whether I think parents should be banned from being board members.

I understand the perceived conflict of interest that being a parent AND a board member can generate, especially when tuition fees are being discussed or when a board member's child has just been disciplined, but these situations can be handled with a sound conflicts of interest policy.

I appreciate the risk of partisanship when parents might focus excessively on their own child's needs or situations, but this can be handled by a solid onboarding program, understanding when to wear different "hats", and ongoing professional development in governance.

I can see the limitations upon diversity and skills imposed by parent-only boards, and in such situations the board might consider a constitutional change (if possible) to allow the addition of non-parent members or observers.

At the end of the day, I think asking whether or not to ban parents from board membership is the wrong question because it starts from a conclusion and works backwards in search of reasons. On the contrary the right questions to ask, irrespective of whether or not board members are parents, are:
- how can we attract the right skills set among board members?
- how do we ensure diversity of age, gender, experiences, ethnicity, perspectives, etc, among board members?
- do we have a sound orientation (onboarding) process for new board members so they understand the extent and limitations of their role as governors?
- do we have a sound conflicts of interest policy and associated practices?
- are we conducting regular performance reviews of all board members?
- has our constitution kept pace with the times and the school's changes?
- are our mission, vision and strategic plan requiring a review and perhaps an update?
- are we engaging in regular professional development in governance to ensure ongoing best practice?

Insight 79

Perfection can be a prison

Sylvaster is one of the more confident, outspoken members of the school board. Known as "Vaster" to his friends, but "Mr Lee" to new and younger members of the Board, he has been a member of the board for only three years. Nonetheless he brings a wealth of experience from his paid service as a member of several corporate boards. The epitome of self-assurance, no-one would ever accuse Sylvaster of humility.

Sylvaster gladly labels himself as a "perfectionist". He sets high standards for himself, and he expects nothing less from others in his professional and social circles – and even his own family. He justifies this craving for perfection by telling himself he is simply striving for excellence. After all, why would anyone NOT want things to be done to the highest standard possible?

The other members of Sylvaster's school board have different perceptions of Sylvaster's perfectionism. Some see his penchant for detail as valuable, offering comments like "every board needs a Sylvaster". Others are deeply irritated by what they see as Sylvaster's insipid fault-finding, prolonging meetings with tedious debates over the precise wording of motions, such as whether or not split infinitives should be permitted, or whether the upper limit for the CFO's spending approval should be $24,000 rather than $25,000. For Sylvaster, delegating anything to others is fraught with risk, because no-one else on the board or in the senior management seems to understand anything as clearly as he does, hence his desire to check and verify everything that anyone else says or suggests.

Now that Sylvaster has been a member of the school board for three years, and has emerged to dominate most of the discussions during that time, several of his fellow members are becoming irritated. At first, they admired his hard work, his insistence on high standards and his precise thought processes. However, the more he has insisted on perfection, the more the other board members have become frustrated. Many are now hesitant to offer opinions because they fear they will be humiliated or criticised. Some have begun second-guessing Sylvaster's opinions so they can fall quickly into line with his views. Endless point-picking, revisions to drafts, then further revisions of drafts, and then revisions of the re-drafts, are draining their energy because nothing ever seems to meet Sylvaster's high expectations. The Chair feels powerless, and more than a little intimidated by Sylvaster, and this allows Sylvaster's apparent authority to expand even further.

Unknown the other members of the board, Sylvaster is also feeling exhausted and overwhelmed. He feels he has to carry the weight of responsibility of the whole board because of others' incompetence, and he can't see a way out of the prison that has been constructed around his perfectionism.

How did Sylvaster come to be in this prison called perfectionism?

Many POIs (People of Influence) in society, like Sylvaster, function in workplaces where precision and high performance are essential. Industries such as engineering, biotechnology, aviation and medicine leave no room for error. Should schools also be places where mistakes are not tolerated? Perhaps they should be in some ways, and yet schools are places of learning, and the most powerful way to learn something new is through the mistakes that are made. Moreover, schools are dynamic and diverse "people places" where ignoring or suppressing the viewpoints and perspectives of others is almost never helpful, even when those opinions fall short of "perfection" in the eyes of some decision-makers in the school.

Many successful leaders became perfectionists because their attention to detail and commitment to high standards have been rewarded in their careers. The problem is that working on a school board requires a different type of leadership that demands working as a team with other people. The individual quest for perfection that serves people like Sylvaster well as a specialist in his own employment can actually hinder them on a school board where task-orientation must be balanced with a mature set of people-skills.

In many organisations, especially those in the corporate sector, failure is not seen as a learning opportunity; it is a career risk. Leaders who have been conditioned to believe that mistakes equal incompetence often struggle to let go of perfectionism and embrace excellence. The 'perfection mindset' demands avoiding mistakes at all cost, whereas an 'excellence mindset' focusses on learning and improving from mistakes.

For those people who are bound in the Prison of Perfection, it may seem that their perfectionism brings comfortable security. Of course, such comfort represents a false sense of security not unlike the Stockholm Syndrome. People like Sylvaster believe that if they check everything, review every decision, and ensure no mistakes slip through, they can be in control of the outcome. As Sylvaster's fellow board members have come to realise, however, this mindset slows everything down, creates bottlenecks, suppresses a free exchange of ideas, and thus stifles innovation and creativity.

By the time Sylvaster realised there was a problem, he found himself in a vicious cycle. As he continued to push for perfection from his fellow board members and the Head of School, frustration grew and everyone he worked with became more and more reluctant to show initiative. As the other board members showed less and less initiative, Sylvaster increasingly felt he had to step in to fix things. The more he stepped in, the more dependent (and frustrated) everyone else became with him, and the less capable they seemed to be in Sylvaster's view. It was becoming a major source of board disagreement and dysfunction.

Perfectionism in leadership creates a paradox. School leaders such as board members and the senior executive sincerely believe they are ensuring quality, but they may actually be eroding trust, collaboration, and efficiency. The longer they retain this mindset, the harder it will be to break.

Once a board member or a school leader realises they are trapped in the Prison of Perfection, breaking free can seem to demand a huge effort, not least because perfection has become an established facet of that person's public identity. So how can an escape from the prison of perfection be achieved?

Initiating this process of release often requires external assistance, such as a quiet conversation over a cup of coffee, or perhaps a "walk in the yard" with the Board Chair. Certainly, the regular process of Board

Performance Reviews should be a powerful and persuasive tool to identify dysfunction with a board's dynamics or the disruption caused by an aberrant board member such as Sylvaster.

The ideal 'prison escape strategy' would be for Sylvaster to understand why progress is preferable to perfection for a school and its board. Fortunately, as is often the case, there is someone who understands this trade-off. The school's Principal, Josepha, does understand the need to balance progress with perfection and has the skills to balance the important priorities of getting tasks done while also caring for people. Of course, no Principal can (or should) ever initiate the process of reforming a board member's behaviour; that is strictly a task for the Board Chair or (preferably) a neutral, independent consultant. Nonetheless, a high functioning Principal can serve as an appropriate role model, leading by example.

Like most school principals, Josepha understands the pressures of having to please multiple constituencies – students, parents, teachers, alumni, the Board, government authorities, and many more – and she has learned that mistakes have consequences. Josepha also understands that her job is not to create perfect outcomes herself – it is to build a team that is capable of delivering excellent work without her constant oversight.

Early in her headship of the school, Josepha decided that rather than reviewing every piece of work herself, she would set clear 'big picture' expectations in advance, delegate, and then trust her team to meet them. She encouraged her executive team to take responsibility for their work, and when mistakes happened, she treated them as learning moments, not failures.

Over time, Josepha's team grew in confidence, took more initiatives, and consistently began to deliver high-quality work without her constant involvement. The executive team was not just working for Josepha; they were working with her as members of a coherent partnership.

Following the most recent board performance review, the Board Chair approached Josepha and asked whether she would be prepared to allow Sylvaster to shadow her for a few days, emphasising this request was not for Sylvaster to interfere but simply to observe. Understandably, Josepha was nervous about the suggestion because it ran the risk of blurring the line between governance and management, but she unselfishly agreed in the hope of streamlining the board's work by diluting Sylvaster's frustrating perfectionism.

Shadowing Josepha proved to be a transformative experience for Sylvaster – a true revelation. He learned how different the culture of schools is compared with the corporate sector, and how insights from his work in the corporate sector need to be tempered if they are to have relevance in the context of a school.

Sylvaster came to realise that effective school leadership is unconcerned with achieving the perfection of flawlessness; it is about delivering high-impact results that help achieve the school's mission as efficiently and humanely as possible. Sylvaster learned that a quest for perfection can actually be a barrier to achieving effective progress. He learned that perfectionism often arises from an unjustified lack of trust in others, and that it is more valuable for a project to be delivered today at 95% than too late at 100%.

Sylvaster learned that mistakes are inevitable, and they should be embraced as opportunities to learn and improve, not seen as failures to be punished. After significant personal reflection, Sylvaster even came to realise the paradox that perfectionism is usually either a reflection of an inflated ego or a deep level of personal insecurity – the reality is that excessive perfectionism cannot arise from a balanced, mature personality, nor does it enhance servant leadership.

This story has a happy ending. Sylvaster escaped from the Prison of Perfectionism and continues serving on the school board, making a far more effective, productive contribution while also halving his input of time and effort. Board meetings now always finish punctually having successfully completing the agenda, and Sylvaster's relations with fellow board members have flourished. Sylvaster's respect and support for Josepha has especially blossomed, and he has invited Josepha to address a meeting of his own corporate board to share her insights into balanced leadership.

Do you have a Sylvaster on your board whose well-intentioned but misguided perfectionism is imprisoning your board's effectiveness? If you do, how do you think your board should address the situation and escape from the prison? Hint: ignoring the problem is not an option!

Original images of cards and characters from the game of Monopoly are © Hasbro Inc., 1936, 1996.

Insight 80

Principled Leadership

"Politics can be made more difficult than it really is. There are three essential tenets. First, take responsibility; second, reject the ideas that distract, divide and discount the nation; and third, argue to the last breath for the ideas and ideals that make the nation a better place. Honesty will, nearly always, win over duplicity."

Those words appeared in a 2013 article written by Bill Kelty, the former secretary of the ACTU (Australian Council of Trade Unions) from 1983 until 2000 and a key person of influence during Australian Labor governments under Prime Ministers Bob Hawke and Paul Keating. It was just one small paragraph in a long newspaper article at the time, but it caught my attention because those same three points could – and should – be made about leadership in a school.

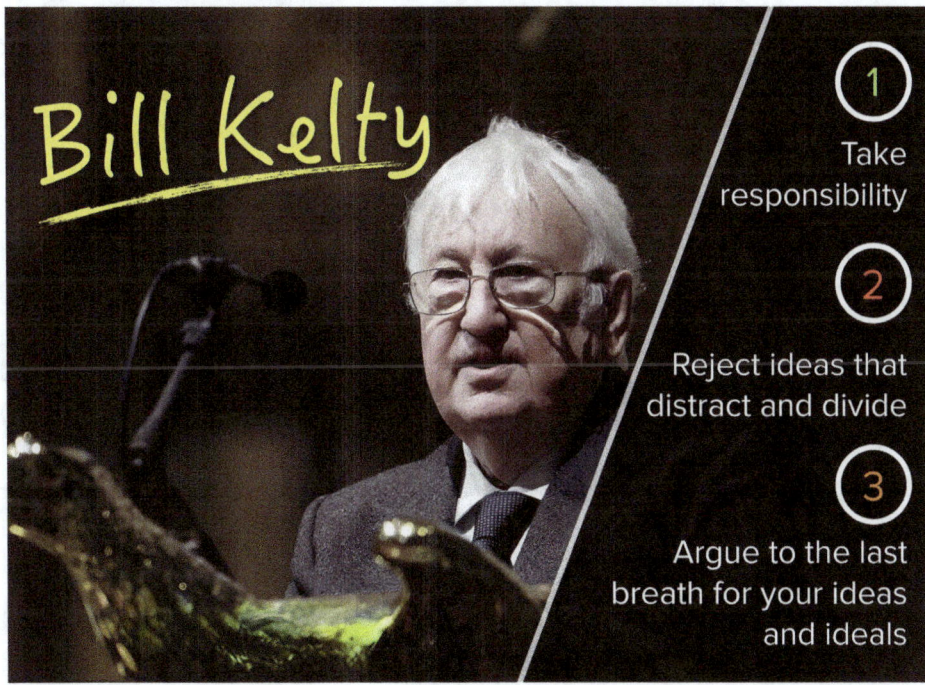

Perhaps surprisingly for the casual observer, school leadership can seem at times to have a similar level of complexity and intrigue as national politics, although (mercifully) at a smaller if no-less-intense scale. This is the case for all levels of school leadership, including school boards and senior executives.

Kelty's first point: take responsibility.

I think there are two facets of taking responsibility – taking responsibility for ourselves and fulfilling our responsibility towards others. However, as the former US Secretary of State, Colin Powell, expressed so eloquently: "Being responsible sometimes means pissing people off". For a leader or aspiring leader whose main but misguided focus is popularity, resistance inevitably leads to inertia, which is why responsible leadership is incompatible with popularity as its driving force. In the words of former Australian Prime Minister Gough Whitlam, sometimes you just have to "crash through or crash".

For some school boards and senior leaders, the alternative to accepting responsibility is trying to shift blame and responsibility towards others. This type of cowardly behaviour is inevitably damaging for any school. Therefore, an important part of taking responsibility as a leader is maintaining a calm, clear-thinking, resolute disposition, even when confronted by opposition, anger and blame.

Whenever a culture of blame is evident in a school, it needs to be addressed and replaced by a culture of responsibility. To paraphrase Harry Truman's famous statement of the US President's ultimate level of responsibility, the buck in a school stops with the Board and the Principal. A culture of blame is never helpful in a school. Schools which function well have a vibrant, healthy culture of collaboration and co-operation, together with a balanced mix of self-responsibility and collective duty towards one another.

Kelty's second point was to reject ideas that distract and divide.

Ideas that distract and divide fall into two main categories – straw man fallacies and "argumentum ad hominem". (I guess there is also a possible third category – lies, deception and misinformation – but as Kelty says, "honesty will, nearly always, win over duplicity", so I won't dwell on that distracting third category here).

A straw man fallacy arises when someone misrepresents an opponent's position, often by exaggerating it or making it more extreme (thus setting up a 'straw man'), and then proceeds to attack the 'straw man' rather than address the real argument. "Argumentum ad hominem" arises when a person attacks an opponent on personal grounds rather than addressing the argument at hand (attacking the person rather than the argument). Sadly, both approaches are as common in schools as they are in wider society.

Differences of opinion and conflicts are inevitable whenever people interact meaningfully, and indeed they are central to a healthy democracy. It is the way in which these differences are handled that indicates the health of that democracy. Whether in a democracy or in a school, conflicts of ideas are to be welcomed, encouraged and embraced, whereas conflicts between people are destructive and divisive, and thus must not be tolerated.

Kelty's third proposition (paraphrased) is that a leader should argue to the last breath for the ideas and ideals that make the school a better place. In the context of a school, those ideals should be articulated through the Mission (the school's enduring purpose), the Vision (priorities in achieving the Mission over the next few years), and the Core Values (or Philosophy).

One of my most influential models for 'arguing to the last breath for ideas and ideals' has been Nelson Mandela. When I was Head of Li Po Chun United World College in Hong Kong, Mandela was my ultimate boss as he was the Honorary President of the UWCs at the time. I would often quote his inspiring words about education in speeches, words such as "Education is the most powerful weapon which you can use to change the world", and more autobiographically, "It is through education that the daughter of a peasant can become a doctor, that a son of a mineworker can become the head of the mine, or that a child of farm workers can become the President of a great nation".

Full disclosure: my photo with Nelson Mandela was taken at Madame Tussauds wax museum in London.

Nelson Mandela has few equals as an example of persistence and determination, given that he spent his entire adult life mobilising his people against apartheid, remaining undeterred through 27 years of imprisonment. Mandela's persistence in patiently arguing for positive change is legendary, and I cannot think of any better role model that I, or my students, or my school board, could have had for "arguing to the last breath for one's ideas and ideals".

Change – anywhere – inevitably provokes a reaction, and this is especially so in schools where inertia and personal interests can sometimes be more deeply entrenched than is the case in profit-focussed enterprises. In my various leadership roles, I have probably found myself in the position of advocating for robust discussions about change, and then managing the ensuing process of change, more than most other educational leaders. Indeed, the reason I first went into education many decades ago was to be a catalyst for bringing about positive change that would benefit young lives. I was therefore encouraged when I read Bill Kelty's third proposition, because the sad reality is that the process of leading others through necessary change can at times be so overwhelmingly disheartening that many school leaders give up on it.

I have written elsewhere about the nature of school leadership (see Insights 8, 91 and 98), observing that anyone in a position of leading a school, either as a board member or as a Principal, has been given an immense privilege. The actions and decisions of school leaders have the potential to influence not only the trajectory of hundreds, or even thousands, of people's careers but also their entire lives. However, with that power comes great responsibility. Being a great leader in a school is not just about achieving goals and hitting targets; it is about creating a positive and supportive environment where everyone can flourish.

The former Prime Minister of Singapore, Lee Kuan Yew, once said, "I do not know of anyone who became a leader as a result of having undergone a leadership course". Given that almost half a trillion US dollars are spent on leadership development programs annually, that is a sobering claim, as is the finding of leadership derailment studies that 93% of leadership development programs fail to meet expectations.

Schools are notorious for NOT preparing their board members and principals for leadership roles. Very few school board members receive any professional development on their role before taking up their positions, and only a minority of schools have adequate formal induction programs for new board members. Similarly, most countries do not have any mandatory requirements for training aspiring principals to become Heads of Schools, although Principals do have more avenues for professional development once appointed than is usual for members of school boards.

The US educational consultant, John Littleford, claims that almost 80% of school principals are fired rather than leaving of their own volition. Correlation does not imply causation, but that statistic begs the question of whether more (or better) professional development for school boards might increase members' reflective awareness of their duties of care and loyalty to their one employee – the Head of School.

Of course, Lee Kwan Yew is right in suggesting that authentic leadership cannot really be taught. True leadership is acquired through the rigours of experience, both in the heat of the moment when a leader is under fire and through the reflective process that follows. Nonetheless, sound training in effective leadership can provide a firm foundation for building the knowledge and skills required by school leaders.

There is an arguably even more important application of Kelty's three tenets than the implications for a school's leadership. Schools exist primarily for the formation of their students, and Kelty's three tenets make an excellent set of guiding principles for students as they go through life.

The topic of developing leadership in students is often a controversial one. Over the years, I have heard strong arguments supporting the idea that every student should be trained for leadership, whether that leadership is of a family, a company or a country. I have also heard equally strong counterarguments claiming that leadership is not for everyone; it is an ability that only a few possess and so it sets children up for inevitable failure to tell them "everyone can be on top" or "you can be whatever you want to be". To a large extent, these arguments tend to be futile because they seldom agree on what the word 'leadership' actually means for young people.

Personally, I believe developing leadership in students does not mean preparing them for political office; it means equipping them with whatever skills they need to become people of influence in whichever sphere of life they find themselves.

If leadership can simply be thought of as being a positive influence to improve the lives of other people, how wonderful it would be if every student graduating from every school (1) took responsibility, (2) rejected ideas that distracted and divided, and (3) argued to their last breath for the ideas and ideals that make the world a better place.

Schools everywhere in the world have the potential – sadly, often untapped – to produce hundreds of thousands of new Nelson Mandelas, each committed to a principled and persistent life of fostering positive change. I cannot think of a more appropriate and enduring legacy for the work of today's school leaders, but it cannot happen unless school board members and senior staff are equipped with the skills and the vision to take responsibility, reject the ideas that distract, divide, and argue to their last breath for the ideas and ideals that make the world a better place.

References:

Kelty, B (2013) A new script needed for Labor and the nation, *Sydney Morning Herald*. 28 March 2013, https://www.smh.com.au/politics/federal/a-new-script-needed-for-labor-and-the-nation-20130327-2gufy.html

Littleford, J (n.d.) *Leadership Of Schools And The Longevity Of Heads*, https://www.jlittleford.com/leadership-of-schools-and-the-longevity-of-heads/

Insight 81

Priorities when finances are beyond tight

Finances are always tight in every school. This is understandable because finances are never sufficient to meet the high aspirations and ideals that school leaders and boards have – and should have – for their schools.

Having said that, there are times in the lives of many schools when finances are beyond tight, times when the financial constraints are so severe that they seem to pose an existential threat that might strangle the school. In such times, how should school leaders and the board prioritise expenditure and financial management?

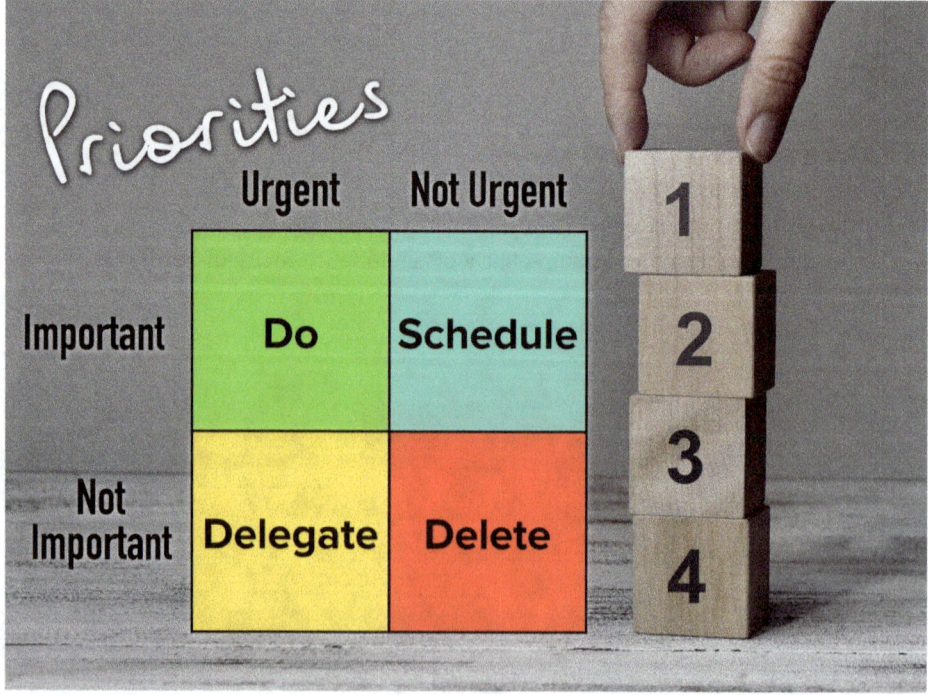

Two key approaches are required that cover two different time frames.

First, in the short-term, priority must be given to making those payments which are most urgent and important. These high-priority immediate expenditures typically fall into six groups:

- Wages and salaries for the staff.
- Expenses related to health and safety, including essential services such as electricity, water and internet services, and repairs to infrastructure.
- Expenses that will result in better performance and reputation, and/or generate higher income in the (hopefully near) future.
- Debt obligations, including expenses for which invoices have already been received.
- Renewal of insurance policies.
- Payments to meet regulatory requirements and obligations, such as licensing fees, accreditation fees, and other expenses necessary to maintain the school's legal status.

Second, in the longer-term, once the immediate crisis has been averted, a more strategic level of thinking is required. Typically, this would involve the board and senior management working together as a team to address six action areas:

- Conduct a full, thorough, critical budget review to identify areas of inefficiency or excess spending which are 'costs' rather than 'investments', combined with long-term financial sustainability planning that includes realistic revenue projections, expense controls and contingency measures that should provide protection against unforeseen future financial crises.
- Ruthlessly pursue new, diverse sources of income to reduce over-reliance on a narrow range of income such as tuition fees and government payments. New incomes sources worth exploring may include sponsorships, partnerships with local businesses, philanthropic giving, grants from NGOs, alumni donations, establishing distance learning, expanding into adult education, rental of school facilities out-of-hours, and many others. Seeking diverse sources of incomes is an area where board members can hopefully tap into their community networks.
- Where possible, try to negotiate cost reductions from suppliers and contractors, and in cases where that is not possible, take the difficult

decision to reduce non-essential programs, optimise energy use, and explore sharing services (and therefore costs) with other schools.

- While acknowledging staff salaries are a priority in any school, the reality is that staff salaries are also typically the single largest expenditure item in most schools. Therefore, times of financial hardship, it would be derelict not to examine staffing levels and consider options such as attrition, voluntary retirement packages, or temporary furloughs to reduce payroll expenses on the essential condition that any changes do not compromise the quality of education.

- If the school has outstanding debts, work with creditors to renegotiate repayment terms or explore debt consolidation options that may ease financial burdens.

- Monitor cash flow management and pay close attention to punctual collection of tuition fees, grants and other income, and perhaps even consider offering cash or other incentives for early payments or instalment plans for families facing financial hardship.

With strategic planning, innovative thinking, transparent and frank communication, collaboration with stakeholders, and a dose of courage, schools can usually overcome financial challenges and achieve long-term sustainability, even when the immediate financial pressures are acute. Of course, each school's approach needs to be tailored to its unique circumstances, but common themes for most schools include targeted cost-saving measures, revenue diversification, and transparent community engagement.

Insight 82

Purpose trumps convenience

In today's society, convenience often trumps purpose, or meaningfulness.

There are many examples of this phenomenon all around us. The rise of multinational retailers such as Amazon at the expense of locally owned, employment-generating stores is one example. Another is the rise of home delivered food or other purchases which save the time it takes to travel to shops, even though travelling to shops provides interaction with other people (however superficial) that psychologists say is important for our mental health. As another example, people in Western societies prefer to drive than take public transport to save time despite the considerably higher financial and environmental costs of doing so. The widespread use of mobile phones to skim news articles and reduce analysis to brief social media posts provides still further evidence.

Yes, the fast road to convenience seems to be winning the battle against the longer, winding, more slippery roadway towards meaningfulness. It should not be that way, especially in schools.

Many school boards are prone to adopt society's widespread embrace of convenience, even though it may come at the cost of purpose. In some ways this is understandable given that most members of school boards are well-meaning, highly motivated but time-impoverished volunteers who are squeezing their board service into their otherwise very full and busy lives, careers and families.

On the other hand, it is important to remember that authentic leadership means giving your best in order to inspire other people to do their best too, getting them to care as much as you do about the things that matter. Leadership involves defining and articulating a purpose that has meaning rather than simple convenience.

Convenience might not seem to be the prevailing priority when board members are sitting through a four-hour long meeting late into the night. However, these are the precise types of occasions when board members should resist any temptation to take short cuts for the sake of convenience, because the consequence will almost certainly be decisions that dilute purpose and meaningfulness.

Every school exists for an inherently noble purpose, a purpose which is hopefully articulated publicly and frequently through the school's mission statement (its statement of enduring purpose). This explicitly articulated, noble purpose should form the foundation of every decision the board makes – after all, what could be more important than steering the school towards achieving its enduring purpose in a clear, intentional manner?

Therefore, the priority of seeking meaning and purpose over convenience applies in every area of board operations and policy setting, especially where fiduciary and other duties are concerned. For example (and obviously), it is important to take the time and consider alternatives when recruiting a new Principal, undertaking a risk audit and analysis of the school, in policy development and review, when undertaking performance reviews of senior and middle managers (and of the board itself), and when considering financial reports, analyses and projections. Due diligence demands that the board takes whatever time is necessary to consider such matters fully and work to enhance the school's purpose and meaningfulness. Short cuts for convenience are not an option.

Similarly, when a school embarks on a process of strategic planning, a risk arises that convenience may overtake significance. Of course, this is not necessarily a deliberate decision by board members, but is more likely a consequence of board members who are in a hurry accepting our society's prevailing, uncritiqued assumption that speed and convenience are inherently good.

It is easy to appreciate the passionate discussions that take place among board members when they focus on the best way to achieve the school's mission. However, having decided on the priorities (or vision) for a new strategic plan, dangers arise as soon as the vision is written down. One initial danger is that the vision risks becoming a diluted, pale reflection of the passionate insights that underpin it simply because a long and passionate discussion has been reduced to a brief sentence or two. Subsequent dangers arise when a poorly articulated vision statement becomes hijacked by those in the school community who may have a different agenda to that of the board, leading to a process of white-anting or well-poisoning.

If a strategic plan is to communicate the board's passion effectively and inspire an entire school community to support it, then the words that are chosen and the visual presentation become critically important. The task of communicating a strategic plan lies well beyond wordsmithing. It requires communication skills of the highest order as the strategic plan will be called upon to define the school's future direction and priorities for the entire school community, prospective clients and the general public.

In public documents such as strategic plans, over-simplification, lack of clarity, poor illustrations, ambiguity, weak expression or just a few words out of place can cause so much confusion that the entire document could easily become an ineffective embarrassment.

The real test of a strategic plan is this – does it articulate a genuinely meaningful pathway towards positive transformation, or is it just a convenient means of ticking a bureaucratic box?

And the way to answer that question is this – is the strategic plan an integral component of the school's day-to-day planning, decision-making, budgeting and direction setting, or does it simply sit on the bookshelf gathering dust?

Sadly, studies have shown that more than 70% of strategic plans in schools are simply dust collectors within a month or two of their completion. Such strategic plans lack both convenience and, much more importantly, meaningfulness.

In everything that a school board does, therefore, purpose and meaningfulness must trump convenience.

Clarity of purpose is essential for boards and school leaders to educate and motivate people so they feel compelled to respond to an invitation to help build the school's future. The mission – the school's enduring purpose – must be central to every decision made by the board and its senior leaders, and it must underpin (implicitly or explicitly) every public statement or promise that is made on behalf of the school.

These days, people (and especially younger people) rightly expect meaning and purpose. They openly ask questions like "what do you value?", "what is your purpose?" and "how do you bring your values to life?". Embracing meaningfulness and purpose is thus the antidote for disengagement because it allows tiny flames of interest to grow into raging fires of enthusiasm and positive action.

Insight 83

Recruiting a new Head of School

No task is more important for a school board than choosing the right Head to fill a vacancy. Once appointed, the next most important task for the board is building and maintaining a relationship of mutual trust between it and the new Head.

Heads up: that word "trust" is the underlying theme of this article for the obvious reason that it really, REALLY matters!

The nature of the role of Head of School is changing rapidly, and it is certainly very different to when I was appointed to my first headship in 1988 at the age of 35. Compliance requirements are more demanding, documentation expectations are more onerous, remuneration and some working conditions in education have declined relative to other industries, parental expectations are expanding, curriculum freedoms are declining, social media is bringing hitherto unknown and uncontrollable risks, and all these factors are additional to the pressures of a global pandemic and the stresses of leadership that have always been omnipresent in leadership.

It is perhaps not surprising that increasing numbers of Heads of Schools are leaving their positions abruptly. NAIS statistics from the United States show that as many as 20% of new Heads leave their jobs after three years or less, while a worrying 42% of Heads have reported a "strained" relationship with their board over the past decade.

The stresses of leading a school are significant, but they are insufficient to explain alarming statistics such as these. In many cases, the problem goes back to the recruitment process, beginning with expectations.

In the unlikely event that every board member actually shares identical expectations with every other board member of what they WANT in a new Head, this will almost certainly differ from what they NEED. Many (perhaps most) search committees develop such an idealistic and unrealistic list of characteristics for a new Head even before they have met the first candidate that (to use a long-standing aphorism) it could only be satisfied by "God, on a good day".

Another mistake that many boards make is to swing the pendulum excessively. In other words, boards seek to recruit whatever qualities, skills and attributes they felt were deficient or missing in the Head who is leaving. This is a recipe for potential instability when the new Head arrives as existing policies are challenged, assumed leadership styles are missed, existing 'comfort zones' are disrupted for long-standing staff, and so on – all of which can be further exacerbated if the Board also requires the new Head to "fix up" a few unfinished issues from their predecessor's tenure.

There is no doubt that an external, neutral consultant, working closely in partnership with the Board's own Search Committee, can help professionalise the recruitment of a new Head. Before engaging with a consultant, it is helpful for the Board to do some preliminary work:

- Make sure the school's mission and vision are clear, as these will provide the "true north" non-negotiable framework and direction for the incoming Head.
- Given the stage reached in the school's history, what type of leader is needed for the next phase of the school's development?
- Agree to be flexible in the forthcoming search as an applicant may provide unanticipated characteristics that would fit in very well with the school's needs.
- Recruit primarily for character and integrity – skills can be developed at a later date.
- Acknowledge any implicit biases among board members, especially regarding the career pathways that bring applicants

into the process – such career pathways are much more diverse than they were a few decades ago.

- Ensure that all board members commit to complete confidentiality during the recruitment process.
- Ensure that all members are open and honest with applicants (and the recruiter!), acknowledging the challenges facing the school and avoiding the tendency to 'sugar coat' the school's situation.
- Form a Search Committee that is intentionally diverse in terms of age, gender, ethnicity and occupational experience, but unified in its enthusiasm for the school's mission and vision.

The next step is to find a recruiting consultant who satisfies several criteria:

- understands (and preferably shares) the school's ethos, mission and values;
- has experience of both the governance and management sides of school leadership;
- possesses high quality qualifications;
- has the interpersonal skills to represent the school positively to applicants;
- has a solid network from which applicants might be drawn; and
- is affordable.

Once a recruiter has been appointed, it is important that the recruiter and the Search Committee function as effective partners, partaking in frank, robust (and always confidential) discussions, asking each other the 'hard questions', adopting a single co-ordinated approach to reference checking, with neither party deferring obsequiously to the other.

It is important not to develop a premature attachment to any particular applicant, especially an internal applicant from within the school. Once a short-list has been curated, it is highly advantageous for the recruiter to visit each of the final applicants in their own schools to see the applicant in the context of their own school culture, to ascertain the respect they are shown by students and staff, and perhaps to conduct confidential interviews with named referees.

Before a final decision is made, it is wise to bring the 'finalists' to visit the school, perhaps on a weekend when there are fewer people present, and to meet with and speak to the whole board. The Search Committee should be ready to make a recommendation, but the final decision must reside with the entire board.

Once an offer has been made and accepted, the process of co-ordinating announcements with the school from which the incoming Head will be departing must be set in place, after which board members can begin the exciting process of generating enthusiasm for the arrival of the new Head, balanced with paying due respect to the achievements of the departing Head.

This is also the period during which a detailed transition plan should be developed to address the Head's professional and personal needs, preferably by a Transition Committee established by the Board specifically for the purpose. In addition to developing a list of priority actions for the new Head, the Transition Committee should also oversee arrangements of introductions to key constituencies such as staff, students, alumni, Heads of nearby schools and local politicians. First impressions can be highly significant, so this potentially fragile process should be carefully managed.

The needs of the incoming Head's family must also be addressed at this time, including easing the pains of relocation such as orientation to a new city, finding a new home (if required) and arranging schools for children (if required). Support for the family should continue to be available for at least the first full school year.

Much more that could – and should - be said about the process of recruiting a new Head. When a board engages a competent recruiter, such information would be expanded and articulated in considerable detail to ensure a common understanding. The process may seem intimidating at first for board members, and there is no doubt that nothing less than the school's future rests on the process and its outcome.

Nonetheless, the selection process invariably becomes more and more exciting as the potential for advancing the school's mission and vision become clearer. Conducted well, the recruitment of a new Head is the most important task any school board ever undertakes.

Insight 84

Related party transactions

For school boards, related party transactions are agreements or arrangements between the school and individuals or organisations that have a close relationship with board members, senior managers, or staff. These transactions can include contracts for services, sales of property, or employment and other agreements involving family members or business associates. While not inherently unethical, related party transactions have to be treated sensitively and transparently because they pose a risk of perceived favouritism, reduced competition, loss of public trust and acceptance of sub-optimal arrangements that are not in the school's best interests.

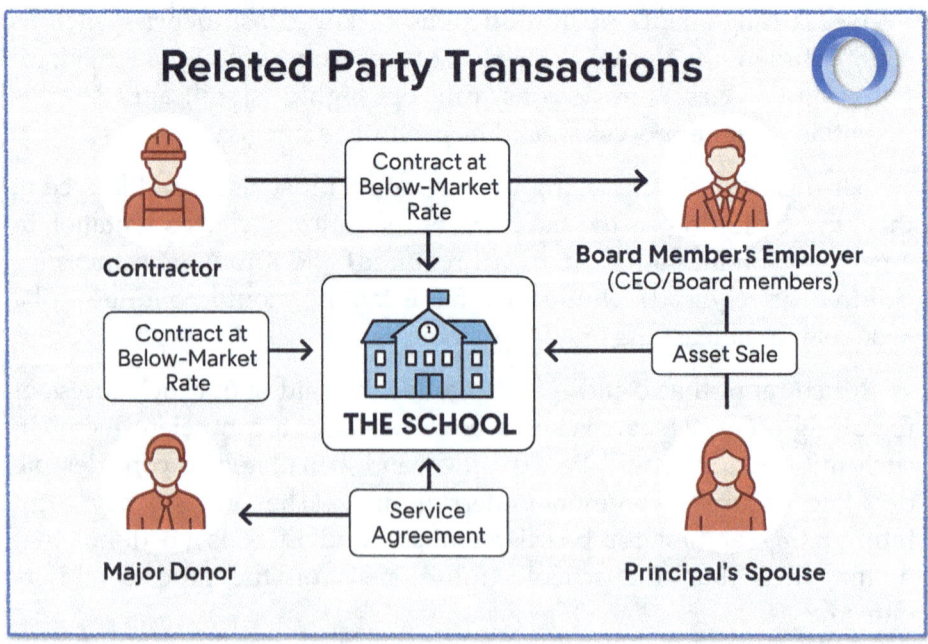

To manage related party transactions effectively, school boards must establish clear policies defining what constitutes a related party and the types of transactions that fall under scrutiny. A sample policy might look something like the document on pages 397 and 398:

RELATED PARTY TRANSACTIONS
Sample Policy

1. Definition

A 'related party transaction' includes any transaction through which a Responsible Person (as defined in the Conflicts of Interest Policy) acting on behalf of the School provides a financial or other tangible benefit to a related party (such as themselves or another Responsible Person for the School or their spouse, other relatives or close associates and other related organisations).

2. Overview

As related party transactions involve conflicts of interest or material personal interests, [Name of]

School has established policies and procedures for financial management including a register of all related party transactions which is validated by an external independent auditor.

[Name of] School's procedures are that:

a. all related party transactions and payments will be conducted on an arm's length basis to ensure that a financial benefit is not given to a related party;

b. the process surrounding those transactions must be transparent and fully documented including the maintenance and audit of a register of related party transactions; and

c. Board approval must be obtained for all related party transactions and payments recognising that the Board can delegate this approval in respect of a class of transactions and on such terms and conditions as the Board sees fit.

3. New transactions

Where the School proposes to enter into a related party transaction, the following procedure applies:

- the relevant responsible officer must inform the Director of Finance about the proposed transaction, including the proposed parties and how they are related, details of the proposed transaction and where arm's length terms may be evidenced;

- the Director of Finance will review the transaction, and consider external legal advice where appropriate in considering the transaction;

- the Director of Finance will inform and advise the Board of the proposed transaction and obtain the Board's approval for the School to undertake the transaction or approval in respect of a class of transactions;

- a register of all Board approvals in respect of related party transactions shall be maintained under the supervision of the Company Secretary and it shall include details of the nature of the transaction, the date of the approval and any key conditions to which the approval is subject; and

- when Board approval is obtained, the transaction must proceed in accordance with any procedures and conditions outlined by the Board.

4. Annual review

At the beginning of each year, the Company Secretary will write to all Responsible Persons as per the sample related party transactions disclosure letter (below).

The register of related party transactions will be updated to reflect these disclosures and submitted for audit by the School's auditor.

RELATED PARTY TRANSACTIONS
Sample Policy - continued

5. Retention of records

The School will ensure that records of related party transactions, including the registers and audit reports thereon, are retained for at least seven years.

GUIDANCE NOTES IN RESPECT OF RELATED PARTY TRANSACTIONS

Who is a related party?

For the purposes of these procedures, the following persons are considered related parties of the School:

- all Responsible Persons and all members of the School's Executive, including their spouses, de facto spouses, parents and children; and
- entities controlled by these persons.

A person or entity is also a related party of the School at a particular time if the person or entity:

- was a related party at any time within the previous six months; or
- the entity believes or has reasonable grounds to believe that it is likely to become a related party of the School at any time in the future.

A full definition is set out in Australian Accounting Standard AASB 124.

What is a financial benefit?

The legal definition of the term 'financial benefit' is broad. A non-exhaustive list of examples includes:

- providing finance or property to a related party;
- buying or leasing an asset from or selling an asset to a related party;
- supplying or receiving services from the related party;
- issuing securities or granting options to the related party; and
- taking up or releasing an obligation of the related party.

A financial benefit includes giving a financial benefit indirectly through an interposed entity and does not require the payment of money. For the purposes of this Policy, reasonable remuneration within parameters approved by the Board is excluded from the definition of "financial benefit".

What makes a transaction "at arm's length"?

A transaction is at arm's length if the relevant parties have dealt with each other as parties normally do when they are not related, so that the outcome of their dealing is a matter of genuine bargaining, and although not necessarily technically an open market price, the terms are those that might reasonably have been agreed between arm's length parties.

When school boards and senior managers take the initiative to identify potential transactions with related parties, they can implement safeguards such as pre-approval requirements, competitive bidding processes, and public disclosure of any related interests. Therefore, an annual declaration can be very helpful in identifying potential related party transactions. Optimal School Governance can provide sample declarations to school boards who require such support.

Related party transactions are a form of conflict of interest (see Insight 23). A practical example of how a related party transaction could arise might be when a school board considers contracting a construction company for school renovations. If a board member's sibling owned or had a significant share in one of the bidding companies, selecting that company would constitute a related party transaction. To ensure fairness, the board member must disclose this relationship and recuse themselves from the board's decision-making process. Furthermore, all bids should be evaluated objectively using standardised criteria to avoid any appearance of impropriety, and complete records retained of the tendering process. A contract should only be awarded to a related party if the evidence is clear that the school's best interests would be served by awarding the contract to the related party rather than to another bidder. In such cases, appropriate evidence would be something like the lowest price (or the best value), or demonstrable, data-based evidence that the quality of service provided by the related party is significantly better for the price than the other bidders have offered.

Regular audits and independent reviews of procurement processes also help school boards identify and manage related party transactions. These audits should include a review of vendor relationships, contracts, and the decision-making processes that led to their approval. School boards can engage external auditors to conduct these reviews, providing an unbiased perspective and helping reinforce public confidence in board members' integrity.

Education and training for school board members and senior managers also plays a critical role in safeguarding against the perils of undeclared related party transactions. Training sessions can raise awareness about the legal and ethical implications of such transactions and reinforce the importance of transparency and accountability.

Ultimately, fostering a culture of ethical decision-making is essential. School board members should consistently communicate their primary obligation as being to serve the educational needs of students and the broader school community, not only now but into the future, and they must demonstrate this unwavering commitment through the decisions that they make.

Insight 85

Resuscitating a bored board

THE BORED BOARD

Many schools' board meetings could be more engaging.

For a school to advance under visionary, energetic, committed leadership, board members and the Principal must be visionary, energetic and committed. And yet some of the board members I deal with when I conduct workshops and large projects confess that although they are excited by the school and the potential of the contributions they can make, they are often bored when they attend board meetings.

Given that every school board meeting should be making decisions that will enhance the formation of young lives and thus shape our society for decades to come, I genuinely find it perplexing that this could ever be described as 'boring'. I would love to think that at the end of every board meeting, every board member goes home and is able to claim:

1. I left the meeting feeling privileged that I am able to serve as part of the collective process to shape the future of this school.
2. I gained a deeper understanding of the work we are doing and I can't wait to tell others about it (while respecting the confidentiality of the meeting, of course).
3. I felt that I was respected by others and that my insights were valued as we worked together to solve problems and create new opportunities to advance our mission and vision.
4. I gained fresh perspectives that help me understand some of the ongoing challenges that we need to address.
5. I feel even more enthusiastic about being an ambassador for the school and I want to raise its profile across my network and in the wider community.
6. I was impressed that the Principal's and other reports were informative, compelling, and inspiring.
7. I learned more about my fellow board members.
8. I thought the meeting was well planned and executed by the Chair.

It is hard to imagine any board member making those eight claims AND also honestly claiming they had been bored. Therefore, what practical steps can a board take collectively to make these eight claims a reality after every meeting?

1. Ensure that every board member understands the school's purpose (its mission) and priorities (its vision) by quoting these at the top of every meeting agenda.
2. Set a clear agenda for every meeting, distribute it well in advance of the meeting together with any documents required for background reading, and stick to the set agenda throughout the meeting.
3. Be mindful of the time commitment of board members by starting and finishing meetings punctually, setting time limits for individual agenda items, disallowing discussion on items not on the agenda, treating items that do not require discussion or decisions "as read" or "for information only", thus keeping the discussion focussed.
4. Encourage respectful disagreement during discussions (because it helps the board to fine-tune its decisions), but eject any attendee from the meeting who shows contempt or disrespect for others.

5. Incorporate interactive elements in the meeting, such as Q&A sessions, group discussions or different styles of presentation, including multimedia where appropriate.
6. Urge every attendee, including the quiet introverts, to contribute to every discussion.
7. Allocate a responsibility to every board member, such as chairing a board committee, liaising with an outside organisation, etc.
8. Introduce breakout sessions to encourage small group discussions and greater individual involvement when exploring options on specific topics.
9. Include personal stories that highlight the impact and significance of statistical information that is presented during regular reporting sessions.
10. Offer regular professional development workshops on best practice in school governance so that board members fully understand their roles and the ways in which they can maximise their 'value added' to the work of the board.
11. Undertake regular board performance reviews to encourage board members in areas that are working well as well as identifying areas where renewed focus might yield significant benefits.
12. Take the time to celebrate the board's (and the school's) achievements and successes.

These 12 points all relate to the conduct of the meeting, either directly or indirectly. There are some additional factors that can support these steps and help facilitate positive meetings:

1. The environment of the meeting room has a huge impact on meeting dynamics. Participants' energy levels increase when there is abundant natural light, good ventilation and a cool-to-moderate temperature.
2. The room must be acoustically sound (excuse the pun), not only to avoid disempowering participants with hearing difficulties, but so everyone can hear everything that is said by everyone else without straining and having to filter out echoes or background noise.
3. Attendees should be arranged so that everyone can see as well as hear everyone else. This is necessary because body language is an important component of communication (for everyone), and in

addition, those with poor hearing are helped by seeing the lip movements of other speakers. In general, oval-shaped tables work best if available.

4. Morning meetings are usually more productive than evening meetings. Meetings that last more than two and a half hours show declining focus and productivity.

5. It is helpful to take a short break every 90 minutes or so participants can use the bathroom, take important phone calls, stretch legs, inhale some fresh air or simply clear their minds.

6. Have refreshments such as water, biscuits, chocolate, tea and coffee available throughout the meeting for participants, recognising that some attendees may not have had time for proper meals before the meeting.

Insight 86

Retaining excellent staff

Every competent school board dreads the thought that one day, its highly talented, highly effective Principal will resign. Similarly, every competent school leader dreads the thought that one or another 'irreplaceable' employee will resign one day. And yet, both scenarios are almost inevitable when we employ highly competent personnel who authentically help the school advance its mission, vision and values.

Every school has its megastars, and both the board and the principal should do everything they can to retain such talent in the school. Some resignations are inevitable for reasons such as family changes, geographical pressures, the desire to make even greater contributions to the educational world, or simply the inner need that many talented people have to take on periodic new challenges.

Of course, no-one – not even a megastar – is irreplaceable. If someone had to be found to fill their role, someone would be found. More significantly, it is highly unlikely that any megastar will remain as long as the board and/or the school's leadership might wish. After all, a school's most competent people will be the ones who are most attractive to other organisations.

Having said this, there are several ways a Principal can raise the retention rates of excellent staff (or retain excellent Principals in the case of the school board).

1. **Focus on mission.**

A school's best leaders and employees are excited by the mission, purpose and ethos of the school. Maintaining a consistent, clear, explicit focus on the mission is a powerful motivator for a school's most effective personnel. For example, one extensive study concluded that "purpose" was the single most important influence on both job satisfaction and retention. As the New York Times reported, "Employees who derive meaning and significance from their work were more than three times as likely to stay with their organisations — the highest single impact of any variable in our survey. These employees also reported 1.7 times higher job satisfaction and they were 1.4 times more engaged at work".

2. **Remunerate generously, or at least fairly.**

School leaders, and indeed all staff in education, deserve to be remunerated in a way that reflects the dignity, the importance and the effort involved in their work. At the very minimum, remuneration must reflect the competitive economy within which schools (both government and non-government) operate. It is a "penny wise, pound foolish" ideology to try and pay staff in schools as little as possible – how can financial meanness towards educators be justified when the future of our society is being formed in the classrooms of our schools today? This principle applies especially to the Principal – having made so much effort to recruit a great Principal, the board has an obligation to compensate that person competitively. This will usually include benefits as well as cash, and should also include opportunities for professional development. The Principal's remuneration should be reviewed regularly, probably on an annual basis. In that context, any board that ignores a Principal's spouse's or partner's needs does so at its peril – very few Principals remain at a school if their spouse or partner is disgruntled.

3. **Remove or discipline incompetent or toxic staff.**

One of the greatest frustrations faced by competent staff is having to work with incompetent staff, or even worse, toxic staff. The cost to a school of tolerating incompetence is greater than the inefficiency and lost productivity caused by that one individual's poor work; a far greater cost arises when excellent staff with high aspirations decide they would prefer to work in an environment where they do not have to tolerate or compensate for the inefficiency of others, or battle their constant undermining and toxicity.

4. **Listen to others and consult widely.**

Unlike corporate institutions, schools function on a highly collegial basis. Professional, highly idealistic educators, leaders and board members all appreciate opportunities to express their views and be heard by others. Although consultation may slow down progressive change, it usually results in more reliable and productive outcomes because it enables a wide range of diverse perspectives to be considered. This is especially so for the school's megastars who will invariably have unique, original, highly worthwhile ideas to offer. Megastars deeply appreciate the invitation to contribute, and moreover, they feel highly affirmed if and when their ideas are acknowledged and put into action.

5. **Create new opportunities.**

High performing school leaders and educators relish new challenges and opportunities, and a wise board will encourage creativity that leads to implementation of soundly researched reforms, especially those that benefit the students. In order to facilitate such energy, it often helps to build curated career paths or make internal promotions for a school's megastars because the position thus created is likely to be a more attractive alternative than leaving for another job elsewhere – a true win-win outcome.

Having made some or all of these efforts to retain excellent staff and leaders, it is inevitable that many will eventually leave at some time. This is not necessarily a negative reflection on the school which is losing its megastar. Indeed, such moves are often very positive reflections on a school which has almost certainly nourished the professionalism of its future leaders who are ready, willing and able to expand their positive influence in the wider educational world. Such is true educational leadership.

Insight 87

Riding a dead horse

I have never seen a School Principal or a Board Member literally try to ride a dead horse. However, I have seen many trying to do so metaphorically.

Spoiler alert – it never ends well.

Riding a dead horse is a metaphor that relates to the grandly named but staggeringly simple "Dead Horse Theory". The theory is straight-forward: "When you discover that you are riding a dead horse, the best strategy is to dismount." In the context of school leadership and governance, the Dead Horse Theory becomes relevant whenever an initiative or a project has failed but is kept alive by wilfully misguided, stubborn, blinkered or ignorant decision-makers.

The Dead Horse Theory has even been dignified by internet memes such as the one at the top of the next page:

At both the board and senior management levels, school leaders often have difficulty abandoning pet projects that are clearly not working or achieving their intended goals.

Why is this important? Perpetuating 'dead horse' projects may well harm the students and staff in the school, either directly or indirectly by directing funds and energy away from genuine areas of need into unproductive areas. Moreover, persisting with 'dead horse' projects can provide an unnecessary educational and marketing advantage to competitor schools, it erodes motivation and commitment from committed staff, and it creates a school-wide culture of avoidance when faced with making difficult decisions. In short, it is a barrier to achieving the most important task of all, which is fulfilling the school's Mission and Vision to meet the needs of its students.

How does this look in practice? In 'dead horse' terms, rather than dismounting from the dead horse, school leaders might choose to add more riders to the horse, feed the horse better hay, schedule daily stand-up meetings to discuss why the horse is no longer moving, form a cross-faculty task force to review the horse-riding strategy, or invest in a new sleek saddle in the hope it will inspire the horse to get up and run. If all else fails, the board may decide to give the horse a new, more aspirational identity – perhaps something like "strategic unicorn".

Why might school leaders be trapped into illogical actions to keep riding a dead horse? Although some people are excited by change, the vast majority of people seem to prefer the comfort zone of inertia. This is particularly the case on school boards where long-serving members may have created their personal 'comfort zones' over many years or where the board has an unbalanced dominance of members from stereotypically conservative occupational backgrounds such as accountants, lawyers and pointedly (according to Jeff Cole at IQPS – the International Quality and Productivity Centre) executive leaders, senior managers, and middle managers.

How can rising a dead horse ever be justified? There are four common justifications heard in schools for trying to retain ineffective projects:

- "We have already invested too much to stop now" – the sunk cost fallacy which implies the mistaken value of throwing good money after bad.

- "We can't admit this was a mistake" – the misplaced fear of reputational damage while ignoring the far greater harm caused by perpetuating the mistake.

- "As long as things are changing, we are making progress" – the confusion of wrongly equating busy-ness with productivity.

- "This project is an essential element of our strategic plan" – the discredited, outdated notion that strategic plans are inflexible and cannot be adapted to account for changes in the school's operating environment.

- "If we can just tinker and fix this little problem, we can get back on track" – the mistaken view that a temporary, quick fix or patch-up will solve the deeper underlying issue.

Of course, "rising a dead horse" is just a metaphor. No-one would ever try to do this in a literal sense, would they?

Well, actually, yes they would. The photo at the top of the next page shows a man who is actually sitting on a dead horse in South 8th Street, Sheboygan, Wisconsin (USA) in the 1870s. Although he is dressed more formally than any school board member I have ever met, it seems like a good visual metaphor of a school board member trying to ride a dead horse – and moving along with the precise speed I would have predicted.

So, how can school principals and board members overcome the temptation to keep riding a dead horse in their school? Leadership in abandoning dead horse projects can be demonstrated by following four courageous steps, uncomfortable though they might be at times:

1. **Ask perceptive, penetrating, challenging questions** – A 'dead horse' project needs to be identified through questions such as "what is the problem we are trying to solve?", "what are the barriers to success we are encountering?", "is this project helping us to achieve our Mission and Vision?", and "if we were considering starting this project today, would we do so?".

2. **Build a culture of transparency** – It is critically important that everyone involved in the school feels safe to identify, analyse and articulate problems, challenging established projects and procedures with justified arguments and observations.

3. **Focus on outcomes rather than activity** – Progress reports must be based on results and outcomes, not how busy everyone has been. Sound project management requires regular reporting based on KPIs that flow from the school's Mission and Vision, not vanity metrics such as the number of hours worked, or meetings attended.

4. **Be prepared to make the brave decision to cut your losses** – Although it is often emotionally difficult to cut ties to a beloved project or a failing product, or to terminate a financial relationship that has turned toxic, doing so is almost always necessary for the vitality of the school.

In the ever-changing world of education, clinging to ineffective projects or toxic relationships is like trying to ride a dead horse – wasted effort, disheartening, and inevitably unproductive. Schools thrive on adaptability, innovation, and a culture of support, and that means having the courage to cut ties with anything that no longer serves the Mission and Vision. By eliminating those factors which drag schools downward, board members and senior management create space for fresh ideas, meaningful collaborations, and a truly dynamic learning environment.

Progress is not about holding on; it's about knowing when to let go.

Disclaimer: No animals were harmed in the writing or illustrating of this article. Historic photo is in the public domain.

Footnote: I have used the expression "riding a dead horse" while acknowledging that the more commonly used expression is "flogging a dead horse", or in the United States, "beating a dead horse". Both idioms mean the same as "riding a dead horse" in the context of the Dead Horse Theory. However, I believe "riding a dead horse" addresses the concern expressed by PETA (People for the Ethical Treatment of Animals) that "flogging a dead horse" introduces unwelcome speciesism into everyday conversation in a way that trivialises cruelty to animals. PETA recommends replacing "flogging a dead horse" with "feeding a fed horse", but I am unconvinced that this suggestion is useful for clarifying the Dead Horse Theory.

Insight 88

Risk management

For a school board, risk can be viewed as anything that impedes, or has the potential of impeding the school achieving its strategic goals. Ensuring that risk is managed effectively is one of the key fiduciary duties of a school board as it seeks to direct and protect the school.

Realistically, there is no way that a school board can establish enough policies and procedures to eliminate every possibility of every risk. It is thus an important task for the board to identify and prioritise possible risks. Board members can never (and should never) have an intimate knowledge of every operational aspect of the school. Therefore, risk identification should be undertaken by a broad, diverse range of people who possess a variety of perspectives. Those involved in this process should include board members, senior management, faculty who are in charge of critical areas, operational staff, and even part-time staff, contractors and volunteers.

RISK MANAGEMENT CHECKLIST

- Clear mission statement
- Crisis management plans
  - Adequate insurance
  - General liability
  - Evacuation
  - School closure
- Directors-and-officers liability

WRITTEN POLICIES ON:

- Blood-borne pathogens
- Conflicts of interest (with forms signed by board members and administrators acknowledging the policy and identifying potential conflicts)
- Personnel: hiring, evaluation, termination
- Staff evaluation and compensation
- Harassment / sexual assault
- Student code of conduct and discipline procedures
- Religious or political activity on campus
- Athletic safety
- Use of school bulletin boards
- Off-campus trips, including issues of adult supervision – locally, nationally and internationally
- Use of buildings and grounds by the school community and outsiders
- Bids required for contracts for goods and services
- Financial management, especially checks and balances
- Investment management
- Admissions
- Campus security (including health and safety)
- Financial aid/scholarships
- Gift acceptance
- Information technology (including social media)
- A system to review policies periodically, both internally and with outside professional assistance
- Up-to-date by-laws (M&As)
- A strategic plan with measurable action plans
- A rolling three-year financial plan
- Bonds for paid staff and volunteers who handle money
- Child protection
- Publications, videos and electronic media that accurately portray the school

Based on NAIS (2010) p.37

It is not the board's responsibility to manage risk on a day-to-day basis. The board's duty is to establish policies that reduce risks and ensure that risks which have been identified are actively monitored by the appropriate personnel in accordance with the policies. The board should then expect regular reports from the Head on the actions taken by faculty and staff to reduce and manage risks, especially in vulnerable spheres such as policies, campus safety and security, publications and everyday practices.

Reputational risk is of growing significance with the rise of social media and instant messaging. Other risks can arise from such diverse sources as deceptive advertising, trustee negligence, poor management of a crisis, missed enrolments targets, forced closure of the campus due to a hazard event, capital availability, actions of competitor schools, leadership change, performance shortfalls, loss of records, among many others. A particular area of risk for the board may arise with the sudden or unexpected absence of the Chair or the Head, and it is important that the board has a clear written protocol in place to cover such an unpredicted event.

The response of some school boards to risk management is to overburden senior management with crippling check-lists and internal controls to measure, monitor and reduce risk. Risk registers that are monitored regularly certainly have their place in the array of risk management tools. In such situations, the intensity of board scrutiny of the school's practices should be inversely related to the quality of internal controls that are in place. As an alternative or supplementary approach, some enterprises overseas have appointed CROs (Chief Risk Officers) to oversee and manage risks on behalf of the board and the senior management.

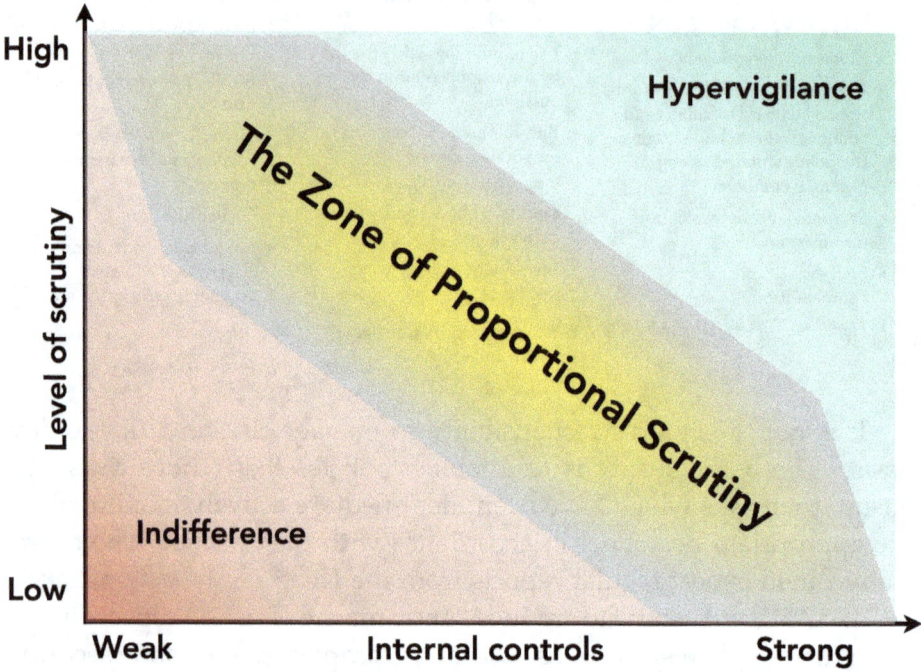

At the very least, managing risk requires that the board undertakes periodic reviews of its own exposure to risk, that it regularly reviews all the school's insurance policies, that it operates in a legal and balanced way that deviates neither into undue risk aversion nor recklessness, and that it monitors the implementation of risk management policies and procedures by the senior management.

School boards traditionally view risk management as a necessary but less-than-welcome duty that is required to safeguard the school from litigation. A smaller number of more enlightened boards embrace risk as a hidden opportunity for the school to gain a strategic advantage. If this view is adopted, then it becomes desirable to identify as many risks as possible, as every risk provides the potential of bringing a new strategic opportunity.

Insight 89

Roots and wings

Perhaps I am someone who identifies patterns even when they are not there, such as when I look up at a cloud in the sky but see the shape of a lion or a map of New Guinea. In the same vein, when I think about the future of education, two broad parallel themes keep recurring in my mind. For want of better labels, I call these two threads 'roots' and 'wings'.

By 'roots', I mean the foundations from which the future will spring. 'Roots' are the ways in which the past nourishes today's experiences and attitudes, mostly for the better, but occasionally in ways that cause anxiety.

By 'wings', I am referring to the freedom we all have to look towards and shape the future. 'Wings' involves creating an environment that is at the cutting edge of best practice which aims to give young people freedom, thus providing the school with the freedom to fly.

'Roots and wings'. To me, this seems like an ideal dual image to provide a framework for schools to plan for the future because it brings together the importance of linking a school's founding principles with its future hopes, aspirations and strategic direction. It reflects the wisdom of a Māori saying that I came to love when I worked in New Zealand some years ago: "You walk into the future looking backwards". In the context of a school's strategic planning process, I might reimagine those words as "Our wings spring from our roots".

What is the significance of this for the people who will develop a new strategic plan – usually the school's senior management and the board?

At the risk of mutilating an old cliché, I sometimes think that the world consists of two kinds of people. Some focus on roots, and others focus on wings.

Speaking personally, I am primarily a 'wings' person, because wings represent the future, and the future both excites and fascinates me. After all, if you are playing football, you need to run to where the ball is going to be, not to where it has already passed. Importantly, however, we must appreciate that unless they are nourished by the 'roots', the 'wings' will lack the strength and tenacity to fly.

In my mind, 'roots and wings' provides a powerful conceptual framework for strategic planning. It is not the mechanism for planning; it is the inspiration that guides the thinking and direction of planning.

When most people plan for the future, they usually begin by examining current deficits or problems. This deficit-centred approach may be intuitive, and it is explicitly advocated by many consultants – generally those who have never worked in a school. Deficit-centred (or problem-focussed) planning has some merit, but it also contains a huge inherent shortcoming that is often overlooked.

The danger is that deficit-centred (or problem-focussed) planning tends to accept existing trend projections and strategic pathways uncritically before proceeding to focus on innovating better ways to accomplish the same outcomes – the very same outcomes that have been identified as today's shortcomings, deficits, or problems. It is a recipe for replication, not transformation.

Doing old things in better ways merely creates a future approach to education that is less mediocre. It is not strategic, nor does it envision authentic change. This is where the 'roots and wings approach' offers a better solution.

To construct a magnificent system requires developing a vision of what constitutes a magnificent system. Anyone who wants to create outstanding education must first imagine it. Continuous improvement and marginal, incremental change - important as these are - are seldom enough.

It has been said that only a small proportion of people in the world actually make things happen. There are significantly more people who watch things happen, and then there is the bulk of humanity who ask 'what just happened?'.

In the same way that effective education shifts students into the first category, an effective process of strategic planning should shift school boards and leaders into the group that "actually makes things happen". Schools need leaders and board members who can initiate positive change. It sounds like a simple goal, but as Leonardo da Vinci said (and Steve Jobs agreed), simplicity is the great sophistication.

So, what is needed to create this powerful process of transformative strategic change? First, a clear 'vision' is needed with a central focus on mission-focussed, student-centred, excellent education. By 'vision', I mean a powerful statement of the priorities required to achieve the school's mission (enduring purpose) in the context of tomorrow's challenges and expectations. To miss this step is to allow the school to drift rudderless into an uncertain future.

Second, there needs to be a strong commitment to 'sustainability'. This includes more than environmental sustainability (which I discuss at length in Insight 67). It includes every form of sustainability including financial sustainability, institutional sustainability, demographic sustainability, curriculum sustainability, governance sustainability, staffing sustainability, technological sustainability, and even personal sustainability. Without sustainability in all its forms, the school simply will not have an enduring future.

Third, there needs to be a firm set of underlying values, balanced with flexibility to change when external circumstances change. This may sound self-contradictory at first, but this simply highlights the fine balance required. Strategic planning requires a foundation (the "roots") of a clear set of principles that articulates what the school believes is 'right' for it as an ethical learning community. This typically includes the school's philosophy, the quality of relationships expected, and key

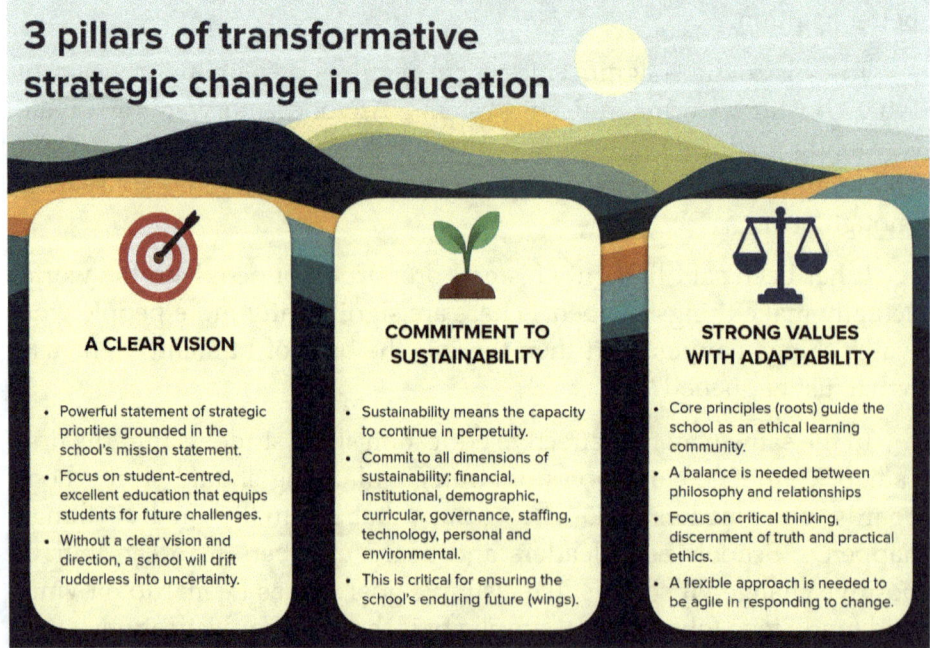

facets of its education, such as (for example) developing intercultural understanding, holistic learning, curriculum balance, global interaction, critical thinking, equipping students with the skills to discern reliable from unreliable information, truth from consensus, the various approaches to ethics, and so on.

The big challenge of strategic planning is that no-one can predict with certainty the skills that will be needed when today's students have been in the workforce for a few decades. We need to prepare students for the world they will enter as adults while being completely unable even to know which occupations have yet to be invented. How could anyone have predicted 30 years ago what many then-students would be doing today, especially in jobs involving Information and Communication Technologies, Artificial Intelligence, nanotechnology, and so on?

What schools must do, therefore, is to help students grow "wings". In other words, schools must equip their students with the creativity, the flexibility, the confidence and the competence to initiate change in original ways by bringing together insights from disparate fields. It is hard to see how a school might honestly claim that it is equipping its students with future-proof skills without including this as a central part of its educational armoury. As PARC researcher Alan Kay famously said, "the best way to predict the future is to invent it". And yet, how many schools' strategic plans emphasise these future-proof skills?

The famous story is told of a man visiting Michelangelo in his studio as he worked with his chisel on a huge block of rough-hewn marble. It was apparently an uninspiring sight, as the work was dusty, messy, and hard. When the man asked Michelangelo what he was doing, he replied: "I'm releasing the angel imprisoned in this marble."

Strategic planning for schools is like that. It is a task that seeks to free people and allow the school to achieve its potential to transform young lives. It means digging deeply into the block of marble to find the roots as a means to unfold and release the angel's wings.

The image on page 415 was used with the kind permission of MTEI, https://www.blogmtei.in/.

Insight 90

School Board Chairs are superheroes who conduct orchestras

Sadly, but unsurprisingly, I have never heard a teacher, parent or student in any school say "Our Board Chair is my superhero".

It's a pity because the research is very clear – there is no more important factor in the success of a school than the Board's and its Chair's performance, which may explain why staff and parents have such high expectations of the Chair of a School Board.

The role of the Board Chair varies from school to school according to the requirements and constraints of the school's constitution. However, a sound job description for a Board Chair should read something like this:

The Chair of the Board will have general oversight of the operation of the Board of Governors and will have general charge of overseeing the execution of the Mission of the School and of the policies and programs adopted by the Board of Governors. Subject to the Board of Governors, the Chair of the Board will speak for the Board. The Chair of the Board will be an officer of the School and a member of the Board Executive Committee. The Chair of the Board will provide advice, guidance and support to the Head of School and work closely with the Head of School to identify issues, agendas and priorities for Board consideration and action. The Chair of the Board will provide oversight and direction to the School's finances and resource management. The Chair of the Board will set the agenda for the Board meetings and preside over all meetings of the Board of Governors. Subject to the Board of Governors, the Chair of the Board may agree upon and execute all legal documents, bonds, contracts and other obligations in the name of the School, and will see that all orders and resolutions of the Board of Governors are carried into effect. The Chair of the Board will also have the usual powers and duties pertaining to the office, together with such other powers and duties as may be assigned by the Board of Governors, resolutions of the Board and/or the Board Charter.

In many ways, this formal description of the role and powers of the Board Chair doesn't really do full justice to the role. The Chair must be knowledgeable about the school – not every tiny operational detail, but its mission, vision, values, and collective purpose as well as its programs, services, constituents, resources, and of course, its challenges. The Chair also needs to have a clear understanding of the school's place in the larger framework of the community it seeks to serve and the still larger sphere of local and national peer organisations. A good board chair will listen to others, lead by example, and be a wise, calming voice in times of turmoil and crisis.

A good board chair is communicative, especially in maintaining frequent and regular contact with the Head of School (generally at least weekly). The Board Chair functions as an effective 'go-between' between the Board and the Head, including looking out for the welfare of the Head of School. Indeed, the Chair's relationship with the Head of School is widely regarded as the single most important relationship in a school.

Most Board Chairs and Heads never struggle to find things to talk about, but a good starting point for a checklist might look like this:
- How effectively is the School's Vision being implemented, and what barriers need to be cleared to make it more effective?
- What is the status of progress in implementing the strategic plan?
- What successes has the school enjoyed?
- Are there any current or evolving changes in relationships with the community?
- What are the current significant trends affecting the school – demographically, financially, educationally, strategically, and in terms of personnel?

- What significant challenges and opportunities is the school facing?
- How is the school's financial health?

The board chair is somewhat like the conductor of a fine orchestra, ensuring that the disparate and diverse elements of the board (its members) are playing the same tune at the same time towards the same end point. Although some board chairs have full control over the composition of the board's membership, most do not, and thus conducting the orchestra first requires the Chair to get to know the members of the orchestra and earn their respect. This process requires diplomatic and empathetic leadership, ideally arranging scheduled conversations from time to time over a coffee (or less ideally, catching up with a board member for a quick chat when the board meeting adjourns for a 5-minute toilet break).

Conversations between the Board Chair and other members of the Board might fruitfully cover points such as:

- What motivated them to join the board.
- How they feel their service on the board is going.
- How they feel the Chair could be more effective.
- Whether there are ways in which board meetings might be improved.
- Expressing appreciation for their service.

In addition to informal 'catch up' conversations, it is important that all board members, including the Chair, are regularly and independently evaluated, and if required, counselled and admonished – while also feeling appreciated and valued of course.

Overall, I think the most important advice I can offer a School Board Chair would be to **lead with integrity, listen with intent, and never lose sight of the students**. Your role is much more than running meetings or managing policies. It is about setting the tone for school-wide collaboration, ensuring every voice is heard, and keeping the board focused on what truly matters most, which is the success and well-being of the students. It isn't always easy, but I encourage Board Chairs to remain neutral but decisive, build strong relationships with your Principal and fellow board members, and remember that transparency builds trust. Finally, and inevitably, embrace the chaos, because in school governance, there is no such thing as a dull moment.

In the grand symphony of the 'school governance orchestra', the Chair of the board is not merely waving a baton; the Chair is conducting a full and sometimes discordant orchestra of opinions, policies, and the occasional off-key controversy. Blending diplomacy with energetic decisiveness like the true superhero shown at the top of this article, Board Chairs navigate the fine balance between visionary leadership and not-so-glamorous budget spreadsheets, all the time striving to maintain a calm voice and a straight face during particularly passionate board discussions. It is a role that demands patience, resilience, diplomacy, experience, and above all a deep love for young people and their educational formation. We know this because no-one would ever agree to join a school board on the basis of the quality of the coffee or take-away meals that are usually served at meetings.

So, to all the School Board Chairs who are reading this – may your meetings be productive, may your board-related e-mails be few, may your personal relationships survive your board service, and may your idealism and sense of humour remain firmly intact.

Footnote: One final comment should be made regarding the title of the role. Throughout this article I have used the word "Chair", which for some people equates to an item of furniture. Many traditionalists prefer "Chairman", which was used for centuries for both men and women. In recent decades, however, the word "Chairman" has increasingly been viewed as antiquated and sexist, leading to the rise of neologisms such as "Chairperson", and less frequently, "Chairwoman". The term "Chairman" dates back to the mid-1600s, at which time the "man" component of the title was known to derive not from the masculine gender but from the Old English word "mangere", meaning "one who manages things" (as in manage a meeting or a shop). The "chair" component of "chairman" therefore pointed to authority, so "Chairman" meant "the person who manages authority" – nothing to do with gender. Despite the historical inaccuracy of linking "Chairman" with masculinity, I'm happy to stay with the term "Chair" for the very practical reason that it has now become, for better or worse, the most commonly used title.

Insight 91

Servant leadership and falling into a river

I would like to share an autobiographical metaphor with you.

From 2004 to 2011 I was Principal of Li Po Chun United World College in Hong Kong. The United World Colleges are arguably the gold standard of altruistic international education. Originally a product of the Cold War imperative to bring together young people from both sides of the Iron Curtain to build a global future of peace and sustainability, the UWC movement has now expanded to a network of 18 schools and colleges, plus more than 150 national committees.

One of the distinctive features of the UWC in Hong Kong while I was Principal was that in November each year we would suspend classes for "China Week", a time in which all our IB1 (Year 11) students travelled into Mainland China in small groups under the care of a teacher to perform service work or personal challenge activities. As Principal I accompanied one of the groups of students every year as the leader of two projects – building toilets and renovating homes in a village of leprosy sufferers in Yunnan province, and helping with the construction of basic medical clinics in poor, remote rural areas of Guizhou province.

In order to initiate the medical clinics project in Guizhou, I travelled to Guizhou in March 2008 with the Chair of my Board and representatives of our partner organisation, the Amity Foundation, visiting several of the villages that lacked adequate medical services.

One of these villages was named Gubin, which is in the Xingshan district of Majiang County.

The start of my visit to Gubin was not auspicious. To enter the settlement of Gubin, we had to cross a creek using an improvised bridge that comprised just two metal pipes, which were very slippery in the rainy conditions on the day. Despite the intimidating view of rushing water beneath me, and in defiance of the old, smooth-soled shoes I was wearing that day, I started to make my way gingerly across the bridge.

To my surprise, I almost managed to reach the far side of the bridge when Gubin's paramedic who was standing at the far end of the bridge decided to reach out to me and offer a polite helping hand. Unfortunately, this meant that as she grabbed my hand, we both lost balance and slipped over the edge, the paramedic falling into the river and me falling half in the river and half on the muddy bank. Apparently, this was the most exciting event that had occurred in Gubin for several decades, and so our fall caused quite a commotion among the local people who immediately rushed to our aid.

The concerned residents of Gubin accompanied the paramedic and me up the hill to the very basic old building that served as the village's current clinic. The local residents were extraordinarily gracious, even to the point of insisting that I accept a dry pair of socks.

My visit to Gubin's clinic was therefore spent huddled over a bowl of hot coals, trying to dry my shoes and muddy clothes while at the same time listening to the paramedic's stories about health care in the village. Like the other clinics I had already visited in Guizhou, the level of equipment was extremely basic, including an old twisted wire coat hanger on the ceiling to hold the intravenous drips.

Yes, there is a point to this anecdote regarding school leadership and the relationship between boards and principals. My point is this: **effective leadership serves the needs of others – it is "authentic servant leadership"**.

When I was sitting in the Gubin medical clinic trying to warm up and dry out, my Board Chair obtained a dish of warm water, knelt down, and proceeded to wash the mud from my feet. It was a simple gesture reminiscent of Jesus washing his disciples' feet (John 13:1-17), and its symbolism had a profound impact upon me.

It is said that servant leadership is a highly effective approach for promoting individual, team and organisational performance as it shifts the focus of people's concern from themselves towards a concern for others, towards serving a mission that is far greater than any individual's ego, thus creating a culture of service.

What is servant leadership? According to Sendjaya et.al. servant leadership comprises six dimensions that can be applied on a daily basis:

Dimension 1 – **Serving followers** – assist others without expecting acknowledgement from higher up.

Dimension 2 – **Being authentic** – act with integrity, be accountable for past actions, and admit mistakes and limitations where required.

Dimension 3 – **Building deep relationships** – Constantly listen to others' opinions, do not take sides or play favourites, and be genuinely interested in people.

Dimension 4 – **Acting ethically** – openly discuss ethical ambiguities, always choose to do the right thing rather than just trying to look good in front of others.

Dimension 5 – **Creating meaning and purpose** – clarify a sense of meaning and purpose that arises from daily routines, help others to connect their work to the bigger picture.

Dimension 6 – **Be a mentor** to others to help them through professional and personal issues, empowering them to make decisions, take risks, and so on

The topic of servant leadership is a huge one that extends far beyond this simple article, but it is a critically important area of understanding for members of school boards and leadership teams.

Servant leadership encompasses nurturing, defending, guiding and empowering followers. Servant leaders are concerned for the needs of their followers; they seek to build up their well-being together with the well-being of the school as whole. A servant leader empowers followers rather than dominating them. A servant leader will have a natural inclination to serve marginalised rather than powerful people. A servant leader is a humble role model who leads others by their own example.

Quoting his own and others' research, Fogarty's doctoral dissertation (2013) found that servant leadership is significantly positively related to intrinsic motivation, trust, and value congruence among the members of an organisation. This suggests strongly that that (a) leader selection criteria should incorporate evidence of effective demonstration of servant leadership behaviours; (b) leader training should incorporate instruction on and guidance in servant leadership behaviours; (c) leadership strategies should incorporate the goal of building volunteer intrinsic motivation; and (d) school boards and leaders should receive regular professional development input to enhance the quality of their own servant leadership.

I can't remember anything during my fall from the bridge into the creek in Gubin – the fall from the bridge down to the muddy river bank remains a complete blank in my memory bank. However, I vividly remember the care shown for me by the residents of Gubin as well as the humble comfort of the servant leadership shown to me by my Board Chair. For me, this remains a compelling metaphor to illustrate the enduring power and supremacy of servant leadership over the challenges and perils that face school leaders routinely on a daily (or sometimes an hourly?) basis.

References:

Eva N, Robin M, Sendjaya S, van Dierendonck D and Liden RC (2019) Servant Leadership: A systematic review and call for future research. *The Leadership Quarterly*, 30(1): 111-132.

Fogarty S (2013) *The Impact of Senior Pastor Leadership Behaviours on Volunteer Motivation* (Doctoral dissertation, Regent University).

Sendjaya S, Eva N, Butar IB, Robin M and Castles S (2017) SLBS-6: Validation of a Short Form of the Servant Leadership Behavior Scale. *Journal of Business Ethics*, 156: 941-956.

Insight 92

Setting tuition fees – the annual agony

Every board of every independent school struggles annually with the question of setting tuition fees for the coming year. If the board does not struggle with setting the "right" tuition fees, then it should.

On one hand, tuition fees determine the affordability of a school to its parents and prospective parents, and thus the enrolment size and the financial elitism of the school.

On the other hand, tuition fees deliver the primary source of income that are needed to pay the staff and provide the resources required to provide a solid learning program in most non-government schools.

Clearly, wisdom is required to ensure a fair balance is achieved between these competing needs. It is far too easy for board members to assert "if the school is full, then the price we are charging must be appropriate". Similarly, it is far too easy for board members to quote individual anecdotal cases as a basis to claim that if fees rise too much then large numbers of loyal families will be forced to withdraw their children.

To address this tension, it is important to separate the issues of **"ability to pay"** from **"willingness to pay"**.

ABILITY TO PAY

Even if a family's profile is perfectly aligned with a school, even if they passionately believe in the school's mission and even if they are excited by the outcomes the school is achieving, they won't be able to attend the school if they can't afford the fees. This raises an important question for board members – how can we identify the ability of our clients to pay the tuition fees?

In an excellent recent article by Mark Mitchell (Vice President of NAIS) published a graph showing the changes in tuition fees for students in independent day-schools in the United States since 1990 as a percentage of family income. He showed the statistics against median family incomes, and also against each quintile of family incomes. For every income group, school fees were shown to have increased over the past three decades as a percentage of family incomes.

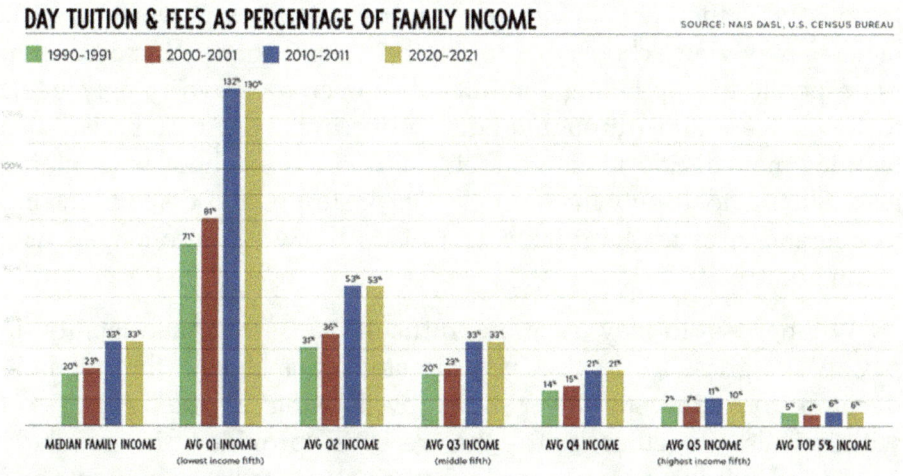

As shown at the top of the next page, he also presented equivalent statistics for boarding tuition fees over the same period, showing that the increases were even greater.

Clearly, if a school's fees are rising faster than the incomes of the families it serves, then the school becomes – by definition – less financially accessible to those families. This can result in decreasing

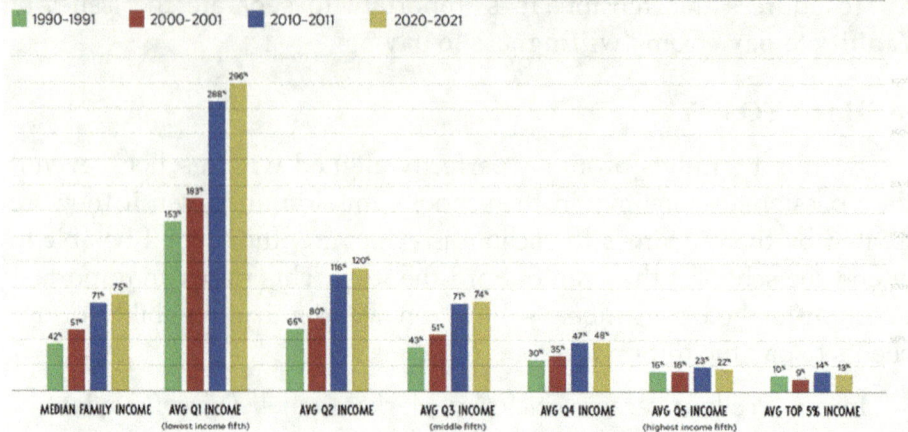

student numbers, greater economic elitism in the school's population, an increase in bad debts, greater pressure for targeted financial aid, and more grumbling in the school community.

WILLINGNESS TO PAY

Even if families are able to pay the tuition fees, there may be reasons why they are unwilling to do so. Perhaps perversely, some families may view schools that freeze their fees or hardly increase them as desperate to stop falling enrolments or, even more worryingly, liable to lower standards through under-resourcing. On that basis, such families may decide to move their children to a school with higher fees. Such schools defy the normal rules of supply-and-demand insofar as demand rises as the price rises (this is known by economists as a Giffin good).

Willingness to pay is more difficult to assess than ability to pay. Willingness to pay can be estimated by analysing the trends in demand for admission over time, by looking at the statistics of withdrawals (together with the reasons provided in regularly conducted exit interviews), and by listening to families' comments and feedback, whether provided informally or through regular school community surveys of the school's performance and culture.

There are also more formal methods to assess willingness to pay, and one notable instrument is Van Westendorp's Price Sensitivity Meter. This simple approach analyses the results of asking a group of participants four price-related questions:

- At what price would you consider the product to be so expensive that you would not consider buying it? (Too expensive)
- At what price would you consider the product to be priced so low that you would feel the quality couldn't be very good? (Too cheap)
- At what price would you consider the product starting to get expensive, so that it is not out of the question, but you would have to give some thought to buying it? (Expensive/High Side)
- At what price would you consider the product to be a bargain—a great buy for the money? (Cheap/Good Value)

Another complication arises due to the impact of competitors. For example, a school may be both affordable and performing strongly, but word-of-mouth conversations among parents may push the idea that a competitor school is doing something that is even better – maybe it has a more charismatic leader, or offers a better educational program such as the IB, or is regarded as more caring for students with special needs, and so on.

At the risk of over-simplifying the complexities of setting fees at the "right" level, if a school needs to help its families to become more able to pay a price, then it might:

- Reduce the tuition fees so that more families can afford the fees.
- Reduce the rate of fee increase so that more families can maintain the pace of the rise.
- Extend more needs-based financial assistance to bring the price charged closer to an affordable level for those families who cannot pay full price (knowing that the "standard" fees level may have to rise slightly to cross-subsidise this assistance.

If a school needs to make the market more willing to pay a price, then it might:

- Increase the value proposition by offering an improved (i.e. lowered) price while keeping outcomes fairly stable (or even improving them).
- Increase value by delivering improved (strengthened) outcomes while keeping the price fairly stable (or even lowering it).

- Improve awareness that the things the school provides are aligned to families' core motivators (the school's values, educational outcomes, care for students, etc), and that this happens without large-scale changes in the fees charged.

The American business magnate and philanthropist Warren Buffet is reported to have said "The single most important decision in evaluating a business is pricing power... If you've got the power to raise prices without losing business to a competitor, you've got a very good business. And if you have to have a prayer session before raising the price by 10%, then you've got a terrible business." He also claimed that "You can determine the strength of a business over time by the amount of agony they go through in raising prices."

"Whether or not you believe a school is (or should be) a business, it must be conducted in a business-like manner"

One can join the never-ending debate over whether schools are (or should be) businesses or not. However, irrespective of which side of that argument you take, it must be conceded that schools must be run in a business-like manner if they are to survive – hence the important annual agony over the decision about tuition fees.

Insight 93

Should board members be required to donate?

Schools have boards to satisfy legal requirements. Even more importantly, though, school boards add value to the organisation and enhance its outcomes. By giving their time generously, and often sacrificially, board members fulfil a complex cocktail of fiduciary and non-fiduciary duties, shape the ethos and identity of the school, oversee the school's operations and the work of the principal, and deal with many complex and often unforeseen challenges.

In the United States, a common additional expectation is that members of school boards will make generous financial donations to their school. Of course, the United States' philanthropic environment is famously quite different from everywhere else in the world.

Very few school boards outside the US have explicit expectations that its members will contribute financially to the school's fundraising. Some schools encourage their board members (like everyone else in the school community) to contribute to fundraising for capital campaigns, such as an appeal to raise funds for a large building project. However, such encouragement is almost never followed through with explicit demands or consequences for not contributing.

One of the dangers of expecting board members to make financial contributions is that financial capacity could become a criterion for board membership. That would be unfortunate as it would make board membership financially elitist and reduce the diversity of perspectives available in board meetings. I would always recommend that board members be recruited for their character, not their wealth.

If a board decided that it wanted to require financial contributions from its board members, this expectation should be stated explicitly before a new board member is recruited, and then annually in the code of conduct that each board member signs. Financial expectations must always be part of the board's "no surprises" culture.

There is a rarer but more sinister situation to consider. There have been cases where individual school board members have made significant donations and then used those donations (or the promises to make them) to advance their own agenda on the board, or even to advance their own seniority on the board. Although such actions could not be classified as 'blackmail' in the legal sense, it is easy to understand how the seductive influence of a substantial donation could sway the votes of other board members.

An associated question is "should board members be reimbursed for board-related expenses?".

In the United States, the usual answer is "No, never". In US schools, board members are almost never reimbursed for their expenses on the basis that board members should not cost the school money. The role of board members in the US is seen to be to enhance the school's financial position, and nothing should dilute this goal.

In most other parts of the world, board members are usually reimbursed for expenses such as travel and accommodation for board meetings, tickets and travel to conferences and events, working meals over meetings with board members or the principal, and entry to school functions such as musical productions or graduation dinners. Less frequently, some boards also reimburse its members for expenses such as credit card fees on their donations and any professional services they provide.

Like any expectations regarding donations, the expectations regarding reimbursements should be explicitly stated and agreed, preferably in writing, to prevent any uncomfortable misunderstandings. For new board members, this should be a component of the induction and orientation program.

Excuse the pun, but most board members will get on board with expectations if they are communicated clearly, explicitly, fairly and transparently.

Insight 94

Should school boards be innovative?

Boards rightly expect excellence from their teachers and administrators. One important aspect of excellence is innovation – implementing change that has been demonstrated to enhance student outcomes. How many board members place these same standards of innovation upon themselves? How many school boards genuinely strive to be innovative in ways that have been demonstrated to enhance their effectiveness in achieving better outcomes?

When I speak with Heads of Schools and describe my role of assisting school boards to preserve and enhance their effectiveness, I typically receive one of three responses:

- **The most common response:** "This work is really needed. My board members just don't realise how far their efforts fall short of best practice. Most of them just continue to operate in the way the board has always operated. They simply don't know how everything should be done. They think they are doing wonderfully well, and no-one (including the Head) is brave enough to tell them how much they need to improve."

- **A less common response:** "My board certainly isn't a glowing model of 'best practice', but we think it's my job as Head of School to guide them towards improvement. I can see what is needed, and more to the point, I'm affordable – my board won't spend money on themselves."

- **The least common response:** "My Board functions extremely well. Meetings are run tightly and efficiently, and they stick to the agenda. They understand the difference between governance and management, and keep them well separated. Board members never put personal interests before those of the school. The board undertakes regular training and orientation for new members, and is highly regarded throughout the school community."

In answer to the second response, it is usually unwise for Heads to take on the role of board improvement, which ought never to be part of the Head's formal job description. Heads who devote energy to board training will often find that:

- Their work is unappreciated, or even viewed suspiciously, and it may erode their political capital;
- It diverts the Head away from the core task of managing the school; and
- It may limit the range of possibilities that the board considers, compared with input from a neutral, external advisor.

As for boards identified as currently functioning well, it is helpful to ask, "Would everyone else in your organisation agree with this summation? And what measures are in place to ensure such perfection is perpetuated?"

The idea of training for school boards to improve effectiveness might seem innovative in some parts of the world. In other parts of the world where it is not only expected, it is often mandated. Independent schools in the US, for example, must be accredited in order to operate, and most accreditation agencies require that board members receive regular – usually annual – external training as a condition of accreditation. This reflects a professional approach to school governance that promotes professionalism, efficiency and effectiveness among board members.

Insight 95

Successful successions

Some school principals remain in their positions until they retire. Others prefer to move on to new challenges every five to seven years or so. Both approaches have their benefits and shortcomings.

Principals who remain in their schools for more than a decade are usually seen as long-serving Heads. They know the school's culture well. They have usually played a part in shaping that culture during the early years of their tenure, and they will have certainly helped to perpetuate it during their later years of service. Long-serving Heads tend to have strong networks of relationships in the school (both for better and for worse), and they usually provide consistent if sometimes traditionalist leadership.

Principals who remain in their schools for less than a decade are usually seen as change-makers. They are usually uncomfortable with the status quo and quickly recognise the potential for improvements that will enhance the school's mission and vision. They tend to implement change quickly and efficiently, even if this is sometimes at the cost of upsetting long-serving, more conservative personnel who feel invested in 'the way things were'. Change-making Heads are motivated by improving a school's practices and infrastructure, and once significant advances have been set in place, they feel the need to move and implement new reforms elsewhere.

Long-term principals usually lead only one or two schools in their career. Change-making principals often lead four, five, six or more schools in their career. In the interests of full disclosure, I was Principal of five schools in four countries during my 25-year career as a school principal, which suggests I was in the "change-maker" category – a label that would be confirmed by the large number of building programs I led and the quantity of educational innovations I initiated.

When I announced I was leaving my third headship (a prestigious boys' school in Australia with a history of over 140 years) to lead an international school in Hong Kong, there was widespread consternation as I was the first Head of that school since 1875 to leave in order to take up another position. All the other Heads of that school in the intervening period (numbering only six) had retired from the role; one had served as Head at the school for 39 years.

The average tenure for School Principals today is seven years, considerably shorter than it was a few decades ago. This reflects the changing role of Heads of Schools, where boards increasingly view effective change management as essential if schools are to retain their relevance to the challenges of our rapidly changing world.

Whether a school operates on a "long-term Heads" or "change-making Heads" model, surprises can – and do – happen. That is why succession planning for the school's headship position is important for a board. It should never be avoided because it is uncomfortable or because the Head might feel threatened. Planning a Head's succession represents an important risk minimisation strategy for an event that one day, sooner or later, must inevitably be required.

Wise succession planning explores three possible scenarios:

Scenario 1 – An immediate departure

Sometimes referred to as the "hit by a bus scenario", it is probably more affirming to label this as the "winning the lottery scenario". By their nature, immediate departures are almost always unplanned and unintended, which makes having an emergency plan in place so important. This plan will usually have a person (or a small team) within the school in mind to assume the responsibilities for leading the school, communicating with the school and wider community, and reporting to the board. It follows from this that any Principal must have a strong leadership team of exceptional, supportive people in place at all times.

Scenario 2 – A planned departure within (say) six months or so

When a Principal leaves within the minimum period (or less) specified in the employment contract, the board may not have sufficient time to conduct a full search process to find a replacement. In such cases, it may be wise for the board to consider appointing an Interim Principal to guide the school through the intermediate period until a permanent replacement can commence duties. Two key issues arise in this scenario for the board. First, is there an external person (such as a retired Head of School) or another suitable person who could be called in for an extended – but not permanent – period of time to cover the search process? Second, is there a suitable consultant who could assist with the appointment of an Interim Head if the board does not have the contacts required?

Scenario 3 – A planned departure two or more years in the future

This is the ideal scenario to plan an orderly succession because it allows sufficient time for the current Head to complete key projects, for a search to be conducted, and for the successful candidate to give and complete an appropriate period of notice in their existing school. A successful succession plan in this scenario allows (a) a Search Committee of the Board to be formed, (b) a professional consultant to be engaged who is sympathetic to the school's mission but also independent, well-connected, and experienced with a wide range of school environments, and (c) a carefully sequenced communications and implementation plan to be established.

Of course, there are no 'guarantees' when it comes to appointing new school principals, but with guidelines in place such as these the chances of a successful succession are greatly enhanced.

Insight 96

Succession planning

Few changes are more disruptive for a school than a change at "the top", or in other words, a change of Principal or Board Chair. Both transitions have the potential to disrupt the smooth operations of the school during an often-lengthy transition period, especially when either position becomes vacant unexpectedly.

According to statistical research conducted both in Australia and overseas, leadership positions across all industries are becoming vacant at unprecedented rates.

Schools and their boards are no exception. However, like most organisations, succession planning is a topic that most boards don't like to think about. Like many elderly people who have ignored making their will, they ignore engaging with the uncomfortable thinking for far too long. School Principals, and to a lesser extent Board Chairs, often don't want to discuss their departure, and their boards are quite comfortable avoiding the conversation.

It is therefore surprising – and paradoxically also unsurprising – that so few boards give serious consideration to leadership succession planning.

What should a board be doing to plan the school's leadership succession, both of its own Board Chair and the School Principal?

The first step in planning a transition is to have someone lined up who can serve in an interim capacity in the event of a sudden or unexpected change. In the case of the Board's leadership, this will probably be another member who has preferably had some experience stepping in for the Chair from time to time, or else has had experience leading boards elsewhere.

In the case of the school's leadership, this person may be a Deputy or sectional leader. Choosing the right person to be an Acting Principal may be politically complicated if it is likely that more than one current employee will become internal applicants, in which case bringing in an experienced external retired Head to serve as Acting Principal in an interregnum capacity is definitely worth considering.

Internal applicants for the Principal's position can present especially complicated situations for the Board. For example, some schools do not allow senior managers within the school (such as the Deputy) to apply because the potential of doing so may provide an incentive for ambitious personnel to undermine the existing Principal. Other schools do allow the Deputy and others to apply on the understanding that if they are appointed – great – but if not, they should resign and leave the school. This may seem harsh, but the thinking is that their relationships with other staff within the school will inevitably have been burned or at least changed through the application process, and in any case, there is a need to avoid any risk they might undermine the successful applicant (whether internal or external) when the appointee begins duties.

Assuming that a Principal's vacancy has not arisen from a firing, a sudden death or an otherwise abrupt transition, the departure of either the Board Chair or the School Principal is an occasion when both should work together and synchronise communications. If the Principal is leaving, the first announcements (which are to the staff, the students and the parents in that order) should be made as quickly as possible after each other by the Board Chair with the Principal present. If the Board Chair is leaving, the urgency of an announcement is reduced, and should be made to the school community by the Principal.

If the Principal is leaving to take up a new position, then the timing of public announcements should be co-ordinated with the other school so that both school communities learn the news simultaneously. This will reduce the likelihood of unhelpful rumour mongering.

After the announcement has been made that the Principal intends to leave, an important duty of the outgoing Principal is to prepare a confidential document for the incoming Principal with a title such as "Here is everything you need to know" that covers all items of unfinished business (especially those involving students or personnel), a personal perspective on priorities for the future (which may differ from the Board's perspective), and which lists the people who are important in the school community (and those who think they're important). This document should be discussed confidentially at some opportune time between the outgoing and incoming Principals.

Much more could be said about leadership transitions, although such detail quickly starts to differ between each particular school and each specific situation.

Insight 97

Term limits

One of the popular workshops I conduct for school boards is titled "Creating and Sustaining Healthy Boards in good times and bad". During that workshop I present research on the characteristics of school boards that have demonstrated characteristics of effective governance that have led to demonstrably higher student achievement.

According to this research, one of these characteristics of healthy school boards is having term limits for their members. For boards in schools that follow US traditions, adopting term limits is unsurprising. For boards in schools that are more within the British tradition, term limits are far less common.

When I touched upon the subject of term limits during a workshop presentation to one school board (in Australia), the conversation between board members went something like this:

Board Member 1: "So John, when does your term end as Board Chair?"

John (the Board Chair): "Well, actually, we don't have term limits here."

Board Member 2: "Really? We just go on and on and on? Not you John, I mean, all of us?"

John (the Board Chair): "We've never really thought about it. I don't think there is anything about term limits in the Constitution. Or maybe there is, I'm not sure. But it doesn't really matter, does it, because how would you all feel if you were forced to stand down?"

Board Member 1: "Sometimes I think it would be relief." (General polite laughter follows).

Board Member 3: "Well, John has been willing to serve as Board Chair now for the past nine years and to be honest, I don't think anyone else here wants the job. More to the point, I doubt any of us could do the work that John has been doing."

What is the biggest issue at play here?

Perhaps it is that board members don't know their own constitution? Perhaps it is that no-one on the board aspires to be Chair?

I think the biggest issue is summed up in the words "I doubt any of us could do the work that John has been doing". Clearly, no succession planning has been done, and the board has no leadership pipeline. The situation was exacerbated because this board operated with very few committees, and the committees it did have were composed entirely of board members, so this common avenue to explore potential new board members (and leaders) was unavailable to them.

How can term limits strengthen board leadership, and what do we mean by term limits? In essence, term limits arise when a board adopts a policy that requires board members to retire when they have served a pre-set number of terms (such as three 3-year terms). Sometimes, term-limit policies may include specific exceptions, such as when a Chair who has reached the term limit may be permitted to remain one extra term to provide institutional memory and support during a new chair's first term of office.

There are (at least) five reasons that term limits can add value to a school board:

- Term limits force boards to seek and actively recruit members with leadership potential.

- Term limits refresh the perspectives available to the board, leading to new ideas and innovation.

- Term limits allow the board to increase the spread and diversity of its membership, thus increasing the board's capacity to network and advocate for the school's position.

- Term limits provide a face-saving structure to manage poorly performing or problematic board members; how else can a weak board member be told politely, face-to-face, that their contribution is deficient without insulting them?

- Term limits give the board flexibility to adapt to changing external forces and needs by giving space to recruit new skills and expertise.

One of the most common objections I hear to introducing term limits is that the board will lose institutional memory. Of course, institutional memory is important for a board, but that is a weak argument when it is used to justify retaining board members (as I have seen) for twenty years and more on a school board. Term limits do not imply that institutional memory should be sacrificed, simply that institutional memory shifts from the board to other bodies such as committees, advisory groups, task forces and "friends of the school" groups. Alternatively, any loss of institutional memory can be minimised by creating a plan that staggers the timing of the term limits, meaning that everyone isn't rotating off the board at the same time.

If a board wishes their school to gain the benefits of introducing term limits, it must be handled in a way that is appropriate for that school's history, mission and demographics. For example, one young school introduced term limits of three years with the option to renew for one more time, but in addition had a limited number of lifetime positions for the school's founders.

Why is this conversation important? A meta-study by Nancy Walser demonstrated that there is a direct, positive relationship between "high quality boards" and higher student achievement. Given that schools exist primarily to benefit the students they serve, every school board should strive to be as effective as possible. Walser identified term limits as one of the characteristics of "high quality boards".

Therefore, for boards that do not have term limits, I suggest it is worth initiating a discussion about the potential benefits that introducing term limits might bring. Naturally objections like "losing institutional memory" and "being chased by a clock" should be included in the discussion; it needs to be a full and frank discussion that is based on the evidence, not sentimentality or emotions.

Term limits may not be the easiest policy to introduce to a school board, and the form they might take will vary from school to school and from board to board, but a competent school board should never have qualms about engaging in important discussions.

Insight 98

The best, most complex job in the world

There is a famous story about former world heavyweight boxing champion, Mohammed Ali. He was on a flight in the US and was refusing to wear his seat belt. When the flight attendant told him to put on the seatbelt, he replied "Superman don't need no seat belt". The flight attendant instantly replied: "Superman don't need no airplane either".

Many school principals feel their boards expect them to be like Superman. They also sense that their staff, their students and their school communities think similarly. Few jobs have the range of complex and often competing constituencies that school principals must keep happy – their boards, parents, students, teachers, staff, alumni, government authorities, accreditation organisations, owners of neighbouring properties, the media, the wider community, politicians, bureaucrats, their families (yes!), and so on. The list may not be quite as long as a national leader, but notwithstanding Winston Churchill's comment that "Headmasters have powers at their disposal with which Prime Ministers have never yet been invested", it is understandable that fewer and fewer applications are received when principals' vacancies are advertised these days compared with a decade or two ago.

As expectations of school principals continue to increase, a real risk arises that these expectations reach the point of becoming unrealistic. You may have never heard the German expression *"Eierlegende Wollmilchsau"*. Literally meaning "egg-laying wool-milk-sow", it describes a pig covered in fluffy fur that lays eggs and produces milk. It is the perfect farm animal that only has advantages, satisfies all needs, and meets all demands by bringing together the best qualities of a hen (laying eggs), sheep (producing wool), cow (giving milk) and pig (eats rubbish and produces bacon). The only shortcoming of the *"Eierlegende Wollmilchsau"* is that it doesn't exist

I wonder whether the ideal school principal is seen by some school boards as resembling the *Eierlegende Wollmilchsau* – perfect in every way except that he or she doesn't really exist.

In the preface to his book Letters from School, the Principal of Westminster School in England from 1970 to 1986, John Rae, wrote feelingly about the scrutiny, often unfair, to which school principals are frequently subjected by parents, school boards and the general community. He observed that *"ours is the one job in society that everyone feels qualified to criticise"*. Paraphrasing the critics, he continued:

> *"We have all been to school. We all know how it's done. It didn't strike us then and it doesn't strike us now as a job requiring much in the way of sophisticated expertise. We wouldn't actually say that any fool could do it, but we think it is largely a case of common sense, an amateur business and not even full-time, given the long holidays and the short working day".*

Rae continued: *"Headmasters and headmistresses are insecure, more so than they look. They regard any criticism of the school as criticism of their leadership, as indeed it is"*.

On the other hand, he also wrote this reflection on being a school principal: *"It must surely be the best job in the world. There is such variety, such unpredictability, and such provocative fascination in dealing with the young"*.

I concur with the full range of Rae's views, contradictory though they may appear. The huge challenge for Principals as they fulfil the duties of "the best job in the world", of course, is that they must try and meet a daunting array of expectations.

Where do I begin? School principals are expected to:

- provide educational, ethical, visionary and pastoral direction;
- ensure financial solvency;
- keep a respectable circle of friends;
- maintain strict discipline (except when a board member's child is involved, in which case they must maintain charity, love, tolerance, forgiveness and gentle nurturing);
- make sure the students learn to do dancing, crafts, cooking, sport and debating as well as developing literacy, numeracy, and understanding sex education'
- personally find and return the lost lunch box;
- prepare detailed regular reports for each board meeting, hoping they will be read by every board member prior to the meeting, and then answering questions at the board meeting from several attendees who were clearly too busy to read the written reports beforehand;
- be courteous, alert, decisive and even friendly around the school, even after a School Board meeting which finished after midnight the night before;
- try to see and cheer for every sports team when it competes against another school;
- set an example by stopping to pick up litter in the school grounds;
- ensure that music, the arts and multiple languages flourish in the school;
- stop the pushing and shoving in lines at the canteen;
- ensure that all the students dress appropriately, neatly and apolitically;
- make sure the buses are on time;

- inspire the students with short addresses at regular assemblies throughout the year;
- maintain students' attention during the long, long speeches at the graduation ceremonies and other end-of-year functions;
- present regular reports at board committee meetings, alumni gatherings and reunions, parent support groups, fund-raising gatherings, and indeed any school event that (like these) is typically held in evenings or on weekends;
- counsel students during intense crises such as a death or divorce in the family - or a break-up with a girlfriend or boyfriend;
- ensure that every member of staff dresses in a professional manner, at least to the standards expected of the students, while emphasising that each teacher is an adult and an individual with due sense of responsibility;
- know every student by name and greet them as such;
- find a system of numbering the rooms and buildings in the school with which everybody can agree;
- keep the school fees as low as possible;
- arrive punctually to every meeting and commitment;
- ensure that every child has the best teacher in every subject;
- ensure that there is no swearing, smoking, drugs, alcohol or pre-marital sex at a party in a private individual's home that is likely to be attended by a student of the school;
- secure the best staff and sack the bad ones;
- identify future building and other capital works needs, and persuade the board accordingly;
- perform two walks around the school each day to "sniff the mood" of the school, drop into classrooms, and "be seen";
- supervise ongoing thorough risk audits to make sure health and safety is always "guaranteed" for every student, employee, contractor and visitor in the school;
- monitor the performance of every employee in the school, either personally or by delegation;

- personally ensure that every student records homework in the handbook every night;
- make sure that every child has access to the computers and musical instruments whenever they wish;
- deal with lawyers and attorneys when they lodge a formal complaint on behalf of a parent claiming their child's failure to learn was the result of the school's failure to teach;
- ensure the school's telephone number is answered quickly and courteously;
- write a regular article for the weekly newsletter, the once-per-term illustrated magazine, and the annual yearbook, in addition to presenting papers at professional conferences and posting frequent positive stories on Facebook and LinkedIn;
- stop students (and staff) driving dangerously;
- prepare copious, detailed reports for accreditation and compliance authorities in the name of "accountability", and then endure multiple follow-up visits and meetings to defend their contents because a box or two was not ticked properly;
- support staff after first perceiving themselves whether or not they need or, indeed, want it by giving them the chance to dump their feelings in total confidence while not allowing accusations against other staff to be heard outside their presence;
- promote the school in the wider community;
- attend conferences and workshops to keep up to date;
- be present, available and on call in the office at all times;
- fix the water, phones or electricity when they malfunction;
- consult widely with everyone who thinks they are important, and listen even more carefully to those who don't;
- keep everyone happy;
- explain to the neighbours why the new building project will not increase traffic congestion, will not create undue noise, dust or excess water to flood their land, and why the lunch wraps which fly over the fence will not choke their pets;
- stop the lunch wraps flying over the fence;

- be a role model as a spouse and parent;
- convince the public that this is the best school for their youngster;
- AND, most challenging of all, to look as though they are interested and enjoying themselves when supervising at a school disco!

I doubt even Winston Churchill had to deal with such a diverse range of responsibilities. However, to be fair, he did have to keep Josef Stalin on side in the effort to defeat the Nazis in World War II, which some might argue (tongue-in-cheek) was akin to the challenge of negotiating many staffing issues in schools today.

It is important for school boards to appreciate the complexity of the demands made upon their Principals these days, and to provide unwavering support for the Principal without hesitation. No Principal should ever feel alone as they lead their school, although sadly many do. School leadership is always a team effort.

In this context, I love the words of Faith Abiodun (UWC International Executive Director) from August 2023: *"Not a single one of us is going to change the world by ourselves. We always do that in community and you have to learn how to do that. Sometimes those really uncomfortable experiences of having your clear ideas being challenged propel you to become a much more conscious member of society. And that is worth fighting for"*.

My concluding message to board members as they work to support the principal is a simple one – we fail as leaders when we expect more from others than we expect from ourselves. If you expect someone to fight for you, you must also fight for them.

Reference:

Rae, J (1988) *Letters from School*, London: Fontana Press.

Thank you to 720.ch for the graphic on page 451 that was adapted for use in this article.

Insight 99

The Board's most important duty

Most members of school boards are keenly aware that they are obliged to perform certain duties.

There are fiduciary duties – the duty of care, the duty of loyalty and the duty of obedience – which are expressed through compliance to legal and financial standards, risk management and program oversight.

There are also non-fiduciary duties which don't have direct legal or financial requirements, but are nonetheless necessary for good governance. These are matters such as development of and adherence to the board's policies, overseeing strategic factors such as demographics and reputation, and so on.

When I work with principals and their boards, it often emerges (indeed, too often!) that one critically important duty is neglected by the board – its duty to care for its principal.

Let's compare three comments I have heard recently from principals about their board's care for them:

- When I was diagnosed with cancer, I resolved that the school would not suffer because of my absence. So I worked right up until the day before my operation, and then I returned to school on the third day after discharge from hospital. In hindsight, that was probably a bit too soon. Having said that, it was disappointing that no-one from the board visited me in hospital, or sent a card or flowers, or even phoned or texted me – and there was not even any mention of my surgery at the next (or any other) board meeting. It made me realise that I was no more valued in their eyes than any other resource or asset in the school such as a desk or a chair.

- It happened at the start of the second year of my headship. The day after I returned from annual leave to begin the new school year, the Chairman of the Board took me aside. He said it was his duty to pass on the concern of some board members that I had spent ten days of my break away on an interstate trip with my family. He told me that my predecessor had always spent his annual leave in the house provided on campus so he could serve as unofficial caretaker and keep an eye on the property while the maintenance staff were away. He informed me that 'the board' expected that this would be my practice henceforth.

- It had been a very difficult year, both for the board and for me. The open revolt by the hostile group of parents against the board's decision to change the rules for election to the board had placed huge strains upon all of us, and especially the Board's Chairperson. My role as principal was a simple one – to be a 'shock absorber' between the angry parents and the board, and to keep the school operating as calmly and as normally as possible. And so it was both surprising and truly humbling when my frazzled Chairperson came in for our weekly meeting on Wednesday morning and said "Everyone on the board understands how difficult this year has been for you and your family. We really appreciate what you've been doing, and we would like you and your family to spend a long weekend at a resort down south at the Board's expense as our way of saying 'thank you'. Just let us know when you want to take the time off and we'll arrange the air tickets and accommodation for you all".

You can probably guess which of these principals reciprocated the loyalty and gratitude that were expressed to them by the board, and which principals decided to start searching for new schools where they might be treated in a more caring or professional manner.

In many ways, the board's duty to care for its principal is arguably its single most important duty. That may sound strange when there are huge legal and financial responsibilities resting upon board members' shoulders. However, it is important to appreciate that almost every facet of the school's health depends to a greater or lesser extent upon the principal's capacity to implement and maintain energetic leadership, and to guide the school along the pathway of the mission and vision set by the board.

It is no coincidence that successful schools are led by great principals (and boards!)

Boards treat their principals poorly at their peril. The costs of losing a principal and initiating a new search and recruitment process are not inconsiderable, especially when unquantifiable but real costs such as loss of institutional memory and interrupted momentum of initiatives and strategies are included.

In my experience working with many schools in various countries over several decades, the principle of reciprocity – "generosity begets generosity" – applies almost universally. It is false economy, ethically as well as financially, for a board not to invest generously in treating its principal well.

Insight 100
The Board's Relationship with the School Community

Managing the Board's relationships with the school community is often one of the more problematic and perplexing aspects of governance. It is a relationship requiring immense sensitivity. For many board members, engaging with the school community can quickly become a matter of 'damned if you do, and damned if you don't'.

At its best, effective two-way engagement between the Board and the community can build collaborative relationships of mutual trust and common purpose with key stakeholders. Such relationships can be very productive in clearing blockages as the school works harmoniously and productively to achieve its shared vision for the future. On the other hand, inappropriate communication between board members and the school community can short-circuit the normal information flows, resulting in mistrust, unawareness, suspicion, rumour-mongering and instability.

Communication between the Board and the community can be broadly categorised as a 'boundaries issue'. This is especially so for board members who are parents, or alumni who may feel competing loyalties towards maintaining Board confidentiality on the one hand and aiding transparent communication with other parents and alumni on the other (especially if the board member was nominated to the

Board by these groups as their representative). Board members who are parents or alumni must, like all other members, place the whole school's interests before their own sectional interests. A good rule-of-thumb here is that board members who are parents need to make decisions that are based on what will be best for their grandchildren, not their children.

There is a growing trend among school boards not to appoint parents as members to avoid the conflicts of loyalties that may arise. One school board I worked with had decided to cease appointing parent representatives. The decision became quite controversial as it was seen to be a change to the school's long-standing tradition of open transparency and strong parent voice.

I advised that the Board should continue with its proposed change, but also establish a new advisory group to the Head comprising parents, teachers, senior students and alumni as a substitute. This initiative enabled the board to engage with the community appropriately, while also giving parents a more direct and effective voice. Furthermore, the initiative provided the Head with an effective new group to use as a sounding board for advice and a significant channel of communication with important elements of the school community.

One way that relations between the board and the community can become dysfunctional is when appropriate conduits of communication are ignored or misused. It is important that board members who receive concerns and hear complaints from parents and others in the community refer those people to the Head or another appropriate senior administrator without becoming involved personally (unless the concerns relate strictly to matters of governance or board practice). By following correct communication protocols, board members can help

maintain the pivotal separation between governance (the role of the board) and management (the responsibility of the Head and the staff).

It is important that the board engages with the school community, and that it does so appropriately. For educational and administrative matters, the Head will be the main conduit of communication – in both directions – between the board and the community. More direct communication from the board (usually through the Chair) will be appropriate for governance matters, but such communications will usually be infrequent, and concern matters of considerable substance.

Insight 101

The board's role in thinking strategically

Very few actions that a school board takes will give it more influence in guiding the school's future and improving the quality of student outcomes than establishing a well-considered strategic vision.

It is therefore surprising that many boards do not really understand what constitutes an effective strategic vision. A 'vision' is not a synonym for the 'mission'; they are interdependent but quite different.

The **mission** of the school is its enduring purpose – why it was established; the unchanging raison d'être of the school. On the other hand, the **vision** derives from the mission. It expresses the 'big picture' priorities of the school over the coming few years while achieving the mission in a contemporary context.

In the 1990s, it was voguish for schools to prepare strategic plans, usually following one or another model that was common in the corporate world at the time. When the currency crises of the early 2000s hit, school leaders realised that strategic plans tended to be too inflexible, and in extreme cases, they even prevented schools from adapting to rapidly changing circumstances and deteriorating financial environments. This insight was reinforced during the COVID-19 global pandemic. In recent years, therefore, schools have found that more flexible **strategic visions** have suited their needs better than the older 'strategic plans'.

A coherent strategic vision will provide the roadmap for the school's immediate and medium-term future, and also provide a framework of operations for the school's management. Therefore, there is (rightly) considerable pressure for boards to consider their strategic visions very carefully. Given the critical importance of getting the strategic vision 'right', most boards wisely engage the services of an external consultant to inform the process, steer it in the right direction and avoid over-burdening board members and the school's management with excessive workload.

When boards begin the process to develop a strategic vision, the starting point must be the mission, as this provides the philosophical, ethical and cultural basis for the school's identity. This is followed by a period of wide consultation, seeking the views of the Head, faculty, staff, parents, students and alumni.

Having completed the consultation and having considered the input carefully, the next step is to identify what the board wants the school to look like, and what it would like the school to be, in (say) five to ten years into the future. Inevitably, there will be a gap between this strategic target and the current state of the school. The strategic vision must therefore articulate the priorities that will shift the school from its current position to its targeted position.

An effective strategic vision must:
- **be achievable;**
- **contain an element of 'stretch';**
- **be ambitious;**
- **contain criteria for measuring (or determining) success of failure;**
- **reflect the ethos and mission of the school and**
- **be concise.**

Note that the strategic vision should not address 'how' the goals should be achieved, as determining the most effective mechanisms to achieve the goals is a task for the Head and the school's faculty and staff. The board's role is to determine and articulate the strategic vision – setting a direction, thus operating within its sphere of governance without straying into the realm of management. Having formulated a strategic vision, the board must then articulate it clearly and widely if it is to be effective.

Of course, the board's role does not cease with the publication of the strategic vision. As described in Insight 76, the board has an ongoing duty to monitor the implementation of the strategic vision, making changes as required to suit changing circumstances. A substantial part of every board meeting should be devoted to this task, and in so doing, the board will fulfil its duty actively and effectively to direct the school's future.

Insight 102

The first hundred days

In Insight 103, I write about **"The Great Resignation"**. One of the consequences of The Great Resignation is that an unusually large number of schools have (or soon will have) new principals.

The first hundred days of a new principalship represents a critically important time. The new Head will (hopefully) be doing lots of listening, consulting and thinking during this period. This is the period when initial impressions are made, impressions that may become quickly entrenched.

How should a new Principal approach the first hundred days, and how should the Board support their new Principal?

Regardless of the circumstances of their predecessor's departure, an incoming Principal almost always starts with enormous goodwill, or what I call political capital. (This is not a universal truth, and the amount of political capital may be smaller if the new Principal is an internal appointment, because internal appointments inevitably begin their new role with a combination of historical baggage and existing relationships).

This large balance of political capital enjoyed by an incoming Principal leads to what is known as the "honeymoon period". After the insecurity of the search period for a new Principal, there is always widespread excitement (and perhaps relief) that after a thorough and exhaustive search, the Board has managed to select the ideal candidate with the right balance of ideological alignment, experience, enthusiasm, character and skills to lead the school into a bright future.

The honeymoon period for a new principal may last a year, or just a month, or even just a day. The first time that a new Principal makes a decision, his or her political capital begins to erode. This is because every decision benefits some constituencies while also disadvantaging other constituencies in either relative or absolute ways. Principals who have been selected to advance a particular board agenda are especially vulnerable to rapid erosion of political capital because they may be forced into making changes prematurely without sufficient consultation or nuanced understandings of the consequences. As a result, they may take anger upon their own shoulders that should really be directed to the Board.

Incoming Principals would be very wise to spend one-on-one time with every staff member – teaching and non-teaching – as quickly as possible, and ideally before they begin official duties. This is an opportunity to learn about every staff member's story, who they are, what they do, why they do it, and what their aspirations are for the future. Like any community, schools work through relationships, so building relationships is an essential foundation for a successful principalship.

Of course, Principals relate to a wide range of constituencies in addition to staff, including board members, parents, students, alumni and the general public. Each constituency rightly demands that their aspirations to be heard and considered. It follows from this that the new Principal should make it an urgent priority to meet with anyone and everyone who is (or may see themselves as) a key stakeholder.

The new Principal's relationship with the board, and especially with the board chair, is of supreme importance. The Head-Chair relationship is rightly regarded as the most important single relationship in any school. Therefore, regular (preferably weekly) meetings should be scheduled to establish a professional working relationship of mutual trust, transparency and a 'no surprises' environment.

Having got to know the people, the next task for a new Principal is getting to know the school thoroughly, inside and out. A good tip for a new Principal is to carry around a small pocket-sized note pad for the first couple of months to note down thoughts and observations as they occur while walking around the school. It is almost inevitable that the new Principal will see and observe things in the first six weeks that will become 'invisible' once familiarity sets in.

Getting to know the school involves more than just casual observation, of course. Familiarity includes developing a thorough understanding of the financial position and the school's programs, policies and procedures.

This all takes time, and some Principals become frustrated when they are constantly interrupted by staff and others coming to the door of their office. As a young Principal I remember being frustrated by these seemingly interminable interruptions to my work, until one day I realised that these people were my "real work" – the paperwork was what I did in between dealing with my real work, which was people.

A third priority area for the first hundred days is training and networking. Very few new Principals have ever been specifically trained for the role; rather they rise through the schooling profession along one of several pathways.

Therefore, a new Principal should commit to networking widely through as many associations as practicable, getting to know other like-minded Principals, as well as engaging in leadership and governance-oriented professional development. Coming to a clear understanding of the board's role of governance and the consequent unique delegation-accountability relationship between the Board and the Principal is arguably the most critically important insight to understand – for both Board and Principal.

It is said that the job of a School Principal is the best in the world.

It can also be one of the most lonely jobs in the world. However, it doesn't have to be that way.

The first hundred days may not necessarily make or break a new headship, but they can profoundly affect its success. The new Principal needs to take the occasional deep breath, pause, and remember to take on only a manageable number of tasks at a time – a number that will almost certainly be fewer than the demands that flood in from those many constituent groups.

Meanwhile the Board's duty is to support the new Principal, both publicly through affirmation and privately by ensuring the new Principal's personal needs are being met. It is in everyone's interests to ensure the new Principal's honeymoon period outlives the first day, the first week, and hopefully the first year in the role.

Insight 103

The great resignation

In mid-July 2022, the Times Educational Supplement reported that 95% of schools in the UK were struggling to recruit teachers, with 43% claiming the problem was "severe". Schools were trying to cope by increasing class sizes, especially in subjects such as Physics, Mathematics, Design and Technology, Chemistry and Computing. Similar patterns of teacher shortages are emerging globally, including in Australia, New Zealand, Uganda, the US and elsewhere.

A year earlier in 2021, mid-way through the most savage impacts of the COVID-19 global pandemic, **"The Great Resignation"** became a topic of widespread speculation and conversation. According to the often-dubious source of Wikipedia, the term was first coined by Anthony Klotz, a professor of management at Mays Business School at Texas A&M University in May 2021 to refer to a predicted mass voluntary resignation of employees. He (and others) predicted that many people would resign due to factors such as wages rising more

slowing than costs of living, frustration with endemic job dissatisfaction, concerns about the safety of working in a pandemic environment, and a desire to change the balance of in-house and remote working.

Whatever individual reasons a person has for joining The Great Resignation, the common theme seems to be a simple one; **it is lack of job satisfaction**.

In my work with School Boards and Principals, I have detected signs that "the Great Resignation" is starting to affect many schools, with some being affected to a significant degree. Some boards are struggling to find good applicants with appropriate credentials and character qualities to fill vacant headships. In turn, Principals are finding it more and more difficult to retain good staff and maintain morale.

The media increasingly highlights stories about the low pay of teachers, the long working hours, the growing struggles of classroom management, the challenges of expanding parental expectations, and the difficulty of attracting intelligent, motivated high school graduates into teaching as a career. The increasing demands of government compliance and accountability add to the impression that education is an increasingly bureaucratic occupation that offers decreasing scope for originality, creativity, and genuine care for students' needs and individual differences.

Interestingly, many educators (including school leaders) who are resigning are not doing so to earn higher salaries; indeed, many are taking a pay cut. They have realised that whatever the level of remuneration, workplace culture is more important than material gain.

If this is true (and anecdotal evidence strongly suggests that it is so), the implications are clear. School boards need to ensure that they are caring adequately and genuinely for their Principal in non-material as well as material ways, including doing their best to make sure the Principal's spouse or partner (if they have one) is also feeling supported in the face of the seemingly excessive demands that are often made of Principals.

Similarly, Principals need to care for their staff genuinely and authentically. It is an often-repeated truism to say that a school's most important resource is its teachers, but it is no less accurate for being repeated so often.

What does this mean in practice? I think there are **three significant factors**.

The first is **culture**.

Culture is often seen as a nebulous, intangible 'thing' that is impossible to define precisely. In schools, culture is central to identity, and is usually defined by the mission statement, the strategic vision and the articulated core values. To ignore culture is to surrender the identity of the school – which is why the SMART evaluation tool was developed to help schools measure their effectiveness in implementing their mission/vision/culture (see Insight 69).

Moreover, ignoring culture will adversely affect the everyday experiences of every employee in the school, starting with the Principal and permeating through every facet of the school. Culture influences the behaviour of every line manager, whether or not credit is given for effort, the extent of help and support available, and who steps up to become the influential role models.

Irrespective of a school's underlying philosophy, two key elements of a positive, effective work culture are **collaboration** and **transparency**.

In a collaborative work culture, everyone works together as a team to get things done. Everyone – the Principal, teachers and non-teaching staff – are trusted as professionals who will perform their job well. Recognition of success and achievement are shared fairly, while leaders and employees have a strong mutual accountability to one another.

Signs of a dysfunctional work culture include people and sections working in silos, individuals who promote their own self-congratulation and importance, fear of making a mistake, micromanagement of staff by managers (or worse, the Board), and widespread gossip, complaining, victimisation, sabotage, and backstabbing.

The stereotype of schools as described by many people in the United Kingdom today. Is this really what Principals must deal with?

It is easy to understand why an educator or school leader might resign to escape such a dysfunctional work culture.

The second area is what I call **source of meaning**.

Everyone is motivated by something meaningful. The source of this meaning may be external or internal, and it may be positive or negative. Positive meaning derives from a mix of passion and purpose – head and heart.

'Meaning' is the driving force behind the effective work of most teachers, educators and members of school boards. For many educators in independent schools, this meaning flows from religious faith and identity, including cultural identity. In other words, authentic meaning – purpose and passion – is found in convictions that are profound, and immeasurably larger than any one individual or institution.

Tensions inevitably arise in schools when the ways in which 'meaning' is expressed or practised fall short of the ideals that are expected or promoted. The word 'hypocrisy' may even be used in corridor conversations.

Of course, everyone finds meaning from many sources apart from work. However, when the importance of workplace-sourced meaning declines for any individual in a school, morale and motivation decline, and an exodus of competent staff often follows. For the Principal, lack of effective support from the Board can motivate a similar course of action.

The third area is **opportunities for personal, professional and values/soul growth**.

No teacher, no Principal and no Board Member is a static, inert being. We all either grow or shrivel depending upon the quality the inputs we receive, the experiences we enjoy (or endure), and the opportunities we have to try new things, meet new people and to serve others.

For most educators (and for every good educator), personal, professional and values/soul growth is more important than salary. Good educators, and good Principals are inherently idealistic and optimistic. This characteristic should never be seen as an opportunity for school boards to squeeze employees in terms of remuneration or expectations of time and effort. Such squeezing stunts growth and can (indeed probably should) become a trigger for unwanted resignations.

Insight 104

The Red Line between Governance and Management

The purpose of a school board is to govern the school. The purpose of the staff and its leadership is to manage the school. The so-called Red Line that divides the roles of Governance and Management is the most basic element of sound leadership in schools – and often the least understood or most ignored.

The Board's duty of Governance arises from its legal authority to exercise power and authority to ensure legal compliance, make sure risk is managed, ensure financial viability, set and monitor the mission, vision and direction of the school, engage and support the Principal, and so on. Governance is thus a future-focussed, collective or group action – the Board's authority arises when it meets and makes resolutions.

The Board delegates authority to the Principal to manage the school's day-to-day operations in such a way that the mission and vision are achieved, financial sustainability is secured, legal requirements are met, risk (including health and safety) are managed effectively, and so on. Of course, the Principal is not expected to achieve this single-handedly, and therefore management involves the delegation of tasks and outcomes to teaching and non-teaching staff, all of whom are recruited and managed as part of the Principal's responsibilities.

A two-way delegation and accountability relationship therefore arises between the Board and the Principal – this is shown in detail in the diagram on page 60. The Board delegates all operational matters to the Principal but remains ultimately accountable to ensure that its mission and objectives are achieved. Therefore, the Principal provides regular reports to the Board on the state of the school, with special emphasis on the strategic goals that the Board has set. This allows the Board as a collective body to monitor the progress of the school in achieving its objectives (and parenthetically also the Principal's effectiveness in implementing their delegated authority).

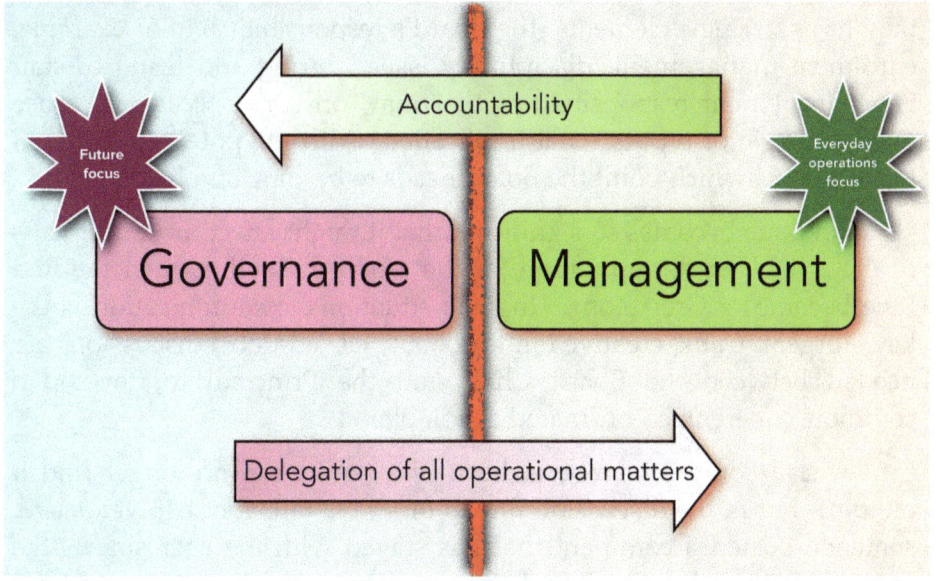

It's all so clear – Boards govern and Principals manage, Boards focus on the future while Principals act in the present, Boards determine the mission and the goals while Principals operationalise and implement the same mission and goals. Discrete roles and responsibilities, separated by a clear, thick, Red Line, but linked by a strong delegation-accountability relationship. It sounds like a formula for perfect teamwork.

WHAT COULD POSSIBLY GO WRONG?

The short answer is "plenty", as many Principals and Board members will attest.

Sometimes, friction arises simply because well-meaning but untrained Board members (or the Principal) don't fully understand the different roles and responsibilities that lie on either side of the Red Line.

On other occasions, a weak or ineffective Board might 'force' a Principal to take on some of the functions of governance. Equally, a weak or ineffective Principal may 'compel' the Board to intrude into aspects of day-to-day operational management, even to the point of micro-management. The relationship works best when a school has a strong Board and an equally strong Principal, each of whom understands their respective roles and responsibilities.

There is also a more subtle reason that complicates the relationship. Some areas of management (the Principal's responsibility) may have strategic elements (the Board's responsibility). For example, enrolment management, disciplinary issues, hiring and firing of staff are management responsibilities that may, on some occasions, cause huge strategic or reputational implications with the potential to derail the school, at which point the Board needs to become involved.

If an issue becomes so significant that it might affect the enrolments of the school, or its reputation, or the school's viability, then the Red Line becomes a Grey Zone. In such situations, communication is the key – urgent, frank, creative (and probably closed-door) discussions are needed between the Board Chair and the Principal to develop a common, coherent, co-ordinated action plan.

I wish I could remember who it was (and I can no longer find it online) – but in the discussion thread of a TED talk about 15 years ago, someone posted a comment that has stayed with me ever since: "the grey areas are where you find the complexity, the humanity, and the truth".

Schools are complex, people-focussed communities where discernment of truth is by definition a key goal. Understanding when the Red Line should be held rigidly in place and when the Grey Zone can and ought to intrude is a key capacity in which the Board and the Principal together can model agile, authentic, effective leadership for staff, students and parents alike.

Insight 105

The Village Venus Effect

There aren't many places left in the world which are so isolated that the residents have had almost no exposure to the outside world. I feel very fortunate to have visited some such places in my research for writing geography textbooks – remote locations such as the Hartmann Valley in northern Namibia where the Himba people live, the upper reaches of the Baliem Valley in West Papua, Indonesia, which is home to the Dani people, and the Omo Valley of southern Ethiopia where several remote tribes such as the Mursi and the Arbore tribes live.

If you were a boy in the un-named village of the Arbore people shown below, you would grow up knowing all the other boys and girls in the settlement. As you emerge from boyhood into young manhood, your perspective of your peers will almost certainly change and mature. One day, if you are brave enough, you might even approach one of the young women in your village and declare "you're the most beautiful girl in the world".

Four girls of the Arbore tribe in southern Ethiopia. The photo was taken by me in 2008 when I visited to undertake field research for a Geography book I was writing at the time.

In terms of the world you have known all your life, you may well be right. You may continue to hold that view for a long time, perhaps until the day comes when you are old enough to venture further afield into the wider world.

As the famous Maltese organisational philosopher and thinker, Edward de Bono, wrote in 1982, "Simply stated, if you're living in small village, the prettiest girl in that village, is essentially, the prettiest girl in the world — in your own perception". This has become known as the Village Venus Effect.

The term "Village Venus Effect" describes a situation where a small, insular community excessively praises and admires a local individual or entity, often beyond the level that is objectively warranted. This admiration can lead to a distorted perception of that individual's or entity's true value or achievements, creating an echo chamber of mutual self-congratulation and complacency. In the context of a school board, the Village Venus Effect can show itself when board members, leaders or administrators are excessively praised and shielded from criticism, leading to a lack of accountability and resistance to change.

The Village Venus Effect can pose a huge but often unrecognised trap for school boards and leaders. In the same way that in Greek mythology Narcissus fell in love with his own reflection in a pool of water, school boards and leaders sometimes fall into the trap of believing their own marketing rhetoric and may become blind to significant shortcomings that ought to be identified and addressed. In colloquial terms, this is sometimes referred to as "drinking your own Kool-aid".

It is easy to understand how the Village Venus Effect (or "collective narcissism") can seduce a board and/or the executive leadership into an unrealistic and unfounded state of complacency. If the Principal or board members stay within their own isolated bubbles and never visit or experience other schools, never network with others who serve in similar roles in other schools, and never undertake any professional development workshops on school governance, they are never challenged by the realities and initiatives of the outside world. Complacency can be particularly insidious, and indeed dangerous, for school boards where most of its members have been serving on that same board for a long period of time (which is an argument for term limits).

Extract from the painting "Echo and Narcissus" (1903) by John William Waterhouse. The painting captures the tragic moment from Greek mythology where Narcissus, entranced by the beauty of his own reflection, is oblivious to the forlorn Echo who watches him in despair. Credit: Google Art Project. Public Domain.

What are some signs that a school board may be falling into the trap of the Village Venus Effect? Warning signs might be comments like these:

- "90% of our board members all attend the same church" (or work at the same place, or are former students who were friends at school, or are members of the same club – you get the idea).
- "Our board meetings are little more than social events focussed on mutual self-congratulation. Certain individuals or groups always seem to receive disproportionate admiration or accolades".
- "Our board functions like an echo chamber where feedback loops repeatedly reinforce positive perceptions, even when they aren't justified".
- "Board members are afraid to hold each other to account because they don't want to hurt others' feelings".
- "Our board is complacent; it is satisfied with the status quo, and lacks the drive to innovate or look for ways to improve".

When a Board becomes unknowingly trapped in the Village Venus Effect, the results can be dramatic – and seldom in a positive way:

- Without critical feedback and external comparisons, the Board is likely to stagnate by failing to identify areas needing improvement, both within the school and in its own operations.
- When over-valued individuals or practices resist necessary change, progress and improvement are hindered.
- A focus on praising an "in-group" of select individuals or groups is likely to cause neglect of others who deserve recognition and support.
- A lack of fully-informed, critical oversight will almost certainly result in poor decision-making and governance, leading to compliance, accountability and accreditation challenges.

Is there hope for a school board (or Principal) that is caught in the Village Venus Effect? The first, hardest, and most difficult step is to take a 'big picture' look inwards from outside the isolated bubble, recognise that collective narcissism may be at work, and then acknowledge with humility that a culture of self-congratulation needs to be replaced by a culture of transparency, accountability and continuous improve-ment. This will happen as diverse perspectives are encouraged and embraced, constructive criticism is welcomed, benchmarking and external reviews are regularly conducted, and authentic merit is celebrated.

Insight 106

Thinking strategically

Most board members I work with clearly understand the importance of strategic thinking for guiding the school's future direction in a sustainable, intentional direction. Having said that, many board members admit that they struggle to understand what it means to **"think strategically"**.

Strategic thinking is **NOT** the same thing as strategic planning, and indeed strategic planning can become an impediment to strategic thinking if not handled appropriately. Many members of school boards feel more confident if they stay within their comfort zone of thinking operationally – planning, monitoring and executing – while at the same time acknowledging that they would like to develop more future-focussed strategic skills.

When we consider "strategic thinking", we should not restrict ourselves to the five-yearly (or so) process of developing a new strategic plan. Strategic thinking should be a normal, regular, ubiquitous component of every board meeting. Every decision a board makes should involve strategic thinking.

However, it is possible that not all board members have a common understanding of the key word – "strategic". The word "strategy" derives from the Greek στρατηγία (strategia), which means "army moving" or "generalship". Like military strategy, effective school board strategy means flexibility in placing resources where needed to achieve the goals that have been identified as key priorities. In other words, being flexible to move resources if circumstances change is "strategic" behaviour.

It follows from this that strategic thinking differs from "everyday" decision-making because it adopts an intentional process which considers data (such as school culture, demographic change, risk factors, and so on) to identify the key priorities required to advance the school's mission.

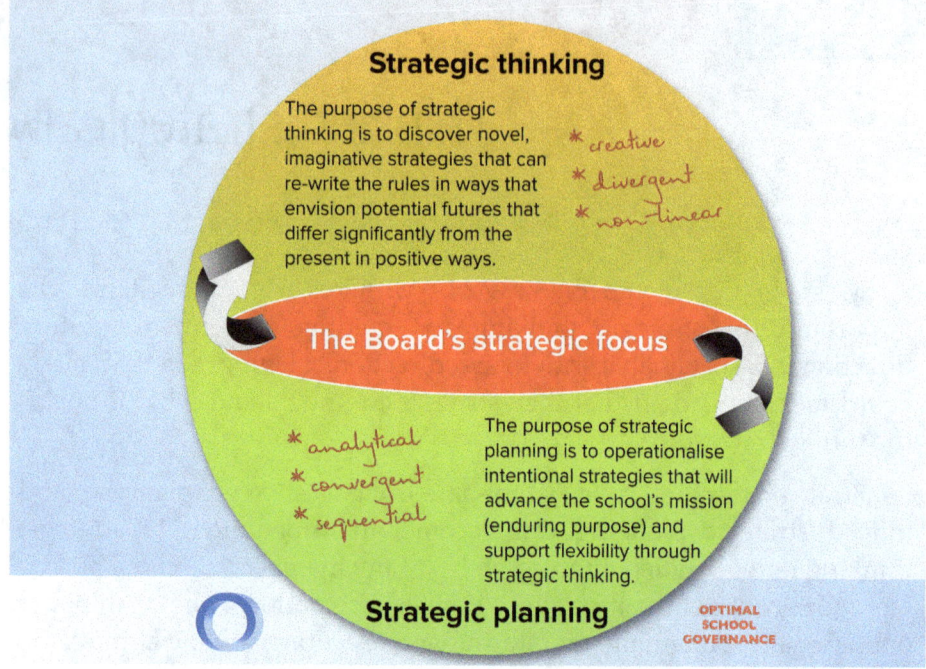

Research persuasively reveals that most people's decision-making processes are consciously or unconsciously biased. Most people pay very little attention to how they make their decisions, but rather they focus solely on the outcomes. We need to understand that we gather knowledge in many disparate ways – our five senses, emotions, intuition, reasoning, language, traditions, beliefs, etc – and each of these ways brings certain advantages and shortcomings that we should recognise and acknowledge.

It is therefore important that when a school's future is being considered – which means every time the board is looking to make a decision – strategic thinking is required. Sound strategic thinking should be neither complicated nor time-consuming; it should simply but explicitly consider all relevant data and perspectives to achieve the best outcomes for the school.

It is said that there are five steps involved in thinking strategically:

1. Clearly articulate the goal or desired outcome: What do we want to achieve? What does success look like?

2. Analyse current understandings: What do we think we know? What are our current assumptions and beliefs? How confident are we that our assumptions are justified?

3. Gather the data: What evidence do we already possess? What additional data do we need? What is the best framework to ensure the data we collect will be objective, thorough and reliable?

4. Establish options: In view of the data, evidence and information available, what are our alternatives?

5. Consider each option from various perspectives: How would the school's different constituencies view this proposal? What are the benefits and challenges of each option?

When various options are being explored by a board, differences of opinion are almost inevitable, especially when various perspectives are considered. Such differences of opinion are valuable – indeed, they are the point of having the discussion! It is, however, essential that while the conflict of ideas is embraced, it must never degenerate into a conflict between people. Mutual respect is essential for clear strategic thinking.

Insight 107

Time management – juggling tasks, coffee cups, and late nights

Let's begin with a short quiz for school principals and senior leaders.

Listed below are 12 statements or questions. Give yourself a point for every statement you have thought or said to yourself over the past month (paraphrases are acceptable):

1. I can't believe how many e-mails arrived today.
2. Is there a 'Delegate' button hidden somewhere in my office that I haven't found yet?
3. Is it possible to survive solely on a diet of coffee and appreciation?
4. I never even managed to pee once the day had started.
5. I've been in back-to-back meetings all day.
6. Do they make a 'Principal Clone' kit? Just asking for a friend… who is me.
7. Is it acceptable to add 'Professional Juggler' to my C.V. for handling all these tasks?
8. Lunch? Who has time for lunch?
9. Yes, I know I said I'd be home by 8pm, but I thought you understood that was a joke.
10. An entire month went by and I never managed to connect with my board chair.
11. There simply aren't enough hours in the day.
12. I'm so busy that I considered joining a time management support group, but I just don't have the time.

If you gave yourself 12 points, then you probably don't have time to read this article (although you really need to!). I suspect many school principals and leaders would be able to score around 8 out 12 with little difficulty. However, that is NOT a badge of honour like the one shown in the photo above – it is a problem that needs to be fixed.

Quickly! Before burnout solves the problem for you.

Having a daily schedule with no blank space IS worn like a badge of honour by far too many school leaders. It is not good for the leader, and it is not good for the school. Not having time to attend to bodily functions, to respond to e-mails, and most importantly of all, to relate meaningfully to staff, students, and even your own family, is almost certainly not the plan you had in mind when you applied for a principalship.

Having been the Principal of five schools myself, I look back and completely understand the pressures upon every school leader. They are insidious and unrelenting.

School Principals have a huge number of often competing constituencies that all demand time and attention – the board, parents, teachers, non-teaching staff, alumni, the wider community, government authorities, contractors, the press and media, volunteers, donors, potential donors – and of course their own family. I have never met a School Principal anywhere in the world who has been able to put hand on heart and declare that their own family never had to make any sacrifices to support their work – which doesn't make it acceptable, of course.

Astute boards understand the vast range and ongoing stress of these pressures and do whatever they can to protect the Principal from excessive demands, providing 'space' for renewal and support in any possible way. Nonetheless, there are limits to the extent that a Board can (or is likely to) say "go home and do less work".

A complicating factor is that most good Principals have a strong disposition to give, and give, and to keep on giving, because they see their vocation as one of servant leadership. Therein lies the tension.

It has been said by many people – Principals are often their own worst enemy when it comes to looking after their personal welfare. No less true but said less frequently is the claim that most constituents in a school have no idea how hard and sacrificially their Principal is working because so much of the Principal's work is done away from their direct vision or the public eye.

The good news is that School Principals have considerable power to improve their time management. Although not every strategy will work for every Principal, some possibilities include the following:

1. **Delegate effectively.** This involves handing over some authority to make decisions to others, accompanied by the expectation and the requirement for explicit accountability for the effectiveness of those decisions. Delegation involves placing trust in others, and I fully appreciate the difficulty some Principals face in doing so, especially considering that the Principal is ultimately accountable to the Board for every aspect of the school's operations. If the Principal can't find any competent staff to perform delegated tasks, then the Principal is the one who has the duty and the responsibility to find and recruit some, and the Board should encourage and financially support such recruitment. It should be noted that as well as relieving the Principal's workload, delegation develops the skills of more junior staff members and prepares them for leadership in due course, and this benefits not only the school but the entire education sector.

2. **Prioritise tasks.** Lists are a great help here; note everything that needs to be done, number the points in order of priority (which may not be the same as order of importance), and then enjoy the satisfaction of crossing items off the list as they are completed.

3. **Set aside blocks of time.** Everyone needs some flexibility in their day to draw breath, to think and reflect (and pray), to go to the washroom, to return an unexpected phone call, or even to renew

oneself professionally by reading a free online article about best practice in school leadership.

4. **Schedule daily 'open door' times.** Being accessible to staff enables issues to be handled when they are just a spark that might lead to a grass fire rather than waiting for it to flare up and become a forest fire. When I was Principal, every staff member knew they could come to my office for an unscheduled chat of up to five minutes about anything at all during the hour after morning tea every day. If they needed more than five minutes, they could schedule an appointment in the usual way. These 'open door' times were additional to the accessibility I provided by being present in the staff common room at morning tea every day, and during my twice-daily walks around the entire campus of the school. If no-one came to see me during some or all of the daily 'open door' times, I had the bonus of some extra time to catch up on other matters.

5. **Learn to say 'no'.** Many Principals find this even harder than delegating because most Principals are by nature people pleasers. Hopefully saying 'no' becomes easier for Principals once they focus on the reality that overcommitment to their work leads to burnout, stress, decreased work effectiveness, short-tempered relationships, poorer family life, and often a shorter life span.

6. **Invest in the Principal's own professional development.** Although professional development takes time away from everyday duties, it should be seen as an investment rather than a cost. This is because professional development refreshes the mind, spurs creativity, and (at its best) enhances leadership and time management skills.

Let me finish with a challenge to every school leader who has read through to the end of this article. Consciously try to improve your time management using the six points above, plus anything else that might work for you. Work through those strategies for six months. Then re-take the 12-point quiz at the start of the article and compare the difference. I would love to receive your feedback on the changes you experience.

Insight 108

Trust and truth – the fraying impact of distrust in schools

In Insight 17 I quoted the profound words of Sissela Bok in her book 'Lying': **"Whatever matters to human beings, trust is the atmosphere in which it thrives"**.

The point she was making is that trust is the essential pre-condition of every healthy and just human relationship. Schools are places built around relationships, so it follows that appreciating the central importance of trust is an essential understanding for every school leader and every board member.

Bok amplifies her focus upon trust by adding "But if I do not trust your word, can I have genuine trust? If there is no confidence in the truthfulness of others, is there any way to assess their fairness, their intentions to help or harm?" She therefore draws an ineradicable bond between trust and truth. Without truth, there is no trust.

I write about the importance of truth in Insights 109 and 112. Telling the truth is important. Even traditional children's stories such as 'the Boy who cried Wolf' and 'Pinocchio' are centred on the importance of telling the truth. For Christians, it is so pre-eminent that it one of the 10 Commandments.

And yet, truth seems to be increasingly elusive in our so-called postmodern, post-truth era. In his book 'Evangelism in a Skeptical World', Sam Chan identifies six cornerstones that define, or characterise, today's postmodern society:

1. People's views are subjective, biased and influenced by their culture, race, history, gender, education, etc.
2. Each truth is free floating and unanchored; all truth is coherence-based and independent of prior truth.
3. All thinking is biased and subjective, so our presuppositions will determine our conclusions.
4. Certainty of knowledge is impossible because all knowledge is historically and culturally determined; no facts are culturally neutral.
5. Science is biased by the consensus of authority figures, so its premises and conclusions cannot be trusted.
6. There is no universal truth.

The sad reality is that malleable concepts of truth such as those outlined by Chan make trust impossible to establish in today's society, including our schools. This is because elastic truth breeds tribalism and suspicion, which are the enemies of community and collective trust. We see tribalism eroding trust to a growing degree in today's politics, which should be a warning for other facets of our society, including schools.

We already see evidence of the erosion of trust in universities and colleges of higher education. Whereas universities were once bastions of free speech where contentious ideas were encouraged and debated until sound arguments could prevail over weaker thinking, postmodernism emphasises people's feelings, prejudices, histories, identities and cultures over rational argument. This leads to intense suspicion of those who are not in "your tribe" and unquestioning acceptance of the claims made by those who are in "your tribe".

It is not unusual to see and hear claims from both sides of the political spectrum being amplified on social media and elsewhere by outbursts of such moral gravity that when anyone disagrees with the claims, then it is assumed – and openly asserted – that this could only be on the basis of antithetical ideological bias.

Ever since the times of Socrates, and more especially since the enlightenment era of the 1600s, debates have traditionally aimed to persuade others through sound, rational arguments. In today's society, debates tend to be focussed not on listening to others but on expressing one's own talking points – usually to people who are unlikely to be open to changing their minds. I have seen some school board meetings descend into the same dynamic. These meetings tend to be divisive, combative, and adversarial. Such discussions almost never resolve the issue at hand, and they invariably damage the level of respect and quality of working relationships among board members.

Board dynamics, and indeed the quality of all relationships in a school community, are highly susceptible to the corrosive, or fraying effects of distrust, contempt, and mutual intimidation. A strong Board Chair must be sensitive to the emergence of such trends on a board and intervene quickly to stifle them should they begin to emerge. There must always be enough time allowed in any board meeting for attendees to treat each other with respect, to listen to one another, to find common ground and to find a just solution to any problem in order to advance the school's mission and vision.

For board dynamics to function effectively, it needs to be assumed that everyone present is acting in good faith for the benefit of the school. In my experience, this is almost always a fair assumption. Having said that, I have seen some situations where board members may seem to be acting in bad faith by placing the interests of the body that nominated them above what is best for school, or where a conflict of interest distorts sound judgement. This highlights the importance of establishing sound policies and practices on conflicts of interest and related parties transactions. It is imperative that such policies are developed, established and agreed during 'normal' calm times, because the middle of a crisis when the issues are causing acute and immediate pressures is precisely the wrong time to start developing such policies.

As mentioned earlier, though, truth is essential for trust. But how can a board member, or a school leader, or even a classroom teacher who is being told by a student that their dog ate their homework, be sure that they are being told the real truth?

The reality is that not all lies in schools are blatant. Some lies can be classified as concealment, while others are fabrication. There are also subtypes within these categories – ambiguities, deliberate confusions, embellishments, exaggerations, omissions, decontextualisations, and so on. As the English mathematician and philosopher Alfred North Whitehead once said, "There are no whole truths; all truths are half-truths". (I can't help thinking that his statement must therefore either be a half-truth or self-contradictory).

Most people think they are very good at spotting liars. They believe that "giveaway" gestures include facial touching, avoiding eye contact, fake smiles, shaky voice, odd noises, random words, and so on. There is some basis for this, although research shows that most people are very bad at differentiating truth from lies.

The challenge of separating truth from lies is becoming even more difficult with the rise of Artificial Intelligence, especially the use of deep fake videos. Deep fake videos are especially insidious because they can show celebrities, politicians or other authority figures who appear so realistic that we are easily convinced they must be real.

However, the seriously consequential danger emerges once we suspect deep fake technology might be in play, because at that point we begin to doubt everything, including what we know is actually real. This type of generalised, widespread doubt and scepticism leads inevitably to chronic mistrust, which as we saw earlier, undermines truth, reality and relationships.

Fortunately, to the best of my knowledge, deep fake videos have never yet been a factor in any school board meeting. Nonetheless, it is not hard to imagine a day when deep fake videos, or even simple old-fashioned lies, distortions of the truth, or broken promises, sow so much doubt in the minds of a school community that trust becomes frayed, loyalty is eroded, and chaos ensues. At this point persuasion is no longer effective, creating a vacuum that can only be filled by suspicion, ideology or emotions.

Trust based upon truth and honesty is the necessary, precious catalyst to every effective relationship we have. Therefore, like every other institution in our society, school boards and leaders must intentionally work to protect and nurture truth and trust as essential foundations of achieving the school's mission and vision.

They should never break a promise. They should never fail to be transparent. They should never lie.

Trust is the litmus test of value and meaning in our lives and common experiences.

References:

Bok, S (1999) *Lying (2nd ed.)*. New York: Vintage.

Chan, S (2018) *Evangelism in a Skeptical World*. Grand Rapids: Zondervan. (see especially chapter 4)

Insight 109

Truths about truth

In this so-called post-truth era, many people seem to feel that truth is negotiable. You can have your truth, she can have her truth, I can have my truth, and according to the common view in society today, they can all have equal validity even if they are mutually inconsistent and incompatible.

This is, of course, just lazy thinking that avoids the need to engage with other people's ideas – their truth claims.

The world doesn't work according to this "multiple truths" viewpoint. I can't go into my bank to withdraw $10,000 when the bank's records show I have $150 in my account, even if my "truth" is that I have the full $10,000.

If I am driving and a police officer stops me to issue a fine for speeding dangerously, I can't reply and claim "my truth is that I was driving safely". (Well, I can, but it won't make any difference, because my "truth" is no more than an unjustified "opinion").

Similarly, school leaders and boards have to operate in the real world where facts mean something. Whether it is disciplining a student, dismissing a teacher, arranging a bank loan for a capital project, or responding to a media attack, the truth of the matter is central to sound decision-making.

In Insight 112, I describe the difference between correspondence truth and coherence truth. School boards and leaders should understand the difference because it will almost invariably result in better decision-making. Two (perhaps surprising) examples illustrate the difference.

Example 1: The Boxers of China

In 1898-1901, a group of nationalistic Chinese men known as the Boxers led a rebellion in Beijing (then Peking) to drive out foreigners. They believed certain martial arts gestures made them immune to bullets.

They were wrong.

They found that immunity to bullets did not work very well in actual battle conditions.

Their belief was sincerely held, but that did not make it "truth". In their case, their belief was coherently true (because they all shared the common belief), but the belief did not correspond to reality.

Example 2: The Tariana of Brazil

The Tariana people are found in the remote upper reaches of the Amazon River basin in Brazil. Only about 100 people speak the Tariana language.

In Tariana, it is grammatically incorrect to make a statement without saying how you know it is true. Because evidence of truth is required, this is known as evidentiality in a language.

Every sentence must contain a marker that indicates on what evidence the statement is based - such as whether the speaker saw it, or heard it, or inferred it from indirect evidence, or learned about it from someone else.

I cannot just say "the dog stole the fish". To speak proper Tariana, I must add a suffix to the end of the verb.....

If I actually saw the dog drag the fish over the grid of the fireplace, I would say "The dog stole *ka* the fish". (*ka* means saw with my own eyes).

If I didn't see the dog take the fish but I heard the noise of a fish falling from the grid, I would say "The dog stole *ma-ka* the fish". (*ma-ka* means heard, smelled or tasted).

If I come into the kitchen and see the fish missing and the dog looking happy and well-fed, I would infer that the dog ate the fish and say "The dog stole *ni-hka* the fish". (*ni-hka* means inferred on the basis of evidence I have seen personally).

If I come and the fish is gone, and my general knowledge says only dogs steal fish, I would say "The dog stole *si-ka* the fish". (*si-ka* marks information made on general assumptions).

If someone else told me what had happened, then in reporting it I would say "The dog stole *bi-di-ka* the fish". (*bi-di-ka* marks information as having been reported by someone else).

In almost every culture in the world, evidentiality is secondary information, but to the Tariana it is basic to communication and understanding. The Tariana are compelled by their language to be precise in telling others how they know something.

When the Tariana speak, they cannot avoid conveying both correspondence and coherence truth.

Wouldn't it be great if students and staff, and even board members, had obligatory evidentials and were compelled by the language they use to say how they know that their claim is true?

Insight 110

Turns are permitted

I have been to North Korea nine times since my first trip there in 2005. I learn new things every time I visit. Moreover, the additional perspective provided by multiple visits deepens my capacity to understand and interpret the changes I witness.

It's the same with the performance reviews I undertake of boards, principals, senior and middle managers. Although a single performance review provides really valuable insights that highlight potential areas for improvement, repeated reviews over a period of time provide truly profound insights into the improvements underway and the possibilities for true excellence.

One of the appealing "constants" for me when I visit Pyongyang, North Korea's capital city, is the ubiquitous presence of traffic police at major intersections. I know Pyongyang has a reputation for having wide deserted streets with no traffic, but the stereotype is untrue – the city may not suffer from the extreme traffic congestion of many other cities, but there is sufficient traffic to warrant some control mechanism.

I took the photos in this Insight on two of my visits to Pyongyang. They shows a policewoman at the intersection of Victory Street and Somun Street near Kim Il Sung Square in the heart of the city, one in summer and one in winter. The baton held out horizontally indicates that a turn through the intersection is permitted.

Maybe it is stretching the analogy somewhat, but I think this is a great metaphor for school boards and leaders to consider when they are developing or implementing a strategic plan.

As many boards and school leaders found during the COVID-19 global pandemic, and even earlier during the Global Financial Crisis of 2008, 'strategic planning' is an oxymoronic term. If you have a fixed plan, it is no longer 'strategic'.

"Strategy" derives from the Greek word στρατηγία (strategia), which means "army moving" or "generalship". Like military strategy, effective school board strategy means placing resources where they are needed and being flexible to move them if circumstances change.

In today's educational environment, flexibility and adaptability are essential. That is why I prefer to focus on an agile 'strategic vision' that is nourished by – and flows directly from – the school's distinctive mission.

If a school is to be strategic (which requires being agile and responsive to changing circumstances), turns are not only permitted – they are necessary.

Insight 111

Values define our identity

Many members of school boards come with experience on other boards, especially in the business sector, but also on other not-for-profit boards. Many Heads of Schools struggle with what they perceive as an overly pragmatic approach by such board members as they continually focus on balance sheets, KPIs, returns of investment, enrolment statistics, and so on. Most Heads readily acknowledge the importance of such matters, but also wish (usually secretly) that board members would balance this with greater attention to the areas of their school that are less readily reduced to statistics.

Albert Einstein is reported to have said "not everything that can be counted counts, and not everything that counts can be counted". In his book *The Little Prince*, Antoine de Saint-Exupéry went further, saying **"It is only with the heart that one can see rightly; what is essential is invisible to the eye"**. It is anecdotally true that very few school board members see with their hearts or focus on what is invisible to the eye.

At the core of "what is invisible and uncountable" lies the school's values. For any school, it is arguably values that define its identity.

If we express this in a way that a stereotypically hard-headed board member from a business background might appreciate, it is the school's values that drive appropriate resource allocation, both human and financial. The process of developing, defining and promulgating the school's values pay dividends in a multitude of other ways.

Values which are clearly articulated, promulgated, and authentically practised will inevitably have a profound influence on the character of students who graduate from a school. Consider the four schools shown in the photos below which have significantly different core values and will produce quite different students from each other.

This monument at Eagle's Nest Christian School, Polokwane, South Africa identifies the core values of (i) prayer (ii) education and (iii) outreach, drawing inspiration from Isaiah 40:31 which reads in part "those who hope in the Lord will renew their strength; they will soar on wings like eagles".

Cultural evening performance at Li Po Chun United World College of Hong Kong. The large banner overlooking the College's central courtyard lists the College's core values: (i) international and intercultural understanding; (ii) celebration of difference; (iii) personal responsibility and integrity; (iv) mutual responsibility and respect; (v) compassion and service; (vi) respect for the environment; (vii) a sense of idealism; (viii) personal challenge; and (ix) action and personal example.

"It's fun to play military games and beat up Americans" is the slogan on this wall display on a staircase landing in the Kindergarten on Chonsamri Co-operative farm, near Kangsŏ, North Korea.

The external walls of the National Institute for Zorig Chusam (a specialist high school for the visual arts in Thimpu, Bhutan) outline the school's commitment to its five core values: (i) quality; (ii) life-long learning; (iii) enterprise, (iv) dignity of labour; and (v) integrity.

Every school has both stated and unstated organisational values that are derived from their beliefs and assumptions about the world, but not every school makes these values a focus of their daily operations. The common element of these four schools shown above is that their well-considered values positions are so highly visible that they cannot be ignored by any teacher or student in the institution. When values can be expressed clearly and authentically in a way that goes to the heart of the school's purpose, it touches people,

This is how the school's values can (as described above) drive resource allocation, both human and financial. Potential parents and students, potential new staff, and even potential new board members, are always interested in what a school stands for. If they can go to the website or browse the school's publications and find a strong statement of values that is supported by a clear mission statement, they are very likely to want to be involved with the school. It may even lead some altruistic individuals to donate money to the school because they are excited by finding a set of values which they share with passion.

Values attract people to schools in ways that more logically oriented documentation such as organisational charts, the model of strategic change, the qualifications list of the staff and the school's history are unlikely to achieve. Schools are institutions where 'heart decisions' often outweigh 'head decisions' because the futures of children are involved.

Values are especially important in attracting suitable new people to join the board. Very few people sign up to serve on a school board because they are excited about the job description or the list of responsibilities. They typically agree to join because they share a set of values and feel a passionate commitment to the mission (enduring purpose) of the school and its immediate vision to accomplish that mission.

It follows from this that the board should periodically review its own performance, not simply in terms of fulfilling its fiduciary and other duties, but especially with respect to its progress and impact in identifying, articulating, promoting and furthering the school's core values. When goals are set for the coming year, an important focus should be exploring practical, intentional, effective ways in which the core values will be advanced.

What makes an excellent values statement? The first point to note is that values are not the same as virtues. Some of the values statements in the photos above confuse the two terms because they include virtues such as kindness and compassion; characteristics which are somewhat generic and which lack a challenge through action.

A strong values statement will be fundamentally unique to the school; it will help to define its identity.

It will embrace the essential characteristics of the school, including its beliefs and assumptions, as well as being somewhat challenging in that it invites the reader to want to find out more about what it means for them.

It will also include the organisational behaviours to which the school commits itself. This will include the ways in which members of the school community will interact with each other as well as ways in the school will interact with the outside world.

It will outline the qualities that make those within the school proud to be a part of the organisation.

Finally, the values statement should be simple, readable, and easy to remember.

Of course, values statements do not write themselves. The process of formulating a strong values statement may seem long and excruciating, especially for board members who are more comfortable analysing balance sheets or stock market reports. Nonetheless, the process of getting a values statement right is one of the most important tasks a board can undertake; it is right up there with recruiting a new Principal in its importance for determining the school's future.

Ideally, to prepare a values statement, a board would begin by assembling a group of people who really understand what the school's purpose includes and display a genuine passion for that mission. This group should comprise just six to ten people drawn from a diverse mix of board members, senior and middle leaders, teaching and non-teaching staff, plus some students and parents. The need for diversity arises because greater diversity increases the range of perspectives offered, and research consistently demonstrates that diverse groups make better (more sustainable, more authentically transformative) decisions than more uniform groups.

The exercise would begin remotely before anyone gathers as a group. After appointing a facilitator to guide the process, the first step is to invite each member of the group – individually at home – to write down (or type) their views on questions such as:

a. why did you first get involved with this school?

b. what do you think are the school's most distinctive features?

c. why do you think people at this school are so happy to be involved?

d. why do you think developing a values statement is so important? and

e. what core values do you personally bring to this discussion?

The value of starting the process on an individual basis is to maximise the originality and creativity of the initial input, avoiding the 'groupthink' dynamic that often occurs in meetings where the first response may steer (or divert) the direction of the ensuing conversation.

All participants then send their answers to the group's facilitator who collates, documents and then distributes the collated responses to each member of the group. This provides everyone with a chance to read and reflect on everyone else's responses at their leisure.

After everyone had a chance to read each other's individual perspectives, the group is assembled for the first time face-to-face and invited to discuss the document that was circulated. Typically, this meeting lasts for about three hours, and is usually highly productive provided everyone has read the collated document before the gathering. Everyone has the opportunity to speak, the discussion is noted, and the expected outcome is a highly effective statement of the school's core values.

I have found that people love being a part of these types of conversations, especially once the momentum gets underway. This applies especially to board members who find they have been freed from routine discussions about fiduciary duties and balance sheets to progress to the things that really matter – the invisible values that define the school's identity.

I'm sure Einstein and Saint-Exupéry would have predicted this, just as I suspect they would have enjoyed participating in a generative discussion to develop your school's vision statement.

Insight 112

What is Truth?

"What is Truth?". I'm sure Pontius Pilate was not the first person to ask that question as he interrogated Jesus Christ (John 18:38). He was almost certainly following the tradition of Greek philosophers such as Socrates, Plato and Aristotle, and the question continues to engage thinkers – and school leaders – today.

Why should we care about having a serious discussion to understand truth? We should because simply complaining about post-truth, or fake news in the abstract, without attempting to define what truth really means, and without examining actionable responses, does not ease our society's emerging culture war. It inflames it.

As a response to this challenge, I would like to offer two personal experiences that relate to this question before circling back to its significance for school boards and senior managers.

Every time I visit Pyongyang, North Korea's capital city, I try to visit the Grand People's Study House. Located in the heart of the city on Kim Il Sung Square, and by far the largest and most extravagant building in this key central location, the Grand People's Study House serves as both the nation's central library and an adult education centre.

The statistics of the building (600 rooms) and the collection of books (some 30 million books, 60% of which are in foreign languages) were mind-boggling. Unusually in North Korea, it has access to the nationally developed intranet (although not the global internet of course).

I recall one visit where I visited a number of reading rooms, a lecture hall and other facilities, all decorated with huge portraits of Kim Il Sung and Kim Jong Il overlooking those who were seated below, before being invited into an English language class. After first observing the class, I was encouraged to engage in small group conversations with the students, which was informative, enjoyable and impressive for the high standard of English spoken by many of the students. I really had put on my thinking cap as I was asked questions such as "what is the difference between a shopping mall and a department store?", "in what ways are theme parks different from amusement parks or fun fairs?" and "why would someone want an electronic organiser when they have a mobile phone?". These students were not the mindless robotic images that are frustratingly and wrongly portrayed so often by the foreign press.

One facility in the Grand People's Study House that particularly appealed to me was the 'ask the expert room'. The idea is that if anyone has any questions about what they are reading or studying, they can go to this special room and ask "an expert who knows everything" about the subject. On the day of my visit, I decided to use this service, as it is not every day that one has the opportunity to speak with "an expert who knows everything". I found the "expert, seemingly quite lonely in his large, spartan office.

I was told the "expert who knows everything" would be able to answer any question, so I decided to pose Pilate's question – "What is Truth?"

He seemed very puzzled by the question. I quickly got the idea that this question is not commonly discussed in North Korea. He furrowed his brow, shuffled in his chair, and after what seemed like an excessively protracted delay responded simply with **"Such questions** *should not exist"*. And that was the end of our discussion on the matter.

This experience in Pyongyang contrasts markedly with the second personal experience I would like to share.

In 1993 I was attending the annual conference of Heads of International Baccalaureate (IB) schools in Buenos Aires, Argentina. In one of the sessions, each of the Vice-Chancellors of Argentine universities was asked to speak for about 5 minutes on the skills that he/she believed schools should be doing better to prepare students more adequately for university. Some spoke about global awareness, some about time management, some about maths and science skills, and so on. The responses were illuminating and well-received.

But one response made an especially deep impression on me, and I suspect upon everyone present. One Vice-Chancellor stood up, looked at us, spoke just one sentence, and sat down again. I have never forgotten this sentence, which was his entire speech (it is not often that I memorise someone's entire speech!).

He simply said this: *"We need students who understand the difference between truth and consensus"*.

This is not the place for a detailed treatise on truth. The essence of the difference, however, is this:

In the **Correspondence Theory of Truth**, a statement is true if and only if it corresponds to a fact. The fact should be independent of language, society and culture. Therefore, "Grass is green" is true if and only if the grass is green.

Truth thus depends on how things are, factually, in the world, not on what an authority says is true or how a person feels. This was the basis of the scientific revolution in the 17th century.

On the other hand, this notion of truth contains some shortcomings. For example, we do not always have enough information to know whether something is a fact. Furthermore, correspondence can't be perfect because of the gap between language and the world. Moreover, truth can't really be determined in isolation from other propositions.

In the **Coherence Theory of Truth**, a statement is true if it is consistent with other true statements within a belief system. Whereas Correspondence truth-seekers go out and look for evidence, adherents of coherence truth sit and think about consistency. Therefore, in the coherence theory of truth, the statement "the world is flat" was once true because it conformed to the broad consensus of how people viewed the world, but it is no longer true.

The Coherence Theory of Truth is a useful approach in legal cases (and school discipline investigations) where all the facts may not be not known. It is effective in situations where empirical evidence may be impossible to obtain or measure, such as the evidence underpinning a religious belief.

However, this notion of truth also contains some shortcomings. For instance, coherence may be necessary for truth, but it is not sufficient. Fairy tales may be coherent but they are not true. Furthermore, any crazy belief or lie can be made to appear coherent and gain consensus if truth is reduced to the level of an opinion poll.

Of course, correspondence and coherence are not the only approaches to finding truth, and other less common approaches include **pragmatism**, **fundamentalism** and **relativism**. Like correspondence and coherence, these approaches also have their own advantages and disadvantages.

The Correspondence Theory of Truth

- A statement is true if and only if it corresponds to a fact.
- The fact should be independent of language, society and culture.
- "Grass is green" is true if and only if the grass the green.
- People who hold the correspondence theory of truth are called REALISTS.

The Coherence Theory of Truth

- A statement is true if it is consistent with other true statements within a belief system.
- People who hold the coherence theory of truth are called ANTI-REALISTS.
- Whereas realists *go out and look for evidence*, anti-realists *sit and think about consistency*.
- For an anti-realist, the statement "the world is flat" was once true because it conformed to the broad consensus of how people viewed the world, but it is no longer true.

The Pragmatic Theory of Truth

- A statement is true if it is useful or works in practice.
- People who hold the pragmatic theory of truth are called PRAGMATISTS.
- Pragmatism does not concern itself with facts or coherence.
- "If it works, it must be true".

Can we know the truth?

You could develop a 3-part test of truth based on the 3 theories of truth by asking:

1. Does it reflect the facts?
2. Is it coherent?
3. Does it work in practice?

School boards and leaders have an obligation to seek truth and to operate within its parameters. As George Orwell said, **"In a time of universal deceit, telling the truth is a revolutionary act"**. But which approach, or approaches, should be followed to discern authentic truth – and in which circumstances?

Given society's accelerating drift towards "post-truth" and "fake news", understanding truth has never been more important.

Insight 113

What new board members should know

Joining a school board can be quite overwhelming, especially at first. It is understandably intimidating to be presented with huge pile of paper (or large digitised files) containing the board's handbook of policies and procedures, minutes of past meetings, financial statements, organisational charts, and so on, together with your obligatory "welcome to the board" card (or e-mail).

Burdensome as these may appear, these documents are necessary because becoming a board member means accepting legal duties and potential liabilities. Being fully informed is not a luxury; it is an expectation.

Let's imagine that you have taken up your place as a new board member, you have received, read and understood the documents, and hopefully have had a tour of the school with the opportunity to meet key people, have some informal conversations and "sniff the mood" of the campus.

You have realised that there will be more work than you had expected, more responsibility than you had been given to understand,

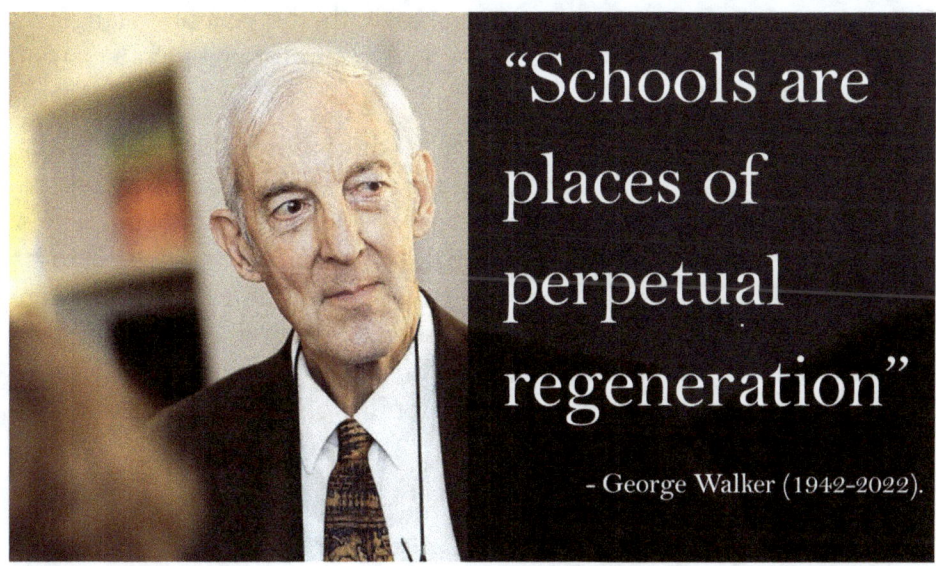

"Schools are places of perpetual regeneration"

- George Walker (1942-2022).

and potentially more frustrations than you might have anticipated. On the other hand, you can see real potential for making positive, substantial and lasting changes that will bring life-enhancing benefits to countless young people whose education has been entrusted to the school by their parents.

Wow! What a joy, privilege and honour you have!

So what is next? I suggest that there are ten things a new board member should know and understand.

1. Joining the board of an independent school is a sacrificial act of servant leadership that is exclusively for the benefit of others. You are called to serve, not to be flattered. Any board member who disagrees with that assertion should probably not be occupying a place at the table.

2. The perspective you bring to the Board is just as valuable at your first board meeting as your 100th meeting – perhaps more so because your views are fresh and untainted by board procedures and protocols, or by the 'comfort zones' that long-standing board members may have erected around themselves.

3. The board is not a disassociated attachment to the school. The board is the future-focussed, mission-driven, strategy-initiating driver and protector of the school's direction and identity. It is an active partner that oversees and monitors the school's day-to-day management and operations, which are responsibilities delegated by the Board to the Principal. In other words, the board is a team player that functions in partnership with the school's staff in a manner that is somewhat akin to the captain (or chief strategist) of the team.

4. It is important that you receive a thorough orientation to the board. This should include coverage of the culture of the school, an intensive explanation of the governance vs management boundaries of decision-making, an explanation of board responsibilities, personal and participation expectations, and important program and administrative information, that enable new trustees to perform effectively without undue delay. Additionally, new board members should sign the board's standard "conflict of interest" and "code of conduct" documents.

5. Although the board's authority is collective (which means it can only make formal decisions when its members gather in a formal meeting with a quorum), informal board work continues between meetings. For example, it is usually expected that board members will be advocates (or even evangelists) for the school when appropriate as they network socially or at work.

6. You are expected to contribute to board solidarity by maintaining the confidentiality of board discussions and publicly support board decisions, irrespective of your personal feelings or how you voted during a board meeting. If you can't publicly support a decision the board has made, your only recourse is to resign from the board.

7. As a board member, many staff and others in the school community are likely to treat you a little differently from your pre-membership existence. They may be more wary of you, perhaps more fearful of you, or maybe even more respectful. It is important that you understand that your authority as a board member exists only when the board meets (as the board's authority is collective), and you cannot make statements (or decisions!) on behalf of the board as an individual. Membership of the school board is never a reason to bully, threaten or abuse members of the school community – remember, servant leadership with unwavering humility is the key.

8. If you need to miss a meeting, you should ensure your apologies are received and recorded. If you are likely to miss two or more meetings in a row, you should advise the Board Chair as a courtesy. Some boards have provisions for automatic removal of board members who miss two meetings without receiving prior dispensation from the Board Chair.

9. It is essential (indeed, a legal requirement) that you avoid situations where your personal interest or the interests of a relative or interests of a close associate may conflict directly or indirectly with board decisions, whether actual, perceived or potential. Any such conflict of interest must be declared and recorded.

10. And finally, enjoy it! There can be few more important or rewarding tasks than building the future of our world. As a board member, you have the capacity to shape that future.

Insight 114

When should board members step down?

Most boards consider the recruitment of new members very carefully. However, a more difficult conversation arises on the question of when a board member should retire or step down.

Board members typically leave school boards for one of four reasons:

Reason 1: Voluntary resignation

This is by far the easiest and most common way that board members leave school boards. The board member decides that it's time and announces that he or she will not seek re-election or re-appointment. The reason that the decision is made by the board member is usually personal – it may be fatigue, it might be family pressures, it may be illness, or it may simply be to make room for 'new blood'. Typically, such departures are accompanied by warm speeches of appreciation and sorrow at the loss of expertise, and everyone remains friends in good standing.

Reason 2: Term limits

Term limits for school boards are less common in some countries (such as Australia) than in others (such as the United States). In essence, term limits arise when a board adopts a policy that requires board members to retire when they have served a pre-set number of terms (such as three 3-year terms). Sometimes, term-limit policies may include specific exceptions, such as when a Chair who has reached the term limit may be permitted to remain one extra term to provide institutional memory and support during a new chair's first term of office. Research into best practice indicates that board effectiveness is enhanced on boards that have introduced term limits.

Reason 3: Unsatisfactory performance by a board member

It is good practice to conduct a performance review of each board member annually. This is additional to and separate from the more encompassing full review of the board's performance as a single entity that is conducted regularly (such as biennially). The aim of individual board member reviews is emphatically not to find fault or grounds for criticism, but to explore emerging areas of interest where board members can contribute effectively and thus avoid drifting into "comfort zone" mentality.

It rarely happens, but ideally the Board Chair should sit down over a coffee with each board member individually at the start of each year and ask how they intend to advance the school's strategic vision in the coming year. At the end of the same year, the Chair would have a follow-up one-on-one chat with each board member to review the year and set goals for the coming year. If the chat reveals that the board member has had no impact during the year, the Chair can and should ease out that member.

More common than the annual chat with the Chair is an anonymous survey of each board member to reflect upon their own performance, together with the performance of the chair and each of their fellow board members. The criteria for such a survey will vary from school board to school board, but a sound list of 20 characteristics of effective board members that emerges from evidence-based research would be something like this:

- Has a strong record of punctual attendance at meetings;
- Is thoroughly prepared for meetings;
- Makes an active and positive contribution to the board's work;
- Makes an active, positive contribution to committee(s);
- Understands and can articulate the school's mission;
- Demonstrates support for the Head of School in public;
- Follows correct established communication protocols;
- Maintains the confidentiality of the board;
- Functions in governance, not straying into management;
- Focuses only on interests of the whole school (not personal, not sectional);
- Seeks to serve the students' interests first;
- Has read the Board Handbook and complies with its provisions;
- Has a strong sense of the importance of ethical behaviour;
- Shows respect to every board member;
- Can work with others in a team-like manner;
- Supports board decisions, even if initially disagreeing;
- Absents themselves when there might be a conflict of interest;
- Is visible in the school community;
- Is open-minded, curious, and asks perceptive questions;
- Has strong leadership abilities and/or potential.

Reason 4: Board member removal

Removing a board member against their will is the least common and least comfortable manner for the departure of school board members. It is rightly regarded as a fairly extreme and 'ultimate' action, and is thus exercised rarely and prudently.

Removal of board members is an action reserved for dire circumstances such as violation of legal duties, a failure to participate adequately, repeated unexplained absences from board meetings, failure to fulfil the written set of board expectations or code of conduct, a violation of the duty of confidentiality or public undermining of a board decision.

Board member removal should be undertaken on a 'no surprises' basis, only after formal board member evaluation and/or prior counselling with the Chair.

A question to consider when a board member must be removed is whether there may be a non-board role suitable for this former board member, such as on an advisory committee. Of course, this may not be possible or appropriate depending upon the reason for the removal.

It is essential that boards have policies in place addressing the recruitment, orientation, regular review, term of office and procedures for the removal of board members. These policy provisions must be in place well before they are needed. The worst possible time to consider developing a policy on board member removal for incompetence, inactivity, ineffectiveness, lack of alignment with board priorities or disreputable activity is when the need actually arises.

Insight **115**

You have been asked to join a school board

Imagine you have been approached to join a school board. You are seen as an ideal candidate who could bring a fresh perspective to board discussions. You have done your own due diligence research, and found that you not only understand but embrace the school's Mission and Core Values. Although busy with work and family commitments, you sense that serving on a school board – and especially THIS school board – could enable you to serve others and make a contribution which benefits hundreds of young people whose education has been entrusted to the school. You realise that some people are attracted to sit on school boards because it looks good on their CVs, but ego is not a factor in your thinking. Rather, you wholeheartedly embrace the idea that being on a school board is a privilege of service to others.

You have been invited to the school for a tour of the campus. Although you expect to see Grade 1 students who ooze cuteness, meet some specially selected celebrity teachers and spend time in the school's newest and most impressive facilities, the focus of your visit

will be a discussion with the Principal and the Board Chair over coffee and cakes prepared and served by some senior Home Science students.

This meeting will present you with a valuable opportunity to observe at first-hand what is usually regarded as "the most important relationship in the school" – the interaction between the Board Chair and the Principal. For example, if the Board Chair hands the task of answering most of the questions over to the Principal, or if the Principal is excessively deferential to the Board Chair, that should be a warning sign that their working relationship lacks the healthy balance required for effective Board-Management relations.

You already understand that any school thrives only when its board is well-led and its day-to-day operations are well-managed. Furthermore, you believe that an effective board is measured not only by statistics, but by its organisation as a learning environment that ensures diverse voices and perspectives are heard and treated with respect.

As someone who is innately curious about everything in life and loves to ask questions, you have decided to prepare for your visit to the school by posing some questions to the Principal and the Board Chair. Some of your questions will be a continuation of your due diligence enquiries, such as the state of the school's finances, its level of debt, its financial viability, its known legal and financial risks, and so on. This discussion does not have to be a boring, mechanical exercise, and might even include a question such as "if the school received an anonymous donation of $25 million next month, what would you do with it?'.

You hope to be inspired by the school and its board, so you have thought of several other questions that you would like to ask the Board Chair in the presence of the Principal. You don't know ahead of time whether you will ask them all because you don't yet know the dynamics of your meeting, but you want to be prepared. So, depending on how the meeting proceeds, these are some of the questions you may ask:

1. "How long have you been Board Chair, and when does your term of office expire?" The answer to this question should initiate a discussion about board stability, composition, and term limits.
2. "What is the board's process for managing the succession of board positions and for the Principal's position?" This question should open up a discussion on how this relates to the desired skills matrix

and priorities for populating the board. It may also allow a frank discussion about the Principal's future plans; if not, any evasive responses may be revealing in themselves.

3. "As Board Chair, how do you manage a board that comprises a diverse set of volunteers?" After a brief description of board members' diversity, this question should provide some insight into board discipline and whether the Chair seems capable of admonishing miscreant board members if, and when, required. This is a key skill in managing effective, efficient, productive, respectful board meetings.

4. "Why do you serve as Board Chair when it is a huge amount of work that is often thankless and done out of sight of others?" This question is designed to gain a personal insight into the Board Chair's personality, motivation, commitment and priorities.

5. "Related to the previous question, how do you measure your own success and the success of the board?" This question should reveal something about the effectiveness of the board's processes for internal and external performance reviews, both of the board as a whole and of individual board members. It should also reveal the extent to which board members feel a sense of belonging and commitment to their board work.

6. "Do you feel board members receive sufficient professional development in governance to perform their tasks effectively?" Whether the answer to this question is 'yes' or 'no', it should provide some important insights into the board's expectations and professionalism.

7. "What do you see as the biggest challenges that the board needs to address in the foreseeable future?" The answer to that question will probably take the rest of the afternoon!

Of course, you may want to share these questions with the Board Chair before your visit to the school to avoid any sense of entrapment. After all, most boards work that operate effectively do so in a transparent, conversational environment of "no surprises" that builds trust and mutual respect; you would probably want to model that same approach as a prospective board member.

Fast forward a few weeks. The school visit went well. You were more excited than you expected to be by the school. As soon as you stepped foot on the campus you were impressed by the relationships you witnessed where students and staff greeted one another as they

walked around. You even saw an older student stop and look after a younger student who had tripped and fallen over. More than any statistical data, these observations told you the school was a safe, happy, respectful environment that staff and students enjoyed being in.

Your meeting with the Principal and Board Chair proved to be a relaxed, almost fun-filled exchange of ideas, hopes and aspirations. You raised a few minor concerns, and these were effectively addressed by the Board Chair and the Principal in a reassuringly co-operative demonstration of teamwork. You agreed to join the board, and to paraphrase the traditional ending a fairy tales, everyone lived happily ever after.

Except – life on school boards is never a fairy tale. The expectation that every experience serving on a school board will be sweetness and light leads to unrealistic, false hopes and inevitably to disappointment. Board service is not the place to find blissful paradise, nor should it be. Board service is selfless commitment to others, a relentless search for truth, a willingness to grapple with the complexity of new and challenging situations, and an unwavering obligation to advance the Mission of the school. It is "a burden of responsibility" that quite literally helps to shape the future of our society.

There are very few forms of service that have such huge potential to make a positive impact upon our future than serving on a school board.

About the author

Dr Stephen Codrington established Optimal School Governance in 2015 as a cutting-edge specialist service to support school boards seeking to govern effectively according to recognised best practice. Since that time he has worked with hundreds of school leaders and board members.

Before establishing this service, Stephen served for 25 years as the Head of five schools in four countries – Australia, New Zealand, Hong Kong and the United States. During that period, as well as serving on the boards of his own schools, he also worked with many other schools (including as an accreditation officer) through organisations such as the Council of International Schools, United World Colleges, the International Baccalaureate, the Western Association of Schools and Colleges, and the Independent Schools Association of the Southwest. He has developed strategic plans for schools, helped with board reviews and restructuring, conducted performance appraisals of senior and middle management, and observed boards at their best and at their worst.

As a result of his diverse experiences, Stephen developed a deep appreciation for the fundamental importance of effective governance in schools. His current work reflects his passion for making school environments as supportive as possible for the flourishing of young hearts and minds. He currently serves as the Chair of the board of Djarragun College (Cairns, Australia), Australia's largest independent school for Aboriginal and Torres Strait Islander students.

During his quarter-century of school headships, Stephen served as the Head of schools that are boarding and day schools, national and international,

single-sex and co-educational, religious and secular, including all age groups, ranging in size from 256 to 1505. The schools where he served as Head were:
- St Paul's Grammar School (Sydney, Australia)
- Kristin School (Auckland, New Zealand)
- Prince Alfred College (Adelaide, Australia)
- Li Po Chun United World College (Hong Kong, China)
- The Awty International School (Houston, Texas, USA)

Stephen has been elected as a Fellow of the Australian College of Educators (ACE), he is a former Chairman of the Heads of Independent Co-educational Schools (HICES), former Vice-President of the Association of Executives of Christian Schools (AECS), and a former President of several academic and teaching associations, including the Geographical Society. In 2014, he was appointed an International Baccalaureate (IB) Ambassador in recognition of his high standing in international education.

His work in and with schools has included financial oversight, fundraising, advising and guiding boards through challenging times, public speaking, hiring faculty, problem solving, strategic planning, cultural and social adaptability, presentation skills, diplomacy, and – reflecting his own view of the importance of education in forming young lives – passionate advocacy for the power of education to transform our world.

From 2018 to 2022, Stephen worked with Alphacrucis College in the position of Director of School Governance and Leadership Development. In this role, he conducted research, professional development and school reviews through the Centre for the Future of Schooling, a research centre within Alphacrucis College. He also spearheaded a self-funded project to raise the quality of teacher training across Sub-Saharan Africa in partnership with several local education providers.

Stephen's wider experience in education includes many years of service as a senior IB examiner, including five years as an IB Deputy Chief Examiner. He is the author of 71 books, including 'Planet Geography', the first text written specifically to support IBDP Geography, which is now in its 9th edition as a set of ten books. His research has taken him to visits in almost 170 countries.

Stephen has spoken widely at various conferences and venues on themes such as change management in schools, best practice in education, building authentic internationalism in schools, and building international links in education. Some of Stephen's most popular presentations include his own personal educational experiences in such diverse locations as North Korea, East Africa, the former Soviet republics of Central Asia, China and Cambodia.

Stephen maintains a personal website at www.stephencodrington.com.

Index

A

Accountability, 68, 69, 164, 181, 193, 399, 459, 471, 474, 480, 489, 510, 511
Accreditation, 29, 56, 154, 232, 368, 381, 439, 454
Adaptive governance, 50, 51-52
Admissions, 92, 413, 414
Advice
 for new Principals, 13-17
 historical (1932), 18-23
Aesthetics, 144, 256
Agendas, board meeting, 95, 346, 361, 362, 401, 439, 447
AI (Artificial Intelligence), 24-28, 491
Alignment
 board culture and management, 94, 96-97
 mission and values, 251, 317, 326, 358, 369, 405, 451, 513
Alumni, 68, 73, 153, 225, 226, 360, 450, 457, 460, 467, 485
Antifragility, 38-41, 156-159
Anxiety, 262, 365, 415
Appraisal *See Evaluation; Performance reviews*
Aristotle, 101-102, 138, 222, 490, 504
Arnold, Dr Thomas, 21
Artificial Intelligence *See AI*
Assessment, 27, 77, 193, 317, 322, 325, 335, 369, 470
Authentic leadership, 42-44, 427
Authenticity, 74, 137, 142, 251, 257, 322, 323, 341, 344, 428, 470, 476, 490, 501
Authority, 21, 44, 59, 60, 66, 68, 85, 89, 105, 106, 112, 149, 153, 219, 221, 225, 227, 257, 304, 308, 310, 340, 345, 367, 368, 372, 374, 408, 412, 428, 451, 467, 469, 474, 488, 511
Autonomy, 31, 45-49, 99, 153, 220, 251

B

Bassett, Pat, 306
Bias, 25, 148, 161, 265, 393, 482, 490

Black Swan events, 50-52
Blame, 29, 66, 69, 70, 97, 179, 223, 259, 320, 378, 379, 391
Board (School)
 agendas, 95, 346, 361, 362, 401, 439, 447
 boredom, 400-403
 Chair, 15, 36, 62, 88, 89, 93, 94, 115, 126, 146-151, 166, 168, 225, 226, 241, 287, 290, 303, 306, 320, 353, 354, 355, 362, 368, 369, 372, 374, 375, 390, 420-423, 444, 447, 460, 467, 476, 480, 490, 513, 514, 515, 517, 518
 committees, 56, 62, 87, 89-93, 153, 225, 242, 277, 278, 355, 447, 453, 514
 community relationship, 459-461
 composition, 86, 164-165, 265, 268, 269, 354, 412, 517
 confidentiality, 56, 88, 152, 226, 308, 320, 360, 365, 394, 510, 511, 514
 disengagement, 35-37
 diversity, 164-165, 267, 268, 306, 366, 510, 517
 donations by members, 435-437
 dysfunction, 83, 135, 166-170, 227, 372, 374, 375, 460
 effectiveness, 29, 30, 36, 83, 85, 86, 87, 89, 135, 154, 164, 171-172, 227, 241, 243, 255, 264, 265, 269, 277, 278, 292, 311, 312, 358, 381, 438, 444, 447, 448, 513
 engagement, 35-37
 evaluation, 30, 56, 86, 87, 92, 95, 154, 225, 312, 375, 448, 513, 514
 innovation, 438-439
 manuals, 53-58, 86, 514
 meetings, 35, 36, 56, 59, 61, 62, 70, 83, 84, 86, 89, 93, 95, 96, 97, 100, 115, 116, 118, 120, 122, 123, 126, 127, 128, 129, 130, 131, 134, 146, 147, 148, 149, 150, 151, 154, 160, 161, 162, 166, 198, 200, 213, 214, 225, 226, 228, 240-243, 275, 276, 278, 297-299, 300, 301, 304, 308, 320, 355, 360, 361, 362, 366, 368, 369, 392, 400-403, 408, 420, 422, 423, 447, 452, 457, 460, 462, 467, 471, 475, 476, 480, 484, 490, 511, 514, 515, 517

members (new), 13, 53, 55, 86, 98, 123, 278, 306, 439, 447, 509-511, 513
members (stepping down), 167, 292, 447, 512-515
parents as members, 366-370
professional development, 79, 81, 86, 87, 242, 381, 402
recruitment, 7, 97, 164, 292, 306, 435, 512, 515
responsibility, 29-30, 56, 60, 61, 63, 70, 164, 224, 306, 368, 372, 378, 379, 412, 450, 474, 510
role, 59-64, 96, 104, 115, 224, 225, 305, 311, 312, 320, 360, 368, 393, 401, 402, 405, 444, 462, 468, 474-476, 510, 513
size, 276-278
staff interaction, 59-64
term limits, 11, 278, 292, 446-449, 479, 513, 517
Boeing, 65-71, 189, 358
Bok, Sissela, 85, 488
Bono (Paul Hewson), 248, 252
Branding, 72-74, 78
Budget, 26, 57, 89, 92, 96, 148, 229, 256, 333, 377, 385, 390, 453
Busby, Dr Richard, 21

C

Cameron, William Bruce, 323, 324
Ceausescu, Nicolae, 284, 286-293
Change management, 94, 132, 135, 141, 152, 154, 221, 225, 227, 242, 257, 259, 260, 261, 262, 267, 268, 341, 344, 351, 358, 418, 438, 440, 441, 453, 476, 480, 517, 521
ChatGPT, 24-28, 202
Chiat, Jay, 45, 49
Child protection, 56, 308, 413
Cicero, 103, 104, 114
Cialdini, Robert, 112
Civility, 83-85, 135, 200, 297
Clarity, 34, 66, 70, 85, 102, 104, 110, 111, 123, 135, 147, 148, 151, 152, 192, 193, 265, 267, 307, 352, 355, 390, 391, 465, 504, 511
Clear, James, 237, 349
Cloke, Kenneth, 118, 120
Cobra Effect, 337-338
Code of Conduct/Practice, 56, 86-88, 435, 510, 515
Codrington, Graeme, 244, 246
Codrington, Stephen, 520-521
CODM (Consensus-Oriented Decision-Making), 131-132
Coherence Theory of Truth, 493, 507
Collaboration, 51, 55, 64, 70, 85, 119, 160, 172, 181, 212, 261, 271, 315, 318, 372, 374, 379, 386, 423, 467, 471
Collegiality, 135-137
Committees *See Board committees*
Communication, 36, 61, 63, 64, 66, 68, 70, 88, 90, 96, 97, 101-114, 146, 147, 148, 149, 189, 191, 193, 197, 198, 200, 201, 202, 205, 220, 221, 225, 226, 233, 234, 235, 236, 250, 266, 267, 291, 297-299, 303, 308, 310, 320, 326, 330, 340, 341, 351, 358, 359, 360, 363, 365, 368, 369, 386, 390, 401, 402, 403, 450, 457, 460, 461, 475, 501, 503, 511
Community
board relationship with, 459-461
engagement, 94, 315, 318, 386, 401
school as, 75-78, 154, 213, 242, 260, 261, 271, 278, 311, 320, 325, 340, 341, 347, 352, 360, 368, 374, 399, 401, 412, 450, 457, 460, 467, 476, 480, 485, 490, 511
Compassion, 34, 105, 157, 177, 209, 499, 501
Compliance, 31, 39, 55, 61, 68, 69, 99, 125, 149, 224, 225, 351, 392, 454, 470, 474, 480, 514
Confidentiality *See Board confidentiality*
Conflict of interest, 24-25, 56, 88, 121-125, 213, 214, 306, 359, 366, 368, 370, 396, 397, 490, 510, 511, 514
Conflict resolution, 87, 115-120, 133, 148, 320
Confucius, 102
Congeniality, 135-137
Consensus, 21, 76, 85, 119, 120, 123, 126-134, 135, 146, 147, 151, 213, 251, 261, 278, 298, 325, 354, 390, 392, 476, 489, 493, 494, 507
Consultants, 30, 94, 114, 141, 290, 308, 341, 375, 393, 442, 462
Contracts, 25, 57, 122, 148, 225, 241, 291, 308, 396, 399, 413, 421, 442, 452, 453
Correspondence Theory of Truth, 493, 507
Courage, 138-142, 209, 303, 352, 374, 386, 408, 411
Crises, 7, 50, 51, 61, 68, 70, 87, 166, 167, 168, 170, 213, 242, 286, 308, 319-321, 358, 385, 390, 453, 490, 507

Culture
  board, 94, 96-97
  organisational/school, 31-34, 44, 62, 70, 75, 78, 87, 94, 95, 135, 136, 137, 153, 154, 159, 173, 181-185, 193, 202, 216, 220, 244, 257, 261, 262, 266, 267, 268, 271, 311, 337, 339-343, 345, 359, 372, 374, 376, 379, 386, 394, 408, 411, 428, 456, 470, 471, 472, 481, 488, 489, 491, 501, 507, 510
  Curriculum, 26, 61, 94, 148, 154, 166, 204, 221, 225, 246, 261, 271, 305, 366, 369, 393, 418, 450

D

Data, 40, 95, 102, 114, 128, 130, 132, 256, 311, 312, 323, 324, 338, 340, 351, 356, 358, 481, 483, 490, 508, 517
De Bono, Edward, 128, 367
Dead Horse Theory, 407-411
Debating skills, 146-151
Decision-making, 25, 30, 33, 36, 51, 59, 62, 68, 83, 85, 87, 89, 90, 91, 95, 101, 102, 104, 112, 113, 115, 121, 123, 126, 127, 130, 131, 132, 135, 147, 148, 152, 154, 156, 164, 168, 170, 172, 211, 212, 213, 214, 221, 224, 225, 227, 231, 241, 251, 261, 265, 267, 269, 271, 303, 306, 311, 314, 315, 316, 317, 320, 322, 323, 338, 344, 346, 351, 358, 359, 372, 374, 381, 393, 395, 398, 399, 401, 408, 411, 412, 414, 418, 450, 455, 457, 474, 480, 482, 493, 501, 504, 510, 511, 515
Delegation, 36, 60, 91, 224, 225, 277, 354, 362, 375, 454, 467, 486, 487
Delphi Technique, 130-131, 132
Derrida, Jacques, 152, 155
Digital age/tools, 53-58, 154, 189, 191, 195, 202, 217, 219, 220, 305
Dismissal *See Firing employees*
Diversity, 109, 115, 164-165, 217, 222, 251, 265, 267, 268, 269, 306, 318, 333, 341, 342, 366, 401, 406, 418, 435, 455, 502, 510, 517
Documentation, 53, 54, 55, 57, 58, 69, 88, 123, 124, 208, 209, 256, 392, 501
Donations *See Board donations; Fundraising*
Dynamic Facilitation, 132

E

Education, future of, 24, 27, 28, 415
Effectiveness *See Board effectiveness*
Effort grades, 173-176
Ego, 83, 161, 345, 376, 428, 516
Einstein, Albert, 498, 503
Empathy, 34, 177-180, 181-185, 422
Engagement *See Board engagement; Community engagement*
Enrolment, 45, 74, 92, 166, 210, 255, 256, 337, 430, 431, 476, 498
Environment *See Sustainability*
Equality, 279-283
Equity, 271, 279-283
Erikson, Erik, 249
Ethics, 31, 44, 56, 63, 68, 69, 86, 87, 88, 94, 99, 102, 103, 107, 112, 123, 135, 142, 152, 154, 168, 171, 186-188, 190, 192, 212, 221, 224, 225, 226, 231, 250, 257, 303, 308, 317, 323, 325, 328, 341, 354, 359, 399, 413, 418, 428, 452, 490, 507, 514
Euphemisms, 66, 189-193
Evaluation
  board, 30, 56, 86, 87, 92, 95, 154, 225, 312, 375, 448, 513, 514
  Principal, 62, 86, 92, 225, 352-356
  staff, 57, 193, 225, 413
Evidentiality, 494, 495
Excellence, 82, 87, 135, 137, 138, 154, 171, 172, 174, 175, 204, 205, 225, 265, 322, 323, 355, 405, 406, 418, 423, 428, 438, 442, 450, 452
Exit, Voice, Loyalty, 166-170
Expectations, 26, 31-34, 69, 87, 94, 98, 150, 219, 221, 251, 266, 267, 306, 324, 365, 366, 369, 405, 420, 428, 440, 450, 452, 470, 510, 513, 515, 517
Expert help, 169, 170

F

F-shaped reading, 194-197
Fairness, 24, 27, 87, 88, 148, 209, 279-283, 396, 488, 489
Fees *See Tuition fees*
Finance, 57, 61, 62, 68, 70, 92, 94, 100, 122, 148, 150, 151, 161, 164, 185, 186, 190, 203-205, 213, 224, 226, 231, 254, 255, 256, 278, 311, 323, 328, 335, 351, 356, 359, 362, 384-386, 392, 413, 418, 422,

435, 450, 452, 467, 474, 498, 501, 509, 517
Firing employees, 143-145, 206-209, 406, 444, 453
Free riding, 210-214
Fundraising, 61, 92, 385, 435, 453
Future of education, 24, 27, 28, 415

G

Generational differences, 215-222
Governance
  adaptive, 50, 51-52
  vs. governing, 231-232
  vs. management, 42-44, 59-64, 86, 96, 152, 224, 231, 303, 311, 312, 320, 360, 361, 362, 368, 369, 375, 401, 439, 460, 474-476, 510, 514
Gradients of Agreement, 127-128

H

Hahn, Kurt, 37, 139, 140, 159
Handbooks *See Board manuals*
Harassment, 56, 413
Head of School *See Principal*
Health and safety, 57, 193, 256, 351, 359, 385, 413, 454
Hirschman, Albert, 166, 169
History, 18, 44, 56, 142, 204, 227, 308, 378, 393, 448, 451, 467, 489, 493
Holidays, 33, 451
Honeymoon period, 13, 33, 465, 468

I

Idealism, 13, 248-252, 264, 323, 365, 378, 423, 470, 473
Identity, 33, 34, 72, 73, 75, 76, 77, 143, 152, 159, 249, 250, 251, 267, 268, 317, 323, 325, 326, 345, 363, 368, 374, 412, 415, 435, 471, 498, 501, 503
Ignatius Loyola, 108
Independent schools, 31, 32, 79, 90, 254, 306, 323, 341, 431, 470, 510
Indigenous populations, 63, 219, 222, 341
Innovation, 31, 39, 45, 70, 87, 89, 112, 159, 181, 217, 246, 260, 267, 269, 313, 354, 374, 408, 411, 438-439, 448
Inspiration, 42, 294, 296, 390

Integrity, 25, 44, 68, 87, 88, 90, 102, 107, 108, 125, 150, 169, 177, 213, 224, 231, 249, 250, 322, 328, 359, 393, 406, 423, 428, 457
Intentional Cultural Change, 257-262
Interaction
  board-staff, 59-64
  intercultural, 340, 341, 419, 499
Interim principals, 33, 442, 463-464
  Interviews, 99, 149, 209, 244, 270-275, 308, 330, 395, 432
Isolation, 75, 158, 291, 477, 479

J

Jargon, 189-193
Jesus Christ, 73, 105-106, 107, 344, 427, 504
Job description (Principal), 57, 353

K

Kant, Immanuel, 187, 212
Kelty, Bill, 377, 379, 381
King Jr, Martin Luther, 111, 120
Knowing when to go, 284-296
Knowledge
  common, 261, 289, 290, 291, 296
  shared, 289, 290, 291
KPIs (Key Performance Indicators), 68, 96, 317, 335, 337, 410, 498

L

Language, 24, 56, 110, 114, 146, 152, 160, 189, 191, 193, 200, 266, 267, 297-299, 300-302, 318, 323, 341, 347, 461, 475, 482, 494, 507
Lao Tzu, 44
Leadership
  authentic, 42-44, 427
  ethical, 69, 186-188
  principled, 377-383
  servant, 93, 379, 424-429
  vs. Management, 42-44, 474-476
Learning from mistakes, 70, 158, 375, 376
  Legal issues, 30, 56, 58, 87, 94, 122, 125, 143, 150, 152, 154, 208, 224, 225, 231, 291, 306, 307, 308, 351, 359, 385, 413, 421, 456, 474, 510, 514
Littleford, John, 293, 381

Loyalty, 21, 64, 103, 166-170, 213, 217, 267, 356, 366, 368, 381, 456, 457, 490
Lying, 85, 148, 307-310, 488

M

Management *See Governance vs. Management; Principal*
Manuals *See Board manuals*
March, James, 126
Marks, Howard, 40
Marketing, 33, 34, 45, 58, 72, 78, 92, 255, 408
Measurement, 30, 100, 317, 322-334, 335-338, 413, 483, 518
Mediation, 115-120
Meetings *See Board meetings*
Mental health, 39, 218, 219, 246
Mission, 16, 30, 31, 33, 34, 36, 51, 56, 60, 61, 72, 73, 74, 88, 94, 95, 96, 97, 101, 108, 131, 132, 135, 142, 143, 144, 148, 151, 152, 154, 156, 158, 159, 164, 168, 186, 188, 192, 203, 204, 207, 213, 219, 221, 224, 225, 226, 231, 246, 250, 251, 254, 256, 257, 259, 261, 264, 269, 291, 303, 305, 306, 308, 314, 317, 320, 322, 323, 324, 325, 326, 327, 328, 331, 332, 333, 341, 344-347, 351, 354, 358, 360, 361, 362, 368, 369, 371, 376, 381, 386, 389, 390, 391, 393, 394, 395, 401, 405, 408, 410, 411, 412, 415, 416, 417, 418, 423, 428, 435, 440, 442, 448, 450, 452, 462, 463, 471, 474, 476, 481, 488, 490, 501, 504, 510, 514
Mission drift, 344-347
Mistakes, 39, 70, 142, 158, 237, 251, 286, 372, 375, 376, 406, 409, 428, 472
Morale, 29, 45, 62, 70, 94, 154, 179, 192, 224, 320, 408, 470, 490
Motivation, 31, 97, 173, 174, 197, 209, 213, 273, 274, 304, 305, 351, 365, 381, 388, 429, 470, 473, 518
Motto, 72, 142, 347

N

NAIS (National Association of Independent Schools), 90, 306, 392
Negativity, 29, 74, 162, 170, 192, 206, 218, 235, 257, 326, 341, 358, 363-365, 406, 441, 457
Nepotism, 359
Networking, 56, 212, 305, 448, 468
Normalisation of deviance, 357-359

O

Office design, 45-49
Onboarding *See Board members (new)*
Online meetings/remote work, 26, 198-202, 224, 268, 306, 308
Operationalising vision, 360-362
Oratory, 101-114
Orientation *See Board members (new)*
Orwell, George, 300, 508

P

Parents
  as board members, 366-370
  expectations, 31, 32, 450, 470
  relationships with, 61, 68, 73, 87, 94, 166, 168, 219, 225, 226, 242, 256, 261, 290, 291, 293, 305, 313, 326, 328, 341, 345, 351, 352, 356, 360, 362, 366, 368, 400, 405, 420, 450, 453, 457, 460, 467, 476, 480, 485, 502, 510, 513, 517
Parkinson's Law, 241
Perfectionism, 371-376
Performance reviews
  board, 30, 56, 86, 87, 92, 95, 154, 225, 312, 375, 448, 513, 514
  Principal, 62, 86, 92, 225, 352-356
  staff, 144, 172, 193, 208, 227, 320, 323, 324, 333, 454
Persuasion, 24, 26, 42, 43, 44, 101-114, 146, 148, 151, 189, 191, 209, 273, 307, 341, 453, 490
Pilate, Pontius, 504, 505
Policies, 26, 29, 30, 51, 53, 56, 57, 58, 61, 62, 68, 69, 87, 88, 94, 113, 117, 121, 122, 123, 125, 131, 143, 148, 149, 151, 152, 154, 166, 186, 187, 192, 206, 213, 225, 231, 241, 242, 255, 300, 306, 311, 317, 351, 359, 362, 368, 369, 370, 374, 381, 390, 396, 397, 398, 399, 405, 413, 414, 421, 456, 467, 474, 490, 509, 515
Post-truth, 300, 489, 493, 508
Powell, Colin, 378
Pragmatism, 34, 138, 248-252, 323, 345, 473, 507
Prescott, CJ, 18, 19, 23

Principal (Head of School)
  advice for new, 13-17
  evaluation/performance review, 62, 86, 92, 225, 352-356
  recruitment, 7, 89, 90, 92, 101, 290, 308, 309, 356, 392-395, 405, 435, 441, 442, 444, 458, 501
  relationship with board/chair, 15, 59-64, 96, 97, 115, 116, 172, 224, 225, 226, 227, 290, 291, 311, 360, 362, 365, 367, 368, 372, 421, 422, 427, 467, 468, 474, 476, 517
  role, 14, 15, 16, 17, 33, 43, 44, 57, 59, 60, 61, 62, 63, 86, 89, 90, 92, 94, 96, 97, 99, 115, 126, 135, 140, 142, 143, 145, 151, 152, 153, 154, 156, 158, 159, 161, 166, 167, 168, 169, 170, 172, 173, 176, 177, 178, 180, 181, 185, 186, 187, 188, 191, 194, 197, 200, 203, 204, 206, 207, 209, 213, 219, 221, 224, 225, 226, 227, 228, 229, 231, 233, 234, 241, 242, 243, 246, 248, 250, 251, 252, 255, 257, 259, 261, 271, 273, 280, 284, 286, 290, 291, 293, 300, 303, 305, 306, 307, 308, 309, 310, 311, 314, 315, 317, 318, 320, 323, 341, 345, 346, 347, 351, 352, 353, 354, 355, 356, 360, 362, 365, 367, 368, 369, 370, 372, 375, 377, 378, 379, 381, 383, 386, 391, 392, 393, 395, 401, 404, 405, 406, 407, 408, 410, 411, 412, 414, 417, 418, 420, 421, 422, 423, 427, 428, 429, 435, 438, 439, 440, 441, 442, 443, 444, 445, 447, 448, 450-455, 456, 457, 458, 460, 462, 463, 465-468, 470, 471, 473, 474, 475, 476, 479, 484, 486, 487, 488, 490, 493, 501, 504, 510, 517, 518
Priorities, 15, 31, 36, 68, 94, 96, 100, 154, 177, 192, 196, 251, 257, 306, 313, 314, 317, 318, 323, 333, 341, 345, 346, 351, 355, 375, 384-386, 395, 401, 405, 418, 421, 444, 462, 463, 510, 513, 515, 517
Productivity, 45-49, 403, 406, 409, 411, 480
Professional development *See Board professional development; Staff professional development*
Purpose, 16, 17, 29, 31, 33, 34, 36, 37, 44, 52, 86, 88, 92, 94, 115, 131, 132, 142, 143, 144, 152, 158, 166, 180, 188, 203, 204, 225, 231, 234, 249, 251, 256, 257, 274, 278, 287, 290, 303, 305, 314, 317, 323, 325, 344, 345, 354, 369, 372, 387-391, 394, 401, 405, 408, 412, 416, 417, 421, 428, 456, 474, 501
Purse strings, 20

Q

Quality, 7, 29, 66, 68, 69, 70, 79, 87, 104, 122, 128, 135, 140, 148, 154, 166, 171, 186, 187, 189, 204, 219, 224, 225, 233, 241, 254, 255, 292, 293, 306, 311, 325, 358, 365, 366, 368, 374, 375, 386, 394, 414, 423, 429, 433, 448, 452, 462, 471, 480, 491
Questions (asking), 27, 32, 34, 83, 88, 94, 105, 106, 118, 130, 135, 146, 149, 151, 164, 191, 241, 249, 270, 271, 272, 274, 275, 303, 304, 354, 375, 388, 391, 393, 452, 504, 505, 514, 517, 518
Quintilian, 107
Quotas, 175

R

Rae, John, 451, 455
Reading reports, 194-197
Reciprocity, 84, 112, 458
Recruitment *See Board recruitment; Principal recruitment; Staff recruitment*
Red Line (Governance/Management), 474-476
Remote meetings/work *See Online meetings*
Resignation, 13, 465, 469-473, 222, 284, 293, 406, 435, 441, 444, 458, 511, 512, 513
Resilience, 38, 51, 141, 156, 157, 158, 159, 217, 219, 220, 286, 319, 423
Respect, 17, 59, 61, 64, 83-85, 115, 117, 133, 135, 136, 152, 160, 166, 219, 221, 224, 225, 226, 246, 273, 274, 278, 298, 305, 314, 318, 320, 328, 351, 367, 368, 372, 374, 376, 378, 401, 406, 423, 427, 457, 460, 467, 483, 490, 499, 514, 517
Responsibility *See Board responsibility*
Retirement, 23, 33, 290, 293, 296, 305, 386, 440, 441, 447
Reviews *See Evaluation; Performance reviews*
Risk management, 30, 51, 57, 70, 88, 94, 99-100, 142, 148, 150, 171, 224, 256, 308, 351, 412-414, 433, 453, 456, 474, 517
Roberts, John, 158
Roots and wings, 415-419

S

Safety, 30, 66, 68, 69, 70, 94, 148, 151, 192, 256, 308, 310, 351, 359, 366, 385, 413, 453, 454, 470, 517
Saint-Exupéry, Antoine de, 498, 503
Salaries, 20, 31, 255, 281, 385, 405, 435, 470, 471, 514
School culture *See Culture*
Self-evaluation (Principal), 354, 356
Servant leadership, 93, 379, 424-429
Six Thinking Hats, 128-130
SMART (Schools Mission Appraisal Reporting Tool), 322-334, 471
Social media, 16, 33, 57, 58, 88, 99, 112, 144, 153, 189, 218, 219, 226, 268, 290, 310, 313, 413
Socrates, 106, 222, 490
Staff
  autonomy, 45-49
  board interaction with, 59-64
  development, 56, 69, 79, 92, 154, 158, 208, 223, 242, 318, 353, 405, 429, 487
  firing/dismissal, 143-145, 206-209, 406, 444, 453
  morale *See Morale*
  recruitment, 60, 143, 145, 207, 242, 251, 307-310, 453
  retention, 404-406
  salaries, 20, 31, 255, 281, 385, 405, 435, 470, 471, 514
Stakeholders, 26, 68, 73, 87, 88, 94, 125, 148, 152, 187, 232, 271, 303, 306, 386, 450, 467
Stevens, Scott, 200
Strategic planning/thinking/vision, 7, 36, 51, 56, 61, 72, 74, 88, 92, 94, 95, 96, 100, 101, 108, 125, 131, 132, 136, 142, 148, 151, 154, 156, 158, 166, 171, 186, 188, 193, 196, 204, 213, 221, 225, 229, 230, 241, 242, 251, 254, 256, 259, 261, 274, 278, 284, 304, 305, 306, 317, 319, 320, 323, 325, 335, 344, 345, 346, 347, 351, 354, 359, 360-362, 366, 368, 369, 385, 386, 389, 390, 391, 395, 401, 408, 409, 412, 413, 414, 416, 417, 418, 421, 456, 462-464, 471, 474, 481-483, 488, 501, 504, 510, 513, 517
Succession planning, 89, 92, 94, 97-99, 164, 440-442, 443-445, 447, 517
Sustainability, 31, 94, 171, 229, 253-256, 313-318, 322, 325, 328, 332, 341, 342, 385, 386, 413, 418, 462, 474

T

Taleb, Nassim Nicholas, 38, 39, 50, 51, 157
Tattoos (as metaphor), 237-239
Teacher shortages, 469
Technology, 24, 26, 27, 28, 39, 54, 57, 152, 164, 191, 217, 218, 219, 220, 221, 246, 271, 313, 418, 419, 450, 491, 492
Term limits *See Board term limits*
Thring, Dr Edward, 22
Time management, 484-487
Tókes, László, 287
Tours (school), 46, 242, 509, 516
Training *See Board professional development; Staff professional development*
Transparency, 25, 62, 64, 66, 68, 84, 87, 88, 97, 101, 123, 124, 125, 154, 168, 213, 214, 232, 261, 306, 359, 363, 386, 396, 399, 408, 410, 423, 437, 459, 460, 467, 471, 480, 490, 492, 511, 518
Trust, 25, 30, 61, 64, 85, 87, 88, 97, 103, 113, 120, 125, 142, 149, 151, 159, 161, 172, 177, 192, 193, 207, 212, 213, 224, 227, 303, 306, 341, 358, 372, 374, 376, 392, 423, 429, 457, 460, 467, 488-492, 518
Truth, 85, 102, 105, 106, 107, 111, 114, 146, 147, 151, 163, 183, 200, 207, 212, 225, 246, 251, 293, 302, 309, 311, 317, 341, 345, 353, 419, 450, 451, 465, 476, 488-492, 493-495, 501, 504-508
Tuition fees, 256, 345, 366, 370, 385, 430-434
Twenge, Jean, 218, 219

U

United World Colleges (UWC), 140, 164, 284, 294, 380, 455, 499
Utilitarianism, 187

V

Values, 16, 31, 33, 34, 44, 56, 68, 72, 73, 91, 94, 101, 102, 104, 106, 107, 121, 122, 142, 144, 148, 152, 153, 154, 157, 158, 161, 166, 171, 184, 186, 187, 192, 194, 204, 217, 221, 224, 225, 227, 231, 246, 250, 251, 256, 257, 259, 264, 267, 273, 275, 278, 281, 290, 291, 303, 305, 306, 314, 320, 322-334, 340, 341, 345, 346, 347, 351, 358, 359, 368, 372, 376, 379, 404,

405, 408, 412, 415, 417, 418, 421, 423, 428, 429, 434, 450, 456, 458, 462, 463, 471, 473, 488, 498-503, 510, 517
Village Venus Effect, 477-480
Vision, 16, 17, 33, 34, 56, 61, 72, 74, 88, 94, 95, 96, 97, 101, 111, 131, 141, 142, 152, 154, 156, 158, 159, 164, 168, 186, 188, 192, 203, 204, 213, 219, 221, 224, 225, 226, 227, 229, 230, 231, 239, 242, 250, 251, 256, 257, 259, 261, 262, 264, 271, 274, 278, 290, 291, 292, 303, 305, 306, 311, 314, 317, 320, 322, 323, 324, 325, 326, 327, 328, 331, 332, 333, 341, 344, 345, 346, 347, 351, 354, 358, 359, 360-362, 368, 369, 372, 381, 386, 389, 390, 391, 393, 394, 395, 401, 404, 405, 408, 410, 411, 412, 415, 417, 418, 420, 421, 450, 452, 456, 458, 462, 463, 471, 474, 476, 481, 488, 490, 501, 503, 510, 513, 517
Volunteers, 52, 70, 99, 160, 313, 388, 412, 429, 518
Voting, 19, 25, 122, 126, 127, 134, 211, 212, 213, 214, 278, 304, 355, 511

W

Walser, Nancy, 448
Weinberger, Caspar, 252
Whitlam, Gough, 110, 378
Whorf, Benjamin Lee, 302
Wings See Roots and wings
Work-life balance, 217, 220, 275, 486

Y

Yarning Circles, 133

Z

Zaleznik, Abraham, 43
Zizek, Slavoj, 319

www.ingramcontent.com/pod-product-compliance
Lightning Source LLC
Chambersburg PA
CBHW071850290426
44110CB00013B/1087